THE PATRICIAS

THE PATRICIAS

The Proud History of a Fighting Regiment

David J. Bercuson

Stoddart

Published in 2001 by Stoddart Publishing Co. Limited
895 Don Mills Road, 400-2 Park Centre, Toronto, Canada, M3C 1W3

Distributed in Canada by:
General Distribution Services Ltd.
325 Humber College Blvd., Toronto, Ontario M9W 7C3
Tel. (416) 213-1919 Fax (416) 213-1917

05 04 03 02 01 2 3 4 5

Canadian Cataloguing in Publication Data

Bercuson, David J., 1945–
The Patricias: the proud history of a fighting regiment

Includes bibliographical references and index.
ISBN 0-7737-3298-5

1. Canada. Canadian Armed Forces. Princess Patricia's Canadian Light Infantry — History.
I. Title.

UA602.P75B47 2001 356'.113'0971 C00-932848-3

Every reasonable effort has been made to obtain reprint permissions. The publisher will gladly receive any information that will help rectify, in subsequent editions, any inadvertent omissions.

Front of jacket illustrations: (top) The Battle of Frezenberg, 8 May 1915, from the original painting by W.B. Wollen in the PPCLI Museum; (bottom) Armoured Personnel Carriers of 1 PPCLI Battle Group on rural patrol in Kosovo, 1999 (courtesy Sgt. V. Striemer, Garrison Imaging, Edmonton). Back of jacket illustration: The Regimental Colour, Princess Patricia's Canadian Light Infantry.

Jacket design: Bill Douglas @ The Bang
Text design: Joseph Gisini / PageWave Graphics Inc.

Princess Patricia's Canadian Light Infantry thank the following organizations that have provided funding for the development of this book: Canada Millennium Partnership Program, DND Millennium Fund, Donner Canadian Foundation.

We acknowledge for their financial support of our publishing program the Canada Council, the Ontario Arts Council, and the Government of Canada through the Book Publishing Industry Development Program (BPIDP).

Printed and bound in Canada

To the everlasting memory of
Andrew Hamilton Gault
1882–1958
A great Canadian, and a great Canadian soldier

CONTENTS

Acknowledgements ix

Introduction **The Ghosts of Bellewaerde Ridge** 1

One **Princess Patricia's Regiment** 19

Two **Wipers** 39

Three **The Salient** 61

Four **Vimy Ridge** 83

Five **The Road to Mons** 103

Six **From Armistice to War** 123

Seven **To War Again** 149

Eight **From Pacino to the Moro** 173

Nine **From Ortona to Victory** 201

Ten **Korea** 239

Eleven **Keeping the Peace** 275

Epilogue **Kosovo, 1999** 301

Maps 304

Roll of Honour 311

Notes 325

Index of Divisions, Brigades, Battalions, and Regiments 339

General Index 341

VP

ACKNOWLEDGEMENTS

THIS BOOK WAS TRULY A TEAM EFFORT AND, ON THE part of the Calgary-based Princess Patricia's Canadian Light Infantry Regimental Heritage Committee, a real labour of love. The Committee — Rod Middleton (Chair), Don Ardelian, Rudy Raidt, and Hub Gray — sought me out and "sold" me to the Patricias as the person they wanted for this project. I am grateful to them for the chance to write this exciting story and to learn as much as I have learned about this unique Canadian family. I am also grateful for their understanding of, and acquiescence to, my insistence that the final decision on what to include — or exclude — in this book be mine alone.

My agent, Linda McKnight, was generous with her time and advice in helping the Patricias make a mutually advantageous publication arrangement with Stoddart. I am pleased to be working with Stoddart again, and especially with Jim Gifford and Susan Goldberg.

Many people worked very hard to prepare research material for my use from the PPCLI Archives and other repositories. Several stalwart members of the regiment gave generously of their time to conduct interviews or to sit and recollect while others did the interviewing. Rebecca Deery spent endless hours transcribing and cataloguing more than 150 audiotapes received from Patricias across Canada. D'Arcy Best, Harry Bloom, Fred Breurkens, Warrant Officer Rick Dumas (2 PPCLI), Hub Gray, Ed Hansen, Del Harrison, Bill Minnis, Brian Munro, Bruce Paxton, Don Ross, Chris Snider, David Snowball, and Ken Villiger conducted interviews.

The PPCLI and I owe much thanks to the University of Victoria Library and Archives for allowing us to acquire copies and use parts of their extensive collection of interview tapes compiled by Dr. Reg Roy. We also owe a debt of thanks to Mark Zuehlke of Victoria for allowing the PPCLI to acquire his interview tapes of Patricias involved in the Battle of Ortona. PPCLI Archivist Corporal Regan MacLeod helped copy key documents in the PPCLI Archives. Don Ardelian and Bob Zubkowski combed virtually the entire PPCLI archival collection in Calgary to identify and copy important research material for this book. Their work saved me literally hundreds of hours of research time and shortened the entire project by many months.

PPCLI Museum curator Lynn Bullock worked hard at the task of document retrieval from outside sources; Rod Middleton, Don Ardelian, Rudy Raidt, and Hub Gray read the manuscript for accuracy and made many key editorial suggestions to me. PPCLI business manager Pam Borland helped raise funds for the project and, assisted by Rudy Raidt, managed it financially. Whitney Lackenbauer did an outstanding job on the index. Sydney Frost sent me hundreds of pages of very useful information, particularly on the war in Sicily.

It is difficult, if not hazardous, to pick any one of these people as having been more generous with their time and patience than any other. Everyone mentioned did what he or she could to make this project a success. I hope all will forgive me, however, for mentioning that, of all those who did contribute, I will always remember the steadfastness and drive of Rod Middleton just a tiny bit more than all the rest.

To my wife, Barrie: I love you more than forever. You are my oxygen, my earth, my sunshine, my rain, and all my sustenance. You are the seasons of my life, and the comfort of my soul, and I will love you until the sky falls.

David J. Bercuson
Rockyview, Alberta
January 2001

Introduction

THE GHOSTS OF BELLEWAERDE RIDGE

CLARKE STADIUM, EDMONTON: 2 JULY 1999. MORE THAN 7,000 people huddled against the cool, wet weather and waited for the tattoo and sunset ceremony that marked the eighty-fifth anniversary of Princess Patricia's Canadian Light Infantry to begin.

It had been an unseasonably cool summer, and this day was no exception. Heavy snow in the mountains to the west coupled with a cold, hard rain most of the day had left a sodden city and a chill everywhere.

The weather did not warm the hearts of the ceremony organizers, nor of the stadium crowds, but in a way the rain and the cold more than fitted the occasion. This was the sort of weather that the Originals — the Patricias who had formed the original regiment in August 1914 — endured day after day in a wet Flanders spring in 1915. There, at a place called Bellewaerde Ridge in the northwest corner of Belgium, they had undergone, and endured, the first major test of their mettle.

The Originals — those who survived Bellewaerde Ridge — and the thousands of other Patricias who followed them to war in the next three and one-half years, are all gone now. Not a single veteran of the First World War remained to mark the eighty-fifth anniversary of the regiment, at least not in body. But those old soldiers will always be with the regiment in spirit, because the PPCLI isn't simply a military formation in today's Canadian Army. It is a regiment of the Canadian Infantry Corps, an extended family of soldiers old, new, and long gone, with roots in the traditions and history of its past. And no part of its past was bloodier, nor more important to the development of the Patricia legacy, than Bellewaerde Ridge.

P.P.C.L.I.

At precisely 7:30 p.m., the military band struck up the regimental march. Led by the scarlet-coated drummers of the PPCLI, resplendent in their white Wolsley helmets; white ceremonial belts; dark blue, red-striped trousers; and gleaming black boots, the participants marched onto the bright grassy field. Brass instruments shone brilliantly in the light cast by the stadium's massive lamps. The crowd applauded. Many knew the words to the Patricia medley by heart. It begins "Has Anyone Seen the Colonel?", a song Patricias have sung in messes and barracks, and on route marches and in parade squares for more than eight decades. The words mock officers and NCOs who enjoy the good life while corporals and privates do the brunt of the fighting and dying.

It was a night to honour history, but even so, very few people in the stadium knew the original version of the last verse of "Has Anyone Seen the Colonel?" The words of that verse are haunting:

Has anyone seen the Old Battalion? We know where it is,
We know where it is, we know where it is.
Has anyone seen the Old Battalion? We know where it is.

It's there on Bellewaerde Ridge.
How do you know?
They stood there, they fought there, there on Bellewaerde Ridge.
They rest there, there on Bellewaerde Ridge.

Bellewaerde Ridge is a low rise near Belgium's northwest border with France, stretching north of the Menin-Iepers freeway, just to the west of a small body of water known as Bellewaerde Lake. It is a gentle ridge of grass, trees, and fertile farmland rising over the flat polder land of Flanders. The traffic roars by at 130 kilometres per hour; almost no one gives this bit of ground a second glance.

Flanders is soaked in the blood of as many as a million men killed attacking, or defending, what was once known as the Ypres Salient. First World War cemeteries lie everywhere. Today, this part of Belgium, known as the Westhoek, or West Corner, is Belgium's answer to Silicon Valley. In late 1999, the Belgian prime minister descended upon the region to open "Flanders Language Valley," an industrial park where small but thriving software companies tackle the challenge of designing computer systems that recognize and respond to human speech in dozens of languages. If they succeed, the keyboard and the mouse will go the way of the quill pen; translation of even the most complex sentences from one language to another will be as quick as an electronic pulse. The software technicians work beneath the gaze of the ghosts of Bellewaerde Ridge.

On the night of 3/4 May 1915, the Old Battalion — some 800 strong — moved into its position below the crest of Bellewaerde Ridge. The men were just settling into defensive positions when the Germans began a massive artillery bombardment followed by infantry assaults that lasted all the next day. The Patricias lost 122 men on 4 May alone. On 5 May, their commanding officer, Lieutenant-Colonel Herbert Buller, was badly wounded. He was replaced in the midst of the fighting by Major Hamilton Gault of Montreal, the Patricias' founder. For the next three days, desultory sniper fire, machine-gun bursts, and the occasional shell-and-mortar blast took their steady toll on the PPCLI, but the men continued to improve trenches and firing pits, mend wire, and carry forward ammunition and supplies.

The morning of 8 May began as the previous mornings had, with sporadic sniper and artillery fire. The first shells rumbled in at about 0700. In their trenches, the Patricias went about their usual morning routine of eating, smoking, and cleaning their weapons. They expected the shelling to die away; it had every other morning since they came to the ridge. Instead, its tempo increased. Explosions soon came so quickly it was hard to tell when one ended and another began. Even then, the shelling intensified. For two hours, the deluge of cordite and steel fragments wore away the walls and parapets of the trenches. It blew in bunkers. It destroyed machine guns and the men who manned them. It tore up barbed wire, and blasted sandbags and timber to bits. Torn and broken bodies cartwheeled through the air. Some men simply disappeared, vapourized by direct hits.

The Patricias hunkered down. They stuck their fingers in their ears. Some men soiled themselves. Others cried to Jesus, or to their mothers, or sweethearts. They grasped desperately at their rifles. They endured the German machine-gun fire raking their positions from the flanks. Then, when the shelling died out, the survivors, rallied by their officers and NCOs, grimly dragged themselves to the remains of their parapets, to the edges of their smashed trenches, and waited for the German infantry.

The grey-clad men in the spiked helmets advanced on the Patricia positions in rows, and died by the hundreds under withering Patricia rifle fire. The German infantry outflanked the Patricias on the left, but the Patricias did not break. Instead they reorganized their line, pulled back into a semicircle, and met the German enfilade head on. When Patricia officers were killed, senior non-commissioned officers stepped in to fill their ranks. When they too were killed, corporals and lance corporals gave the orders.

Ammunition ran short, was replenished by men risking their lives to drag cases of grenades or boxes of ammunition forward, then ran short again. There was no water and almost no food.

Still the Patricias held. All day and into the night, as gun barrels grew too hot to touch and ammunition disappeared at a ghastly rate — and as, one by one, Patricias died or were severely wounded — the regiment held. The German attack faltered, then died. By nightfall, the danger of a complete German breakthrough abated. A British battalion relieved the Patricias after dark.

The Patricias had saved the line, and maybe even the entire Ypres Salient, but the cost was appalling. Out of all the rifle companies, only four officers and 150 men were left standing at the end of the battle; 392 had been killed or wounded, or were missing. The regiment's founder, Major Hamilton Gault, had himself been hit twice. He had lain in extreme pain for most of the day while the fighting swirled around him, and refused attention or evacuation until others were cared for. When Gault and the survivors of the day's battle left their positions at nightfall, they left the core of the Originals behind — the ghosts of Bellewaerde Ridge.[1]

P.P.C.L.I.

The Patricias who went to war in the fall of 1914 were unique in a number of ways. Virtually all of them had been soldiers before. The strong presence of western Canadians in their ranks gave them a distinctly western flavour. They were also the first formation from Canada to enter the battle zone.

More than anything, however, the method of their founding, and their distinguished royal patron, marked the Patricias apart from other regiments. They were the only privately funded Canadian regiment established in the First World War; Montreal millionaire Hamilton Gault, who became its Senior Major, bore the initial costs of raising the regiment. The PPCLI was also the only Canadian regiment to go into action with its own camp colour, hand-made especially for it by Princess Patricia of Connaught, the daughter of the Governor General, who also gave them her name. The Patricias, therefore, went to war with a distinct identity and culture and a strong regimental spirit.

Soldiers are different from everyone else in society. They are the men (and now women too) who are sometimes called upon by their country to bear arms and use deadly force in order to secure the nation's borders and pursue its goals and interests. Since the dawn of time, soldiers have donned battle garb and wielded weapons to fulfill the same basic task: to kill other soldiers in war, soldiers who have done them no personal harm but whom their nation has declared "enemies." In performing that bloody and solemn task, they must, of course, deliberately place themselves in jeopardy of life and limb. Canadians sometimes forget that militaries, including their own, exist for only two related purposes — to fight wars and to prepare to fight wars. They do not exist to fight floods, repair ice storm damage, or act as peacekeepers. Armies can do all those things, and the Canadian army has done them all well. But armies are fundamentally about war and killing and, at bottom, soldiering is the occupation of meting out, and accepting, death. Despite all the devices of modern technology that promise to give tomorrow's soldier a greater capacity both to kill and to survive, the essence of battle has never changed, and will not change.

The harsh realities of war pose a major challenge for armies: how to steel soldiers for the horrors they will endure when they arrive at the place and time of battle, when other soldiers come to kill them. In the British army, and in those armies such as the Canadian whose traditions are rooted in those of the Redcoats, the regimental tradition has evolved to meet that challenge.

It is not known when the first regiments appeared in organized armies, but the Roman army often raised its legions from specific places in the Roman Empire or from selected tribes or peoples. As well, the Romans gave their legions distinct standards, symbols, and names. The premise behind these actions was to instill pride in a particular legion, and to bind the soldiers in it together in war so that they would fight and die for each other. Centuries later, when regiments began to appear in European armies, they were often privately raised. Their benefactor, usually a nobleman, supplied them with weapons, uniforms, helmets, and other accoutrements, and loaned his name or that of his house to the regimental standard. It was thought then and is still strongly thought now by those who believe in the regimental tradition, that cohesion is the key to a regiment's survival in battle. It seems to be a fact proven in countless wars that men-at-arms fight more resolutely for their extended regimental families than they do for kings, presidents, or such abstract notions as "making the world safe for democracy."

To distinguish themselves from other, similar, bodies of fighting men, regiments of the past adopted particular battle flags, called "colours"; special insignia; distinct uniforms; and sometimes even their own names for ranks. Often, they developed their own drill and training practices. They nurtured difference not only in the way they dressed and fought, but in the way their officers comported themselves in barracks, at regimental celebrations, or in public. In the British Army, "Guards" or cavalry regiments often imposed strict physical requirements so that all the guardsmen or cavalrymen would be of the same height and build.

Two centuries ago, some armies were as much loose formations of regiments as they were a single fighting force. As late as the 1980s, the British army was so steeped in the regimental tradition that it could still have been considered a creation of its regiments. That was never the case in Canada, where the military predated the creation of infantry regiments. But however regiments are formed, and whatever characteristics they take even in the modern, integrated militaries of today, they still strive to be unique, to distinguish themselves and the members of their regimental families. In the Canadian army, the regiment is still the soldier's first home and his military clan. It is his or her source of pride and strength. A soldier knows that even if he or she does not survive, the regiment will live on and draw strength from the sacrifice. For the Patricias, the regimental family still includes the long-gone soldiers of Bellewaerde Ridge, as much as it does its 2nd Battalion, which held off Croatian soldiers in the Medak Pocket in Croatia in 1993.

P.P.C.L.I.

The army that Canadian Minister of Militia Sam Hughes put together in the late summer and early fall of 1914 was not a regimentally based army. In his desire to send a Canadian contingent overseas as quickly as possible, Hughes scrapped the army's mobilization plans and instituted one of his own. The army's plan had provided for the militia regiments across Canada to recruit themselves up to strength, and then send battalions to a central training area to be organized into larger formations.[2] Instead, Hughes ordered the militia regiments simply to sign up volunteers and put them on to trains to Camp Valcartier without delay. At Valcartier, the volunteers were formed into anonymous numbered battalions, such as the 27th Battalion, the 10th Battalion, or the 50th Battalion, of the Canadian Expeditionary Force (CEF), the official name bestowed by the Canadian government on the entire formation dispatched overseas in the First World War. Thus, the PPCLI, with its distinct name and camp colour, stood out from its very beginnings.

The Patricias were "first in the field" from Canada, though initially attached to a British brigade and only later to the Canadian Corps, a tactical unit of the CEF formed in 1915 from the 1st and 2nd Canadian Divisions.[3] The Patricias' performance in battle throughout the First World War reflected their star quality. The regiment's founder, Hamilton Gault, was himself wounded three times, and lost his left leg at Sanctuary Wood in 1916. He took command a number of times, when the battalion CO was killed or badly wounded, an event that happened far too often: of the six men destined to command the regiment in the First World War, three were killed in action and two (including Gault) were wounded. Five of the six were awarded the Distinguished Service Order (DSO) at least once. Francis Farquhar, the Patricias' first Commanding Officer, already possessed a DSO when the war broke out. Three Patricias were awarded the Victoria Cross, and 366 other decorations, awards, or distinctions were handed out to members of the regiment in the First World War. Much of the regiment's success might well be attributed to the practice, initiated by Farquhar, of promoting from within the ranks. For example, the Patricias' CO in the last three weeks of the war — Acting Lieutenant-Colonel A.G. Pearson — had enlisted as a private in Winnipeg in August 1914. This practice had the effect of ensuring that officers were not only thoroughly familiar with the duties and responsibilities of all infantrymen from the ground up, but also with the fast-developing regimental traditions of steadfastness and innovation.

The PPCLI amassed twenty-one regimental battle honours in the First World War, but those honours came at a terrible cost. By the end of the war the regiment had suffered 4,076 casualties, 1,272 of them killed in action.

At the end of the war, the large and very proficient Canadian Corps melted away, but the Patricias survived. Designated as one of Canada's three Permanent Force (PF) infantry regiments (the others were the Royal Canadian Regiment and the Royal 22e Régiment), the PPCLI was later sent west to establish its home bases in Manitoba and British Columbia. Thus began its close ties to the Canadian west, and a further evolution of its character. Because so many of its recruits came from the west, and because its prime task in the years between the First and Second World Wars was to train western Canadian militiamen, it gained a reputation as an open, friendly, and somewhat informal regiment.

Like the rest of the Canadian military, the PPCLI suffered from chronic budget cutting, undermanning, and poor equipment in this era. The governments of the day let the Canadian military languish. The PPCLI, for example, remained at about half its peacetime establishment for most of the period. Its weaponry, uniforms, and training were First World War vintage. Because the PF Canadian officer corps was so tiny, soldiers had little chance of promotion. The Canadian Army devoted most of its time and its few resources to rudimentary training; its infantry regiments could do little more than the basic tasks of training part-time soldiers and focusing on keeping regimental traditions alive. The officer corps could do little to prepare for the mobile war of infantry, fast armour, and tactical aircraft that would engulf the world in 1939.

As a PF regiment, the PPCLI was activated at the very beginning of the Second World War, and formed part of the 2nd Canadian Infantry Brigade of the 1st Canadian Infantry Division — the "red patch" division. The PPCLI left Canada with twenty-six officers and 781 other ranks in December 1939, and trained in the United Kingdom until July 1943, when it took part in the British and American landings on the south coast of Sicily. From then until the end of the war, almost always under the command of Lieutenant-Colonel Cameron Ware, the PPCLI was in the thick of the fight, in battles at places such as Leonforte, Agira, the Moro River, Ortona, the Liri Valley, and the Hitler and Gothic lines. They were then transferred to northwest Europe to take part in the First Canadian Army's last great attack of the war, the liberation of western Holland. The Second World War added more battle honours to the regiment, but many more names to the list of regimental dead: 273 officers and other ranks were killed or died of wounds, and 1,076 were wounded.

The Patricias' reputation for being first in the field was upheld in Korea in late 1950. The 2nd Battalion, also known as 2 PPCLI, was recruited specially for service in the Korean War under Lieutenant-Colonel Jim Stone, and arrived as Canada's initial contribution to the ground war there. In April 1951, 2 PPCLI held off and blunted a major Chinese attack against Hill 677, just to the west of the Korean village of Kap'yong. For an entire night, the surrounded Patricias beat back the Chinese attack, held the position, and kept open the road to the rear of the village. In conjunction with the other two formations that succeeded in holding the Chinese at Kap'yong — Company A of the US 72nd Heavy Tank Battalion and the 3rd Battalion, Royal Australian Regiment — 2 PPCLI was awarded a US Presidential Distinguished Unit Citation, and another battle honour for the regimental colour.

Most Canadians do not know that the Patricias came under fire once again in the bitter civil war that marked the break-up of Yugoslavia in the early and mid-1990s. In early 1993, 2 PPCLI under the command of Lieutenant-Colonel Jim Calvin was sent into "Sector South," the Krajina region that borders eastern Croatia and western Bosnia. Ordered to keep warring Croatian and Serbian forces apart, the Patricias stood off a full-fledged assault by Croatians on what was then known as the Medak Pocket. Though more than 40 percent of the Patricias were augmentees — soldiers from militia units who volunteered for a tour — they turned back the Croatians, helping to contain a renewed round of ethnic cleansing. For this action, 2 PPCLI was awarded the United Nations Unit Citation.

P.P.C.L.I.

The marking of regimental birthdays is an important part of celebrating a regiment's achievements; the celebration in Edmonton of the eighty-fifth anniversary of the founding of the Patricias, on the weekend of 2–4 July 1999, was thus an occasion for festivity and reflection. More than 1,100 Patricias — serving members, veterans, and their families — took part in the event; some 750 had travelled to Edmonton for the celebration. They started to arrive from across Canada, the United States, and the United Kingdom at mid-week.

The anniversary celebrations began on Friday night, with the tattoo and sunset ceremony. On Saturday, the Patricias were treated to a large static display of the latest military equipment, including the new Light Armoured Vehicle, with all of its technical gear, infrared detection systems, and armament. Bad weather forced the cancellation of the parachute drop by the Third Battalion's Parachute Company, to the disappointment of many an old jumper in the crowd. The highlight of the weekend took place that afternoon, with the "Trooping the Colour" ceremony; Lady Patricia, the Countess Mountbatten of Burma, Colonel-in-Chief of the PPCLI, took the salute alongside Major-General C.W. Hewson, Colonel of the Regiment. Dinner and a dance closed the day's activities. On Sunday morning, the Colonel-in-Chief dedicated the new Hamilton Gault Memorial Park, a fitting close to the eighty-fifth anniversary celebrations.

No First World War veterans were alive to share the celebration, but more than a handful of Second World War Patricias were in attendance. One was eighty-year-old Don Munro, from Calgary, who had transferred to the Patricias from the Calgary Highlanders early in the Second World War to swap the tedium of English training-camp life for a chance to take part in the Allied assault on Sicily. After receiving his commission as a fresh, young lieutenant, Munro slogged up the Italian peninsula alongside the rest of the Patricias before joining the main body of the Canadian Army in Holland in the last months of the war. At the celebration, he met Don Gower, a fellow infantryman, whom he hadn't seen in fifty-four years.

Korean War veterans were more common at the eighty-fifth anniversary, being on average some five years younger than those who fought in the Second World War. They too, however, are fast disappearing. Seventy-one-year-old Oscar Lacombe of Two Hills, Alberta, who served in Korea in 1951, told one newspaper reporter that about nine of his comrades had died since the eightieth anniversary celebrations. "On the ninetieth," he mused, "there'll be a slew of us gone again."[4] Others in attendance served with the Patricias in Europe during the Cold War, in Cyprus and the Middle East during the heydays of Canadian peacekeeping operations, or more recently in former Yugoslavia.

Anniversaries of the regiment's founding are important, but so too the biannual orientation weekends for young officers — dubbed the "Ric-a-Dam-Doo" — and the Regimental Museum and Archives at the Museum of the Regiments in Calgary. At Ric-a-Dam-Doo weekends, junior officers meet Patricia veterans, learn Patricia traditions, and are taught about Patricia battles and campaigns. The weekends always end with a tour of the regimental museum.

The Heritage Committee, working in conjunction with Regimental Headquarters (RHQ) at Base Edmonton, undertakes the main task of maintaining PPCLI traditions. RHQ publishes *The Regimental Manual,* which lays out the exact order of regimental organization, its constitution and by-laws, its awards and honours, and virtually every detail of regimental life not determined by the Canadian Forces. This practice is consistent with those of all Canadian army regiments, which have their "regimental," or ceremonial and traditional, side, and their strictly military side. When a battalion of the PPCLI takes to the field, it is armed, equipped, and clothed in essentially the same manner as Canada's other infantry battalions. Its operating procedures, rules of engagement, organization, and fighting doctrine are also the same. The soldiers wear their regimental cap badges, and a shoulder title that marks their regiment, but to the untrained eye, they are indistinguishable from any other Canadian infantry. In the field, the distinct traditions of the regiment, and even of the battalion, are motivating factors, sources of strength, and bonds of loyalty, but they are not readily visible.

And yet in the field or not, RHQ and dozens of Patricias now on civvy street keep the regimental uniqueness alive. The regiment's, and even each individual battalion's, special history and traditions are emphasized at the more ceremonial occasions, such as tattoos, parades, mess dinners, or change-of-command ceremonies.

P.P.C.L.I.

On 1 July 1999, as the eighty-fifth anniversary weekend approached, Patricia pride was on display at another Edmonton location. At Edmonton International Airport, some thirty kilometres south of the city, the Patricias of Alpha Company, 1 PPCLI, were saying their final farewells to their families. Alpha Company was bound for Skopje, Macedonia, to pick up their equipment, already shipped by sea, before heading north into Kosovo. The NATO bombing campaign against Yugoslavia had just ended and NATO needed to deploy as many infantry units as possible into Kosovo, as quickly as possible, to enforce the terms of the NATO-Yugoslav ceasefire that had ended the bombing. Canada had sent an armoured reconnaissance squadron, a helicopter squadron, and support troops to Macedonia the previous May, but the Patricias were the first Canadian infantry to be sent into the war-torn province.

Under normal conditions, a Canadian infantry battalion takes up to ninety days to ready itself for deployment after receiving a warning order from National Defence Headquarters. But not this time. Alpha Company had been informed only on 11 June that it was going to Kosovo. But "thanks to the high level of operational readiness," as the CO of 1 PPCLI described it, the company was ready in three weeks.[5] Colonel Andrew Leslie, outgoing Commander of 1st Canadian Mechanized Brigade, responsible for overall training of the brigade and its formations — including 1 PPCLI — told the departing troops, "Arguably you are the best mechanized company Canada has produced in decades."[6] They were, and so was the rest of the 1 PPCLI Battle Group that followed them into Kosovo five weeks later. They were as well equipped, and well trained, as any NATO mechanized infantry battalion deploying to the Balkans. Their professionalism shone through upon their arrival as they spread out into their operational zone near Pristina. Within hours, the Patricias were mounting patrols, providing security for forensic teams examining war crimes sites, searching for and emptying illegal arms caches, and enforcing the mandate of NATO's KFOR (Kosovo Force) to police and enforce the ceasefire agreements.

P.P.C.L.I.

Canada's regular soldiers today are fully professional. They have committed themselves to soldiering for their country, and they train and prepare constantly for the day that they may deploy overseas in the national interest. All the preparation in the world, however, doesn't make their parting any easier. They and their families accept the inevitable — that potentially dangerous foreign operations are a part of their lives — but leaving is always difficult. There is a pattern to departures, and the soldiers and their families followed it on the afternoon of 1 July 1999. They gathered in an aircraft hangar at the airport. A line was drawn across the floor of the building: one side of the hangar for the departing troops, the other for their families. The soldiers and their families entered the building together. The kids grabbed a juice box or two and played among the personal packs and other equipment lying on the hangar floor. Some gaped at the troops in their uniforms; others were used to the ritual. One little girl asked her dad, "Is this the costume you're going to wear in Kosovo?"[7]

The soldiers and their wives or husbands hugged often, and spoke to each other softly. Alpha Company's unusually short warning period was especially hard on the 40 to 50 percent of the departing troops who were married. Sergeant David Pusch told one reporter: "I want to stay home and be with my family. You're constantly wondering if they're going to be all right. But I know I have to go. I have a lot of excitement about going over and I'll help out as much as I can."[8] Brenda Leonard, wife of a warrant officer, put it this way: "He's been gone so many times we're used to it. We know they know what they're doing. I'm sure they'll be fine. [But] it kind of messed up our plans for the next eight months."[9]

As arrival time neared, the departing troops slowly moved to their side of the hangar while their families moved to theirs. Then the wives (and a few husbands) and children began to leave the building, to drift to their cars and drive back to their homes, most near CFB Edmonton, some on it. They would not likely see their loved ones until just before Christmas. They knew that Kosovo was a dangerous place, and that almost a dozen Canadians had already died on active service in the Balkans since the start of the Yugoslav civil war in 1992. But their spouses were soldiers, and risk came with the job. For those at home, the challenge was to cope with kids, and households, and all the ordinary bumps in the everyday road of life that people must cope with, without their partners to help. For the departing soldiers boarding the long flight to Macedonia, there were thoughts of home, of course, but excitement about the days ahead.

"It's always different," Corporal Mike Tait, with three overseas tours under his belt, told a reporter. "But it's still the same rush, walking into the unknown."[10]

On 3 July 1999, some thirty-six hours after their departure from Edmonton, and after a nine-hour delay at CFB Trenton, Alpha Company pulled in to Glogovac, Kosovo, to begin setting up their two camps. It was hot, with daytime temperatures soaring to almost fifty degrees Celsius, and it was dusty. The signs of the recent fighting were all around them. Their 200-square-kilometre area of responsibility was, in the words of their company commander, "one of the most heavily damaged areas of Kosovo . . . the scene of many atrocities." Alpha Company set out immediately to establish their dominance in the area, getting to know the terrain, the people, and the "key players." They patrolled in vehicles and on foot. They set up checkpoints. They secured the perimeters around their camps, and some watched silently as forensic teams unearthed grisly remains from mass graves.

At almost the same time as the first of the Patricias arrived in Glogovac, Lady Patricia, the Countess Mountbatten of Burma, was reviewing her regiment from the front of a slow-moving Jeep at Base Edmonton. More than 2,000 spectators watched as 500 soldiers stood ramrod straight, their C7 automatic rifles at shoulder arms, as the Jeep passed along their ranks. This was the closing ceremony of the eighty-fifth anniversary, the traditional "trooping the colour." The rite dates back to the Middle Ages, when the smoke and confusion of battle made it difficult to rally a regiment; the soldiers always knew where their commanding officer was when they could spot the colour. "You always needed a rallying point," Captain Steve Newman explained to the press. "We still troop the colour so the troops understand that they're watching their history go by and it's now up to them to maintain that history and add to it."[11]

Eighty-five years earlier, on 23 August 1914, the Old Battalion had received the camp colour — the Ric-a-Dam-Doo, they dubbed it as they would their future orientation weekends and their song — from Princess Patricia in Lansdowne Park, Ottawa. These soldiers were a vastly different breed from those who trooped the colour on 3 July 1999. Today's warfare of high-intensity air/land battle, with weapons of tremendous destructive power, bombs guided to their targets by Global Positioning System satellites, and instant communications, is also very different from the war the Old Battalion set off to fight so long ago. But the essence of soldiering has not changed since the dawn of time. At bottom it is always about war, and war is always about fighting, killing, and dying for a cause or beliefs larger than any one person. From its very origins to now, therefore, the story of the PPCLI is one of a fighting regiment, born in the First World War, steeled in battle in two world wars, Korea, and a hundred deadly encounters since Korea, always proud of its fighting tradition.

Chapter 1

PRINCESS PATRICIA'S REGIMENT

PRINCESS PATRICIA'S CANADIAN LIGHT INFANTRY WAS touched by destiny from the very start. The regiment's founder, Hamilton Gault, was a millionaire Montreal businessman who has been called the true embodiment of the citizen soldier — the militiaman with a full civilian life who also dedicated himself to the defence of his country in time of need.[1] Gault and his glamorous wife Marguerite had been favourites of the vice-regal court of the Governor General of Canada, Arthur the Duke of Connaught, since the duke's arrival in Canada in 1911. The duke was the first royal person to occupy the post of governor general, and, for a time, his vice-regal court became the centre of Ottawa's social life. The Gaults were part of the inner circle, well placed and well connected. Gault's private fortune came from business interests his family had founded and then expanded in the mid-nineteenth century after their arrival from Britain. Hamilton, or "Hammie" as his friends and close associates called him, was a man of action as well as of means. He loved the outdoors. He hunted and fished and rode and hiked and climbed. His youth, his husky build, his wealth, his rugged good looks, and his enthusiasm all added to his charisma. As one man who served with him in the early years of the First World War wrote about Gault: "everyone who knew him — or even just saw him — was imbued with his personality. It was an extraordinary thing that cannot be explained. I have seen a thousand people stand up when he came into a hall — people who did not know him — thrilled by his presence."[2]

When war broke out in 1899 between Britain and its Empire on the one side and the two Boer republics of the Transvaal and the Orange Free State on the other, Gault had volunteered for action. He had been an officer in the 5th Royal Scots, a Montreal militia regiment that had been asked to nominate three officers for service. He left Canada in early 1902 with the 2nd Regiment, Canadian Mounted Rifles (2 CMR). Most of Gault's service with the Mounted Rifles consisted of patrolling and escorting supply columns. The war was in its final stages at that point, and only a few Boer guerillas still held out against the now inevitable British victory. Despite seeing only limited action in the seven months or so he spent with the CMR, Gault, in the words of his biographer, "had seen enough of war to confirm his military ambitions."[3]

Gault was barely seventeen when the South African war broke out. His desire to join up was, no doubt, as much a craving for adventure as it was a reflection of his attachment to the British Empire. He was carefree, had no real responsibilities, and was young and fit. But in the late summer of 1914, in the weeks after the assassination of the Archduke of Austria and his wife in Sarajevo on 28 June, Gault's circumstances were entirely different. He had a personal fortune of some $20 million in today's currency, and he was a husband and the head of a large group of companies. He was also a member of all the important social and sporting clubs of the day. A man of his age, with his wealth, connections, and family and business responsibilities, did not have to go to war in 1914. And even if

Gault had been inclined to don a uniform — he was an officer of the Black Watch (Royal Highland Regiment) of Canada — he needn't have looked for anything adventurous. He might have done yeoman service in a safe staff job, or recruited and trained the much younger men who were more suited than he was for war — in body, if not in spirit. But shying away from adventure was not Hamilton Gault's way. When Austria issued an ultimatum to Serbia on 23 July to virtually surrender its independence or face invasion, war suddenly seemed close. Gault was determined to do whatever he could in the defence of the Empire he so deeply loved.

Gault was an Empire patriot. He was proud of his native Canada, and well aware of the blessings of opportunity that Canada had bestowed on his family. He never tired of exploring the rugged beauty of his country. But he was also a strong believer in the blessings of British liberty and, what he might have called the "civilizing" influence of the British Empire in the world. At the dawn of the twenty-first century, when Canadians are busy forging an independent and unique national heritage, it is easy to be cynical about, even amused by, men such as Gault. If it is easy, however, it is only so because the subsequent history of the twentieth century — a century of war, slaughter, and atrocity — has bred cynicism and undermined the sort of idealism that motivated men like him. Gault might have lived an empty life of ease and leisure for the rest of his days. He chose another course.

The Princess Patricia's Canadian Light Infantry came to life sometime in the last week of July 1914, when Gault decided to follow the example set by Lord Strathcona at the outbreak of the Boer War in 1899 and pay to raise an entire regiment. At first Gault wanted to raise a cavalry regiment. When he discussed his proposal with Minister of Militia and Defence Colonel Sam Hughes on 3 August, however, Hughes persuaded him that infantry would be more useful. Gault returned to Montreal the next day, the day that London declared war on Germany. He soon received a telegram from Lieutenant-Colonel Francis Farquhar, DSO, military secretary to the Governor General. Gault had met Farquhar at the viceregal court and had been impressed by the Lieutenant-Colonel's thoroughly professional but gentlemanly manner. Farquhar's message was short but concise: "Come up at once, have got idea." Thus began the collaboration that produced the PPCLI.

The raising of the new regiment was Gault's idea, but Farquhar had a strong influence on the shape of the PPCLI. Born the son of a baronet in London in 1874, Francis Farquhar, "Fanny" to his friends, had been schooled at Eton before joining the famous Coldstream Guards regiment in the spring of 1896. He attended Army Staff College before leaving for South Africa in October 1899. There, he served with distinction, winning the Distinguished Service Order (DSO) before returning to the United Kingdom in December 1900. His next overseas posting was China, where he served during the Boxer Rebellion, learning a passable Mandarin. Posted to Somaliland for a year in 1903/04, he returned to London to marry Lady Evelyn Hely-Hutchinson and start a family. By the time he was sent to Canada in October 1913 to head up the Duke of Connaught's small military advisory staff, he was the father of two daughters.

Farquhar was intelligent, slim, and tall at five feet, eleven inches. His delicate, "piano player" hands were a particularly distinguishing feature about him. He treated his staff with respect; his soldiers had called him the "KCO," for "kind commanding officer." At the time, the governor general was, in effect, the British high commissioner, or ambassador, to Canada. Farquhar's job was not unlike a military attaché in an embassy today. It was a good position, prestigious and no doubt interesting enough, but Farquhar was a professional soldier; for him, the pull of war was irresistible. Like Gault, he feared the war would be short, and was eager to get out of his commitment to the governor general and overseas into action as quickly as possible.

Gault and Farquhar met in Ottawa on the evening of 5 August 1914. At that meeting, Farquhar told Gault that since Sam Hughes was already rushing to assemble a Canadian contingent for service in France, and would not allow Gault to take any active members of the Canadian militia into his regiment, they ought to "make use of the many men now in Canada who have seen service and who are not at present enlisted in any unit." Such veterans would have the advantage of being able to "shake down quickly,"[4] and get to the front faster than the rest of the soldiers coming from Canada. Farquhar volunteered to command the formation if he could be relieved of his duties at Government House; Gault would be the regiment's senior major and second in command. Gault eagerly agreed. He also approved Farquhar's suggestion that the new formation be named after the Princess Patricia of Connaught, the Governor General's daughter. The princess not only agreed, but also offered to provide the regiment with a camp colour. This colour was not intended as an official regimental colour, approved by both heraldic and military authorities. Rather, it was meant to symbolize the princess and her ties to the men of her regiment.

Princess Patricia's Canadian Light Infantry was not in any way a true "light infantry" regiment, as Gault himself admitted, but he thought the name gave added dash to the formation, and so it did.[5] The princess was a canny choice to symbolize the regiment. Surviving paintings of her from the First World War era show her to have been a woman of extraordinary beauty. One young officer, J.H. Stewart, of Harrowsmith, Ontario, certainly thought so after meeting her for the first time at a social occasion at Government House in early June 1914:

> Blue blood cannot make a woman beautiful; but something must have intervened, for she is the most beautiful one of her sex that I have ever seen. There is some attraction about tall women that their sisters do not possess . . . and she is six feet tall, slim and

> straight, lithe and graceful as a fawn, long-armed and clean-hipped with the stride of a Goddess; if it were not for the sweetest of smiles she would be a model Juno.[6]

What could have been more chivalrous than for men like Stewart to rally to the side of a beautiful princess and carry her colour into battle? This was a regimental beginning that might have been conjured up by Sir Walter Scott. For Stewart, as for many others, however, the tale had a tragic ending. He was killed near Armentières in June 1915.

The agreement that Gault and the government of Canada soon worked out was simple enough. The Department of Militia and Defence would expedite the raising of the regiment by paying the transportation costs of volunteers to come to Ottawa, where the regiment would concentrate. Gault would pay the government "the sum of one hundred thousand dollars" (about $1 million in today's money) to cover the initial cost of raising and equipping the regiment; thereafter, the government would pay all the bills.[7] It would also provide "clothing, arms, ammunition, equipment, transport, horses, stationery, and all other articles laid down for the war outfit of a Battalion," and would then transport the unit overseas.[8] Gault's new regiment would have the same establishment, or structure, as any other battalion in the Canadian or British armies. These conditions were laid out in a special Regimental Charter signed on 10 August by Gault and Sir Sam Hughes. No Commonwealth regiment was ever again raised in this manner.

The ink on the agreement barely had time to dry before posters and recruiting notices began to appear across the country. Men headed toward the Lansdowne Park exhibition grounds in Ottawa. Formal recruiting began 11 August 1914. Among the first to join were three more of the Governor General's military staff, personally recruited by Farquhar. Captain Herbert Buller, formerly of the British army's Rifle Brigade, made a perfect battalion adjutant. Where Farquhar was inclined to be soft-spoken, Buller was more bellicose. Captains D.O. Newton and Raymond Pelly, late of the Loyal North Lancashire Regiment, also organized and recruited for the Patricias, though they continued to serve at Government House for another few weeks.

Another veteran of the South African war, Agar Adamson, then forty-nine and blind in one eye, was as eager to go to war again as Gault. Adamson had served with Strathcona's Horse (later Lord Strathcona's Horse) in the Transvaal. After the war, he and his wife, Mabel Cawthra, had settled in Toronto. Mabel was well to do, and had started a business for her husband, but Agar was not a man of commerce. He focused his energies instead on his social life and outdoor activities like riding and athletics. For him, this war was one last chance for great adventure. He despaired that a man of his age and such obvious physical handicap might not be accepted into Hughes's army, so Adamson tried the PPCLI. He approached Gault through Arthur Sladen, private secretary to the Governor General, with an offer to serve; Farquhar agreed, and Adamson was rewarded with a captaincy in No. 3 Company.

Talbot Papineau has been called "the most unlikely Patricia of all."[9] He was thirty-one years old when the war broke out, and he had had no prior military experience whatsoever. He was the great-grandson of Louis-Joseph Papineau, who had led revolts in Lower Canada against British colonial rule in 1837 and 1838 before fleeing into exile in the United States. Talbot's cousin was Henri Bourassa, fiery leader of the Parti Nationaliste in the Canadian House of Commons. In the late 1890s, Bourassa had been touted as the obvious successor to then–Prime Minister Wilfrid Laurier as titular political head of Quebec, but he broke with Laurier when the latter agreed to send Canadian troops to the South African war in 1899. Bourassa was not, at first, opposed to the war against Germany in 1914, but he believed strongly that there was too much imperial sentiment in Canada, and that such sentiment posed grave dangers to Canada's francophone population.

Talbot Papineau, in contrast, was moved by his strong belief that this war was Canada's opportunity to achieve both full political maturity and independence within the Empire, and a place among the nations of the world. Unlike Bourassa — and the vast majority of French Quebec — Talbot was Protestant. He was the inheritor of both the French Roman Catholic mores of his great-grandfather and the British-Protestant traditions of his mother, and was as "Canadian" as anyone could be in that colonial era. In an open letter to his cousin, published in Montreal in July 1916, Papineau called the war "the great national opportunity for Canada." He believed that if Canada played a full part in the war, "a strong, self-reliant spirit of Canadian nationality" and a "broadened outlook" would develop in its people.[10] He eventually proved correct on both counts.

A man of great personal charisma, the totally untried Papineau soon became, by all accounts, one of the Patricias' most respected, even beloved, officers. One officer who served with him later wrote: "In my opinion, he was the outstanding officer in the Princess Pats when I served with them . . . One could see at a glance that he was the ideal successor to Sir Wilfrid Laurier."[11] Another remembered: "What an orator he was, what language, what emphasis, what gestures, in a class all by himself and how beautifully delivered his speeches were, so fervent in his campaign."[12] For much of the war, Papineau carried on a remarkable personal correspondence with Beatrice Fox, a Philadelphian who wrote him originally as an unknown pen pal. The two became something akin to long-distance lovers before the correspondence suddenly ended in 1917.

The recruiting campaign brought some 3,000 volunteers to Ottawa from across Canada. Each one eventually fell under Farquhar's personal scrutiny; he hand-picked every one of the original 1,098 men. One of the first he selected was W.S. Marsden, a staff sergeant in the Canadian army's corps of military staff clerks. Marsden was summoned to Connaught's residence to be appointed

Regimental Sergeant Major with Regimental Number 1. "We sent out our call. We had no difficulty in getting the number of men we required," he would later remember.[13] Marsden reported twice weekly to Farquhar until Farquhar was given his permanent release from the Governor General's staff.

Another early volunteer was William "Hookey" Walker, age thirty, who had served with the King's Royal Rifle Corps in the United Kingdom before seeing action in South Africa and at Rawalpindi, on the India-Afghan border. When his regiment returned to England in 1907, he retired from the army, then set out for Canada. He settled in Toronto, joined the militia, and worked at odd jobs until 4 August 1914, when he started out for the University Avenue armoury to enlist once again. As an ex-cavalryman, he originally wanted to join a Canadian militia regiment. He met an old friend, however, who told him about the PPCLI, which was "recruiting men with past service."[14] Walker enlisted the next day and was assigned regimental Number 100.[15]

F.G. Young was another Torontonian who signed up. Young had been a private in a British Territorial (reserve) regiment, the London Irish Rifles. Technically, he did not qualify for service with the Patricias because he had not been with a regular army formation. He tried to bluff his way past his initial interview, but the recruiter caught him out. "I told him I was an Imperial Territorial," he would later recall:

> After a bit of humming and hawing, [the recruiter] said, "Well, umm, were you classed as a shot?" I said, "Yes." He said, "What class?" I said, "First class." He said "Oh!" and he wrote in the book and said, "Your number in the regiment is 196." And I knew that he'd taken me in and I said, "Thank you." And he said, "You won't be thanking me in a few months' time."[16]

The Patricias had a decidedly western flavour from the very beginning, with large numbers of volunteers coming from the Prairie provinces and as far away as British Columbia. The western aspect could be attributed to a few factors. For one thing, men of British birth proved the most eager group to serve, and many thousands of those had arrived in Canada since the turn of the century to try their luck in the west. For another, these farmhands, cowboys, and miners were younger and more likely to be single than the veterans of Imperial wars, who had settled in Ontario and started to raise families. One group of young men from Regina, members of an organization known as the "Legion of Frontiersmen," decided to enlist together. They slipped aboard two passenger cars waiting on a siding in that city, and then talked CPR employee George "Smokey" Thompson, and two other CPR workers, to attach the cars to an eastbound train full of Patricia volunteers from Calgary. Thompson did as they asked, then got aboard himself.

One of the Calgary volunteers, also a Frontiersman, was W.J. Popey, who recalled:

> We left Calgary as the 15th and 16th Platoons, under Lieutenant Gray and Lieutenant Fitzgerald. Gray in Frontiersman uniform (Mountie-type Stetsons, neckerchiefs, and khaki shirts), Fitzgerald in cowboy hat and spurs. In the first section of the 16th Platoon none had any previous military experience except Corporal Cooper, who later became Sergeant. We were known as the boy scout section.[17]

Perhaps the most colourful of the western volunteers was Jim Christie. He had been a trapper and a guide in the Rockies, and had had the bad fortune of meeting a grizzly bear along one of his trap lines in northern BC. He managed to kill the bear, but not before it mangled his lower jaw. For a month, he struggled in pain through the bush until he reached a hospital, where a silver plate was inserted in his jaw. Christie was a crack shot, and became the PPCLI's first sniper.

Tracy Richardson, twenty-two, was a soldier of fortune from

Broken Bow, Nebraska. He left a job with a Louisiana oil company in 1909 to wander from war to war in the tropics of central and South America. In Nicaragua, he fought with a rag-tag guerilla army against dictator José Santos Zelaya. Then it was off to Venezuela and Honduras before joining Pancho Villa in Mexico. When war broke out in Europe, Richardson headed to Canada to enlist in the Patricias.

Jack Munro, from Cochrane, Ontario, was well known to those who followed sports. He was the Canadian boxer who had knocked out one-time heavyweight champion Jack Jeffries. The quartermaster had trouble finding a uniform to fit Munro's huge chest, so he walked around Lansdowne Park for weeks in a grey civilian suit and fedora.

One of the strangest contingents of volunteers arrived in Ottawa unannounced. The Edmonton Pipe Band, led by Pipe-Major Jock Colville, had been clothed and equipped by the St. Andrew's Society of Edmonton and sent east to join the Patricias. When Colville met Farquhar at the Ottawa railway station, he announced that the band had come to pipe the regiment to France and back. Farquhar took them on strength as stretcher-bearers. Despite his original plan, Farquhar had to accept these and other men without regular (full-time) army experience. Otherwise, the Patricias would not have been able to raise the necessary numbers; tens of thousands of volunteers were crowding armouries across Canada to sign up for the Canadian contingent, and the Patricias could not recruit them.

As volunteers arrived at Lansdowne Park in Ottawa, they were clothed, equipped, and put up wherever there was room. W.H. Marsden would later remember, "As the companies arrived we were ready with bundles of uniforms to fit the men. We had engaged quite a number of civilian tailors to alter the uniforms as they were needed."[18] The quarters were catch-as-catch-can. H.P. Maddison found himself sleeping in an exhibition hall. "We were quartered in

Machinery Hall," he remembered, "where we tried to sleep on the racks. Each morning, at a very ungodly hour, the pipe band would wind their way between the racks, and in the glass enclosure, the noise was deafening."[19]

Since the Patricias were to be attached to either a Canadian or British brigade, Farquhar formed the volunteers into a standard Canadian infantry battalion, which was, in fact, exactly the same size and structure as a British army battalion when the war began. "At that time a new drill had been adopted in the Regular Army at home," Marsden recalled. "The old standard of eight companies [to a battalion] had been reduced to four, into a mass formation. Col. Farquhar had been supplied with a few circular forms and after a few attempts we were all set to form a battalion."[20]

The battalion consisted of 1,098 officers and men, or "other ranks," in total. It contained four rifle companies with six officers and 221 other ranks each, and a headquarters company with six officers and ninety-three other ranks. Companies were commanded by majors with a captain on strength as company second-in-command, or 2IC in military parlance. A company sergeant major (CSM) and a company quartermaster sergeant (CQMS) rounded out the headquarters. Each rifle company was divided into four platoons, each of which was commanded by a lieutenant with a sergeant as 2IC. Each platoon, in turn, was made up of four sections, each commanded by a junior non-commissioned officer with the rank of corporal. It was standard British — and thus also Canadian — infantry doctrine at the start of the war that battalions generally advanced en masse, with sections, platoons, and companies acting as one. Not until later in the war did Canadian and British infantry battalions begin to assign different and sometimes specialized tasks, even down to the section level of command.

By 19 August 1914, Farquhar had completed his selection: 1,098 men were chosen. Fully 1,049 of them had had regular or reserve military service of some kind, and 456 of them had been in a war. They collectively held 771 decorations or medals for courage or meritorious service.[21] Every British army regiment but one was represented among their ranks. The vast majority (more than 90 percent) of the Originals, as they were soon called, were British born, an even higher ratio of British- to Canadian-born than the contingent gathering under Hughes's direction at Camp Valcartier.

Since the Patricias were equipped by the Canadian Department of Militia and Defence, they received the same kit as the battalions being formed at Camp Valcartier. Much of it was useless. The boots were substandard and quickly wore out in the field. The men's entrenching tool, the McAdam shield/shovel, came from a Sam Hughes brainwave — a shovel that could also be used as a shield by riflemen in the prone position. It was heavy and useless, and was soon discarded. But the most egregious case of sending men to war with the wrong kit concerned the Ross rifle. Hughes selected the .303 Ross for Canadian troops even though it had been tested and found wanting by both the Royal North West Mounted Police and the militia. It was a fine sporting firearm, but it was no infantry weapon. A straight-pull lever worked its action, and it jammed easily with heavy usage or under dirty conditions. The Patricias received and trained on the Ross prior to departing from Canada. Although it was anticipated that they would be placed in a British brigade upon arrival at the front, and British soldiers were armed with the robust Lee-Enfield, Hughes reasoned that both rifles used the same calibre bullet, and thus the discrepancy would not be noticeable. Besides, the Ross was being manufactured by the thousands under a Government of Canada contract, and Lee-Enfields were in extremely short supply in both Canada and the United Kingdom.

The Ross rifle (and the McAdam shield/shovel) was not Sir Sam Hughes's only debacle. Convinced that he had a great military mind, Hughes had not, however, been appointed Minister of Militia and Defence because he was a great soldier, though he had fought in the Boer War, but because he had been a faithful political ally of the prime minister. In fact he was pig-headed and ignorant of effective military organization. He also hated professional soldiers, French-Canadians, and Roman Catholics. His mobilization scheme created major chaos at Camp Valcartier and his reinforcement scheme left thousands of soldiers in the UK doing essentially nothing while front line units cried out for reinforcements. Borden finally bowed to pressure and sacked him in November 1916.

At a church parade on Sunday 23 August 1914, under lowering skies, the Patricias received their colour. Tom Firth never forgot that afternoon: "The Regiment . . . paraded with band and pipers and then formed three sides of a square in front of the Grand Stand. Between the Regiment and the stand were the Duchess of Connaught, Princess Patricia and their ladies-in-waiting."[22] The princess' father, the Governor General, was also there. After the service, the princess passed quietly among the men, "shaking hands, questioning them and generally making herself personally acquainted with the men of the Regiment which [bore] her name."[23] Then the princess presented the colour to Colonel Farquhar. She had designed and made it herself — maroon with a circle of dark blue cloth in the centre, on which she had embroidered her initials and her coronet in gold thread. The staff on which the colour was mounted was cut from a tree growing on the grounds of Government House. As she passed the colour to Colonel Farquhar, Princess Patricia's voice carried across the grounds: "I have great pleasure in presenting you with these colours, which I have worked myself. I hope they will be associated with what I believe will be a distinguished corps. I shall follow the fortunes of you all with the deepest interest, and I heartily wish every man good luck and a safe return."[24]

The colour instantly took on an almost magical quality for the Patricias. While it was not an "official" regimental colour, approved by the Crown's representatives, it was still a "camp" colour — a symbol, a rallying point, a reminder of the uniqueness of this regiment — and all the more valuable to the men because it came from the hands of the princess they championed. As Andre Bieler, who joined the Patricias later in the war, would remember: "We were very proud of that flag, which was very seldom used. It was nearly always carried bundled up in its sheath."[25] Someone dubbed it the "Ric-a-Dam-Doo," apparently a Gaelic phrase. To this day no one knows for certain the true meaning of the words, but there is a chance that Gault himself may have given Princess Patricia's camp colour its nickname. He has previously served with the Black Watch (Royal Highland Regiment of Canada), the Canadian descendant of the Scottish Highland regiment that had remained loyal to the Crown during the eighteenth century Jacobin rebellion in Scotland. The Gaelic name for the Black Watch is *Freicedan Dubh*, which, when pronounced, sounds much like "Ric-a-Dam-Doo."

Looking back from the perspective of almost a century, it is easy to see something both quaint and tragic about the glorious and romantic beginnings of the Patricias. Gault and Farquhar, and the thousands of other men who rushed to Ottawa to join the new regiment, were living symbols of the heroic defenders of the British Empire that filled the pages of G.A. Henty's pulp novels, or *Boy's Own* magazine. They were the men whom Rudyard Kipling wrote about "on the road to Mandalay," the soldiers who "took up the white man's burden" to protect the far reaches of the Empire, from the Khyber Pass to the Sudan. They thought that heroism, noble values, and the ability to drill and shoot would be enough to carry them to victory. But they were wrong.

The Patricias were not prepared for the mass and random slaughter of modern industrialized war. Only a bare handful of observers who wrote about war in the late nineteenth and early twentieth centuries had forecast that the Industrial Revolution would transform war, emptying it of any Homeric glory it might have had, and replacing it with the drudgery and terror of the slaughterhouse.[26]

On 6 January 1915, Francis Farquhar led the PPCLI into the Ypres Salient. The regiment's journey from Ottawa had been long but mostly uneventful. In late August, cheering throngs saw the Patricias through the streets of Ottawa and Montreal to dockside, where they boarded the SS *Megantic* for Britain. But the *Megantic* was ordered to stop at Quebec City by the Navy authorities, who wanted the entire Canadian contingent to sail in convoy. Sam Hughes tried to get the Patricias to wait out their time at Camp Valcartier, but Gault and Farquhar were not eager for the regiment to mix with the raw Canadian recruits at the camp, and they did not want Hughes to strip away the Patricias' best men. So they arranged encampment at Lévis, near Quebec City, from 30 August to 29 September. There, Farquhar continued to train the battalion in musketry, insisting on a standard of performance no less than that of the British Expeditionary Force (BEF). That standard was fifteen rounds a minute of well-aimed fire from their bolt-action rifles. In that "mad minute," as it was called, a well-trained infantry battalion could put in the order of 7,500 rounds down range. When the Germans first encountered the "mad minute" at Mons, they were convinced that the British were firing at them with machine guns.

While Farquhar took care of training, Gault organized victualing and supplies. He contracted with the same order of nuns that had knitted badges for Wolfe's troops during the British siege of Quebec in 1759 to produce red wool shoulder flashes for the men, with the letters PPCLI embroidered on them in white.

The regiment sailed 27 September aboard SS *Royal George*, disembarking at Devonport in the United Kingdom on 18 October. For the next month, the men suffered the cold, wet weather on Salisbury Plain as Gault and Farquhar pulled strings to get them into action as soon as possible. Gault convinced British Major-General

E.A.H. Alderson, designated the commander of the soon-to-be-formed 1st Canadian Division, that the PPCLI was ready to fight without further training or conditioning. In mid-November 1915, the PPCLI joined the 80th Brigade of the 27th British Division, and prepared to embark for the Ypres Salient. Since the regiment was now attached to the BEF, their Ross rifles were replaced by standard-issue Lee-Enfields before they left Southampton for Le Havre, France, on 20 December. This switch was to prove fortunate in battles to come. The Patricias left Le Havre in French cattle cars designed for forty men or ten horses. Then they marched from Hazebrouck to Bailleul to Dickebusch, about three kilometres southwest of Ypres. Their Canadian-made boots fell apart en route. Sergeant G.W. Candy later remembered: "We had to march forty-two miles with about a pack of sixty, seventy pounds on our back with no shoes on. No boots of any kind to speak of . . . I saw men walking with bleeding feet, going on these cobblestones. We could not get boots."[27]

The closer the Patricias got to Ypres, the louder became the rumble of the guns. The men passed ruined farmhouses, partially destroyed villages, and hastily set-up rear defensive positions. They passed ammunition storage dumps, artillery batteries, and a steady trickle of wounded and sick men going to the rear for treatment. The march ended on the afternoon of 6 January at Dickebusch, about five kilometres southwest of Ypres, not far from the front. Here, the Patricias waited in divisional reserve position until nightfall, when French Army guides took them into the line east of the ruined hamlet of Vierstraat. For their first exposure to trench warfare, they were to replace a French regiment in what was thought to be a relatively quiet sector of the line.

The trenches on the western front had been dug in the late fall of 1914 after the failure of the first major German offensive of the war. When mass machine-gun fire and heavy shelling made it virtually impossible for soldiers to survive above ground, they dug lines of trenches parallel to the front. There were usually three trench lines, which were connected to each other and to the rear by communications trenches. As months and even years passed, the trenches on both sides were deepened and strengthened, while underground dugouts were usually built to provide shelter from the weather as well as from enemy fire. Front line trenches had "saps" or short trenches reaching forward towards no-man's land for use as latrines or listening posts. Trenches were generally dug in zigzag pattern, or with half-square shaped traverses to stop the enemy from being able to shoot all the way up the trench line. Trenches could be deep and relatively safe when dug in dry terrain, well above the water table, but in areas with poor drainage or high water tables — especially in Flanders — they were often little more than shallow drainage ditches.

After dark, the Patricias moved out. At first the going was easy, though hazardous, as William Roffey later remembered: "[We marched] up a fairly stiff gradient with the famous poplar trees, line after line on each side of the road. And to cheer us up, we were told how the Durham Light Infantry battalion had marched on that same road just a few weeks prior to our going up there and were annihilated. That was a comforting thought."[28]

The Patricias saw ruins on every side in the light cast by flares and exploding shells. As one man wrote home, "every few minutes the whole country would be brilliantly lighted up with the flares both sides were using . . . the crackle of rifle fire got nearer."[29] They tried to follow each other in silence, lest they reveal to the nearby enemy that a replacement *in situ* was being carried out. They were attempting one of the most dangerous manoeuvres in warfare, when the defenders pull out of a forward position and their relief moves in. Some of the French soldiers sent to guide them got lost; one group of Patricias wandered around in front of the German trenches for two hours. Eventually, the men reached the line and began to size up their situation. Stanley Jones was struck by the strangeness of the landscape:

> On the left of our line the German trenches were only 50 yards away; on the right only 100 yards. By the light of the flares both sides could be distinctly seen with the two rows of wire entanglements between . . . The approach on our side was an open sea of mud, intersected with old wire, abandoned trenches, shell holes strewn with unexploded "Jack Johnsons" [German shells].[30]

Jones and the others quickly discovered that their positions provided little cover from machine-gun or artillery fire. This was no well-prepared line of deep, dry trenches with regularly placed dugouts and saps. The line here was really no line at all, but a series of long, unconnected, shallow, waterlogged, slit trenches. "The earth is so soft it constantly undermines and the parapets fall down," Jones wrote home; "There is no drainage or overhead cover, and we stick over the knees in cold water and mud, absolutely plastered from head to feet. The rifles fill with mud and many cannot be fired. The men cannot walk about, and after sitting in this cramped position for some hours, many men cannot get on their feet, and eventually have to be carried out."[31] Corpses in various stages of decomposition lay everywhere. Rats fed on the corpses or scampered over the men as they tried to sleep.

Dawn arrived, and with it a sight Walter Draycott never forgot: "We gazed out on our 'abode of discontent and misery.' What a sight! How male species of the human family could live under such conditions would baffle the keenest student." It was impossible to move about safely in daylight in the "filthy, water-logged, stinking muddy ditch."[32] There were no dugouts. Constantly in water, the men could not prepare hot food, could not keep dry. There were no sandbags to build up the edges of the trenches, no corrugated iron to shore up their sides. But worse, the trenches were exposed to German fire from the higher and better-sited German positions to the south. Whenever the Germans pumped their trenches dry, even more water flowed into the Patricia positions.[33] Draycott later wrote: "Who can realize the sensation of standing in a muddy, clayey, watery, rat-infested stinking trench for several days without shelter of any kind?"[34]

Vierstraat was a "quiet" sector, but inevitably the Patricias suffered their first casualties. Soon after their first daybreak in the line, the Germans welcomed the Patricias to the war with a heavy bombardment: "Guns of every size and kind roared and spit back and forth," Jones wrote, "ripping up great holes in the earth and throwing mud and water high in the air. We escaped annihilation by only a few feet as the main bursts of Shrapnel just cleared us."[35] Being shelled was both the most unnerving experience a man could have — and the deadliest — but during their first days in the trenches, all the Patricia dead were killed by German snipers. Sergeant Lewis Scott never forgot the moment two of the first Patricias died: "We warned all ranks to keep their heads down . . . I heard a private named MacNeish say to his chum MacNeil . . . 'Mac, look at the bastards, they're bailing out too.' Just at that time a rifle shot came and when I got to where they were, MacNeish had been shot through the mouth and the front of MacNeil's face behind had been taken right off."[36] Captain D.O. Newton was the PPCLI's first officer fatality. Shot in the stomach on 7 January, he died the next day.

For green units like the PPCLI, it was standard practice to limit initial exposure to trench warfare to about forty-eight hours. The Patricias were relieved on the night of 8 January by the 3rd Battalion of the King's Royal Rifles, exactly five months to the day after the War Office in London had given Gault its official approval of his request to raise a new regiment. The Patricias got off lightly with but four killed and nine wounded; most of their casualties came from trench foot and exposure. But they were very quickly learning that Flanders was not the South African veldt or the Somali desert. Here, machine guns, artillery, mass rifle fire, and huge railway guns that fired shells weighing 400 kilograms from thirty kilometres away made this war very impersonal. They were about as far removed from the glamour of their beginnings as they could possibly be.

Chapter 2

WIPERS

BY THE OUTBREAK OF THE FIRST WORLD WAR, THE BELGIAN city of Ypres was still an important crossroads in Flanders, but its earlier glory had faded. For some 700 years the town had been the centre of a thriving cloth trade. The wealthy merchants of Ypres bought the fine wool and intricate lace made by hand in the town, or in the hamlets and farms of the surrounding countryside, and sold the products to all of Europe and beyond. They built magnificent stone and brick houses for their families and, as befitted the wealthy, supported the construction of awesome religious and public buildings, such as St. Martin's Church, dubbed "the cathedral" by British soldiers, and the famous Cloth Hall, built in the thirteenth century. The stylish buildings that faced the central market square equalled any in Europe; the spires of Ypres could be seen for miles around.

The beginning of industrialization in the early nineteenth century led to a decline in the fortunes of the town, and of the merchant classes whose wealth had been so conspicuously demonstrated.

But in August 1914, Ypres became important once again. In accordance with their Schlieffen Plan, designed to bring about a quick victory over France, the German armies were on the move from the western German border, through Belgium, to sweep around Paris. The German commanders believed that the Schlieffen Plan was the key to winning a two-front war by reducing France in the west while holding Russia in the east, then massing the German army in the east to destroy Russia. To fulfill the plan's precise timetable, the Germans had to march along France's channel coast and through neutral Belgium. For the German armies, then, all roads led west, and all crossroads had to be secured.

The Germans were first delayed at Mons, Belgium, on 22 August, when they ran into the small, but superbly trained hundred-thousand-man British Expeditionary Force (BEF). That "contemptible little army," as the Kaiser had dubbed it, inflicted heavy casualties on the Germans before the latter virtually wiped it out. The Germans then continued their inexorable pace until commander Helmut von Moltke ordered his armies to swing southeast in front of Paris instead of around it, and exposed his right flank to the French along the Marne River. The French counterattacked on 7 September and drove back the Germans. There followed a month or so of move and counter-move, as the Germans attempted to remount an offensive to the west, while the French and what was left of the BEF, quickly reinforced by formations of reservists (Territorials), blocked their every effort.

The Germans captured Ypres on 7 October 1914, and completed the conquest of Antwerp and most of the rest of Belgium three days later. On 14 October, the British counterattacked, and recaptured Ypres and the low ridges that formed a natural defensive crescent to the north, west, and south of the town. The Cloth Hall was badly damaged by shellfire, but most of the town was untouched by the fighting that raged around it. This British-held semicircle of territory formed a salient in a German line that stretched from the North Sea to the Swiss border. The Germans were determined to reduce this salient, and to retake Ypres. They made the first of three major efforts to do so on 20 October, when German army commander General von Falkenhayn — successor to von Moltke — threw some of his very best troops at the Allies. The French defended the northern part of the salient, and the British the east and south. The main German thrust was aimed at the BEF, which again suffered very heavy casualties — more than 58,000 killed, wounded, or missing — but stopped the Germans from taking Ypres.

When the First Battle of Ypres ended, the Germans occupied most of the surrounding ground, including the heights of the ridges. From there they kept up a steady fire on the town, using massive railway guns and other heavy artillery to destroy the cathedral and Cloth Hall, which was used as an observation point for the British artillery, and to carry out a steady but systematic destruction of the rest of Ypres. Eventually, the British and Belgians ordered all civilians out of the salient; Ypres was reduced to a pile of rubble. As long as the town remained, however, it was the centre of the salient's defence, the junction of the lines of supply and communication that brought food, ammunition, medical supplies, and reinforcements from the rear. It was the last bit of civilization men passed through when they went into, or came out of, the line, the last refuge where "Tommies" or "Poilus" — the "grunts," or ordinary soldiers — could go for a few hours of escape from the killing along the front. Instead of trying to pronounce the town's Flemish name, the Tommies dubbed it "Wipers."

The Ypres Salient was one of the most important strategic positions on the entire western front. Over the course of the war, three major battles were fought over it, and a million men lost their lives trying to attack or defend it. As one account put it, the region became a theatre showing some of the most horrible scenes of the First World War. The Allies had to hold it because it was one of the last bits of Belgium not occupied by Germany, because it was the only defensive position standing between the Germans and the Channel ports of Dunkirk and Calais, and because this little bit of ground poking into the German lines was a potential jumping-off place for future Allied counterattacks aimed at recapturing Antwerp. The blood-soaked Ypres Salient was destined to be the scene of battle for the Patricias for much of the first two years of the war.

P.P.C.L.I.

As the Patricias completed their first stint in the trenches near Vierstraat on 8 January 1914, Lieutenant-Colonel Farquhar sized up the situation. He was worried about this new style of warfare. Despite his battalion's light casualties, he could easily see that losses were going to be far higher than anyone had expected. Agar Adamson had been left in London to organize a draft of 500 reserves for the PPCLI, but he seemed daunted by his dealings with the British military bureaucracy. In a letter dated 13 January 1915, Farquhar urged him to action: "I hope soon to hear definitely that this draft is on its way . . . you really must do your utmost. I know the very irksome job you have to do but the best solution is to go at it baldheaded . . . Diffidence be damned, my boy."[1]

On 15 January, the Patricias entered the trenches again, this time in the vicinity of St. Eloi on the southern rim of the Ypres Salient. St. Eloi was a crossroads about five kilometres south of Ypres on the important Ypres-Armentières road. The trenches in front of St. Eloi occupied about 1,500 metres of front, but they did not form a continuous line — it was impossible to build one in the waterlogged ground. Instead the trenches were about sixty to one hundred metres in length, sited so as to provide each other with supporting fire. These wholly inadequate defensive positions were to be the Patricias' home for most of the late winter and early spring, as they followed the by-now regular rotation pattern of front-line rifle battalions: three or four days in the line followed by three or four days in brigade or divisional reserve (well back of the line), a few days in "close support" in the second line of trenches, then a return to the front line. On 26 January, for example, the Patricias left the St. Eloi trenches and marched back to Dickebusch for forty-eight hours of rest, reinforcement, and relief from the constant dangers of the front. They returned to St. Eloi to take up a supporting position on the twenty-eighth, and then relieved the 3rd Battalion of the King's Royal Rifles in the front lines on the thirtieth. In these first weeks and months they learned how to live and fight in the rat-infested hell of the trenches.

The trenches near St. Eloi were actually worse than those the battalion had first defended in early January. Private F.G. Young later described them this way: "there was a little ridge at the crossroads of St. Eloi village and it went down a slope across some marshy meadows and in these marshy meadows were dug the trenches."[2] When it was dry, or cold, the trench bottoms were covered in muddy slime. When it rained, water rose to thigh level in some parts. The trenches were small and invariably crowded. "We got into the trenches," Sergeant G.W. Candy recalled. "Where one man should have stood . . . we found that we were standing about eight men in the trench. It was a quagmire within two or three hours . . . pouring rain all the time."[3] Waterlogged trenches caused thousands of cases of trench foot in the Allied lines each month. Standing in water for days on end, boots and socks deteriorated — and so did the men's feet. If not treated quickly, trench foot rendered the feet swollen and painful, and impossible to stand on. It was a crippling affliction, but how could men dry their feet in trenches full of water? Lieutenant-Colonel Hugh Niven later described one way of coping: "Men would sit opposite each other, you'd take off his boots and his socks and the other man would rub them with a towel, dry them, put on another pair of socks and hurry on with the boots. It had to be done in thirty seconds or you never got your boots on again while you were alive."[4] Another regular ritual was close inspection of clothes and blankets for the ubiquitous lice that had taken up habitation on the men's bodies and under their skin.

In daylight hours, anyone who poked his head above the trench parapets died. In the small, cramped, waterlogged St. Eloi trenches, the men lived in a constant crouch, moving with difficulty in the water or thick mud on the trench bottom, eating cold rations, trying vainly to rest or sleep. Trying to build up parapets or parados (mounds of earth on the rear edge of the trench) was futile because of the soft, muddy ground. There was only mud to fill sandbags, and when these bags of mud were piled atop each other on the edge of the trenches, they simply flattened out or slid into the trenches. The men always had a general "stand to," or alert, at sunrise and sunset, in case the German infantry should try a surprise attack. Since it was too dangerous to move about in the open, the normal rhythms of life were reversed: sleep if possible by day, work at night. After dark, the men emerged carefully to crawl over the parapets and try to retrieve wounded, improve wire, dig new saps or communications trenches, or fill and pile sandbags.

So many men had been killed at the salient since the initial German offensive the previous fall that it was almost impossible to dig anywhere and not uncover rotting French or German corpses. Some had been hastily buried by comrades or by the enemy; others had been buried by shellfire. Death had become commonplace, and the dead were just dead and nothing more. "Whenever we move to a new place," one Patricia wrote,

> [we] get the boys at work digging . . . they often find dead Frenchmen barely covered by a few inches of earth. Talking of dead Frenchmen you would hardly credit it but they are very careless over the burial of their dead and [at] night time they often describe the way to a certain trench by a dead one here, two there, and so on. It is not very comfortable when on your own to fall over these gentlemen as having been dead quite a while they exude an odour quite the reverse of pleasant.[5]

There is a common misconception about the trench warfare of the First World War: that it was mass slaughter every day, without let-up, for the men in the lines. Slaughter there certainly was — in mis-planned, badly conceived, poorly executed attacks, or as men tried to hold fast against heavy enemy shelling or mass infantry attacks. But for the most part, death came through a random shell here, or a sniper bullet there. This random loss was called wastage. "Firing, firing, firing. Casualties all the time," one Patricia later recalled. "From the very first day you got to learn to take casualties as part of the ration of the day . . . We had casualties everyday . . . Every battalion in the trench was expecting them at anytime."[6]

The infantry could not do much about the German shelling, though the Canadians soon learned to distinguish one form of German artillery fire from another. They adapted the nicknames the Tommies applied to the different calibres of enemy shells to describe the Germans' fire. High explosive shells were called "Black Marias," after English police patrol wagons; "Jack Johnsons," after the African-American heavyweight boxer; or "coal boxes." Shrapnel shells were "whiz bangs" or "whistling Willies." Trench mortar shells were called "rum jars."[7]

If the infantry couldn't do much about the shelling, they could do something about snipers, however, and Farquhar quickly hit on the idea of designating soldiers especially skilled at shooting to form special sniper units. Jim Christie, from the BC Rockies, was the first Patricia sniper. He studied his craft diligently, keeping a small pocket journal with notes he took on sniping lessons he learned by trial and error. "[S]niper scopes must be practised with to give any degree of comfort and accuracy," he jotted down at one point. "Paint muzzle of rifle khaki, or smear with mud," he wrote at another.[8] Christie and others soon learned to work carefully and methodically in tracking down German marksmen. One German sniper hid in a hedge at night and regularly fired into the Patricia positions. A sergeant from Regina marked his position by the rifle flashes. Then, using field glasses, he selected a hiding spot about twenty metres from the sniper's position. He snuck out after dark, waited for the German to shoot, then killed him when he rose up momentarily to study the effect of his shot.[9]

Farquhar was a tower of strength to the men in those first weeks in combat. Though slight of build and soft-spoken, he exuded strength and confidence. Whatever his inner thoughts and fears — and he must have had them — he knew the vital importance of the men's belief that he would get them through the ordeal. Many years later, one Patricia recalled the night that Farquhar and Captain H.C. Buller helped a working party string barbed wire in no-man's land: "We crawled out and laid wire out in front. Well, of course, that isn't normally a colonel's job, but he did it just to set an example. We, of course, thought the world of him."[10] Another Patricia never forgot how "each night, at each fresh alarm, that gallant gentleman came among his men to inspire them with the freshness of his own courage. His ever ready smile bespoke the tender heart which thrived despite a lifetime of soldier training."[11] These sentimental words, written by a man from a generation that still spoke of courage, honour, loyalty, or sacrifice without embarrassment, sums up the deep love and devotion that Farquhar earned from his soldiers.

Farquhar proved to be an innovative and imaginative field commander. His establishment of special sniper sections was one of the first instances of adapting traditional infantry roles to the specialized needs of trench warfare. He frequently promoted men from the ranks as commissioned officers, believing that recent combat experience and knowledge of regimental doctrine were at least as important as prior military rank. He could promote men more easily in the Patricias than he might have been able to in other Canadian battalions because so many of the Originals were ex-British army servicemen, and better prepared for combat than were the raw militiamen or green recruits of the Canadian Division. Farquhar encouraged the men to innovate on their own, to experiment with new weapons and even to fashion new ones, like jam or bully-beef tins filled with nails and explosives, which the Patricias used until regular hand grenades became available. And on 28 February 1915, Farquhar ordered the very first trench raid against an enemy position by any Canadian battalion.

The Canadian Division, and later the divisions of the Canadian Corps, eventually became known on the western front for their daring trench raids. One history of the Canadian Corps points to trench raids as the prime means by which the Canadians eventually learned how to overcome the stalemate of trench warfare and mount successful attacks on a much larger scale.[12] Trench raids were small, set-piece attacks. They generally followed a prescribed order. A company-size force would sneak up on the German trenches under cover of darkness. At a pre-arranged moment, two parties of raiders would block off a section of enemy trench using rifle fire or grenades, while another party leaped into the trench. The men jumping into the trenches were assigned specialized tasks. Some were to keep the enemy at bay, others to take prisoners, gather intelligence, or wire bunkers or dugouts to blow up on departure. Then, before the enemy could recover, the raiders would pull out and return to their own trenches as quickly as possible. Successful trench raiding took specialized training, split-second timing, stealth, and nerves of steel.

The Patricias mounted their first trench raid on the night of 27/28 February 1915. Seventy-five men in three groups of raiders were involved. The attackers assembled at a group of destroyed buildings known as Shelley's Farm, just behind two Patricia trenches. Gault and "Shorty" Colquhoun, the sniping officer, crawled forward between Patricia trenches 21 and 22 to spy out the German positions. Gault went left and returned several minutes later to report all clear. Colquhoun went right — and disappeared.

He was trapped by a German working party. Farquhar decided to go ahead anyway, and the men moved out at 0515, just before dawn. They crept through the gap between trenches 21 and 22, and headed for a newly dug German sap, or forward-firing trench, that threatened several Patricia defensive positions. Then, they rushed the German sap. One party cut off the communications trenches connecting the sap to the main German trench; one cleared the sap itself with grenades and rifle fire; and the third destroyed as much of the position as they could before pulling out. Both Gault and Papineau took part in the raid; Papineau emerged unscathed, but Gault was shot through the wrist.[13] He was patched up at a medical facility, and eventually returned to the line.

The raid revealed some surprising information; the German trenches were much better-constructed, and drier; they had better-prepared defensive positions and a better way of dealing with water than the Patricias; and they used a different method of stringing wire than the British and Canadians, one far less dangerous. Instead of hanging wire on stakes noisily driven into the ground at night by mallets, the Germans used long steel screws, which they turned silently with axe handles. This method was quickly copied.

The first raid was just that — a first. Success was mixed, with about twenty casualties on both sides. But it was, in effect, the first Canadian attack of the war, and it improved Patricia morale tremendously.

On the night of 19/20 March 1915 the Patricias were in position in the St. Eloi trenches, due to be relieved by the 3rd Battalion of the King's Royal Rifles. As he always did, Farquhar took the CO of the relieving battalion to the front line to give him a full picture of the situation before the battalions exchanged positions. It was especially important that he do so this evening because the Patricias had made some significant improvements to the trenches under Farquhar's direction. Sergeant Louis Scott watched the two men as they proceeded:

> We were draining a front line trench . . . Colonel Farquhar was with the Colonel of the Rifle Brigade. They came up on an inspection tour to observe what was going on. He moved out just a little ahead of me, talking to the Rifle Brigade Colonel, when suddenly we heard him go down. He was shot with a stray bullet . . . We did what we could for him but obviously he needed to be into a dressing station and I ordered Sergeant Maclean and Sergeant MacMorris of my company with a stretcher to take him out to the dressing station at Vermacil, which they did. Regretfully, he died there.[14]

Lieutenant-Colonel Francis Douglas Farquhar, DSO, was buried on the evening of 20 March at the growing PPCLI cemetery at the nearby crossroads of Voormezeele. Captain Buller assumed command of the battalion with the rank of Temporary Lieutenant-Colonel. Although Farquhar had not been responsible for the original idea of raising a unique regiment for service at the western front, he had had by far the greatest impact on how the Patricias were raised, prepared, trained, and brought into action. Gault could not have fulfilled his dream without Farquhar. The day after Farquhar was laid to rest, Talbot Papineau wrote to Lady Evelyn Farquhar:

> Last night we paid our last respects to the Colonel. It was the first beautiful evening we have had. The lovely sunset still slightly tinged the sky. A new moon and the stars were quiet and clear overhead. A warm stillness and peacefulness seemed with us . . . yet just beyond there was the constant crackle of rifles, now and then the whine of a bullet or the loud explosion of a bomb. Peace upon one side, war upon the other . . . There is not a man in the Regiment who does not feel a great and personal loss. No other man in so short a time could have won so much respect and affection. As a Canadian I feel a national debt of gratitude to him. An Imperial officer who could have commanded the highest position in the English army, he accepted

> the task of creating, as well as commanding, a new and untried Canadian Regiment . . . He is no longer with us, but his influence and his memory will endure with the life of the Regiment.[15]

And so it has.

P.P.C.L.I.

In the second year of the Great War, spring came to the Ypres Salient, to a Flemish countryside drastically transformed. The rich farmland had been scarred by hundreds of kilometres of trenches and thousands of shell craters. Yet the local farmers whose farms were outside the immediate combat zone still went out every day to tend to their vegetables, or bring their milk and cream to the market in town. Virtually deserted the previous November, Ypres itself seemed to recover with each warming day. Some townspeople had been evacuated, but refugees from occupied Belgium still streamed into the town, as did thousands of soldiers, mostly British, some Canadian, destined for the front. Ypres had been scarred by the fighting that had raged around it the previous fall, but it still rang with the comings and goings of daily life.

By mid-April 1915, still grieving Francis Farquhar's death, Princess Patricia's Canadian Light Infantry occupied trenches along the southern edge of Polygon Wood, some ten kilometres due east of Ypres. They were good enough trenches as trenches went, deep, passably dry, and well laid out. But the front line lay below a German-held height of land, and the communications trenches that led back to the support line ran uphill. The positions lacked traverses and firesteps,[16] though they were well sandbagged, and gave good protection against the occasional German shell.

Shortly after Farquhar's death, the always taciturn, even stolid, H.C. "Teta" Buller was promoted to Temporary Lieutenant-Colonel and placed in command of the regiment. Gault had been second in command under Farquhar, but could not command because of his wrist, wounded in the February trench raid. Buller was well qualified for command from his tenure as regimental adjutant and his experience as a company commander. He was also the only Patricia officer who had not become a casualty of the late-winter trench skirmishing and shelling. A thoroughly professional soldier, Buller did not possess Farquhar's instinctive touch with the troops, but he was, nevertheless, an exceedingly good tactician, with a talent for selecting good defensive ground and predicting the enemy's likely lines of approach. Lieutenant H.W. Niven, who had done a commendable job as battalion transport officer, became Buller's adjutant.

The PPCLI's routine varied little after Farquhar's death. As part of the 80th Brigade of the British 27th Division, they took turns spelling the brigade's infantry formations in the trenches. And they continued to suffer a steady drain on their strength, as their men were killed or wounded in handfuls by snipers and shellfire, or afflicted with one of a number of serious physical infirmities such as trench foot. In a period of less than three months, for example, by the time the PPCLI left the breastworks at St. Eloi, the day after Farquhar was buried, some 238 of their number had been killed or wounded, and probably another 200 or so were in hospital due to illness or what was then known as "shell shock." Some 300 of the men who had stood on the parade square at Lansdowne Park in Ottawa that wet afternoon the previous August were permanently or temporarily gone. And yet the PPCLI had still not seen a general action.

On 17 April 1915, the Patricias climbed from their defensive positions along the southern edge of Polygon Wood and headed for billets in Ypres. For the next several days, they were to form the Brigade Reserve, the firemen to be called back to the front by Brigade HQ should any sudden threat develop in the 80th Brigade sector. Excited by the prospect of a few nights in warm beds with clean sheets, and the wine and beer and other hospitalities that Ypres still enjoyed, the men were eager for their short respite. They knew that the Germans still threw the odd shell at the town, but what place near the front was truly safe? Besides, Ypres was far from the medium howitzers and the field guns that formed the bulk of the German artillery in this sector.

At mid-morning on 20 April, however, the shelling suddenly grew more frequent, and heavier than usual. Tens of kilometres to the east, the German army's forty-two-centimetre Big Bertha howitzers, capable of throwing a shell weighing a tonne some forty kilometres, opened fire on Ypres. One Ypres merchant recorded the moment in his diary: "20 April. Calm until 11 a.m. While I was at the post office counter a dozen shells fell all of a sudden. I took shelter right away in the cellars and went out at mid-day to see what had happened."[17] What he saw was the beginning of the Second Battle of Ypres, which would see the town's virtual destruction.

"The . . . barracks at Ypres were all brick, with tile roofs and 'Belgian' blocks for paving," Patricia H.P. Maddison later wrote. "When Fritzie hit anywhere new there, they got a lot of ready-made shrapnel."[18] At first it was simply hit or miss; if a "Big Bertha" shell landed anywhere near a soldier, he'd be blown to bits. If it missed, it generally took the German gunners up to twenty minutes to swab out the barrel, reload a shell, charge it, then fire it. But they soon added more Big Berthas and a number of thirty-eight-centimetre guns to the bombardment, and the shells began to fall thick and fast. Entire rows of houses were blown down at a time. The huge shells blew massive craters in the cobblestone squares. Stones, masonry, and wood fell in torrents from the remnants of the cathedral and Cloth Hall. Block by block, the city was reduced to rubble.

"Tuesday 20th, Inf[antry] b[arrac]ks at Ypres shelled badly in afternoon by 15 in [shells]," Patricia F.E. Godwin scribbled in his pocket diary. "Ordered out of b[arrac]ks at 4. Laid in hedge until time to leave."[19]

"Believe it or not," J.W. Vaughan wrote, "we . . . laid over by the railway tracks and watched Ypres being shelled to bits."[20]

Within hours of the first massive shelling, the Patricias were on the move to a much safer place — their trenches at Polygon Wood. "Still shelling the town," Private J.J. Burke recorded after they left. "Feel a lot easier in fire trench."[21] Towards the end of the day, the regiment relieved the 4th Battalion of the Rifle Brigade on the edge of Polygon Wood. They were safer there than in Ypres, but not by much, as German artillery fire increased all around the salient perimeter.

The German decision to level Ypres was not made capriciously, nor merely for the sake of wanton destruction. It was part of a much larger plan aimed at breaking the stalemate on the western front by driving westward through the Ypres Salient to take the port of Boulogne on the Channel coast and cut the supply line from the United Kingdom to the Allied armies fighting in Flanders. To accomplish this task, the Germans mustered eleven divisions consisting of troops mainly from Saxony and Wurtemburg. The plan was to attack the salient on its northern flank using a new weapon: gas. Their attack, which fell on the late afternoon of 22 April, when the winds were favourable, was directed against the salient defences about seven kilometres due north of Ypres. The main thrust fell against two French colonial divisions to the immediate left of the 1st Canadian Division. The German infantry was preceded by a thick, slowly moving cloud of green chlorine gas released from thousands of gas cylinders that had been implanted near the German trenches.

The Allies had had more than a few signs of the impending gas attack, but none of their troops were equipped to handle it. The heavier-than-air gas drifted into trenches and dugouts as it was moved along by the breeze. The French colonial divisions to the left of the Canadians broke, leaving the Canadian left flank exposed. The Canadians battled to hold their turned flank, using urine-soaked cloths tied over their noses to impede the effect of the gas. This strategy was not very effective, but it was the best protection they had against the gas. The defence of their positions during the afternoon was very costly. So were the 2nd Canadian Brigade's night counterattack to close the gap in the line, and the days that followed, especially the twenty-fourth, when the Germans mounted a direct gas attack against the Canadians. Over the course of what became known as the 2nd Battle of Ypres, the 1st Canadian Division lost more than half its effective strength in killed, wounded, or captured, though it played an important part in stopping a potential Allied rout.

The Patricias took no part in the defence of the northern flank of the salient, but they were directly affected both by the battle and its outcome. Because the German attack was such a close call, 27th Division, like other British divisions in the salient, kept its reserves close for the ten days or so that the fighting raged. Normal trench rotations were suspended, and the PPCLI stayed in their positions for twelve days without relief. That was a long time for men right under the enemy's noses, with little sleep, bad rations, and in constant danger. During those twelve days, the Patricias suffered eighty casualties. Added to the normal physical and psychological dangers of a prolonged stint in the lines was the worry that they too might be gassed.

In fact, the noxious fumes of chlorine gas occasionally drifted towards the Patricia positions. The men were quickly told what to do in the event that more lethal concentrations of gas were used against them: "We were in the trenches when the original gas attack took place," Sergeant Louis Scott later remembered. "We got traces of it coming our way . . . We were . . . eventually provided with a little square piece of flannel with a piece of elastic. This we were told to urinate on and place over our nose and mouth . . ."[22] If no flannel was available, the Patricias were instructed to urinate on a handkerchief and push it down their throats. "It gave you a very sickly feeling," Patricia H.R. Herbert wrote, "and more so when you had to use the other fellow's urine."[23]

By sheer luck of the draw, the Patricias were fortunate that in the whole course of the war, only sixty-nine members of the regiment were gassed, mostly by German gas shells. Some of those casualties were completely avoidable. At one point in mid-September 1916, during the later phases of the Battle of the Somme, for example, gas shells exploded in the PPCLI positions. The men quickly donned their gas masks only to hear one brand-new lieutenant proclaim, "You can't see Germans counterattacking with those damned things on," and order them off; five or six men became gas casualties and one was still being treated many years later.[24]

The first phase of the 2nd Battle of Ypres played out through ten days of German attacks and British, Canadian, and French counterattacks until the afternoon of 2 May, when the last German assault on the northern flank petered out. The Germans failed to break through to Ypres, but they did succeed in pushing back the northern defence lines some three to four kilometres, and they captured the important towns of Langemarck, Gravenstaffel, St. Julien, and Pilckem. The British lines on the eastern edge of the salient were no longer viable, as another German push from the north could endanger the left flank and place the troops there at risk of being cut off. The only solution was to shrink the entire perimeter, pulling back on both the east and the south to new and tighter defensive lines closer to Ypres. For the Patricias, this meant a withdrawal of about three kilometres from the southeast edge of Polygon Wood to new positions just to the east of Bellewaerde Lake. There, they would occupy trenches along a north-south axis facing the crest of Bellewaerde Ridge.

On 1 May 1915, preparations for the withdrawal and redeployment of the Ypres Salient began along the front. It was crucial to work on the new defensive positions at night so that prowling enemy aircraft could not see the men during the day. It was equally important to plan the actual pullback, scheduled for the early morning hours of 4 May, in such a way that the Germans would not be immediately aware that their enemy had broken contact and withdrawn. If the Germans did get a whiff of what was to come, they would shell the retreating men in the open, quickly occupy the old trench lines, then pursue the men over open ground, denying them cover and affording them little chance to get to their new trenches and organize themselves for defence.

On the first two nights of May, parties of Patricias slipped back to the new positions to dig what they could before the pullback. Agar Adamson, who had arrived at the front in late February, was deeply skeptical of the positioning of the new defence line and how effective the strategy might be. He wrote to his wife: "A line further back about two miles from here . . . was started last night and our orders are to be ready tonight to fall back and occupy them, if we get the order. This will straighten the line; but will give the Germans, in places, more than two miles of new ground and very good position."[25] As was the case with much of the trench line on the Ypres Salient's perimeter, the Germans would have the high ground, the British and Canadians the low — and the wet trenches that invariably went with it.

The new defence line was only partly ready as the 1st Canadian Division and the 28th and 27th British Divisions readied themselves for the pullback. The new trenches were shallow and, in the words of the regiment's official historian, Ralph Hodder-Williams, "without parapet or parados to speak of, and in some places too wet to be occupied."[26] No communications trenches had been dug as yet, just lines drawn on the ground indicating where they should be. The support trench was not so much a trench as "a ditch behind a hedge."[27] The divisions planned to begin to improve these defences as soon as they were occupied so that they would give somewhat better protection against German shelling and possible infantry attack in the hours just after the repositioning. Two questions circulated in everyone's minds: how long would it take the Germans to learn of the withdrawal, and, once they did, would they attack immediately or concentrate on digging their own new forward trenches and preparing new defensive positions?

Just after full dark on the night of 3 May, the pullback began over several kilometres of front. Against the rumble of distant artillery fire and the intermittent crackle of far-away machine guns and sniper fire, 12,000 infantry quietly left their trenches in shifts and made their way across five kilometres of open ground to their new defensive positions. There was the occasional clink of a sling against a rifle butt, or of water bottles or other bits of kit knocking against each other, and the sound of rustling as the men moved over the ground in crouching rushes. But the move was made in remarkable silence, while those who made up the rear guard fired sporadic shots at the German trenches to give the impression that the British and Canadian positions were still fully manned. Private J.J. Burke was one of the last Patricias to leave the old trenches: "In the afternoon of the 3rd, Corporal Smith . . . came along the trench and said . . . 'you stay behind tonight.' I believe there were about twelve men, an officer, and Smithy who stayed behind. [We] would fire a shot at the enemy trench, walk down the trench about ten yards and fire another shot."[28]

Charlie Peacock, an Original, was also assigned as a rear guard that night:

> P[riva]te. O'Brien and myself were detailed and left the trench shortly before zero hour . . . We started to crawl back and after a while I discovered that O'Brien was not following and so went back. His pack was caught in some old barbed wire and when I pulled out my jack knife to cut the straps he protested vigorously but I had to do it. Next morning . . . I asked him why he didn't want to have his pack cut and he replied "It had a picture of my best girl and I didn't want to leave it hanging on the wire for Fritz to get."[29]

The three divisions completed their withdrawal around 0300 on 4 May without the loss of a single man. Some of the troops set to work immediately, trying to make what improvements they could to their defences before daylight. Others manned machine-gun posts and firing positions and waited for dawn. German patrols quickly discovered the now-empty forward trenches, and the German high command ordered an immediate advance-to-contact. Shortly before 0600, shouts of "Here they come!" resounded along the Patricia line. The Germans came in ones and twos at first, cautiously probing forward for the new trenches. Then came the main torrent. Joe Brice never forgot the spectacle: "It was not long before we saw the Germans coming out of our side of Polygon Woods. They were marching [twenty-four] abreast, when they split up and went left and right and got into extended order. We waited until they got within rifle range and held them down awhile, and when they got their artillery up, boy didn't they give us hell!"[30]

This was the start of a bombardment that lasted an entire day. The German infantry needed to prepare new forward trenches and couldn't do it under constant Patricia and British fire. German artillery, therefore, pounded the new defensive positions while the German soldiers dug and wired trenches on the reverse slopes of Bellewaerde Ridge and Westhoek Ridge just to its east. "Enemy shelled hell out of us all day," one Patricia recorded in a small diary.[31]

It was "the heaviest bombardment of the war," Adamson wrote his wife, "knocking our trenches to pieces in many places . . . the shellfire kept up until 9 p.m. . . . all we could do was to lie at the bottom of our trenches till your turn came for a shell."[32]

"Very heavy shelling all day," the regimental war diarist recorded. "PPCLI suffered 122 casualties before relief at night by 2nd [King's Scottish Light Infantry]."[33] By then, the Germans were well entrenched and had placed snipers and machine gunners in the ruins of a number of farm buildings that overlooked the new Patricia positions. "It was a very bad day," Adamson wrote, "and we got the worst of it at every turn."[34]

In the early morning of 6 May, the Patricias pulled back about three kilometres to take up reserve positions at a spot known as "Hellfire Corner," a small crossroads on the Ypres-Menin road. They were dug in to the north side of a railway embankment when German artillery began to search them out again. Most of the men endured it however they could, focusing their thoughts on mothers, loved ones, things trivial, or sometimes nothing at all. But some could not endure it. They had been twelve days in the line before their withdrawal and they had been under shellfire ever since. While having some minor wounds attended to at a dressing station close to Ypres, Private Joe Brice met a fellow soldier "who was speechless with shell shock." He managed to get him some cocoa and bread and jam; it was the last he ever saw of him.[35]

"My nerves are a bit shaken," another Patricia noted in his diary on 5 May. "Cannot set my mind to write a letter but will write as soon as things get a bit quiet if all goes well. Am feeling very tired and sore."[36]

The Germans occasionally mixed some gas shells in with their high explosives, forcing the Patricias to don their new respirators. On 5 May, Temporary Lieutenant-Colonel Buller was struck in the eye by a shell splinter, and evacuated. Lieutenant Niven remained as Adjutant and Adamson took over as second in command. The next night, the Patricias went back into the line.

Gault spent most of the seventh of May moving about under shellfire and dodging bullets as he inspected his positions. The defences were not good. The battalion's part of the line was across Bellewaerde Lake from 80th Brigade HQ, which meant that communications and supply lines ran around the lake. The PPCLI was responsible for some 600 yards of trench, most of which was at the bottom of a slope. The front trench was not continuous. It was also wet, shallow, and dominated by the Germans on Bellewaerde Ridge. The support trench, about a hundred metres to the rear of the front line, was in passable shape, but the communications trench that linked the two was incomplete, shallow, and exposed to German fire over much of its length. The entire position was open to German artillery; little of the area could not be spotted by a forward observer with a good pair of binoculars. Gault knew it was hopeless to improve the position under the constant shelling, so he did the best he could to deploy his men effectively. He placed two of his companies in the front trench, No. 3 Company on the right, to link with the 4th King's Royal Rifles, and No. 4 Company on the left, to link with the 83rd Brigade. The other two rifle companies were held in reserve in the support trench. After nightfall on 7 May, Gault ordered No. 1 Company to switch positions with No. 3, and No. 2 to switch with No. 4. Then, two hours after midnight on 8 May, Gault and Niven completed their last reconnaissance of the day and fell asleep under the root of a large tree to the rear of the support trench.

Chapter 3

THE SALIENT

AT ABOUT 0600 ON 8 MAY 1915, THE GERMANS' NORMALLY sporadic shelling into the Ypres Salient suddenly increased to a torrent of medium and heavy shells. The firestorm raged over the entire Patricia position, then concentrated on Nos. 1 and 2 Companies in the front trench. The barrage marked yet another German attempt to reduce the salient, this time from the east. The German plan was simple: three of its corps would attack the line from north to south. The 26th Reserve Corps would hit the British lines between a position known as "Mouse Trap Farm" and the village of Frezenberg, atop Frezenberg Ridge. The 27th Reserve Corps — on the main axis of attack — would strike at roughly the boundary between the 83rd and 80th British brigades, and the 15th Corps would attack between Bellewaerde and Zillebeke lakes, about two kilometres to the south of the PPCLI positions.

W.J. Popey was in the Patricias' No. 2 Company position when the heavy shelling began: "We were rudely awakened the morning of the [eighth] by a shell bursting in our lean-to artillery dugout," he later remembered:

> One man, I forget his name, sat with his head off. He had been cleaning his rifle. Most of us had been hit by fragments of shrapnel. We all rushed out and got into the trench. A piece [of shrapnel] had cut through my belt and was rubbing my side. Wright dug it out and I helped some of the others. From that time on it was hell, so many things happened. The shells landed thick and fast. We were down hugging the ground.[1]

Jimmy Vaughan, another soldier in the forward positions, was stung by the ferocity of the attack: "Everything was blown to pieces. There were no trenches left . . . [we] were fighting on nerve."[2]

The German guns virtually wiped out the No. 1 Company positions; No. 2 Company was left in little better shape. Half of the Patricias' effective machine-gun strength (two out of four guns) was blown out of action almost immediately. Shrapnel killed and maimed men; high explosives destroyed positions and blew away wire. Machine-gun fire swept over the PPCLI like driven rain. Gault ordered every able-bodied man who could fire a rifle into the support trench, and sent a brief message to Brigade HQ over the still uncut telephone line. It read, simply, "very very heavy shelling."[3] He followed up that message with a written note detailing the situation, announcing his intention to hold and even counterattack if necessary, and asking for two machine guns to replace those he had lost. By the time the message reached its destination, the first German infantry advance had started.

Convinced that no man could possibly be left alive in the churned-up earth that had once been the trenches of the two forward companies, the German infantry climbed up and advanced against the Patricia front lines. Private T. Richardson was handling the machine-gun range finder in one of the PPCLI positions: "I had a splendid view of the German advance. We couldn't miss them. Our machine guns did terrible execution. But still the Germans came on. Their ranks seemed inexhaustible. It became a sort of nightmare of slaughtering wave after wave of Germans and seeing fresh waves advance over the bodies of the dead."[4]

Sergeant Louis Scott was with No. 2 Company: "After a severe bombardment which depleted our very frail trenches and destroyed 75 [percent] of our personnel, the Germans advanced . . . They came forward in fan formation carrying their full equipment, evidently intending to stay . . . We had a splendid field of fire for a while and were enabled to hold the Hun in position. But not for long."[5]

Private Vaughan was wounded by a shell splinter:

> I was just laying there in the trench, what there was of it and Lieutenant Papineau came along . . . One of my buddies had already ripped my puttees off and slit my pants down because I was hit in the leg and my leg had started to swell. Lieutenant Papineau looked at it and he shoved a cigarette in my mouth and lit it and said, "Don't worry Vaughan, we'll get you out just as fast as we can." I said, "That's fine, sir." But I lay there for six hours.[6]

With sustained rifle and machine-gun fire, the survivors of No. 2 Company drove back the first German attack and gave as much fire support as they could to their comrades on the right. But No. 1 Company was too shredded to offer anything like firm resistance and was forced to give way after a few minutes. The Germans came on, firing and throwing grenades and killing anyone in their path. "They reached our trench and the dogs bayoneted our wounded," one survivor later remembered.[7] On the left flank of the Patricia positions, the scene was even grimmer as the 83rd Brigade of the 28th British Division took the full force of the attack and began to collapse. By 1000 or so, the Germans had swept close to a kilometre beyond Frezenberg, turning the PPCLI's left flank. With the lake at their backs, and bolstered by their own spirit and the strong will of Gault, Niven, Adamson, and the surviving company commanders, the Patricias fought back. As Hugh Niven would later put it: "With Hamilton Gault there, nobody could think of retiring. Just something out of this world. Nobody knows why, but it gave everyone a tremendous lot of courage that nobody else in the world could give to the other regiments."[8]

What Niven and only a few others in the regiment knew, however, was that Gault had been badly wounded. Just after the first German infantry attack, his left arm had been hit by shrapnel. He was hit again in the left thigh, much more seriously, about a half-hour later. Hustled to a position in the support trench, Gault passed in and out of consciousness as the battle raged around him. He refused any suggestion that he be evacuated ahead of any other of the wounded. With Gault out of action, Adamson took command. Soon, he too was hit, in the left shoulder. Still, he carried on, reorganizing the Patricia defences on the left flank with rifle and machine-gun fire covering the gap left by the now departed 83rd Brigade. At the same time, he struggled to help bring ammunition to his beleaguered men: "Even today I can see Capt[ain] Adamson with one arm hanging down getting ammunition from the dead and dying and handing it to us," Bill Popey would remember many years later.[9] Under Adamson's leadership, the Patricias held.

At about 1030, a PPCLI counterattack succeeded in driving back the Germans from the No. 1 Company positions, while men firing from the support trenches and the survivors of No. 2 Company sent a firestorm of machine-gun and rifle bullets into the Germans. But the situation of both forward companies was becoming more desperate by the minute. No. 2 Company was open on both flanks and virtually isolated due to the all-but-impassable condition of the support trench; No. 1 Company could not hold even against a weak German thrust. Adamson ordered both companies back to the supporting trench. With a handful of officers providing covering fire, the few remaining survivors of No. 1 Company crawled back over open ground. No. 2 Company followed, making its way down the corpse-choked support trench.

At noon, some salvation. A second company of the Rifle Brigade[10] worked their way forward to the PPCLI, bringing two machine guns and carrying thousands of rounds of small-arms ammunition. They struggled under their loads as they moved up. Adamson deployed the machine guns and most of the Rifle Brigade men on the PPCLI's left flank, then ordered a counterattack to attempt a link-up with British troops on the other side of the gap. But there weren't enough reinforcements to carry off the link-up, and the drive stalled very quickly: "Orders came to get in touch with the unit on the left, the Monmouth Regiment," Popey later recalled. "Crawling over the dead and dying I couldn't find anyone from whom I could get information. I reported to either [Lieutenant] Clarke or [Sergeant] Beaton (am not sure which) that Germans were going over to the rear."[11]

Adamson could not close the gap with men, but he sited the machine guns to dominate the open ground with fire. At the same time, he added to the firepower of the riflemen in the support trench. No one can say how many more German assaults were turned back by the dwindling number of able-bodied Patricia riflemen in that support trench over the next few hours, nor how many Germans were killed or wounded in the process. But when a platoon from the Shropshires went forward to reinforce the PPCLI at about 1500, the Germans launched their last major attack of the day. One PPCLI runner met the Shropshires just below Bellewaerde Lake, some 200 metres from the PPCLI positions. As they passed him, they doffed their hats and said, "Goodbye Princess Pats, we are going to our deaths like you." The runner — Private G.W. Candy — remembered being "overwhelmed and could not suppress [his] tears."[12]

Adamson, weakened by his wound, quickly broke up the

Shropshire platoon and placed the men wherever they were needed in the PPCLI trench. Then, as the German attack petered out and the fighting slackened, he turned command over to Lieutenant Niven, who held the Patricias in position until after dark. They were relieved by the 3rd Battalion, King's Royal Rifles, at about 2330. As Niven led the Patricias out, the camp colour that Princess Patricia had worked came back with them. "The Colour had been buried in a dugout," Popey later recalled. "We were marching away when someone thought of the Colour. Charlie Palmer and I were sent back to recover them."[13]

The banner had been shot through, possibly when Regimental Sergeant Major (RSM) William Jordan uncased it during the thick of the morning action and waved it from atop a parapet until shot in the head. Jordan was badly wounded, but survived to receive the Distinguished Conduct Medal for his courage and leadership in the day's heavy fighting. Adamson received the Distinguished Service Order (DSO). Most Patricias did not survive the battle unscathed. Between 22 April and 17 May, 700 of all ranks were killed, wounded, or missing. Niven led four officers and 150 men out of the support trench and back along the Ypres-Menin road on the night of 8/9 May 1915. The official history of the PPCLI lists 392 killed, wounded, or missing in the day's fighting.

It is easy to claim, after the fact, that the PPCLI saved the Ypres Salient by holding fast on the lower slope of Bellewaerde Ridge on 8 May, and that Ypres might have fallen otherwise. But no one can ever know what the outcome *might* have been, despite all the words of praise written about the Patricias by higher commanders in the days after the battle. What did happen, however, was remarkable enough. A battalion that had never seen a general action, made up of older veterans shored up by younger reservists, a battalion virtually worn out, and worn down by long periods under fire, threw back a major German attack on its own front. Outflanked, outnumbered, outgunned, the Patricias did not break; they did not allow the enemy to pass. It is no wonder then, as the official history records, that as the bedraggled band of Patricia survivors pulled back on the night of the battle, soldiers from the 80th Brigade lined the road and "swept off their caps to the Colour and cheered and cheered again."[14]

P.P.C.L.I.

The formation that Niven led off the Bellewaerde Ridge was barely the size of a single company. Thus, the battle marked the end of the Originals, and the beginning of a radical transformation to the regiment that Gault and Farquhar had built at Lansdowne Park in the summer of 1914. The most important task now awaiting Acting CO Major R.T. Pelly, who took command from Niven on 15 May, was to rebuild. One option Pelly proposed to Niven, Papineau, and Gault in early June was to have the regiment join the 2nd Canadian Division, which was then being transported to the front. But Gault was not yet prepared to allow his Patricias to become just another battalion in Sir Sam Hughes's army. Then, another option presented itself: the Patricia defence of Bellewaerde Ridge had added immeasurably to their reputation as an "elite" formation, and temporary salvation was on the way in the form of the first of the "university companies," which had started to recruit in Montreal even before the battle.

The University Companies, also known as the McGill Companies because they originated on the McGill University campus, were rooted in the McGill contingent of the Canadian Officers' Training Corps (COTC), established by the Department of Militia and Defence in 1912. McGill had been a logical choice for Canada's first COTC because the university's faculty of applied science had offered a course of study that qualified students for commissions in the Canadian militia or, under certain conditions, in the British army. The idea of channelling McGill volunteers directly to the PPCLI as soldiers rather than officers only was first raised in April 1915 by two McGill graduates, Percival Molson and George McDonald, who proposed to Sam Hughes that a company of McGill men be raised specifically for the Patricias. Hughes agreed, and recruiting began. Soon students from the University of Toronto and other universities clamoured to join. A training camp was set up at Niagara in May 1915 to begin to prepare students to become soldiers. The recruits who volunteered for the University Companies were not, of course, the first nor the only university men to join the Canadian army; many thousands of students poured into recruiting depots at the start of the war and many thousands more joined as soon as they came of age. In fact, a large number of McGill students formed the backbone of two siege artillery batteries before the war ended. The Student Union at McGill became the main recruitment depot for the "University Companies Reinforcing PPCLI," as they were officially called. Eventually 1,239 reinforcements were sent to the Patricias in six company-sized drafts.

The university companies added to the uniqueness of the PPCLI. At a time when few Canadians completed high school, the average educational level of these drafts was much higher than that of the nation as a whole. In fact, most, if not a majority, of these men would have easily qualified for commissions had they not volunteered specifically for service with the Patricias. Many of the university men took a sort of perverse pride in not seeking to join the commissioned ranks, however, and deliberately chose to fight shoulder to shoulder with working men, farmers, day labourers, and store clerks. For them, the war was a crusade to save the world from German militarism and to construct a better and more just society. Some thought it almost profane to use their class position or education to get a leg up on the men with whom they would share the trenches. So the new PPCLI became a somewhat strange mix of war-weary veterans, mostly working-class in origin, and fresh-faced, educated, young Canadians, most of whom were men of means by the standards of 1915. By the end of the war, just over three-quarters of these university recruits had been killed or wounded.

The new recruits had little time for serious training in Canada. As one McGill volunteer later remembered, "We . . . drilled on the McGill campus, marched around and over the mountain, fired our rifles in the CPR Windsor indoor ranges, and lived at the McGill Union and Molson's Hall."[15] The serious training for trench warfare began in the United Kingdom, on Salisbury Plain, under the watchful eye of men such as Captain John Collins. R.G. Barclay, who went to the United Kingdom with the fifth university company, never forgot the first time he saw Collins: "His face, into which he promptly stuck a short black pipe, can only be described as an 'Irish Mug,' and when he spoke there was the suggestion of the green fields of Erin . . ." Like the proverbial drill sergeant, Collins could be very tough on his charges, but also very understanding. And, when they finished their training, he let them know how much they had really meant to him when he told them, "Gentlemen; it is with feelings of sincere regret that I find myself compelled to surrender the control and guidance of a body of men whom I have learned to love."[16]

The first part of the trip to Flanders could be quite comfortable, especially for those moving up in the summer of 1915, probably the calmest period of the war on the western front. One university man wrote home: "From Rouen we moved up the line to our next stop, a place near Armentières, to join the rest of the Battalion. We traveled in great style, in second-class coaches with blue upholstering and lace curtains and thought that soldiering was fine."[17] The official history of the PPCLI says that the old veterans and the young idealists "got on together — the one eager to learn, the other to teach."[18] No doubt, this was true of the majority. But sometimes the initial meetings were more problematic than the official history was prepared to admit. McGill student Andre Bieler would later recall: "When we arrived the Regiment was . . . shattered . . . they had had quite a lot of reinforcements . . . all positions of command, all NCOs, were taken up, quite rightly . . . by the veterans . . . we came in as an outside group against an absolute fortress of non-admittance."[19]

The first university company joined the PPCLI on 28 July 1915, when the battalion was in rest camp at Petit Moulin Farm. At that stage of the war, the Germans were fully occupied with the campaign against Russia on the eastern front, while the British and French high commands were content simply to defend the Ypres Salient and harass the Germans farther south on the western front. From 2 June 1915 to 12 January 1916, the PPCLI was in the trenches just five times. When it did rotate to the front, it was usually to places such as Rue du Bois, near Armentières, which was "very quiet," in the words of the war diarist. The Patricias spent most of August 1915 in that sector. Even the weather co-operated, with warm sunny days and little rain. Life was about as pleasant as it could be under the circumstances. Only a handful of men fell victim to enemy fire. On 17 October, Gault, now sufficiently recovered, rejoined the regiment. He was still the central source of the regiment's pride and spirit, and he quickly resumed his previous position as Senior Major.

The University Companies gave the Patricias a few more months of independence from Sam Hughes's army, but as the summer of 1915 dragged on it was increasingly obvious to all involved that their special status could not last. For one thing, the British intended to transfer the 27th Division to Salonika to reinforce their campaign against Turkey. As a formation drawing its reinforcements from Canada, and whose operating costs were paid by the Canadian government, the Patricias could not accompany the division to the Middle East, where they would be far from Canadian authority or reinforcements. The Patricias were given a choice: join another British brigade on the western front or become part of the newly forming 3rd Canadian Division. Since the majority of the men now hailed from Canada, the choice was obvious: Pelly and Gault consulted Buller, almost fully recovered but for the loss of his eye, and all agreed that the Patricias should join the newly formed Canadian Corps, created 13 September 1915.

On 8 November 1915, the PPCLI marched away from the 80th British Brigade and encamped at Flixecourt, where it remained for several days before embarking on a nine-hour train journey to the Canadian Corps headquarters near Caestre. Here, on 25 November, some twenty kilometres southeast of Ypres, they were welcomed by Lieutenant-General Sir Edwin A. Alderson, GOC the Canadian Corps. Pelly left to become CO of the 8th Royal Irish Regiment, and Buller returned to command on 7 December. On 22 December, the Patricias, along with the Royal Canadian Regiment (RCR) and the 42nd and 49th Battalions CEF (from Montreal and Edmonton, respectively), formally joined the 7th Canadian Brigade. The PPCLI was the only one of the four formations with any combat experience. The two numbered battalions were brand new from Canada via the United Kingdom, while the RCR had spent all of the war up to that point helping to garrison Bermuda. The 7th Canadian Brigade joined with the 8th and 9th Canadian Brigades to form the 3rd Canadian Division under the command of Major General M.S. Mercer.

P.P.C.L.I.

In the first few months of 1916 the Patricias returned to a more regular rotation in and out of the front trenches. For the most part, they helped man defences to the east of the small crossroads town of Kemmel, situated west of the Armentières-Ypres road, south of the main bulge of the Ypres Salient. On four separate occasions in a winter that saw unusual cold and snow, they followed the 49th Battalion into the trenches before going into brigade or divisional reserve. But in early April 1916, the brigade moved north, back into the salient, to take up positions in the trenches just to the east of the tiny village of Hooge, astride the Menin-Ypres road.

Hooge marked the Patricias' return to the daily horrors of trench warfare on the western front. Here, the Germans held the high ground to the east, their trenches running through the grounds of the once magnificent Hooge Chateau. The Canadian positions were constantly wet; they had been dug in a stinking polder that almost always smelled like a sewer. The lines were within grenade distance of each other, and German snipers lurked in the ruins of the chateau and the Chateau Wood that dominated the position. Once again, the battalion suffered daily casualties. In one case, the life of Private Bobby Annan was simply thrown away by an inexperienced captain who ordered him and two others to do a reconnaissance into no-man's land. One of the men present that night later wrote:

> Everyone in the listening post knew it was simply suicide to approach the German lines at that point and the corporal in charge of the post advised against the reconnaissance but was overruled. It was understood that any of the men who might return safely would get leave or a decoration . . . No sooner had the three men slipped over the parapet then they were seen in the glare of the Very lights . . . and German machine guns opened up.[20]

Annan's two comrades made it back, but Annan was fatally wounded.

The officer commanding No. 1 Company in the spring of 1916 was Stanley Livingston Jones, one of the more remarkable officers to have served in the regiment since it first took shape. Jones was commissioned as a lieutenant before the Patricias left Canada. On 25 January 1915, when the Patricias were just being introduced to the realities of life along the perimeter of the Ypres Salient near St. Eloi, he was wounded by shellfire. He recuperated in England, where his wife, Louise, joined him. Louise Jones secured a post at a military hospital so she could be with her husband during his convalescence and close to him after he left for the front. They were very much in love.

Livingston wrote to Louise regularly. His letters were always chatty, with news of the front, but they sometimes also described the irony of a beneficent nature providing the context for the violence of war. "We have had a very quiet warm day," he wrote on 22 May 1915: "Birds singing, farmers working and but for the rumble of the big guns and the passing of troops, one could hardly dream we were in a war."

"I am sitting outside my 'lean-to' smoking my new cherry pipe and enjoying the cool breeze and sunshine," he wrote the next day. "Overhead the aeroplanes buzz and the guns always rumble. Last night there was a heavy bombardment, and I rather expected we should be called out but we were left in peace."

Livingston also wrote Louise to let her know that he was all right in both body and spirit:

> When you do get my letters I hope they will compensate somewhat for your worries — which must cease right now, dear, as we are both in the keeping of Divine Providence which is as much assured us now as in peace, don't you feel so dear? Keep your mind occupied with good books, your hands with knitting and your heart with love and faith and your life will not be barren in spite of all.[21]

Livingston's letters soon formed a diary of life at the front, both the horrors and uncertainties of war and the ways that ordinary mortals coped with the pressure. On 15 October 1915, he wrote: "Such a sweet letter from you tonight. I can fight the Germans so much better, dear, when I know you are cheerful, and we are fighting them all the time here, we have no false sentiments about the matter but are out all the time to kill the other fellow before he kills us." On 6 March 1916, another letter: "The post was good to me tonight, your two letters of the 2nd and 3rd with snaps and your box. The snaps are very good and I shall treasure them . . . A large number of our officers are keen successful business men and make plans for killing huns with the same brains they would use in conducting a difficult law suit."

Two days later, Stanley wrote again: "This morning the entire country is covered with about six inches of soft, flakey [*sic*] snow, a really beautiful sight with the branches of all the trees outlined in glistening white." On 18 March, after the snow had melted, he told Louise: "I've been driving a pill around a cow pasture with a mashie and a ball belonging to Lieutenant McDonald. He is an expert so I didn't shine."

In his letters, Livingston told Louise that the "game" was "getting more scientific every day." The infantry was receiving new, smaller trench mortars capable of pumping ten rounds into the air at the same time. The artillery, meanwhile, was being equipped "with an electric listening device, which by the sound a shell makes passing through the air, the sound of the firing of the gun and the bursting of the shell, is able to locate the gun which fired the shell."[22] The Canadian Corps was also receiving its initial allotments of new Lewis light machine guns, light enough for a man to carry as he moved forward to the attack, giving him tremendous extra firepower. By the end of the war the soldiers of the Canadian Corps (one of the most innovative and best led formations on the western front) would be equipped with one automatic weapon for every thirteen men — as opposed to one for every sixty-one men in a British corps. The Canadians learned much faster than the British how important it was to establish and maintain superiority in firepower in order to overcome enemy trench defences.[23] In that sense, the PPCLI transfer to the Canadian Corps in late 1915 was auspicious.

In the early hours of 1 June 1916, the PPCLI relieved the 49th Battalion in the trenches of Sanctuary Wood. Their portion of the line stretched south for about a kilometre, from a position known as "the Appendix," just over 300 metres south of the Menin Road, to the junction of a main communications trench dubbed "Warrington Avenue." The Patricia front trench ended at the Appendix, which bordered a swampy area in the woods known, appropriately enough, as "the Gap." On the north side of the Gap, the RCR held the trenches between Hooge and the Hooge Chateau. On their right flank, the Patricias linked with the 4th Canadian Mounted Rifles, which guarded the approach to a ridge line that pointed westward from the front Canadian lines. Known as "Observatory Ridge," it was the only dominating height of land in Allied hands along the eastern edge of the Ypres Salient.

By this period of the war, trenches had long become a permanent feature of life at the front. Popular myth holds that one single line of main front trench stretched from the North Sea to the Swiss border. In reality, factors such as terrain, the need to dig trenches where they offered the best protection, and the need to provide back-up defences and communications between forward and support trenches gave the trench system a complex and elaborate structure. This was especially true in places such as Sanctuary Wood, where the trenches were dug in woody areas and sited with a view to avoiding detection by the enemy's roving artillery observation or photo reconnaissance aircraft. To distinguish between one trench and another, the men soon gave them names, which were often reminders of popular streets back home. "Warrington Avenue" and "Gourock Road" were the two main support trenches in Sanctuary Wood, for example, and "Charing Cross Road" was another trench. Sometimes the names were deliberately ironic: "Lovers' Walk" was a portion of the main support trench on the western edge of Sanctuary Wood.

As the Patricias moved into position on 31 May, they were

unaware that they were directly in the way of a major German attack that had been in planning for several weeks. To this day, controversy circulates as to the reason why the German high command sanctioned a heavy attack in the Ypres sector at the time. Perhaps it was because of the obvious British and French preparations for a major breakthrough attack on the Somme. But whatever the German aim, they made thorough preparations for the assault. Three regiments (a German regiment was roughly equivalent to a Canadian brigade) — the 120th, the 121st, and 125th Wurtemberg Reserve regiments — were pulled out of the line for several weeks for special assault training. They were armed with recently introduced flamethrowers, and backed by a major buildup of heavy trench mortars. The most important step the Germans took before the attack, however, was to deploy an unusually large number of artillery pieces, from field guns to the very heavy Big Berthas, to dominate the battle zone by artillery fire. The Germans were well aware that the British Expeditionary Force was deploying the bulk of its artillery along the Somme.

Buller worried about Observatory Ridge; anyone with a good eye for terrain would. If the Germans could somehow take the ridge, they would be in an excellent position to outflank the Patricias and dominate the two kilometres from the ridge to the Menin Road. On the morning of 2 June 1916, Buller deployed his battalion. No. 2 Company, under H.W. Niven, recently promoted to Captain, was on the left front; No. 1 Company, under Major Stanley Livingston Jones, was on the right. Jones's company was anchored on a double trench position known as "The Loop." Buller held No. 4 Company in the "R Line" (the main support trench, located about 500 to 1,000 metres behind the front trench) behind No. 2 Company. No. 3 Company was held in Warrington Avenue, the main communications trench connecting the R Line with the front behind Jones's company.

The main German attack of what is known to history as the

Battle of Mount Sorrel began at 0900 on 2 June 1916, when 3rd Canadian Division positions atop Mount Sorrel were devastated by a sudden and heavy German artillery barrage combined with the explosion of four huge mines underneath their positions. Divisional commander Major General Malcolm S. Mercer was among those killed in the initial explosions. At the same time, the Germans launched a flanking attack against Sanctuary Wood, where the PPCLI was dug in.

"It was the fiercest bombardment which has ever taken place in the British front line," one Patricia later remembered. "Our line was reduced to nothing."

"They kept coming over — coal boxes, whiz-bangs and high explosives of all sorts and shrapnel. By ten o'clock we began to get a bit interested for there were no signs of let-up," wrote R.C. Bradford. "About that time [Sergeant] Cooper ran past the dugout and asked if we were alright at the same time commenting: 'there is many a man at home would give five thousand dollars to see what's going on now.'"[24]

It was the first time Private N.A. Keys had ever experienced heavy shelling: "I was genuinely afraid but do not know whether or not I displayed it," he recalled. "When the bombardment ceased, we issued out of our billet . . . Two casualties were visible, [Lieutenant] Fyfe whose head had been blown off . . . and Sergeant Blackburn . . . [who] lay writhing on the ground with his stomach torn open." Keys was himself badly wounded by shellfire shortly after.[25]

The bombardment virtually wiped out the Patricias' two front companies. In No. 1 Company, Jones was wounded in the back of his left shoulder and in his left side. His orderly and another man dragged him to safety in a mineshaft, but were forced to pull back when the German infantry overran the position. Niven's company had been heavily pounded, but not nearly as badly as Jones's. His men readied themselves for the German attack as the bombardment tailed off at about 1300, but with the virtual disappearance of No. 1 Company, both flanks were open. In the R Line, Warrington Avenue, and at battalion HQ, the shelling killed or wounded nearly half the men. On the right of the PPCLI positions, the Canadian Mounted Rifles had been devastated. The way was open for the Wurtembergers to make their way up Observatory Ridge.

When the German infantry rose to the attack at about 1300, they were certain that nothing could have survived the bombardment that preceded them. Working forward methodically over the broken ground, they raked the remnants of No. 1 Company with machine-gun bullets and sprayed them with liquid fire from their flamethrowers. The six survivors scrambled over open ground to what they thought was the relative safety of Warrington Avenue. But that trench was rapidly becoming a ditch of death as the German infantry pushed up it shooting, loosing streams of flame, and throwing grenades as they moved toward the intersection of Warrington Avenue and Gourock Road, with the R Line just beyond.

Isolated in their front position, Niven's men poured thousands of rounds of rifle and machine-gun ammunition into the Gap on their left and towards the right rear of the German troops moving through the now abandoned No. 1 Company position. Harry Cochrane had just finished bringing a message from his CO to the Regimantal Sergeant Major (RSM), and was scrambling back to his company position, when the German infantry drew near:

> I dug out an old rifle, got the action cleaned, and charged it with ten rounds and happened to look towards the German lines through one of the holes caused by a trench mortar, and here comes the Germans in the hundreds. I nailed four who were closest to me . . . when my parapet was all on fire [with] heavy black smoke. Naturally I didn't want to be burned to death so I started for a part where there was no fire. I got about fifteen feet when some German saw me and handed me my packet through the left lung from the back. It came out very near the heart.[26]

Cochrane lay in a mud puddle at the bottom of a small crater for three hours until he was found by a German Red Cross man who took him prisoner and began tending to his wounds.

The German push up Warrington Avenue and Gourock Road endangered the entire Patricia position. The men of No. 3 Company fought tenaciously for every metre of trench. Buller ordered a blocking position to be set up; he sent two No. 4 Company platoons to position themselves to the north of Observatory Ridge to resist a possible German thrust down the slope and into the rear of the PPCLI. Gault did what he could to help reinforce the block at the head of Warrington Avenue, but he was blown off his feet. Badly wounded, he was carried to a fire trench in the Lover's Walk section of the R Line. No. 3 Company rallied and began to push the Germans back down Warrington Avenue. They were not fast enough for Buller, however, who jumped out of the Warrington Avenue trench to encourage his men to make better progress. His dramatic gesture worked, but he was shot dead almost immediately.

Adjutant Captain A.G. Martin assumed command until Major Donald Gray of No. 4 Company could be summoned to battalion HQ. In the smoke and confusion, these two men directed a link-up between the No. 3 Company infantry, pushing back toward the front trench, and the survivors of No. 2 Company, still resisting with every bullet and ounce of strength.

At about 1500, the Germans seemed to stop their advance along Observatory Ridge and hold in place almost everywhere else, though they made three more attacks against the No. 2 Company position in mid-afternoon. By then, Niven had been wounded. Lieutenant G.B. Glassco eventually took his place, and directed No. 2 Company's withdrawal from its position after nightfall. They pulled out just before daybreak on 3 June, taking all their weapons, stores, and ammunition with them, and carrying all the wounded except two, who were unconscious and dying. They came back over open ground but suffered not a single casualty.

For several days after the PPCLI's ordeal on 2 June, the fighting raged. Both sides attacked and counterattacked until the front stabilized once more around 13 June. The Canadians re-took Observatory Ridge on 14 June. As with so many battles in the first three years of the First World War, little was accomplished for the thousands of lives lost. Once again the Patricias were left shattered. Most of the University Company drafts who had arrived to shore up the regiment were killed or wounded at Sanctuary Wood. Gault would lose his leg. Buller and five other officers were dead, and 388 other ranks were dead, wounded, or missing. About a week after the battle, Louise Jones received news of her husband from Eugene P. Buonaparte, who had come over with the 5th University Company and been captured in the battle. In a note written in French, Buonaparte told Louise that her husband had died in a German army hospital on the afternoon of 8 June: "The doctors did all they could to save him. But in vain. An internal haemorrage [*sic*] and the loss of blood killed him . . . This afternoon [he] has been buried with all military honour in the garden of this Convent Hospital in the City of Moorseele, Belgium."[27]

One of the missing Patricias was Private Stanton McGreer of the 2nd University Company, who had disappeared just after the bombardment destroyed the No. 1 Company positions. His uncle, Colonel A.H. McGreer, a senior army chaplain, set out to find him. The colonel's journey started late on 2 June, when news of the battle reached him. He set out for Headquarters of 3rd Canadian Division. There, he heard the startling news that the divisional commander was missing (in fact, he had died of wounds suffered during the opening barrage) and that the PPCLI had been in the thick of the fight. For two more days he searched casualty clearing and dressing stations and spoke to Patricias who might have had some idea of his nephew's whereabouts. After the Patricias had been pulled back into reserve, he met a member of McGreer's platoon who had survived the battle. But still, he heard no news of his nephew.

On the night of 4/5 June, Colonel McGreer left PPCLI HQ and set out on horseback for the field hospital at Brandhoek. "It was a dark cheerless night with a light mist falling," he wrote his brother, Stanton's father: "The star shells lit up the road beyond Poperinghe for a few seconds only to die away and leave the darkness darker still. Transport columns, ammunition waggons moved to and from the trenches on either side of the road, the drivers calling out 'keep to the right' at regular intervals of a few seconds to avoid collisions." Later that night, he encountered McGreer's platoon commander, who told him that Stanton had not only survived the 2 June battle, but was sure to receive a "mention in dispatches" for the heroism he had displayed when the German infantry had attacked.[28] The commander also described how he and Stanton had been sharing a covered bit of trench in the midst of a bombardment the morning after the battle when a shell had exploded, driving a large piece of wood into the young private's left leg. "He was taken to a dug out, splints were put on the leg and I hope he'll be alright," the lieutenant added. By then it was well past midnight, and Colonel McGreer ended his search for the night.

McGreer found his nephew the next day in a casualty clearing station near Ypres. "I was setting out for Zillebeke . . . when I met Major Creegan and Major Beattie," he wrote. "After a few words with them I went in and met the first of a long line of stretcher cases which had been lying out some of them in the open for three, four, five days. I enquired who each one was as I passed and finally heard the name for which I yearned 'McGreer'. My feelings were too strong to express in words." For two days the colonel helped care for the young man while doing his best to perform his own solemn duties in the midst of a battle still raging. But Private Stanton had developed gas gangrene. Although his left leg was amputated above the knee on 7 June, he died early the next day. He was buried shortly thereafter.

"How sacred the spot which shields Stanton's body," wrote

Chapter 4

VIMY RIDGE

By 1 July 1916, the British and French troops had waited for days in trenches between the Ancre and Somme Rivers, just a few kilometres to the north and east of the little French town of Albert, while their artillery poured a torrent of shells at the enemy. General Sir Henry Rawlinson, commander of the British Fourth Army, assured everyone that when the bombardment ceased, there wouldn't be any Germans left; the Allied infantry would climb out of their trenches and walk to victory in the Battle of the Somme.

The French army HQ first conceived of the Battle of the Somme in December 1915, as a combined British and French breakthrough attack against the middle of the main German defence line. The idea of the attack was simple — a massive buildup of troops, artillery, and supplies at the junction of the British and French forces in the vicinity of Albert would create an unstoppable momentum after the German positions had been reduced by the heaviest bombardment of the war. No new tactics were to be employed and no innovations used in the attack. Sheer drive would win the day.

It did not. The shelling was indeed heavy, but most of the British and French shells were of the wrong kind and inadequate for destroying the large, barbed-wire barriers that the Germans habitually erected. They were also the wrong type to penetrate deeply into the German bunkers. The buildup was an obvious warning to the Germans that a major attack was coming, and they planned for that attack by bringing up masses of reserves. The Germans were determined to contest every metre of ground and turn the impending struggle into a giant battle of attrition. When the shelling stopped, they rose from their bunkers, set up their machine guns, and waited for the attackers.

In the British sector, one hundred thousand men climbed from their trenches. They formed slow-moving waves of infantry and advanced towards the supposedly destroyed German defences. This was classic attack en masse: entire battalions were drawn into line. No effort was made to divide the attacking force into companies or platoons to give each other cover or to use the terrain to advantage, bomb, or Lewis-gun their way forward. Each man was burdened with dozens of kilograms of ammunition, rations, entrenching tools, blankets, and other equipment that would be useless in the first hours of the advance.

The Tommies were slaughtered by the German machine guns. When the sun set many hours later, the British army had been reduced by more than 57,000 casualties, of whom close to half had been killed in action. They gained almost no ground, but British commander Douglas Haig pressed the attack anyway in the days, weeks, and even months that followed. He converted the planned breakthrough battle into a battle of attrition, in which the British and their Empire allies, such as the Australians, lost several thousand men a day for close to three months. Given Haig's determination to pour lives into the Somme battlefields, it was inevitable that the Canadian Corps would have its turn.

Towards the end of August 1916 the Canadian Corps began its transfer to the Somme. Battalion by battalion, the Canadians left their positions near Ypres, marched dozens of kilometres over hot, dusty roads to railheads, then boarded trains to ride the seventy or so kilometres from the Ypres Salient to the vicinity of Albert. The corps now consisted of four full divisions, though the 4th was newly arrived and stayed near the salient to complete its battle inoculation. Commanded by Sir Julian Byng, the corps, always tough and innovative, had emerged from the dark days of the second Battle of Ypres and the St. Eloi Craters stronger than ever. Arthur Currie, in command of the 1st Division, had shown himself to be a superior divisional commander in the closing stages of the Battle of Mount Sorrel, after the PPCLI had withdrawn from the bloodbath of Sanctuary Wood. Ordered by Byng to recover all the ground lost to the Germans since the start of their offensive, Currie's counterattack on 12 June was marked by careful planning, excellent coordination of infantry and artillery, and inspired leadership. Losses were heavy on both sides, but the Canadians pushed the Germans back to where they had been on 4 June.

Much recent analysis examines the reasons why the Canadian Corps became such a crack fighting force in such a short time — essentially between the spring of 1916 and the attack against Vimy Ridge on 9 April 1917.[1] The basic reason is straightforward: this group of one-time amateur soldiers was not burdened with the outmoded fighting doctrine or class rigidity of the British army. In their inventiveness and innovation, they came to reflect the Canadian society in which they were rooted. They emerged, essentially, as a small national army representing a young colony-becoming-a-nation. Canadian commanders knew they could not fight battles of attrition and throw away tens of thousands of lives; they searched for methods of using new technology, in tactically innovative ways, to *save* lives. They began to innovate in infantry-artillery co-operation

Gault underestimated Adamson's determination to have someone else command the Patricias; Pelly agreed to return at Adamson's "special request"[4] and came back to take command on 3 August 1916.

On 15 August, the Patricias left the front trenches on the eastern side of Sanctuary Wood and began successive moves by road, and sometimes by train, to reserve positions further and further back of the line. On 7 September they boarded trains for the long trip south to Albert. "After a march of eleven miles yesterday afternoon," Adamson wrote to his wife, Mabel, "we entrained, arriving at five o'clock this morning and marched a few miles and went into billets — in a beautiful little French village . . . The weather is beautiful. We have no orders, but the general idea is that we remain here three or four days and then march up to the line."[5] When he wrote again three days later, the PPCLI had moved closer to the front and into somewhat less comfortable quarters: "Starting at 5 a.m. today, we marched 13 miles and are now in huts of a very dirty description."[6] One Patricia was deeply impressed by the rats on the Somme. A.E. Potts wrote later: "You could put a piece of bacon or a piece of cheese on the end of your bayonet and . . . just shoot the rats when they came . . . I can remember the rats running over you. I can remember waking once when a rat was biting me on the hand."[7]

The closer the PPCLI got to the active front, the more men, horses, trucks, field parks, aid posts, artillery dumps, and other equipment and installations they saw. "There are signs of great activity all about here, tremendous numbers of troops coming in or going out," Adamson told Mabel.

"Have never seen such an enormous amount of men and equipment in my life before, as far as the eye can see," Patricia A.L. Potentier wrote home. "Thousands of guns and enormous quantities of ammunition."[8]

In this large collection of war-waging paraphernalia were "caterpillars," the likes of which the men had never before seen.

These were about nine metres long, four metres wide, and three-and-a-half metres high. They carried a commander and a crew of seven men to operate the gears and engine, and man the machine guns and six-pounder quick-firing guns mounted inside them. These "tanks" had been under development in the United Kingdom for close to two years, and were a closely held secret until now. Designed to withstand and suppress enemy machine guns, penetrate enemy wire, and lead the infantry in attack, they were slow and subject to frequent mechanical breakdown, but they would eventually revolutionize warfare.

At the beginning of the second week of September 1916, the second phase of the Battle of the Somme was about to begin. In late August, the first Canadian formations to arrive were assigned the job of reinforcing and then relieving troops of 1st Anzac Corps in a part of the battlefield known as Pozières Ridge, south and east of the town of Courcelette. In fact, however, the Canadians had been brought to the Somme to take part in a renewal of the original offensive, due to begin in mid-September. The first attack, on 1 July, had made agonizingly slow progress at a cost of tens of thousands of lives with little gain. The first German defensive line had eventually been taken, but the second line, which ran about three kilometres southwest of Courcelette, was largely intact. Haig intended to use the fresh Canadian troops, the tanks, and a relatively new innovation in artillery tactics known as the "creeping barrage" to attack northeast along the Albert-Bapaume road. The troops, Haig planned, would capture Courcelette, then launch a mighty effort to reach and take the last German defensive line to the northeast of the town, and perhaps even Bapaume itself.

On 14 September, as the 2nd and 3rd Canadian Divisions prepared for the attack, the PPCLI remained in bivouac in the "Brickfields" to the west of Pozières. Turner's 2nd Division was to drive northeast along the Albert-Bapaume road to a point south of Courcelette in the vicinity of a feature known as "the Sugar Factory," while Major-General Louis Lipsett's 3rd Division was to cover the left flank of the main thrust with a holding attack north of Pozières towards the Zollern Redoubt, the key German defensive position to the west of Courcelette. Lipsett's 7th Canadian Infantry Brigade, including the PPCLI, was to be held in Corps reserve until needed.

The attack began at 0620 on 15 September. The 2nd Division quickly made good progress; at Canadian Corps headquarters, Byng decided to follow up as rapidly as possible and issued warning orders to his two reserve brigades, the 5th and the 7th, to be ready to attack by late afternoon. The 5th was to advance up the Albert-Bapaume road into Courcelette itself, while the 7th was to capture a key German trench known as Fabeck Graben. They were then to push on to take a second trench, Zollern Graben, which connected the Zollern Redoubt to the western outskirts of Courcelette.

Pelly knew little of the role that 7th Brigade would play until early in the afternoon when he was given the plan of attack. The plan was a mess. The Patricias would have four hours to move from their reserve position to the "Chalk Pits," about a kilometre south of Pozières, and then from the Chalk Pits to their start line in Sugar Trench, about a kilometre southwest of Courcelette. They were to be in position by 1800 and remain there as the artillery pounded their objective. They were to attack Fabeck Graben as soon as the artillery lifted at 1815.

It is no trick in peacetime to stroll over a few kilometres of gently rolling ground on a warm, dry day. But the distance between the Chalk Pits and the start line was almost five kilometres, and the Patricias had to advance over hilly terrain badly broken up by heavy shelling. The closer the men got to Courcelette, the heavier came the German artillery fire. To make matters worse, they were never sure exactly where they were. As the official historian noted: "There was little . . . to go upon . . . the Patricias were jumping off into unknown enemy country with no guidance but a dubious aeroplane map."[9]

The Patricias left the Albert brickfields at approximately 1400 and moved up the Albert-Bapaume road, arriving at the Chalk Pits about an hour later. Pelly thought the battalion would have a few hours of rest before advancing to the start line, so he authorized the field kitchens to set up and prepare some hot food. Most of the men managed to eat before the PPCLI was ordered to move again at 1630; the Patricias had only ninety minutes to get from the Chalk Pits to Sugar Trench. The battalion moved north, crossed the Albert-Bapaume road, and then turned east to descend single file through rugged terrain to a feature known as the Windmill. No. 3 Company was in the lead. A.R. Milne, who had been assigned to lead the regiment into Sugar Trench, recalled: "We were astonished to see [the regiment] coming over the crest of the ridge . . . a long winding single file led by Major Charlie Stewart, who when we met, inquired without slackening his rapid pace the whereabouts of 'Sugar Trench.' With my arm I indicated straight down the continuation on the slightly sunken road in which we were . . ."[10]

As Stewart's men led the regiment past the Windmill, German shells began to explode among them. About 40 percent of No. 4 Company were killed or wounded within minutes; Major S.F. Martin, the company commander, was killed along with the company sergeant-major. To make matters worse, Stewart couldn't find Sugar Trench. He led his men along the sunken road, past the turn-off point for the trench, and into no-man's land in front of the objective. When he looked up to see Courcelette burning off to his right, he realized he had gone too far and that his men were facing north instead of northwest. Under German observation, the men scrambled into a rough line facing the Zollern Graben trench and dug down. As they redeployed over open ground, they were surprised by several German soldiers. F.J. Kendall later recalled: "Suddenly, about thirty yards in front of us, a dozen or so bandages were waving in German hands. The Fritzies were throwing away their equipment and yelling, "Kamerad! Kamerad!"[11] The Patricias took about seventy-five prisoners before their main attack even began. But nothing else about the attack would be so easy.

The Canadian barrage was already falling when, at about 1815, Stewart got his men straightened out. To his left he caught sight of the 49th Battalion, set to advance on the PPCLI's left flank, and guessed which direction to move his men to get them into the first German trench. When the shelling stopped, the Patricias rushed forward, catching machine-gun and rifle fire from the outskirts of Courcelette to their right. A.L. Potentier was carrying eight panniers of Lewis-gun ammunition, as well as his own rifle, as he scrambled toward the German trench: "I got mine through the hip. It felt as if someone had hit me with a hammer. I went spinning around about four times and fell in a big shell hole. I tore my field dressing out and clapped it on the wound. I lay in the shell hole until it was dark. God it was awful. Dead and dying were lying everywhere."[12]

German slugs tore into Nos. 3 and No. 1 Companies; virtually all the officers and about half the men went down within minutes, but a handful of bombers from No. 3 Company and two platoons of No. 1 Company managed to get a foothold in the trench, as did most of the 49th Battalion. The Germans still held a 200-metre section of trench. Dozens of Patricia wounded lay untended and thirsty in shell holes and communications trenches. "It was pitiful to hear the wounded moaning," Potentier later recalled. W.M. Oliver was luckier than many of these men:

> I went over with the first wave, but after I had gone about 50 yards or so I got hit in the arm, but I thought it didn't matter, and that, if I went back to the dressing station, I should be thought trying to get away from the danger zone. Or in other words, scared. So I crawled as best I could through a communication trench and went on ahead, which proved to be the better choice, as numbers were killed who were on their way to the dressing station.[13]

Throughout the evening and into the night Stewart directed his men in digging a new forward trench a few dozen metres south of and parallel to the German-held portion of Fabeck Graben. At about 1500 on 16 September the Patricias and the 49th Battalion attacked the Germans from both flanks and the front, machine-gunning and grenading their way into the German position. The Germans surrendered: Canadians held the entire Fabeck Graben. As the official historian later wrote: "The Regiment now garrisoned between 300 and 400 yards of good deep trench littered with dead, wounded and equipment."[14] Some effort was made to push beyond to the Zollern Graben position, but the Patricias were much too weak at that point to mount a successful attack. In the roughly twenty-four hours since leaving the Chalk Pits, the Regiment suffered 307 casualties. The proportion of killed to wounded was much higher than usual because of the heavy machine-gun fire directed at them from Courcelette. At 1600 on 16 September, the 7th Brigade was relieved.

The Patricias spent the next three weeks in reserve, rebuilding their strength while forming working parties to improve the roads near Albert or bring up supplies and ammunition. In the meantime, the autumn rains began to fall across Picardy, turning the Somme battlefield into a morass of mud. Patricia Stanley Davis wrote home: "What interests me most is mud. Dog gone yellow mud . . . when I get back I am not going to walk any more than 1/4 of a mile a day and then I shall walk on pavement."[15] Mud had become a constant of life for Davis, but so too had death. "I have lost some great friends here," he wrote. "Someone goes pretty nearly every minute. And once dead a man seems so peaceful. The body is no more use and he departs. I don't fear death the least bit, I never did much and since coming over here I have got so that I can rather see its good points and death has no terror for me."[16]

On 8 October, as the Somme fighting continued, the Patricias were assigned as brigade reserve in an attack on Regina Trench, about one-and-a-half kilometres north of Courcelette. The 49th Battalion and the Royal Canadian Regiment (RCR) led the attack. Pelly was at brigade headquarters that day, so Adamson assumed command. The assault was an abject failure; the attacking battalions ran into thick belts of uncut German wire and were slaughtered. The tragedy, however, was a blessing in disguise for the Patricias, who never got directly into the fight because of it. Instead, they held themselves ready for a possible German counterattack and launched a few grenade-throwing forays into secondary trench objectives while their sister battalions took heavy losses. The Patricias suffered eighty casualties until they were relieved by the 4th Canadian Mounted Rifles in the evening. Adamson summed the day up this way:

> The army had become too sanguine and gave us [the 7th Brigade] a job that was almost impossible to carry out and also did not give us enough support and in many cases, though not in ours, the Artillery had not cut the wire, the men being shot to pieces trying to get through it . . . The RCR lost every officer, killed, wounded, or taken prisoner, they sent in, except the C.O. and Adjutant.[17]

Two days later, on 10 October, the 3rd Canadian Division pulled out of the Somme battle and, in company with the 1st and 2nd Divisions, headed for the Vimy Ridge area, some thirty-five kilometres north of Bapaume. For the better part of two weeks, thousands of Canadian infantry marched north over the muddy roads of Picardy while the unfortunates of the 4th Canadian Division stayed behind for their introduction to trench warfare in the waning days of the fighting on the Somme. The last battles to the east of Albert were fought in the snow and cold of November, before Haig suspended the attacks for the winter.

The Patricias arrived at Neuville-St.-Vaast, a few kilometres west of Vimy Ridge, on 23 October 1916. Pelly then left the Patricias for good, passing command to Adamson four days before the regiment entered the front line at the foot of the ridge. For the next four-and-a-half months, the routine of trench life was broken only by the usual rotations and a series of small trench raids designed to snatch prisoners, gather intelligence, and test German defences.

P.P.C.L.I.

The PPCLI had started life as a regiment of old Imperials. It had been transformed by the infusion of the educated young men of the University Companies and by almost a year's worth of soldiers arriving from across Canada in reinforcement drafts. By the spring of 1917, the PPCLI emerged as a cross-section of English-speaking Canadian manhood. The RCR was similarly unnumbered, and boasted a history several decades and one war (the Boer War) longer than the PPCLI. But the Patricias' unique founding and the regiment's attachment to Hamilton Gault and its patron, the Princess Patricia, still marked it as somewhat different from the other battalions, numbered or not, of the Canadian Corps. Their gradual assimilation into the Canadian Corps, however, was no bad thing: the PPCLI more and more reflected the innovative intelligence, the gritty determination, the sheer courage, and the irreverent spirit of its young country.

That spirit was nowhere more evident than in The Patricia Comedy Company, famous throughout the Canadian Corps by the spring of 1917. It thrived on performing farcical take-offs of high-ranking Patricia officers. In one famous Comedy Company skit, the Acting Provost Marshal, a very near-sighted man who was constantly arresting the wrong soldiers, was depicted entering his London flat eager to see his wife. On spying a woman sitting on a man's knee, he concluded that his wife was being unfaithful and shot the couple, only to discover that he was in the wrong apartment.

Agar Adamson was the Comedy Company's favourite target. In the words of Patricia runner Howard Ferguson, Adamson was a man of "peculiarities and eccentricities." The men called him AAA, or "Ackty Ack"; Ferguson thought he spent entirely too much time writing long letters to Princess Patricia. Adamson was quite aware of his reputation as an eccentric, and probably cultivated it. In mid-March 1917, Adamson wrote to Mabel somewhat proudly that the Comedy Company had done a take-off of him. In the skit, he was caricatured as addressing the battalion with the following words: "any man who does not know enough to take care of himself and allows a woman to ruin his fighting efficiency to the Regiment, and finds himself in No. 9 (this is the big venereal hospital) is not fit to be called a man and ought to be strangled as a creature with a woman's apron string."[18]

P.P.C.L.I.

Vimy Ridge runs northwest to southeast for about six kilometres between the French towns of Lens and Arras. In 1917, it formed a German salient into the British lines; although it was only some 145 metres above sea level at its highest point, it dominated the flat country for many kilometres around. It gave the Germans a tremendous vantage point from which to observe Allied movement to the west and dominate the region with artillery fire. Vimy had been assaulted three times by French troops in late 1914 and 1915 with no result except the loss of some 200,000 men. Given its importance, the Germans spared no effort to defend Vimy Ridge, with three trench lines and dozens of bunkers, machine-gun positions, and strongpoints. The Germans were beginning to experiment with defence-in-depth by the spring of 1917 — leaving the front lines lightly defended while concentrating the bulk of their troops to the rear in position to counterattack almost immediately — but the man commanding the German troops at Vimy, General von Falkenhausen, was a man of the old school. Although he placed his reserves well back of the first trench line, the bulk of his troops were entrenched in the second and third lines and at the top of the ridge. His artillery was sited on the far side of the ridge where he thought it was undetectable by his enemy.

Lieutenant-General Julian Byng learned in the fall of 1916 that the Canadian Corps would have to capture Vimy Ridge in an early spring holding attack while the British Third Army launched a two-corps attack eastward along the Scarpe River from Arras. To help prepare for the attack against these formidable positions, Byng sent Arthur Currie to find out how the French had started to learn how to overcome trench warfare in the brutal battles around Verdun. Currie wrote a long report on what he discovered, and Byng implemented virtually all of the changes Currie recommended. The Canadian Corps reorganized its attacking formations, which were to be made up of three self-contained platoons, with Lewis gunners, bombers, snipers, and scouts to aid the riflemen. Attacking units were trained in how to support each other and how to leapfrog towards an objective, instead of attacking in waves. It became standard practice for the corps to make extensive use of maps and aerial photographs to show junior leaders where to go and how to get there when attacking. Finally, there would henceforth be extensive preparation for infantry advances in coordination with artillery, while the men designated to attack were not to perform exhausting labouring duties in the hours leading up to the assault.

The Patricias were withdrawn from the line on 7 February 1917, and sent some twenty kilometres northwest to the vicinity of Bruay to begin training for the assault on the ridge. The preparations were painstakingly detailed. A large clay model of the ridge was built and carefully studied by the Canadian officers, while a full-scale mock-up, with German defensive positions well marked with flags and tape, was used to familiarize the troops with their objectives. Aerial surveillance photographs and maps were distributed to all attacking formations. The regiment practiced its particular role in the coming attack for almost five weeks before returning to the line. At the same time, the entire corps prepared carefully for the attack. German guns were located with sounding devices and aerial reconnaissance; more than 80 percent were to be systematically destroyed by British and Canadian fire. Tunnels, equipped with lights, were dug in the chalk to the west of the ridge to allow many of the attacking troops to move forward in perfect safety just before the assault. Rooms for aid posts, communications centres, and command posts were carved into the sides of the tunnels. Plans were laid for a creeping artillery barrage that would lay a curtain of fire ahead of the attacking Canadians and lift at ninety-metre intervals every three minutes.

The attack was planned for early in the morning of 9 April 1917. The Canadian Corps divisions lined up in position for the attack by numbers: from the 1st Division in the south to the 4th Division in the north. The battalions were placed in order of seniority from the right. The 4th Division, on the far left flank of the attack, had the shortest distance to cover to reach its objectives but had to travel over the steepest and best-defended terrain. Its prime job was to capture the highest point on the ridge, Hill 145, which dominated the left flank of the 3rd Division's attack zone. The 3rd Division was to secure the height of the ridge and move into the Bois de la Folie, a wooded area on the eastern slope above the village of Petit Vimy. The Patricias would attack along a 250-metre front between the 42nd Battalion, on the 3rd Division's far left flank, and the RCR. The tunnel in their sector was Grange Tunnel. They would enter the tunnel the evening of 8 April and wait until the pre-dawn hours of Easter Monday. They were then to exit the tunnel, line up in their jumping-off trench, and, on signal, advance straight up across a line of large craters to take Famine Trench, about 700 yards from the start line, as their first objective. Britt Trench, a small section of the second line, about 500 yards further on, was their final objective.

Beginning on 20 March 1917, the British and Canadian artillery pounded the German positions atop Vimy. German guns and strongpoints were specifically targeted, and a new fuse allowed wholesale destruction of German barbed wire. The bombardment intensified on 2 April but stopped altogether on the evening of 8 April; the final bombardment, one of the most intense of the war, was scheduled for zero hour at 0530. After dark on 8 April the Patricias filed into Grange Tunnel. At first, the men seemed in high spirits. Bill Miller recalled: "Some were trying to sing, some were playing cards, all milling around, smoking, wondering what time it was, and 'How's the weather?' . . . in our section. Some trying to sleep and for sport, some trying to play with, or killing, rats."[19] But as the night wore on, the enormity of what was about to happen settled over the men. "The usual high spirits and optimistic banter suffocated in the oppressive atmosphere [of the tunnel] and tempers flared over trifles," F.E. Conley later remembered.[20]

At midnight, the NCOs awakened anyone who was sleeping. It was time to get ready. "We fixed our equipment . . . formed up quickly and marched off to the jumping off trench," Sergeant A.A. Bonar recalled. "A pale moon was shining through the quickly moving clouds."[21] "Many of us had a feeling of giddiness and nausea as we pulled in great lung fulls [*sic*] of fresh air," Conley recalled. "I noticed some who staggered slightly. Spirits were still low." The men were given hot food. Then Conley spotted a small party moving along the trench dispensing the rum ration. "Down the line came that panacea to top all panaceas, the rum issue. And it was an unbelievably generous one, about triple the ordinary . . . now, gone were gloom and apathy. A wave of quick and confident elation followed the magic-medicine down the line."[22]

At about 0400 the wind picked up and shifted into the northwest, driving sleet and snow into the eyes of the watchful defenders. Then, as the first grey streaks of dawn appeared over the ridge, the corps machine gunners opened fire, hosing bullets onto the crest line. "The staccato tat-tat-tat of the machine gun bullets filled the air," Bonar remembered. "It was as if great hailstones were being swept in fierce tumultuous gusts against large plate-glass windows. This continued for one minute. Then zero hour."[23] Those who were there never forgot the thunderous barrage that began precisely at 0530. "It looked like the doors of a thousand blast furnaces had been opened by one gargantuan lever," Bonar wrote. A wall of explosions swept up the sides of the ridge, "the whole sky alight and the noise deafening," Bill Miller remembered. He was a drummer in the PPCLI band that Adamson had ordered to pipe the men "over the top" in the first moments of the attack. Led by the pipers and bandsmen, and with senior NCOs blowing whistles atop the parapet, Nos. 1 and 3 Companies of the Patricias and some 15,000 other men of the leading assault companies rose as one and advanced up Vimy Ridge.

Miller and the other bandsmen "got about twenty . . . y[ar]ds in the snow and mud, returning to the tunnel with [their] instruments, then carried on all day as stretcher bearers and attended to the wounded."[24] The rest of the Patricias continued the arduous climb over broken ground in the driving sleet. Andre Bieler was one of them: "We were loaded with wire, we were loaded with tools . . . it was difficult to advance especially because of the craters which we had to go down into and up again."[25]

George Hancox recalled: "We started to go forward following the lip of the crater and past the German outposts[,] which by then were non existent. Heavily laden we lumbered along through the maze of shell holes over the obliterated German front line, past more and bigger shell holes until we reached the main German defensive line, which was the first objective."[26]

Virtually all the Germans in the path of the Patricias had been killed, wounded, or rendered senseless by the final bombardment, but the going was still tough: "It was extremely difficult for companies to maintain their direction and distance and not lose contact with the battalions on their flanks," Bonar wrote. "The heavy smoke contributed to this difficulty."[27]

All along the 3rd Division front, the attacking infantry followed the creeping barrage into and over smashed and battered German positions. German soldiers surrendered by the dozens. The two lead Patricia assault companies were quickly followed by Nos. 2 and 4 Companies, who charged up the slope mere minutes after the initial assault wave left the trench. All four companies reached their initial objective, Famine Trench, within an incredible thirty minutes. They tumbled in, consolidated their position, then pushed on, according to the official history, "advancing at a steady walk, started off with almost a parade ground alignment."[28] This time there was more opposition from the by-now fully alert defenders; many officers in No. 4 Company went down. But in less than half an hour, they were at Britt Trench. They suffered fewer than fifty casualties altogether, took 150 prisoners, and cleared the crest of the ridge. In their new position, they discovered the entrance to a German bunker. It was fitted with mirrors, washbasins, and chairs. There were bunks, some of which were covered with fine blankets, and dozens of bottles of wine and mineral water.

The Patricias had completed their assigned task, as had most of the attacking companies of the 1st, 2nd, and 3rd Divisions, in record time with relatively few casualties. It was a great victory, but the battle was not over yet. The 4th Division had the shortest distance to cover, but Hill 145 was strongly held by the Germans and one of 4th Division's attacking battalions had suffered severe losses in a raid prior to the battle. The initial attack on Hill 145 failed; this left the left flank of the 7th Brigade open to withering German machine-gun and rifle fire. The Germans began to exact a heavy toll. Then the German artillery joined the battle. From 1500 on 9 April until the early morning hours of the tenth, the Patricias and the rest of the brigade took mounting casualties from gun and shellfire while trying to improve their new defensive positions in Bois de la Folie. Adamson wrote his wife later that day: "We took all our objectives yesterday pushing off at 5:30 A.M. in a rainstorm.

The 4th Division on our left, not yet in line with us, having failed in two attempts to gain their objective. We have our flank in the air and are suffering from enfilade fire in newly dug trenches . . . I think we can hang on. Our Brigade did splendidly . . ."[29]

There was nothing to do but hold on, dig in, and hope that 4th Division would capture its objectives before the enfilading fire decimated the Patricias. In the first five hours of the assault, the Patricias had suffered only fifty casualties; by 1030 on 10 April they had taken 165 more. The two forward-most companies were being hard hit and were dangerously disorganized. Relief came in the late afternoon: Hill 145 was taken, and the 4th Division closed up to its final objectives. The Patricias were relieved the next day. They left eighty-three dead on Vimy Ridge and brought 139 other casualties out with them. The Canadian Corps as a whole suffered 3,598 killed and 7,004 wounded in the two-and-a-half-day battle, but at least the losses had not been incurred in yet another senseless attack. Vimy Ridge was a brilliant success for the Canadian Corps.

P.P.C.L.I.

The Canadians' new prowess in the art of war was fittingly symbolized by Arthur Currie's promotion to commander of the Canadian Corps on 8 June 1917. After the Vimy battle there was no longer any need to fill the Corps Commander's job with a British officer. Currie was Byng's logical successor. An unlikely success as a soldier, he appeared awkward, almost pear-shaped, in uniform, and he sat a horse badly. He was stiff and formal when speaking to large groups of men on parade, but he cared deeply about his men. He took great pains to keep casualties low and was alive to the new technological developments and attack techniques that were changing the nature of the war. Indeed, he helped pioneer some of them. Few Allied generals could match him in tactical planning. Currie passionately believed in the national mission of the Canadian Corps and strongly opposed periodic efforts by his British

Chapter 5

THE ROAD TO MONS

THE CANADIAN CORPS STAYED ON THE VIMY RIDGE UNTIL the third week of October 1917. It was, for the most part, a quiet period, but random danger still lurked. On 5 July, for example, Captain Percival Molson and Lieutenant D. MacLean were standing together in a front-line trench when both were killed with a single random German shell. MacLean had joined the Patricias in late July 1915 as part of the 1st University Company, had been mentioned in despatches, and then commissioned from the ranks. Molson came from one of Montreal's wealthiest families and had been instrumental in organizing the University Companies as reinforcement formations for the PPCLI. Adamson mourned his loss as a man "with an extraordinary sense of honour."[1]

The 3rd and 4th Canadian Divisions were held in Corps reserve during the bloody battle for Hill 70; thus, the Patricias took no part in it. Hill 70 was a key position dominating the important coal-mining city of Lens, and had to be taken before a major attack could be launched on Lens itself. The 1st and 2nd Canadian Divisions attacked Hill 70 in the pre-dawn darkness of 15 August 1917. Due to careful preparation, the attack was successful; most Canadian units were on their final objectives by 0600. The Germans counterattacked later in the day and the battle continued for three more days. The attacking divisions suffered 3,500 casualties on the first day alone. Currie called Hill 70 "the hardest battle in which the Corps . . . participated." Not long after, the corps pulled out of the Vimy area and shifted north, back into the Ypres Salient to join the Battle of Passchendaele, which had been raging since mid-July.

Like the Battle of the Somme, Passchendaele was a costly campaign of attrition, initially conceived by Sir Douglas Haig as a breakthrough attack. Haig had planned this third Battle of Ypres as a war-winning offensive from the Ypres Salient towards the Flemish coast. It was to strike a massive blow at Germany at a time when the French army was virtually paralyzed by internal unrest, and the Russians were on the verge of collapse. Haig's overall strategy called for the British Fifth Army to attack from the vicinity of Ypres northeast to Passchendaele village and the ridge beyond — a distance of about ten kilometres — then sweep north toward Ostend on the Flemish coast. When it reached Ostend, the Fifth Army was to be met by troops of the British Fourth Army, put ashore by the Royal Navy in an amphibious operation. The two armies would then link up to capture Zeebrugge and work their way eastward along the North Sea coast. As with many of Haig's plans, this one was too ambitious; it took almost no account of the terrain that would have to be captured. Worse, Haig insisted on pressing the offensive forward long after the initial attacks had lost momentum, turning a bold stroke into a bloody slugging match.

In the first weeks of the campaign, the British, Australians, and New Zealanders slogged their way forward in the face of heavy German resistance. Casualties mounted alarmingly. The British and their Commonwealth Allies were pushing uphill against a defensive belt of trenches, strongpoints, and thick-walled concrete pillboxes with interlocking fields of fire that the Germans had been building for two-and-a-half years. The millions of shells fired in the eastern part of the Ypres Salient since the fall of 1914 had destroyed virtually every canal and watercourse draining the polder, wiping out villages, farms, copses, and woods. Once a picturesque scene of pleasant rural villages and rich, green farmland, Flanders was now an immense quagmire of deep, sucking mud, pockmarked by shell craters and strewn with the half-buried, decomposed corpses of men and animals. After two months of fighting in this mess, and tens of thousands of casualties, Haig's forces had pushed about half the distance from their starting point to Passchendaele. There was almost nothing left of the town, but the all-important ridge beyond it loomed menacingly. In early October, Haig called on Currie to bring the Canadian Corps into the fight. Currie was very reluctant to agree, but set a number of conditions for Canadian participation: the Canadian Corps must fight together; it would not fight under the Fifth Army, whose commander Currie thought incompetent, but under the Second Army; and he and his staff must have sufficient time to prepare the attack. Since Currie was now a national commander with an ultimate right to refuse an assignment, Haig had to agree.

After the corps moved into the front lines to the west of Passchendaele village, Currie and his staff rushed to complete both plans and preparations for the attack. Their ultimate objective was the village and the ridge beyond it. Currie decided to launch three "bite and hold" attacks, each aiming to capture some 500 metres of ground, with several days of careful preparation before each attack. The Canadians built proper roads to bring up supplies, drained as much of the land as possible prior to the fight, and put together an extensive artillery plan. The 7th Brigade, which the Patricias had joined in December 1915, did not participate in the first attack, carried out by the 3rd and 4th Divisions on 26 October and lasting two days. The heavy bombardment, and the Canadians' knack for taking the pillboxes from behind, brought success at the cost of 2,481 men dead or wounded.

Two days later, the 7th Brigade prepared to take part in the second phase of the attack. On the afternoon of 28 October, the Patricias moved from their reserve positions near Ypres to Gravenstafel village. There, they began preparations for an early-morning attack on 30 October along the north side of a creek called the Ravebeek to Meetcheele Ridge. This ridge formed the end of a spur that led into Passchendaele village from the west. Those Patricias who recorded their thoughts for posterity were appalled at the condition of the battlefield: "I shall never forget the forbidding sight of the shell holes on every side, many of them filled with blood," Howard Ferguson would later recall. "It was wet, rainy and miserable."[2]

"The battalion went up the line by duckboard walks with about 650 [men] in strength," R.W. Wilson remembered. "The mud holes were bottomless and it never stopped raining while the shell fire seemed to come from the front, sides and even rear of the Ypres salient."[3]

Andre Bieler came to curse the very name of the village they were about to die for:

> Passchendaele . . . just the name and the spelling of that place is revolting . . . The frozen, stinking mud on both sides of the boardwalk. If a horse got off the board walk, he would sink into that mud and struggle would only make him go deeper until he was shot. We were so loaded with wire and tools that if a man fell, it was the most difficult thing to get him out . . . hell is warm, hell is flames . . . frozen to death in the dark was Passchendaele.[4]

The second phase of Currie's offensive involved the 7th and 8th Brigades of the 3rd Division on the north side of the Ravebeek, and the 12th Brigade of the 4th Division south of the creek. The Patricias would spearhead the 7th Brigade attack with their right flank in the thick bog along the creek's north bank and their left flank on the Gravenstafel-Passchendaele road, some 500 metres to the north. The right flank of the start line was dominated by a German pillbox dubbed "Snipe Hall," which had forced a halt to the Canadian attack in that sector two days earlier. This time it was different. No. 4 Company snuck out in the early-morning hours of 29 October, manoeuvred in the dark over some 500 yards of badly torn-up ground, and stormed the pillbox. The entire garrison of some twelve men surrendered. The start line was secure.

The second phase of the Canadian attack resumed behind a massive creeping barrage at 0550 on 30 October. The Patricias were led by No. 2 Company on the right, under command of Captain M. Ten Broeke, and No. 3 Company on the left, commanded by Major Talbot Papineau. The other two companies followed close behind. It had not rained heavily that morning, but the mud had not dried to any significant degree, making it impossible for the regimental pipers to play the men over the top as they had done at Vimy. The Patricias climbed from their forward trench at zero hour and struggled to follow the slowly moving barrage; they were met immediately by a storm of machine-gun fire. At 0553, the Germans opened their defensive barrage on the slowly advancing Canadian infantry. Papineau looked over the battlefield as he climbed from his trench and said to Niven, the battalion second in command, "You know, Hughie, this is suicide." Moments later a shell blew him in half.[5]

As the men struggled toward their first objective, a pillbox dubbed Duck Lodge, they were, in the words of one witness, "mowed down like wheat."[6] Virtually all the officers were hit within the first hour. The Patricias pushed ahead, but the 49th Battalion on their left flank was unable to keep up. The plan called for the two battalions to coordinate an assault against the heavily defended Meetcheele Ridge, but the handful of Patricias who reached that point reached it alone. One pillbox in particular, on the crest of the Meetcheele Ridge, was the key to the defences. Lieutenant Hugh McKenzie, a Patricia attached to the 7th Machine Gun company, hurriedly put a plan together; he and a small party of men would divert the German machine gunners' attention while others would try to take the position from the flank and rear. One of those others was Sergeant G.H. Mullin, who charged the pillbox, bombed out a handful of snipers in front of it, and leaped onto its roof. With bullets ripping through his overcoat, he shot two machine gunners with his revolver and then assaulted the entrance. The Germans surrendered. The night before this feat, while Mullin was distributing the evening's rum ration, he had told one of his men, "I'm fed up to the teeth. Tomorrow morning it's either a wooden cross or a VC for me."[7] For single-handedly capturing the pillbox, he was awarded one of the first two PPCLI Victoria Crosses; the other went posthumously to McKenzie, who did not survive his suicidal effort to draw the Germans' fire.

The Patricias took and held the ridge, but they were unable to push on to their final objective, Graf Farm, only some 300 metres to their right. There were simply too few men left standing. Adamson ordered the assault called off and the men to dig in for the inevitable German counterattacks. There were at least two such assaults later that day. In addition, sniper fire from the uncaptured Graf Farm position to their right front continued to take its toll into the night and the next day, until the Patricias were relieved by the 42nd Battalion on 1 November. Of the 600 or so who started out on the morning of 30 October, 159 had been killed and 204 wounded, most within the first few hours. Adamson was stunned by the losses. Regimental runner Andre Bieler remembered seeing him at battalion HQ "in such a state of tension . . . the loss of a regiment [*sic*] was just too much."[8] Two days after the Patricias pulled out of the battle, Adamson wrote Mabel: "The ground we gained and held against two counterattacks and continuing artillery bombardment is of some importance, as the ridge we took is a commanding one . . . The higher authorities are themselves out in expressing to us their appreciation of our efforts, but I can't help wondering if the position gained was worth the awful sacrifice of life."[9]

Adamson was not the only one who might have wondered. Currie's soldiers went on to capture the village of Passchendaele on 6 November, and the ridge beyond four days later. On 14 November, British troops began to relieve the Canadians who returned shortly afterward to the vicinity of Vimy Ridge. The Canadian Corps suffered 15,654 killed and wounded in the fighting. Among them were a thousand whose bodies were never recovered from the Flanders mud. All told, the Battle of Passchendaele cost Britain and its Allies 275,000 casualties, of whom 70,000 were killed for a gain of about ten kilometres. One recent history of the battle estimates that the British Expeditionary Force lost the equivalent of ten to twelve divisions out of sixty. More important, perhaps, was the tremendous blow to the morale of those who survived. One British soldier who survived later recounted how the reinforcements "shambled up past the guns with dragging steps and the expressions of men who knew they were going to certain death. No words of greeting passed as they slouched along; in sullen sacrifice they filed past one by one to the sacrifice." Canadian Prime Minister Robert Borden had had enough of Haig. At a meeting in London in early 1918 he told British Prime Minister David Lloyd George, "If there is a repetition of the battle of Passchendaele, not a Canadian soldier will leave the shores of Canada so long as the Canadian people entrust the government of their country to my hands."[10]

P.P.C.L.I.

Although the men who suffered through the Battle of Passchendaele could not know it, two momentous political events in the spring and fall of 1917 would inevitably lead to the end of the war. The first event was the United States' declaration of war against the

Austrian and German Central Powers in April 1917; the second was the Bolshevik Revolution in Russia and the end of the war on the eastern front. The US army had not fought a war in more than a decade and was unready for the special horrors of the western front; eventually, however, American troops and factories would greatly increase the fighting power of the Allied Forces in France and Flanders, and help break the stalemate. For a time, it appeared as if the United States' entry into the war would be offset by the Bolshevik seizure of power in Russia and the subsequent Treaty of Brest-Litovsk, which freed dozens of German divisions for service on the western front. The German High Command hoped it would, and shifted massive amounts of war material and tens of thousands of troops to the western front for one last major attack. It launched the attack — the "Michael" offensive — on 21 March 1918, and dealt the Allies a shocking blow.

The Michael offensive was different from any large assault previously mounted by either side on the western front up to that time. The Germans had learned important lessons about surprise, flexibility, and mobile warfare since the great stalemate battles of 1916. Using heavily armed, specially trained "storm" (assault) troops, under cover of fog and supported by accurate shellfire, the German attackers flowed around Allied forward positions and isolated them for those following behind to mop up. Aircraft and mobile machine guns supported their advances, and the Germans made rapid headway towards Paris, concentrating on the British Fifth Army and the French First and Third armies. In the first weeks of the campaign, thousands of panicked French and British troops clogged the roads in headlong retreat.

The Germans launched four successive attacks on the western front, beginning on 21 March. Fortunately for the Allies, German strategic capabilities did not match the new tactics the German army used on the ground. Each of the four German attacks was made in a different sector, so instead of reinforcing success, the overall

German effort was dissipated. The weaknesses in their strategy did not become evident, however, until after the Germans approached the Marne on their third attack and threatened Paris for the second time in the war. They were close enough to bombard Paris with their Big Berthas, but they were defeated by General Phillipe Petain's French troops at the Second Battle of the Marne. By the beginning of August 1918, however, much of the German army's strength had been sapped by the failed offensive. At the same time, the arrival of the Americans, and the increasingly effective Royal Navy blockade of Germany, undermined military and civilian morale. The time grew ripe for a major Allied breakthrough attack. Haig selected the Australian and Canadian Corps to spearhead the attack of the Fourth British and First French armies. It would come on 8 August 1918, launched from the front lines, about ten kilometres east of the city of Amiens.

With the end of the Battle of Passchendaele, the Patricias left the Ypres Salient for good on 20 November 1917; 750 of them had been killed in the salient since their first arrival in early January 1915. They moved south again to the vicinity of Vimy Ridge, where they were to pass a cold and wet few months in what had become a very quiet sector. On 22 February came news that King George V had appointed Princess Patricia of Connaught as colonel-in-chief of the regiment. The announcement might not have meant very much to the young Canadians who had been filling PPCLI ranks and changing the character of the regiment since the Battle of Sanctuary Wood; what they did not know was that the appointment had been accepted only on condition that the PPCLI join the Royal Canadian Regiment as a Permanent Force formation of the Canadian army after the war.[11]

The Canadian Corps were for the most part spectators when the Michael offensive began; the main German thrust was far to the south of the Canadian sector. That was all to the good as far as the Patricias were concerned, because serious disagreements about who was to command the regiment had surfaced when Agar Adamson relinquished command on 27 March 1918. Adamson had turned fifty-two on Christmas Day, 1917, and by the end of the following March had been in command of the Patricias for seventeen months. They had been difficult months, with two major battles at Vimy Ridge and Passchendaele. Adamson had ordered dozens of his officers and hundreds of his men to their deaths in battle. The strain was tremendous. In the Second World War, Lieutenant-General G.G. "Guy" Simonds, who commanded II Canadian Corps for more than a year in northwest Europe, put the useful life of an infantry battalion commander at only four months. One of Canada's greatest soldiers ever, Simonds believed that the burden of command at that level was more than anyone could bear for any longer; Adamson was just worn out. But who was to succeed?

The obvious successor was Major Charles Stewart, second in command, and the last remaining Original officer with the regiment. Although Gault admitted that Stewart "would fight the battalion boldly and well in any kind of action,"[12] he also believed that Stewart was not enough of a gentleman to lead the battalion out of the line. He wanted the job himself and was sorely disappointed to learn that few of the officers and senior NCOs shared his enthusiasm for his return. Tragically, because of the murderous nature of the war, Gault was a virtual stranger to the PPCLI by March 1918. He had spent more than a year away from the regiment after his grievous wounds at Sanctuary Wood. After his return in early June 1917, he had twice filled in for Adamson, once for a period of six weeks in the fall of 1917. But if those temporary commands had demonstrated anything, it was that he was no longer fit to command a fighting battalion. No man was more devoted to Gault than Talbot Papineau, but even he had written his mother in the fall of 1917: "I think with regret that it would be a mistake for him to attempt to command the Battalion permanently, and even his temporary command is a mistake as it is upsetting & nobody knows just where they stand."[13]

Adamson was angry at the regiment's apparent rejection of its founder, and blamed Stewart for sowing dissent. But the battalion had changed greatly since Gault's departure after Sanctuary Wood, and it demanded a fit man, with extensive and recent combat experience, to lead it through the hell of war. Maybe Stewart wasn't refined enough to be a peacetime regimental commander, or to attend soirees at the Governor General's mansion in Ottawa. But good mess manners were not crucial qualities in places like Passchendaele. Brigadier General Hugh Dyer, OC of the 7th Brigade, refused to support Gault. He wanted Stewart to command. Gault toyed with the idea of protesting to Divisional Commander General Louis Lipsett, then decided that such a move would badly divide regimental leadership. He accepted his fate. The burden of command fell upon Stewart.

In early May 1918, the Patricias left the lines near Vimy to begin training for the August offensive. They and the other infantry formations of the Canadian Corps had to learn how to attack in coordination with aircraft and tanks, while sharpening the assault skills they had acquired since 1916. In the new style of warfare, heavily armed infantry were to move rapidly through holes smashed in enemy defences by artillery, armour, or ground-attack planes, and strike deep into the enemy's rear to disrupt supply and communications. Special units of "moppers up" were to follow the assaulting troops, much in the manner the Germans had used in their spring offensives.

In this "new-style" warfare, it was especially important for officers to learn how to control and coordinate troop movements and for signallers to maintain telephone or wireless communications in fluid battlefield situations. Signaller J.E. Duggan found his training schedule much like a vacation:

> I am now out of the line, in a peaceful, quiet village and my bed is a hay-wagon in an open-work barn . . . I cannot say how long

> I will be here or when I will go up the line again . . . the weather these May days is painfully exquisite, and the hills and valleys and plains and woods of old France are one wild dream of beauty . . . We are supposed to be resting out here and in the morning we do a bit of signalling. In the afternoon, we play baseball and other games.[14]

It was not all a lark, however. The rigours of training increased through the spring and summer. At the same time, the great influenza pandemic that struck down millions of people around the globe did not pass by the Patricias. The war diary entry of 1 June 1918 noted: "many sick owing to epidemic of influenza."[15] At least a tenth of the battalion was down with the flu by the end of June.

The Amiens attack opened on the morning of 8 August, with two British, three Australian, and three Canadian divisions on a twenty-kilometre front. The attack started with the usual artillery bombardment, but then moved forward with tanks and ground-attack aircraft closely supporting the advancing infantry. This time, there was no Passchendaele. This time, the Canadians and Australians rolled forward some thirteen kilometres on the first day alone. This time, the attack moved forward for four days, with German resistance stiffening as the assaulting troops moved deeper into the German lines. But unlike the Somme and Passchendaele, the attack halted when momentum was lost; there would be no grinding battle of attrition. The strategy of the attack and the tactics used produced a stunning Allied victory, punched a major hole in the German lines, and initiated the last hundred days of the war.

Currie held the 3rd Division in reserve on the first day of the Battle of Amiens. When it moved into action, the 7th Brigade remained in divisional reserve. It was the Patricias' job to mop up points of resistance that the assaulting units had bypassed, and to take prisoners. J.E. Duggan remembered, "Not far ahead were barrack buildings for German troops and, as we approached, German soldiers came tumbling out in all stages of undress, but mostly in their underwear. They surrendered in droves." Duggan's company continued its advance over landscape that had been devastated by Canadian and British artillery and came to a grotesque sight: "silhouetted against the sky, in lonely desolation, was an ordinary looking horse-drawn wagon, with a grey horse standing up in the shafts, two German soldiers in life-like attitudes on the driver's high seat, and a large cage, full of pigeons, in the back. All of them — men, horse and pigeons — were stone dead."[16]

The Patricias moved up to front-line positions in front of the village of Parvillers late at night on 11 August, and joined the fight the next day. No. 3 Company led an attack on German trenches south of the town, making good progress until slowed by a shortage of grenades. They hunkered down in the captured trenches overnight, but were heavily attacked by German troops in the early-morning hours of the thirteenth.

Parvillers was an important crossroads on the reverse slope of a gentle ridge, and the key to an extensive network of German trenches. The Germans badly wanted to keep it. Four days after the initial shock of the opening attack, they were rallying sufficient reserves to hit back hard at any further Canadian advances. At least three companies of German infantry moved toward the Patricia-held trench, and No. 3 Company was quickly cut off. With German attackers drawing near on two sides, the Patricias had to pull out. As the company retreated down the trench, a platoon found itself in grave danger of being overrun. Platoon Sergeant Robert Spall grabbed a Lewis gun and leaped on to the parapet, pouring pannier after pannier of .303 bullets into the German troops. They went down by the dozens. Spall then jumped back into the trench and led his platoon to the safety of a sap some seventy-five metres from the attackers. He grabbed a second Lewis gun, scrambled on to the parapet again, and again loosed a stream of bullets into the Germans. He held them long enough for the platoon to get away, and then was shot dead. His posthumous Victoria Cross was the third and final VC won by a Patricia in the war.

Spall was only the most conspicuous, however, of the several outstanding Patricias covering the withdrawal from Parvillers. The beleaguered Patricia company straggled back to the main battalion positions, killing many Germans as it did so. But the Canadians were as determined to gain Parvillers as the Germans were to hold it, and the next day, 14 August, the Patricias attacked again, this time with Nos. 1 and 4 Companies moving directly into the middle of town. Once again the Germans counterattacked. They drove the Patricias back to the western edge of the hamlet, where the line was held until nightfall. Then, the RCR assaulted through the Patricia positions and completed the capture of the town.

With casualties beginning to mount for every additional metre gained, Currie decided that the original momentum of the attack was spent and that it was best to continue the offensive on some other part of the front. The Battle of Amiens was called off on 15 August, and the PPCLI pulled out of the lines to head north to the Arras sector with the rest of the Canadian Corps to prepare for the next blow at the German army. The Patricias sustained 152 dead and wounded in the battle, mostly in the fight for Parvillers, but the entire Canadian Corps suffered close to ten thousand casualties.

There would be no rest for the Germans. Amiens was the first heavy blow; Allied strategy now called for repeated attacks to keep the Germans disorganized, and the momentum of the great offensive going. On 26 August, the 2nd and 3rd Canadian Divisions with the British 51st Highland Division, under Currie's command, launched a drive eastward from the Arras front up the Scarpe River valley. It was, in effect, the opening phase of the British effort to either smash through or somehow outflank the massive German defences of the Hindenburg line. They drove through the fortified Drocourt-Queant line before crossing the half-completed waterway called the Canal du Nord. The 3rd Division's 7th and 8th

Brigades led the way. The main Patricia objectives were the village of Pelves, just south of the Scarpe River, and Jigsaw Wood, a few kilometres beyond the village. The grinding fight for Pelves went on most of the twenty-seventh, but the Patricias were unsuccessful in driving the Germans out of the village. The Germans broke the next day. The war diarist wrote: "The P.P.C.L.I. crossed Jigsaw Valley, cleared Jigsaw Wood, and consolidated a line beyond it under heavy bombardment."[17] Relieved that night, the Patricias had suffered a further 197 killed or wounded.

The Canadian Corps smashed through the Drocourt-Queant line at a cost of more than 5,600 casualties. The Canal du Nord was next. Under construction when the war broke out, it was designed to link the coal-producing regions south of Douai with Ypres and the Flemish coast. In early September 1918, parts of the canal were flooded with foul-smelling marsh water, while others were bone dry but filled with the debris of war. The canal was a formidable defensive obstacle, made stronger by masses of German wire, dugouts, shelters, trenches, and fortified machine-gun positions on its east bank. Once past the Canal du Nord, however, the city of Cambrai was there for the taking.

The 3rd Division was in reserve once again when the Canadian Corps attacked across the Canal du Nord on 27 September. The assault went well, and the canal was crossed in short order. The Patricias joined the battle early on the morning of the twenty-eighth and worked their way forward to support an RCR advance on the north side of the Arras-Cambrai road. As they passed through the hamlet of Raillencourt, they were heavily shelled. Stewart was killed; Captain J.N. Edgar was forced to take command. Edgar led the battalion across a light railway in preparation for an attack across the Cambrai-Douai road and into the village of Tilloy, situated about two kilometres to the north of Cambrai, at the foot of Tilloy Hill. The village commanded three main roads leading into Cambrai and the track bed of the Cambrai-Douai railway. It also lay at the foot of a steep, seventy-five-metre hill that dominated Cambrai and the Scheldt canal. To secure the northern approach to Cambrai, the division had to take the hill or hold the village. Lipsett chose the latter course and assigned the task to his 7th and 9th Brigades.

At twilight on 28 September, the Patricias and the 49th Battalion pushed off towards their objective. They made good time until they ran into two well-concealed belts of barbed wire, swept by German machine guns, on the west side of the Cambrai-Douai road. Patricias dove down in front of the wire and tried to work their way forward. Few made it. J.E. Duggan was one of them. He found himself facing German machine guns embedded in the railway embankment in front of Tilloy. Suddenly a German flare went up:

> We threw ourselves flat and returned the enemy fire . . . I lay on the grass, with no protection, and the bullets just cut the grass to pieces in front of me. My water bottle was hit in three places, and I had my coat sleeve torn and my arm scratched by bullets . . . I remember looking down at myself and saying, "[W]ell, I wonder how soon I'll get it?" Suddenly the firing stopped (without rhyme or reason), it was completely dark, and the few of us who were left got out of there.[18]

On 29 September, Captain G.W. Little took temporary command of the regiment. The Patricias stayed at their previous day's start line while the 42nd and 49th battalions advanced on Tilloy. They were no more successful than the Patricias had been, and Little prepared his troops for yet another attack the following day. This time, the much-weakened PPCLI went forward with the 49th Battalion and the Royal Canadian Regiment. The RCR outflanked the German wire, crossed the Cambrai-Douai road, and swept past the railway embankment that had held up Duggan two nights before. The Patricias and the 49th dug the Germans out of the railway embankment, killing many, and moved into Tilloy. They cleared the village and pushed up to the base of Tilloy Hill. There they stayed, ducking German machine-gun fire from positions on the hill until the early afternoon on 1 October, when they were relieved. They had accomplished their mission at a cost of sixty-six dead and 293 wounded. The fight to secure the northern approach to Cambrai was one of the costliest Patricia battles of the war.

The Allied offensives rolled on after Tilloy; Cambrai was taken quickly and the Canadian Corps launched a major new attack from Cambrai toward Mons on 8 October. But the Patricias had been badly mauled at Tilloy and were once again forced to rebuild. A new commanding officer, Captain (Acting Major) A.G. Pearson, was appointed on 16 October with the rank of Acting Lieutenant-Colonel. Pearson had joined the Patricias as a private. By the time the Patricias fought at Vimy Ridge, he had been awarded the Distinguished Conduct Medal and been promoted to Captain. On 9 April 1917, he had commanded one of the PPCLI's two forward-assaulting companies and had been wounded. He epitomized those Canadian Corps officers who had risen from the ranks and whose leadership in combat had uniquely qualified them for field command.

The Patricias were back in the front lines in early November as the Canadian Corps drove northeast from Cambrai, across the French-Belgian border, to Mons, where the BEF had first tangled with the advancing armies of the Kaiser in August 1914. By now, the Hindenburg line was broken in two places, German soldiers were surrendering en masse, the German navy was in revolt, and high-ranking German officers and members of the Socialist opposition in Berlin were demanding that the Kaiser sue for peace. In front of Mons, however, the fighting continued. The Germans doggedly defended a by-now lost cause and came back again and again to counterattack the advancing Canadians. But the Canadians were not to be denied. The Patricias and the other Canadian formations pressed forward "at great pace"[19] through the outskirts of Mons. On 10 November, the Patricias were relieved in the front lines by the RCR, but No. 4 Company elected to stay in the line under command of the 42nd Battalion as that formation and the RCR crossed the canal that bordered the city and fought their way to within sight of the central railway station. W.J. "Bill" Popey was the officer who commanded 13 Platoon of No. 4 Company when it crossed the canal and into the city. Popey had left Calgary in early August 1914 to join the PPCLI in Ottawa; he was one of the very few left of the Originals.

On the night of 10 November, Popey and his platoon were locked in heavy street fighting in the centre of the city when orders came from 42nd Battalion HQ to pull his men back and get them into billets for the night:

> John Christie and I went to the big hotel past the depot, an old man let us in through the downstairs door. We got into an old-fashioned white-sheeted bed in our clothes with our boots on. We awakened at 11:15. John looking out the window said, "My God Bill, the Germans must be back." We went downstairs. The old proprietor met us, kissed and hugged us both and gave us a bottle of champagne each. This was the first we had heard of the Armistice.[20]

Popey had beaten the odds only to sleep through the end of the war.

For the Canadians, the war ended in Mons, where it had begun for the British Expeditionary Force in 1914. The end came quickly, virtually without warning, when the Kaiser abdicated and the new Social Democratic government in Berlin sued for peace. The German army might well have struggled on for many months over the winter of 1918/19, but German morale was largely broken by the tremendous drain on manpower and the steadily tightening British blockade. The Americans had not done especially well in their first major battles, but they would learn, and tens of thousands more were arriving from the United States every month.

The French army was worn out. Indeed, the greatest burden of the fighting in the last hundred days had fallen on the British and most specially on the Canadian Corps, which, unlike many British and Australian formations, kept its manpower up to strength. The Canadian Corps suffered terrible casualties in those last hundred days, and the Patricias contributed their share of the butcher's bill.

Only 102 men of the 1,098 who had left Ottawa in August 1914 to follow Francis Farquhar and Hamilton Gault to war had been Canadians. Few of those men survived the war; fewer still remained with the PPCLI from beginning to end. When 3rd Division paraded to salute Arthur Currie in the centre of Mons on the afternoon of 11 November, thoughts of home and survival were no doubt uppermost in the minds of the men who were left. The PPCLI suffered 4,076 killed, wounded, and missing in the course of the war, in effect replacing itself four times over. Three commanding officers had been killed in action. But three Patricias had been awarded the Victoria Cross for gallantry, while 366 other decorations had been distributed to members of the regiment. First in the field, the PPCLI fought in virtually every major battle that the BEF and the CEF engaged in on the western front in the course of the war. Gault's dream had been fulfilled in war; the challenges of peace awaited.

Chapter 6

FROM ARMISTICE TO WAR

THE PATRICIAS STAYED IN THE RUINED CITY OF MONS FOR a month after the armistice. It was a time to celebrate the sheer joy of living, to eat and drink, to make love, to play and party long into nights that no longer held the terror of trench raids or shellfire. Some men hiked the countryside around Mons, over miles of recently harvested fields and across irrigation canals into the tiny stone villages that seemed to sit astride every crossroads. Others wrote home, read newspapers and magazines, or took correspondence courses through the Khaki University of Canada, established in 1917. Everyone thought of home, and of the time when they would begin their journey back to families, girlfriends, children, wives . . . Canada.

The sudden peace was almost jarring. The soldiers were now without real purpose; with no more battles to fight, they were really just civilians in uniform who wanted to go home. The army did what it could to keep them busy with sports, trips, dances, lectures, and plays. The Dumbells, an army concert troupe, trekked from camp to camp in the cool autumn weather to help keep spirits up. In some formations, however, senior officers could think of nothing better to do but reimpose the peacetime routine of barracks life — polishing, cleaning, making beds, physical training, route marches, and parade-square drilling. Most of the soldiers resented the excessive time and effort they had to spend on these small and generally irrelevant details, and the excessive discipline that went with them; Second World War soldiers would dub this stuff "chickenshit." The men had not survived shelling and gassing, enemy fire, and the loss of close comrades just to prove to their officers and senior NCOs that they could turn out for morning inspection with gleaming buttons or properly shined boots.

The Patricias had fired their last shots of the war under the command of Acting Lieutenant-Colonel A.G. Pearson, who had assumed command on 16 October after Major Charles Stewart had been killed in action. Pearson was not well, and he had no desire to continue to command after the armistice. He and Brigadier John A. Clark, who had succeeded Brigadier General Hugh Dyer on 12 September, urged Hamilton Gault to return to command. But Gault was resentful. Dyer had not considered him fit to take command after Agar Adamson had left the battalion, and most of the officers had seemed to want Stewart. Gault also felt slighted by the invitation to take the battalion on after the fighting was over. Yet he could not resist the honour of bringing his Patricias back to Canada; on 22 November he resumed command at a parade in Mons. Shortly after, however, he went on leave.[1] Pearson took over temporarily as acting CO.

The regiment Gault commanded in late November 1918 was a very different formation from the one he and Farquhar had left Canada with four years earlier. The Patricias at the end of the war were hardened combat veterans, to be sure, with a proud record of achieving the near impossible under fire. They were amongst the best fighting soldiers Canada had ever produced. But these

Patricias were younger; more of them had been born and raised in Canada, and they were less respectful than the Originals of the symbols of authority. They were also different men. Over the course of the war, 5,086 men served with the regiment, the vast majority coming in as replacements for those killed or badly wounded. Among officers, casualties were close to 100 percent.[2] When the regiment officially demobilized in March 1919, fewer than fifty Originals remained.

Almost all of the newer men were products of the meritocracy that Arthur Currie and others had built when they had made the Canadian Corps into one of the finest fighting formations ever. In the Canadian army of late 1918, leaders were respected not so much for the rank badges they wore but for what they had accomplished under fire. Shortly after the fighting stopped, many of those leaders, including Gault, disappeared — on leave, to take courses, to take other formations, or even to be repatriated early for one reason or another. The Patricias did not know — or respect — many of the new officers who joined the regiment just after the armistice. They resented taking orders from soldiers who had never been under fire, and felt the bonds of their regiment weaken when led by men ignorant of the Patricia heritage, or who had not suffered the wounds of war with them. Thus, discontent grew in this proud and battle-hardened regiment.

John A. Clark, who had succeeded Dyer as brigade commander, was one other major source of the trouble brewing in the PPCLI and, indeed, much of the 7th Brigade. Clark was a lawyer and militia officer from Vancouver who had risen to command the 72nd Battalion (Seaforth Highlanders) before succeeding Dyer. He had been a success as a battalion commander but he proved incapable as a brigade commander. He had proven barely competent to handle his formation during battle. Many of the officers and other ranks blamed him for the high casualties the brigade had suffered in the last ninety days of the war, especially at Tilloy, where Stewart had been killed. As Clark would write many years later, "I was quite a young Brigade commander . . . I was [thirty-two] at the time and most of these COs were older than I was and I felt more or less a stranger in the brigade." After Tilloy, he recalled, "Our losses were heavy. I felt somehow, that I had failed in the leadership that the troops were entitled to."[3]

On 11 December 1918, under Clark's command, the Patricias donned full packs, put on their helmets, slung their rifles, and marched out of Mons.[4] They did not head north, or even northwest, toward a channel port for embarkation to Canada, but northeast, in the direction of Brussels. They didn't know it, but they were headed for the 7th Brigade concentration point at Nivelles. They marched across the Belgian countryside for two days in cold but clear weather. As they marched, their packs, rifles, and helmets seemed to grow heavier. The men grew increasingly resentful. No one in authority had told them what they had in store. They had no real idea where they were going, or why. The rumour spread that they might be headed for occupation duty in Germany.

Most of the Patricias endured the march and the lack of news with the same determination that had got them through the fighting. For a sullen few, however, each step was further proof that no one cared about them, or that the army would not play fair in deciding who had priority in going home. They reached Nivelles about midday on 13 December. Within hours, the battalion was swept up in a revolt that shook the 7th Brigade to its very foundations.

The Canadian army had started to plan for demobilization at the end of 1916. Both the Department of Militia and Defence in Ottawa and the Department of Overseas Military Forces of Canada in London were determined that the return of the nation's soldiers would be carried out in the fairest way possible. As a general rule, those who had gone to Europe earliest should have been the first to return. But in many cases that policy was easier proclaimed than carried out. For example, the 1st and 2nd Divisions had been earmarked for temporary occupation duty in Belgium after the war, which meant that the 3rd Division, which included the Patricias, would head back to Canada ahead of them. This arrangement was certainly fair to the Patricias, who had been "first in the field," but other 3rd Division battalions had entered action much later than the units that made up the two occupational divisions. In addition, many Military Service Act conscripts were part of the 3rd Division. These men had not volunteered but had been drafted in late 1917. Sending them home early created tremendous resentment.

Other difficulties developed. The government wanted married men to go home earlier than single men, for reasons of family and because it was thought they would find employment more easily. Shipping was not a problem — there were enough ships to move 50,000 men a month — but the Canadian railways could not handle more than about 30,000 men a month. Finally, disagreements arose over the route to be taken home. Currie wanted his fighting battalions to return home as units, back to the towns and cities they had departed from, so the men who had fought together could be demobilized together. Again, debates were held: should the men return to Canada directly from France? Or should they go through the United Kingdom, where many had close friends and relatives? In January 1919, a Canadian Embarkation Camp, capable of handling 6,000 men at a time, was established at Le Havre. Canadian units then began to fall back towards Le Havre, where they were sent by ship to camps in the United Kingdom, then home to Canada.

Given the size of the Canadian forces overseas and the rail transport difficulties in Canada, the transfer home went remarkably well: by April 1919, fully two-thirds of the men had reached Canada. Little real effort, however, was made to explain the complex demobilization and transportation procedures to the ordinary foot soldiers, or to inform them of how well the process was unfolding. Given the idleness of the brigade, the lack of news, the men's eagerness to get back, and the wildfire-like spread of rumours, the unrest that started to break out in the 7th Brigade as early as 13 December ought to have been expected. It was not. In the ensuing seven months riots and mutiny broke out not only in the 7th Brigade at Nivelles, but also in the 3rd Brigade, Canadian Garrison Artillery, at Boussu, near Mons, and in many of the concentration areas in the United Kingdom. The official history of the Canadian Expeditionary Force records thirteen instances of such disturbances in the United Kingdom alone between November 1918 and June 1919; the worst was at Kinmel Park in early March 1919, when 800 Canadian soldiers rioted for two days, leaving five men dead and twenty-three wounded.[5]

The mutiny at Nivelles began in the late afternoon of 13 December, after the Patricias had arrived. Throughout the brigade, the atmosphere of resentment grew stronger; the men were angry at having been made to undertake a two-day route march under full pack, and at the lack of information as to their destination. Some would claim then and later that some of the men had been radicalized by the examples of the Bolshevik Revolution in Russia and the sailors' revolts in Germany. While that may well have been the case with a few, no doubt the majority of rebels were just browned-off soldiers who had had enough of Brigadier General Clark's inept and heavy-handed command. Toward evening, a crowd of between one and two hundred soldiers from the brigade gathered near Brigade Headquarters in the Nivelles town square. There, a few self-appointed leaders harangued them and tried to whip the dissatisfaction into a full-scale mutiny.[6]

One of the men in the crowd was Patricia infantryman Eric Knight. He had shared the growing discontent and disillusion in regimental ranks since the end of the war. More than two decades later he wrote Gault:

> The minute you went away, it wasn't a [regiment] with another set [of officers] in command — it was an integrated whole, put together in a white-hot blast furnace during five years — that had had the most important mechanisms removed . . . What was the use of defeating Prussianism if we reached the victory only to find ourselves not understood . . . and controlled only by a variation of the Prussianism that we had, we supposed, come to defeat . . . We were homesick perhaps; but most of all we were outraged that the intangible mechanism of an organization that was the cumulation of all our individual prides had gone dead.[7]

In Knight's mind — and doubtless others in the regiment felt the same way — the Patricias he had risked his life for had virtually ceased to exist. The revolt was a testament both to the strength of the regiment's pride and to the failure of a regimental leadership that had survived the challenge of war only to appear to melt away in peacetime.

Knight and a small group of men in the crowd demanded to see Brigadier General Clark. They went into his headquarters and found him despondent. "I was tremendously sorry for him," Knight later wrote.[8] He ought not to have been: Clark's only advice to the divisional commander was to use force to quell the revolt. He listened but refused to accede to the soldiers' demands to ease up on route marches and peacetime discipline. The crowd dispersed, but gathered again the next morning before parade. They then visited the three battalion encampments to encourage the men to attend a mass meeting at the town square. When the PPCLI was called out for morning parade at 0900, one whole company was missing, along with dozens of men from the other companies. The men were dismissed back to billets while officers and senior NCOs milled about, trying to decide what to do.

Things grew hotter by the minute. Knots of soldiers from the town square returned to the battalion billets to urge more men to join the revolt. Rumours circulated that British artillery was being brought up to fire on the town, just as French artillery had when that army had experienced a spate of revolts in 1917. Some of the men broke into battalion guardrooms to release prisoners, virtually all of whom had been detained on minor disciplinary charges. The guards did not resist. There was no gunfire, however. Calmer heads started to prevail at both divisional and brigade headquarters, and among the crowd, as men such as Knight faced the brutal fact that a full-scale soldiers' revolt could only end with arrests, long prison terms, and possibly even firing squads.[9]

In the afternoon, Clark ordered Pearson to march the Patricias north, to the hamlet of Genval. Most of the private soldiers refused to march; the rifle companies were "sadly under strength"[10] as the regiment set out. As many as half the battalion stayed in their billets in Nivelles; Stewart and most of the officers and NCOs had little choice but to leave them behind. Towards the end of the day, however, the rebels lost heart. They were tired and hungry and alone. No doubt many feared their fate. Knight took a bicycle, rode to Genval to locate battalion headquarters, and then returned to Nivelles. It was time to end the mutiny. He later wrote: "We lined up, marched off . . . and never felt so hungry in our lives . . ." When the bedraggled column reached Genval at about 2100, a company sergeant-major "ran down the street and told us to go back because we were all going to be shot." Knight was "so angry and tired with everyone and their stupidity by that time" that he didn't care: "We went right on into billets."[11]

Although 15 September passed without incident, everyone knew that Gault was rushing back, and would not be easily placated. He arrived a day later; Knight recalled the moment:

> Then, as I had expected, the voice of Olympus . . . sounded, and you were back, coming down the street of Genval with your eyebrows in a straight line, and I knew someone was in for hell, and I didn't want it to be me . . . when you lined us up in the hotel

> and started talking to us, and told us what fools we had been — it was all over, and some of the men actually began crying.[12]

Gault ripped into the officers and senior NCOs. In a pointed challenge to the griping, he ordered the entire battalion to parade in full marching order, loaded down with packs and rifles, grenades and extra ammunition, Lewis guns and Stokes mortars, and shovels and canteens. He then mounted his horse to lead them on a perfectly pointless twenty-mile route march.[13] A few men grumbled and complained, and wondered if they should obey. Knight set them straight: "I told them they should say their merry prayers every night for a long time that that was all we had to do, and the best thing they could do was like it."[14] Like it or not, the Patricias followed Gault out and back, bellowing "Ric-a-Dam-Doo" as they re-entered the town in step hours later. Gault had saved the PPCLI from ignominy.

By taking quick and decisive action in challenging the malcontents for control of the regiment, Gault may also have saved the Patricias from disappearing. After Sam Hughes had been forced into retirement in 1916, the government and the Department of Militia and Defence had turned their attention to the related tasks of fixing Hughes's crazy reinforcement scheme (so as to provide a steady flow of new men into front-line units) and deciding which units to perpetuate after the war. The first challenge had been accomplished by spring 1917. The second was not seriously taken up until the end of the war was in sight. Then, a formal committee was established to recommend upon how to decide the fates of the numbered battalions and how to preserve their respective battle heritages in existing militia units. Sir William Dillon Otter, one of Canada's most distinguished soldiers, led the committee.

The PPCLI's fate also came under review after 1916. At some point in the period 1916–1918 a decision was reached, probably at the cabinet level, that the Patricias would join the Permanent Force

(PF) after the war. Until 1914, the Royal Canadian Regiment, which traced its roots back to 1883, had been the only PF infantry regiment. But in the post-war era, there was simply no way that one PF regiment could both provide Canada with a credible, trained, ready-use force *and* carry out nationwide militia training at the same time. Thus, it was decided that the RCR would establish companies in Ontario and the Maritimes, while the PPCLI would cover the west.

The PPCLI was an easy choice for perpetuation: it was not a numbered battalion, it drew its recruits from across the nation, it had been established under royal patronage, and it had a distinguished battle record. Gault's connections in Ottawa, Montreal, and Toronto no doubt helped. So did the Governor General. When he departed Canada in 1918, he exacted further assurances from Prime Minister Robert Borden that the regiment named after his daughter would survive the war.[15] It is possible, however, that if the Nivelles mutiny had progressed much further, the government's plans for the PPCLI might have changed. Perpetuating a regiment with a history of mutiny and rebellion would have been an entirely different matter than honouring a regiment covered in glory.

Much of the Otter Committee's work fell by the wayside in post-war Canada, but one of its most important recommendations was taken up. This was the suggestion that the 22nd Battalion of the CEF, recruited almost entirely from francophone Quebec, Ontario, and New Brunswick, be remobilized and reorganized as an infantry regiment in the post-war PF (officially referred to as the Permanent Active Militia). Thus, on 1 April 1920, the fighting heritage of the 22nd Battalion was passed to the new 22nd Regiment, which was then redesignated the Royal 22e Régiment on 1 June 1921. Canada's permanent post-war army would thus consist of the PPCLI in the west, the RCR in Ontario and the Maritimes, and the Royal 22e Régiment in Quebec. It was a good balance

Lieutenant-Colonel A. Hamilton Gault, DSO, founder of the PPCLI. From the portrait by Glyn Philpott (1919).

Captain H.C. Buller, Adjutant, and Lieutenant-Colonel Francis Farquhar, DSO, Commanding Officer, with the camp colour at Lansdowne Park, Ottawa, August 1914. Farquhar was later killed at St. Eloi on 20 March 1915. Buller, who succeeded him, was killed at Sanctuary Wood on 2 June 1916.

First World War trenches. A soldier's Funke Hole on the left provided some shelter from shelling and the elements.

The battlefield — scene of death and desolation. German shells burst on the horizon.

No. 2 Company PPCLI at rest from a route march.

The ruins of the village of Courcelette. The Patricias fought a furious battle to seize this objective in September 1916.

Patricias parade in celebration of the great victory at Vimy Ridge, April 1917.

On 21 February 1919 at Bramshott Camp in England, Princess Patricia attaches a wreath of laurel in silver gilt to the pike of her colour in recognition of the regiment's heroic service in the Great War.

Hamilton Gault leads the Regiment in a salute to their Colonel-in-Chief with a rousing cheer on 21 February 1919.

The Patricias' proud return to Ottawa, 19 March 1919.

On 14 November 1939, B Company of the Patricias march from Work Point Barracks, Esquimalt, to the Victoria CPR ferry dock to join the regiment in Winnipeg prior to its move overseas.

The Lady Patricia Ramsay, accompanied by Lieutenant-Colonel W.G. Colquhoun, MC, and Hamilton Gault, inspect the regiment at Morval Barracks, England, 10 February 1940.

In the early 1940s, training in England always included long route marches. This platoon has just completed a seventy-mile march.

Lieutenant-Colonel Cameron B. Ware assumed command of the regiment in August 1943, and would lead the Patricias until June 1944 in some of the toughest fighting in Italy.

Privates J. Craddock, J. Jones, and W. Swift admire a liberated fresh egg, not often seen in the rations, at Sicily, 21 August 1943.

Privates Llasevich and Plamondon of No. 8 Platoon clean a Bren light machine gun and Lee-Enfield rifle during a rest from the front.

Beneath the hilltop town of Agira, Sicily, gun crews pose with one of their six-pounder anti-tank guns. Andy Schaen holds the shell.

Lance Corporal Konyk and Private J. Miller enjoy a quick lunch, 21 August 1943, Sicily.

A three-inch mortar position in Italy, summer 1944. Lack of camouflage indicates that there was little threat of enemy air activity.

A quiet time on the line in Italy, summer 1944.

Major J. Leach coordinates supporting gunfire with his artillery Forward Observation Officer, Lieutenant P.F. Evans, and his signaller, Lance Bombardier K. Wharton, Italy 1944.

Lance Corporal R. Middleton, MM, with Red Cross armband, supervises a casualty evacuation, Italy 1944.

En route to new battlefields, the regiment sails from Leghorn, Italy, for Marseille, France, to join 1st Canadian Army in northwest Europe, 21 March 1945.

and might have maintained Canada's army at an adequate state of readiness but for the basic abandonment of Canada's soldiers by post-war governments.

After quelling the revolt at Nivelles, Gault's immediate task was to bring his regiment home. Before that, however, he initiated the extended, but vitally necessary, task of recording in word and tradition a unique PPCLI regimental heritage, extracted from the events and personalities that had led to the regiment's formation and, of course, from its achievements in the war. Patricia symbols, heroes, and stories would now be enshrined in regimental lore.

The process of recording the regimental heritage began with the consecration of the camp colour. On 28 January 1919, in the hamlet of St. Leger, Belgium, just a few kilometres from the French border and the outskirts of the industrial city of Roubaix, the regiment formed up in a hollow square on the snow-covered parade ground, with the Ric-a-Dam-Doo draped over the piled drums. The camp flag that Princess Patricia had given to the regiment at Lansdowne Park in Ottawa on 23 August 1914 had survived every battle the regiment had fought. Gault had decided to have it consecrated in a religious ceremony reminiscent of those that had sanctified regimental symbols for hundreds of years. Major the Reverend T. McCarthy, MC, chaplain to the Patricias for most of the war, officiated by blessing the flag, which, as far as the regiment was concerned, was now their "official" regimental colour. The colour was then presented to the Senior Subaltern, Lieutenant A.N.B. Mortimer, MC, who knelt on one knee to receive it. The regiment then re-formed in a single line facing Mortimer and the rest of the colour party. They presented arms as the Regimental Pipe Band played a slow march, while Mortimer bore the consecrated colour to its place in the line. The flag consecrated, on 7 February 1919, the Patricias boarded the troopship *Dieppe* at Le Havre for the crossing to Weymouth, in the United Kingdom.

The Patricias spent a month in Britain. There, they visited with friends and family and attended ceremonial events while the army processed demobilization papers and put the men through medical examinations to discover who would be eligible for disability pensions and who would not. On 21 February, Princess Patricia inspected her regiment at Bramshott Camp. It was likely to be a long time, if ever, before she'd see many of these men again. She read a message of farewell and placed a wreath of laurel in silver gilt on the staff of the colour. Six days later, a PPCLI Guard of Honour attended her wedding to Commander A. Ramsay, DSO, RN, at Westminster Abbey. All officers and a representative group of NCOs also attended.

On 8 March, the Patricias left the United Kingdom aboard the SS *Carmania;* they reached Halifax nine days later. Though Gault had invitations to parade the regiment through the streets of Montreal, and even New York, army procedure was strict and allowed for no exceptions. All the battalions of the Canadian Corps had achieved outstanding war records and all were to end their wartime lives in the same fashion: they were to go directly to the places from which they had been recruited. There, they would be dismissed from army service amidst crowds of friends and family, who would welcome them home. Gault understood the protocol, but he was heartbroken that this band of brothers was about to dissolve before his very eyes. On the morning of 19 March, the PPCLI arrived in Ottawa. Led by a detachment of PPCLI veterans, they paraded through the cheering throng to Connaught Square for an official greeting by the Governor General, then on to Lansdowne Park. Few dry eyes could be found among these battle-hardened men, and there were many lumps in many throats, but they paraded with magnificent discipline. At the park, they stood as one for the last time as Gault read out a final order of the day. He reviewed the brief history of the Patricias, and paid tribute to Farquhar, Buller, and Stewart. Then, barely able to control his emotions, he proclaimed:

> I believe we have all returned to Canada better fitted to take up the duties and responsibilities of citizenship in the country we love so well. Difficult days may lie before us . . . but if they are faced with the same steadfastness of purpose which has characterized the years we have passed through, I feel confident that you will succeed in whatever you may undertake to do.[16]

Gault then dismissed his regiment. J.E. Duggan never forgot the moment: "I remember the last glimpse I had of Colonel Gault in Ottawa the day the battalion was disbanded . . . I saw him sitting in a small room with his head in his hands, and I believe he was crying. His heart was in that battalion."[17] Gault knew that the Patricia legacy would continue as a Permanent Force battalion, but it would be a very different formation from the one that had stood fast at Bellewaerde Ridge and fought its way into Mons.

P.P.C.L.I.

On 1 April 1919, the PPCLI was resurrected as a regiment of the Permanent Active Militia of Canada. Gault was battalion CO. A handful of officers and senior NCOs had elected to stay in the post-war army and make their lives as Patricias. At first, Regimental Headquarters (RHQ) was located at or near Toronto, or London, Ontario, but the PPCLI was destined for the west. In April 1920, D Company moved to Winnipeg and settled in at Fort Osborne Barracks; eight months later, Headquarters Company and A Company joined it. B Company moved to Work Point Barracks at Esquimalt, BC, at the same time. For the rest of the inter-war period, the Patricias would remain physically divided. RHQ was at Fort Osborne Barracks; A and D Companies were assigned to train the militia in Manitoba and Saskatchewan; and B Company would train the militia in British Columbia and Alberta. B Company would also provide a small but permanent infantry presence for the sprawling Esquimalt naval base. The regiment was not able to train as a single unit until 1927. Thereafter, it concentrated only three more times before the war, each time at Camp Sarcee near Calgary. The fourth PPCLI company, C Company, was not organized until the mobilization of 1939.

The Canadian armed forces were virtually unarmed for most of the inter-war period. Various recommendations to maintain a healthy military fell by the wayside as successive Canadian governments chopped defence budgets and then chopped them again. The first significant wave of cuts came right after the war; the second later in the 1920s, and the third and deepest during the early years of the Great Depression. It was impossible for the nation to mount a credible defence or to prepare for a possible war under such constraints. Both the Permanent Force and the militia remained drastically under strength for almost two decades. During that time, the three PF regiments remained at about two-thirds below authorized strength, each averaging about 250 to 350 officers and men. Whenever the government handed down a fresh round of cuts, more men were dismissed from PF service, pay was cut, and training time was chopped.

The PF's two most important tasks for most of the inter-war period were to "aid to the civil power" and train the militia. In the first instance, the government called out the Patricias to keep order on five separate occasions. In the largest deployment, one hundred officers and men from the PPCLI travelled across the country to help restore order during an especially prolonged and widespread strike in the Cape Breton coalfields in 1923. The duty could not have been especially tasteful for soldiers whose lives, ambitions, and concerns were not much different from those of the strikers they might have to shoot. The Great Depression was a period of much social unrest in Canada, and the troops were put on the alert on many occasions.

Effective militia training was almost impossible in those years. The militia had no modern equipment, and the ideas underlying their training were as outmoded as their kit. The mounted regiments practiced cavalry charges, for example; the infantry practiced defence against those charges. But then, they could not have drilled in armoured warfare, infantry-artillery co-operation, or large-scale manoeuvre, because they did not have the means to do so. In the highest echelons of the Canadian army, few officers were prescient enough to think about the major changes that technology would bring to future wars. Armoured tactics, rapid deployment of infantry, and air-ground co-operation in attack had all changed the face of war, even while the Patricias were fighting their way toward Germany in the late summer and fall of 1918. Yet there was little discussion of these developments. The basic Canadian defence plan for much of the late 1920s called for a cavalry attack into the U.S. Midwest in the event of war between Canada and the United States!

One Patricia officer would later recall of that period: "I hate to think of what the Canadian government did to the militia in those early days. It wasn't good. They had nothing. They had a rifle, a bayonet and the odd Lewis gun and the odd machine gun . . . but other than that those poor sods had nothing and we had to do the best we could with what we had."[18]

Difficult or not, the job of instructing the militia was important and unending. Every Patricia officer and every man with the rank of corporal and above was trained as an instructor. They ran the officers' courses in western Canadian universities, at the "Royal" or official army schools at Fort Osborne or Work Point Barracks, at the provisional schools set up in towns and cities across the Prairies and in BC, and at the Small Arms School at Calgary.[19]

Throughout the fall, winter, and spring months of the inter-war years, the Patricias assigned personnel to try to teach the militia the rudiments of soldiering at local armouries across the west. These lessons usually took place on Wednesday nights and Saturday afternoons. In red-brick structures on cold nights, the lights burned late as clerks, ranch hands, streetcar drivers, farm boys, or salesmen donned ill-fitting uniforms to practice parade drill on worn, scuffed hardwood floors. With arms shouldered, they turned this way and that to shouted commands, while the PF instructors shook their heads and set themselves to try again. Sometimes there would be rifle practice, with Lee-Enfields modified to shoot .22-calibre bullets in armoury basements. In the summer, western militia units gathered at Camp Hughes or Camp Shilo, both of which were near Brandon, Manitoba, or at Camp Sarcee, near Calgary, for up to two weeks of intensive training. At these summer encampments, the men could fire First World War–vintage Lewis guns, or Stokes mortars, or learn how to operate some of the other basic military equipment. Camp Sarcee could be very pleasant in the summer. Located in the foothills of the Rockies, it was always cool at night, with plenty of water and ample shade trees to provide relief from the heat of the day. Hughes and Shilo in the summer were another matter: hot, dry, dusty, and swarming with flies and mosquitoes. At Shilo, the men "washed" their eating utensils in sand piles because there was not enough water to clean them.

None of the winter drilling or summer training did the militia any harm; they learned a modicum of military discipline, a bit of military law, and some of the traditions of their regiments, and developed camaraderie. The militia training also introduced the Patricias to those parts of the west outside their barracks gates, and westerners to the PPCLI. Sydney Frost, for example, was from Saskatoon. He joined the PPCLI from Royal Military College in 1940, and chose the Patricias in part because of his father's acquaintance with the regiment:

> One of my father's great friends was [Colonel] Arthur Potts, who had served with the Patricias in the Great War. Through [Colonel] Potts and other military friends, father often met serving PPCLI officers who visited Saskatoon in the course of their duties . . . They sometimes came to the house on quite unofficial business and I would get a glimpse of their fancy mess kits from my dug-out in the kitchen.[20]

Although they still wore the uniforms of the First World War on a daily basis, the Patricias could turn themselves out for official ceremonial parades as smartly as any regiment anywhere. The ceremonial and formal uniforms of the day were impressive, and first class in every way. Soldiers would parade in their high-necked scarlet tunics; navy-blue, red-striped trousers; white Wolsley helmets; white belts; and rifle slings. Their brass buttons, medals, and collar badges gleamed. The white-gloved officers would be similarly attired, with gold shoulder boards and shiny swords. Garbed for formal functions or mess dinners, the officers would wear open-front, scarlet mess jackets; navy-blue trousers; white wing-collared shirts; and black bow ties. Officers purchased this mess kit from their pay. Soldiers could purchase, or rent from company stores, a smart brass-buttoned, navy-blue, high-collar tunic and trousers for "walking out" or formal occasions.

Life in the inter-war army was mostly a mundane round of spring small-arms training at a nearby camp, summer encampments or courses, guard duty or recruit training whenever possible, and Christmas and New Year's festivities. In the depths of winter, the men were kept busy running the Royal and provisional schools and studying for promotional exams. Some officers studied for staff college exams. Training was a mix of musketry practice, learning Lewis and Vickers machine guns and mortars, and going on long route marches, a practice the army still considered one of the best ways of keeping men in shape. Sports provided the main outlet to relieve the tedium of training. The Patricias excelled in many games. Boxing was popular throughout the PPCLI. Soccer was prevalent in B Company in Esquimalt, while hockey was the favourite sport in the Winnipeg-based companies. Gymnastics and physical training (PT) were great crowd pleasers; the Patricias often mounted exhibitions of these sports in Winnipeg's Assiniboine Park.

The army spent an average of only $900 per man per year on kit, training, rations, accommodations, pay, and pensions. Basic pay during those years was $1.10 per day; it was not a king's ransom, but it compared favourably to the average hourly wages of western urban labourers, cowboys, or farmhands. For Jock Mackie, the money was better than many other Canadians were earning: "In those days that was like a million. My dad was only making [twenty-five] cents an hour . . . $1.10 a day and all you could eat . . . and your medical, your dental, we felt like millionaires."[21] For Sydney McKay, joining the Patricias was a major step up in both status and wealth: "I was working for the Marconi Company as an office boy, polishing doorknobs and being the gopher at three dollars a month. When I joined the army, I started off at $1.30 a day which we . . . calculated quickly to $39 a month and on top of that I was being fed and clothed. So I was definitely impressed with my step up in life."[22]

If the pay was good for a young man just starting out, after the onset of the Great Depression, the guaranteed three square meals a day were even better. "Our food was always good," John Cave later recalled. "We got eggs maybe twice a week. We got red lead and bacon, which is tomatoes and bacon . . . We got porridge every morning. We'd have pork chops on a Wednesday night for supper . . . All the food was good and lots of it."[23] For married men, and there were few of those, army life was more difficult. The regiment allowed only one-tenth of its men to be married at any time, and those men had to have permission. They received a 50 percent supplement to their regular pay, which usually amounted to about fifteen dollars a month, and they were allotted space in married quarters.

With so little money being spent on defence, true modernization of the Canadian army was impossible. On 2 September 1931, a portent of things to come arrived in Winnipeg — five new Carden-Lloyd Armoured Machine Gun Carriers. A sixth followed later in the year. Here, finally, was a modern piece of kit: a small, tracked, open, armour-plated vehicle, slung low, that carried a driver and a machine gunner. But there were only twelve such carriers in the entire army, and they were soon taken away from the infantry and given to the cavalry regiments, which were beginning to convert from horses to fighting vehicles.

On 20 February 1920, Gault retired from active army service and went to live in the United Kingdom. On his retirement, he was appointed Honorary Lieutenant-Colonel of the regiment. Although the serving commanding officers called upon him often to offer advice, Lieutenant-Colonel C.R.E. Willets, DSO, ADC, assumed the day-to-day command of the Patricias. Willets came to the Patricias from the RCR, which he had commanded during the First World War. He had proven a courageous and imaginative leader. As well, he was one of the very few PF combat veterans in the early 1920s. After Willets left the PPCLI in early 1927, three First World War PPCLI veterans commanded in turn. M.R. Ten Broeke, MC, had joined the Patricias in France in March 1915 and risen to the rank of major. He had elected to stay in the PF with the regiment when it was reorganized in the spring of 1919. Broeke served as regimental CO until January 1932, when he was succeeded by H.W. Niven, DSO and bar, MC.

One of the Originals, Niven had briefly commanded the Patricias at Bellewaerde Ridge in 1915, when he was left as the regiment's senior surviving officer. Like Ten Broeke, he decided to remain with the Patricias when the regiment made the transition from the CEF to a PF battalion. He commanded from January 1932 to February 1937, departing at the very beginning of the pre-war build-up of the Canadian army. W.G. "Shorty" Colquhoun, CBE MC — he was nearly seven feet tall — commanded the regiment from February 1937 to September 1940, taking the PPCLI to England at the start of the Second World War. Colquhoun was also an Original. He had been captured by the Germans in 1915 and sat out the rest of the war in a POW camp, although he had made several attempts to escape. Like Niven and Ten Broeke, he had stayed with the Patricias when they became a PF battalion. These five COs laid the foundations for the PPCLI's regimental heritage and traditions. Gault would forever after be referred to as The Founder.

During the inter-war years, the Patricias also received their official colour. Gault had arranged for Princess Patricia to design and create the original camp colour, and had had it consecrated in Belgium in January 1919. The original colour, however, was never meant to be an official regimental colour and was not acceptable to the Royal College of Heralds. Frayed and tattered by war, it was encased and retired in 1922 and replaced by a second colour, presented to the regiment by Governor General Viscount Byng of Vimy at a solemn parade in Winnipeg that year. Byng also gave the regiment a silk Union flag for use as a King's colour. In April of 1934, the Patricias would at last receive their official colours — a new King's colour and a regimental colour designed according to the College of Heralds' rules and bearing the regiment's battle honours, commemorating the Patricia battles of the Great War. Presented by Governor General the Earl of Bessborough, these colours would be carried proudly by the regiment until 1959, when they were replaced once more.

A regiment's colours lie at the heart of regimental tradition. But traditions are created or evolve in other ways as well. In 1924, the PPCLI chose the Rifle Brigade (Prince Consort's Own) as its "allied" regiment, linked with it in both lore and tradition. The Patricias had fought alongside the Rifle Brigade when they were attached to the British army's 80th Brigade during the first year of the war; thus, the union of the two regiments was more than fitting. In addition to selecting an allied regiment, the PPCLI formulated its rules of regimental tradition. In every Canadian army regiment, those rules stipulate mess dress, badges, regimental songs, ceremonial orders, the order and decorum of mess dinners, the design of regimental flags and pennants, and all other manner of ceremony. The Canadian army, in a tradition inherited from the British, provides its formations with the means to prepare for and fight wars. But it is the regiment that has the task of building family loyalty and traditions through symbols, ceremonies, and the teaching of regimental heritage. The PPCLI was a brand-new regiment compared to the RCR, and certainly an infant alongside venerable British army regiments such as the Rifle Brigade. There had been almost no time to tend to the regimental side of Patricia life before the war, and no time during it. But the blood shed in that war and the battles survived formed the basis of the traditions that were solidified in the inter-war years.

P.P.C.L.I.

In the mid-1930s, world tensions increased as the distant thunder of war rumbled on far horizons. Japan moved into Manchuria in 1931. Neither North America nor Europe heeded that death knell of the League of Nations and the dream of perpetual post-war peace. China was too far away to really matter; the Japanese aggression was virtually ignored. By 1935, however, few of the leaders of the world's handful of democracies could deny that world peace was in for a rough time. In that year, Italy invaded Ethiopia, while the League of Nations stood by, paralyzed. Germany was already in the process of tearing up the Treaty of Versailles, and pushing ahead to full-scale rearmament under Nazi leader Adolph Hitler. In 1936, Germany re-militarized the Rhineland. In 1937, Japan launched an all-out war against China. In 1938, Austria joined Germany in a Nazi-led union of the two German-speaking nations, while Hitler succeeded in carving off a large chunk of Czechoslovakia (with the blessing of Britain and France) at Munich in September of that year.

The Canadian government began to wake from its long slumber in 1935. When Chief of the General Staff A.G.L. McNaughton resigned his post that year, he reported that Canada was virtually defenceless. This was the low point of Canadian inter-war defence preparedness. Both the militia and the PF were well below establishment. The army had a bare handful of modern vehicles: no tanks, no modern infantry weapons, almost no artillery or up-to-date signalling equipment. Though tiny, the navy was in slightly better shape, but the air force was equally obsolete. Thereafter, slowly and reluctantly, but steadily, the government began to feed more money to defence. In the fiscal year 1934/35, the Department of National Defence (formerly the Department of Militia and Defence) received only $26 million, which was increased to approximately $30 million in the next two fiscal years. Then, in 1937/38 and 1938/39, the defence budget grew to $36 million annually. By the time the annual federal budget was introduced into Parliament in early 1939, it was obvious that war was looming on the horizon; defence appropriations ballooned to almost $65 million.[24]

At first, neither the militia nor the PF expanded greatly. There were 51,418 militiamen enrolled at the end of 1938, the same number of part-time soldiers there had been in 1931 and just over half the authorized establishment. Training time increased marginally, as did militia preparedness. The PF, which had fewer than 3,700 men in 1931, increased to 4,261 by the summer of 1939, also well below establishment. Still, the men who drifted into the Patricias in the late 1930s became the backbone of the senior NCO ranks when the PPCLI finally went into action in the summer of 1943. Ken Arril left his home in Port Arthur in 1938, and took a train to Winnipeg to join the PPCLI. "I remember getting off the train and getting out to Fort Osborne Barracks in an old bloody streetcar," he later recalled:

> I walked across the parade square . . . to the cinder block building there and I had a suitcase and a bag of some kind. I saw a man standing there sweeping the floor . . . Being a naive young man, I said, "Well, is this where I join up?" This fellow just

> stopped his sweeping, put the broom very slowly against the wall, reached into his back pocket, took out his wallet and handed me a car ticket . . . and said "Go home boy."[25]

But Arril stayed, went to war as a Patricia, then served in the First Canadian Parachute Battalion.

Don Parrott grew up in Grandview, Manitoba, and was living in Dauphin, Manitoba, in the late winter of 1938 when he decided to become a Patricia: "I joined the PPCLI on the [eighteenth] of March, 1938 . . . There was twelve of us accepted in a [training] squad of recruits right in Winnipeg. We had . . . to clean the floors and scrub everything and make sure everything was in top shape."[26]

Gilbert Hyde, from Moose Jaw, Saskatchewan, was a bandsman in a militia regiment. In late 1937, he wrote the PPCLI to inquire about joining up. He was just seventeen years old. After a few months, he received a reply inviting him to Winnipeg: "I had to pay my own way to Winnipeg. They didn't pay. So I went down there and I joined. The real reason I was able to get in at that time was because they wanted band members because . . . the King and Queen were coming to visit Canada in '39."[27]

P.P.C.L.I.

By 1938, the regiment had 352 men on strength, still below war establishment but above the 250 or so who had soldiered at Work Point and Fort Osborne Barracks for most of the previous decade. After a somewhat cursory examination and physical, the new recruits were attested and sworn in by the Adjutant, Captain G.E. Walls, who explained the pay system — so much per day with bonuses of ten cents a day for being able to use Morse code, five cents for proficiency in shooting, and five cents for passing Grade 8 entrance examinations. The recruits were then assigned a regimental number and given a pay book. After the paperwork was done, they went to the Quartermaster for two summer and two winter uniforms, a greatcoat, a rubber groundsheet cape, a steel helmet, and a Lee-Enfield rifle. They could buy their dress uniform (or rent it on special occasions).[28] Then it was time to begin basic training.

The Permanent Force regiments gave their own recruits basic training at their home bases. In the PPCLI, recruits were formed into training squads named after famous PPCLI battles. There was a Frezenberg squad, a Vimy squad, and so on. The recruits learned basic drill, regimental tradition, and how to handle basic infantry weapons such as Lewis guns and two- and three-inch mortars, in addition to their own rifles. They were taught how the Patricias had won battles in the First World War: "We got lectures on battles, PPCLI battles, every Friday afternoon," Parrott later recalled. "Amusing lectures . . . and they'd take us and show us on the sand tables how the battles went."[29]

Recruits were considered initially proficient when they passed their Tests of Elementary Training, or TsOET. Then they actually began to learn how to use some of the weapons. By the late 1930s, there was usually enough money to get to the rifle range at least four times a year, to expend machine-gun and mortar ammunition at Camps Shilo and Sarcee, and even to fire the odd round from the new (but already obsolete) Boyes anti-tank rifle. After individual training, the recruits learned basic infantry section tactics; they embarked on company-level training after they were permanently assigned to their respective rifle companies. At Shilo and Sarcee, the men might get close to a Carden-Lloyd carrier, or some other fighting vehicle, like the very first Vickers tanks, which began to appear in 1938.

The training was, no doubt, great fun to men who relished the military life. But there was more to military life than training, as Gilbert Hyde recalled: "I ended up on kitchen duty . . . I learned how to peel potatoes . . . I peeled potatoes, I peeled the peelings, and I peeled the peelings again . . . In those days you didn't waste anything."[30]

As Canada's small army slowly reorganized its defences in late 1938 and early 1939, Europe plunged towards war. In March 1939, Hitler unilaterally scrapped the Munich Agreement that British Prime Minister Neville Chamberlain had called "peace in our time," and occupied all of Czechoslovakia. Then Hitler began to make demands on Poland for the return to Germany of the Polish Corridor to the Baltic Sea, that part of West Prussia torn from Germany after the First World War. Britain and France now knew that Hitler could not be trusted, and decided to resist any further German demands, by war if necessary. A treaty was concluded with Poland, binding Britain and France to declare war on Germany if Germany attacked Poland. Hitler took the gamble on 1 September 1939. After concluding the Nazi-Soviet Pact on 24 August, he launched an all-out attack against Poland. Britain and France issued an ultimatum seeking German withdrawal by 3 September; when the deadline came and went, they declared war on Germany.

Canada took no part in the diplomatic manoeuvres that culminated in war. The Canadian military was not ready to fight. But the government of William Lyon Mackenzie King knew full well that Canadians would never stand by and allow Britain to fight Germany alone. In the late 1930s, and for some decades after, the ties of history, culture, family, and trade that bound Canada to Britain were still very strong. Besides, even the Canadian government had finally come to recognize the grave threat Hitler and Nazism posed to the international order and to democratic systems. As events unfolded in Europe, Canada took steps to move itself to a state of basic wartime readiness.

In 1937, a revised version of Defence Scheme No. 3 (first drawn up in 1932) became the basic framework for Canadian mobilization. The plan called for the initial mobilization of two Canadian divisions, one of which would concentrate first, and become the core of an expeditionary force, while the other waited in Canada. The expeditionary force was designated the "Mobile

Chapter 7

TO WAR AGAIN

DONALD F. PARROTT WAS ON LEAVE FROM FORT OSBORNE Barracks that last Labour Day of peace in 1939. His enlistment in the PPCLI was due to expire a few days after his return, but the German attack on Poland changed his plans: "I had intended to apply for my Army discharge . . . to return to work at the Madsen Red Lake Gold Mines," he later recalled. When he arrived back at the barracks, he made ready to re-enter civilian life: "I . . . turned in my pass, put away my civilian clothes and put on my uniform to be ready to go to the Regimental Orderly Room the next day to apply for my discharge." But as soon as Lieutenant-Colonel W.G. "Shorty" Colquhoun announced that the PPCLI was about to be mobilized, Parrott decided to volunteer. He went straight to the orderly room, submitted his discharge papers from the PPCLI as a regiment in Canada's peacetime Permanent Force, and then enlisted immediately into the PPCLI of the "Canadian Active Service Force," activated 1 September 1939. He joined "for the duration of hostilities."[1]

Canada entered the Second World War with a Byzantine recruitment policy that would only grow more complicated. Because the country had been torn apart by conscription in the First World War, every Canadian government from the end of the war until 1942 pledged not to resort to the draft again. As war had loomed closer in early 1939, the Liberal government of Prime Minister William Lyon Mackenzie King and the Conservative official Opposition had both repeated these anti-conscription pledges.

When Canada began to mobilize its first overseas contingents in early September 1939, it created a "Canadian Active Service Force" (later called simply "The Canadian Army Overseas"), made up entirely of men who had volunteered for overseas military service. When Parrott and the other 350 or so PF soldiers who made up the PPCLI on 1 September 1939 made the decision to go overseas with the regiment, they had to pass out of the PF and volunteer for the Canadian Active Service Force. The same held for the soldiers in all the PF regiments in Canada, and for militia regiments like the Seaforth Highlanders of Canada, based in Vancouver, or the Edmonton Regiment (formerly the 49th Battalion, CEF, and later the Loyal Edmonton Regiment).

In this initial mobilization of Canadian troops, the government followed its Defence Scheme No. 3, which provided for an overseas expeditionary force of two infantry divisions and a Canadian Corps headquarters to command them. The 1st, 2nd, and 3rd Canadian Infantry Brigades provided the fighting core of the 1st Canadian Infantry Division. Each of these brigades was composed of three infantry battalions, a medium machine-gun and heavy-mortar battalion, a tank regiment, a field artillery regiment, and other "organic," or attached, troops. The army assigned all its PF regiments to these three brigades: the Royal Canadian Regiment went into the 1st Brigade, the PPCLI into the 2nd, and the Royal 22e Régiment into the 3rd. The PPCLI's sister regiments in the 2nd Brigade were both western formations — the Seaforth

Highlanders of Canada and the Edmonton Regiment. Brigadier George Pearkes, who had won a Victoria Cross in the First World War, initially commanded the 2nd Brigade. The brigade, however, went into action in Sicily in July 1943 under the command of Brigadier Chris Vokes.

On 3 September 1939, "Shorty" Colquhoun returned to Winnipeg from the Small Arms School in Calgary, and immediately got down to preparing his battalion for war. The regiment was as unready as the rest of Canada's military forces at the beginning of September. The entire PF was just over 4,100 men strong; none of the three PF infantry regiments were even close to their war establishment strength of 835 all ranks. None as yet were equipped with the newest-model Lee-Enfield No. 4 Mk I rifle, a bolt-action rifle that was an improved version of the First World War–era Lee-Enfield. The standard light machine gun still in use was the First World War Lewis gun. Virtually no mortars of any kind were available, and no modern uniforms or boots. The army suffered from a shortage of helmets, trucks, small vehicles, radio equipment, medical supplies, even field kitchens. They had on order some 7,000 new, very good, light machine guns — the Bren gun — to replace the obsolete Lewis gun, but only twenty-three had been received.

Colquhoun's first job was to recruit up to war establishment strength. Although plans were laid as early as 7 September 1939 for the Esquimalt contingent to join the rest of the regiment at Fort Osborne Barracks, the movement was delayed while a fourth company was raised on the West Coast and recruitment began to move into high gear in both Winnipeg and Victoria. Most of the regiment's initial contingent of officers were veterans of the First World War and, like Colquhoun, wore decorations for bravery under fire on their tunics. These old soldiers had experienced war first hand and understood the basic disciplinary and morale requirements for a crack infantry formation. Virtually none of them would see combat in this war, however; age, infirmity, or outmoded ideas of how to wage a modern war eventually disqualified them from action.

The Patricias opened recruitment offices in Winnipeg and Vancouver on 10 September 1939; nine days later, the government confirmed that it was actively considering the dispatch of the 1st Division to the United Kingdom. On 28 September, Army Headquarters in Ottawa formally announced that the division would depart Canada as soon as possible under the command of Major General A.G.L. McNaughton. The Patricias found recruitment slow in the first two weeks of September, both because of the uncertainty of the government's overall mobilization plans and the opening of competing recruiting offices by militia regiments across the west. Unlike the initial rush of enthusiasm that had accompanied Canada's entry into the First World War, the men who came forward in the fall of 1939 did so with a far more sober attitude toward war. One PPCLI recruiting officer reported "a complete absence of jingoism and war excitement" among the men who waited patiently in the recruiting lines. These men were volunteering "with full realization of their responsibilities."[2] After Ypres, Passchendaele, and the other meat-grinder battles of the First World War, few could have any illusions of war as a glorious adventure.

When government plans to mobilize the 1st and 2nd Divisions and to send the 1st Division overseas became clearer, Patricia ranks filled up quickly; the regiment was practically at full strength by the end of October. At the same time, Colquhoun received orders to send eighteen officers, seven warrant officers, and twenty-eight NCOs to western militia units to supervise their recruiting and initial training. As PF soldiers, the Patricias' experience was much in demand. Over the next four weeks, more Patricia officers departed for staff courses or were sent to augment western militia regiments. Other officers, such as R.A. "Bob" Lindsay, arrived to replenish Patricia ranks from militia regiments. The new officers were younger and more physically ready for the rigours of war. They were eager, but they needed time to learn soldiering, as well as the ways of their new regiment.

Among the hundreds of men who arrived at Fort Osborne Barracks every week to join up were Patricias who had served before and who returned to accompany the regiment to war. Other men came from western Canadian militia regiments not yet mobilized for either the 1st or 2nd Divisions. Some of the men were un- or underemployed and sought primarily to improve their pay, put a roof over their heads, and eat regularly; Canada was still in the last throes of the Great Depression. Others were young men who sought adventure, travel, and excitement, or whose imagined view of war was still that of a glorious enterprise, not to be missed. Some were even idealists who had followed the mounting diplomatic crises in Europe with concern; they were determined to do all within their power to stop Hitler. As in all wars, motives were mixed. And, as with all armies at war, motives were soon forgotten as fighting units prepared for combat and eventually engaged the enemy.

On 15 November 1939, B and D Companies from the West Coast, under the command of Major J.N. Edgar, arrived at Fort Osborne Barracks. Welcomed officially by the PPCLI band, their unofficial greeting from their rivals in A and C Companies was somewhat more raucous, as George Grant would later remember: "Was that ever a fight that night! They were rolling beer barrels all over the place . . . I was called out with the rest of the guys that weren't getting into trouble to stop this battle between these companies from the West Coast and Winnipeg. It was a son-of-a-bitch of a battle . . . an awful bloody mess."[3]

The barracks had little room to billet these new men, and neither the time nor the space to train them. The men who had joined the Patricias before the war had already been through basic training, which included parade-square drill; military discipline; and shooting, dismantling, cleaning, and reassembling their rifles and other basic infantry weapons. Some had even had formation training of a sort with militia regiments in summer encampments. But it was almost impossible for the brand-new Patricias to undergo any real training, as Felix Carierre would later recall: "[We had] zero training in Canada because we had no uniforms . . . no boots . . . no [modern] military equipment. They had run out of old World War One stuff and they were waiting for the new battle dress . . . new boots. So the only training I did encounter was firing a .303 rifle at the ranges to see if we could hold a rifle."[4] Colquhoun's men received their new boots and the new rugged and practical battledress uniform in late October. The boots were a mixed blessing to the men; they were now called upon day after day to attempt long route marches.

Training men to be soldiers is a long and difficult process, and the Canadian army was not up to the job in the fall of 1939. About the only things a man could be trained in at Fort Osborne Barracks were standing at attention, marching, parade drill, marksmanship, first aid, and other simple military tasks. Day after day, the growing ranks of men did pushups, knee bends, stretches, jumping jacks, and lots of running. And they marched. The army wanted lots of route marches, which, it claimed, kept the men fit. Mostly, however, marching kept the men occupied. Several times a week, the Patricias donned full packs, dressed as warmly as they could in their First World War–era uniforms and coats, and marched out the gates of the Fort Osborne Barracks. They marched for miles through Winnipeg's glorious fall weather, along country roads while farmers harvested their grain, into the first days of winter, as the first heavy snows came and ice coated the highways and byways of southern Manitoba. They became adept at covering fifteen, twenty, even thirty miles a day, but they learned nothing of small-unit tactics such as how to advance to contact with the enemy, use terrain to advantage, follow a barrage, or move into battle with tanks. When they and the other infantry battalions of the 1st Division began to gather in Halifax in mid-December for the voyage to the United Kingdom, they looked like soldiers, and even marched like soldiers, but they were not ready for war.

P.P.C.L.I.

On 17 December 1939, several dozen streetcars arrived on the tracks that ran right alongside Fort Osborne Barracks. The Patricias loaded their regimental baggage into the cars, then piled aboard to ride through the streets of Winnipeg to the Canadian Pacific Railway freight yard on Higgins Street. Sydney McKay remembered: "After we put all our equipment on board the train, we were allowed to get off and say our goodbyes to family or friends. It was a beautiful day. I don't really know what the temperature was but there was very little snow."[5] For three days and nights, the regiment travelled east on two special trains, moving as fast as the Canadian winter — with snow on the tracks, freezing cold, and steam lines that seized up regularly — would allow. Finally, they arrived at Halifax, where they boarded the 39,000-ton transport steamer HMT *Orama,* a former P&O passenger liner now in the service of His Majesty as a troop transport. On 21 December, the main Patricia contingent of 808 officers and men left Canada for war; others had preceded them, or would follow shortly to make up the full complement of about one thousand men.

The *Orama* was one ship in one of the first large convoys of the war, carrying the bulk of the 1st Canadian Division to the United Kingdom. Escorted by three Royal Navy and French navy battleships, and a host of smaller escort vessels, the convoy steamed eastward at high speed to avoid German U-boats or surface raiders. The *Orama* was still fitted out as a luxury liner; the Patricias had very little to complain about when it came to food and accommodation: "Tables, waiters, beds, couldn't believe it," Jock Mackie remembered. "I'll never forget the first breakfast they brought out. The English love on Sunday a herring. Ooohhh, I just couldn't. They were amazed that we turned down herring. I said, 'Just give me some bacon and eggs.'"[6] But crossing the North Atlantic in winter is rarely a pleasant experience: "The day after Christmas we sailed into gale-force winds with fifty-foot-high waves," Don Parrott later wrote. "Our troopship was very high and took a pronounced roll sideways. The up-and-down motion made us frightfully seasick as the sea cascaded down our decks four feet deep. I was thrown out of bed by the roll of the ship and lay on the floor for four days unable to get up or eat anything."[7]

The storm subsided as the convoy approached the coast of Scotland. Just after noon on 30 December 1939, the *Orama* tied up at Greenock, Scotland. By nightfall, men and gear were speeding southward by train, through the blackout, to Farnborough, about thirty kilometres southwest of London. There, they disembarked in the midst of a large staging area built around the same Aldershot Camp that had temporarily housed so many Canadian soldiers in the First World War. They were greeted by Brigadier Pearkes and none other than Lieutenant-Colonel Hamilton Gault, who had assumed command of the Canadian Reinforcement Depot in the United Kingdom. From Farnborough, they marched a few kilometres northwest to Cove, where they settled into Morval Barracks. They found the barracks rooms' steam pipes frozen solid; the insides of the wooden buildings were almost as cold as the weather outside.

Unlike their forebears, who had arrived in the United Kingdom with Gault and Farquhar in late 1914, few of these Patricias had spent any significant portion of their adult lives in Britain. Thus the regiment's first months of war, from the time they arrived on the second-to-last day of the year until the German invasion of Norway in April 1940 (the period known to history as "the phony war"), involved nothing more dangerous than getting used to their barely heated barracks, British army food, the sodden and dreary winter of south England, and the strange drinking habits of the local population, whose pubs closed at ten o'clock at night. Sergeant Lou

Holten was one of the NCOs responsible for what the Patricias ate. Shortly after the regiment arrived, he discovered the British army penchant for serving fatty mutton stew to its soldiers:

> I went in to see the British cooks . . . had a look . . . and told 'em, "Get rid of that fat, our troops don't like it." So then I went to the Sergeant's mess, had my supper there, and then I heard later on there was a riot over there . . . I told that [British mess] sergeant, "See, you wouldn't goddamn believe me." Then, after that, I never served mutton stew to anybody, anytime.[8]

Though the food was awful, Britain held great fascination at that early time of the war when Nazi bombers were not continually droning overhead. Felix Carriere long remembered his first visit to London, which occurred shortly after the Patricias had settled in to Morval Barracks:

> Everyone was so good to us because here we were, the heroic Canadians . . . back again after twenty years . . . We walked around mostly. You carried a helmet and a respirator. If you didn't have this, you were in jail . . . But you just walked around and found places: Trafalgar Square, Nelson's Column, and Big Ben. All things you might have read about . . . now there they were, standing in front of you.[9]

London was less than an hour from the barracks by train, but when their passes were of short duration, the men visited the local villages to take in the quaint, thatch-roofed, whitewashed houses; meet the local girls at dances; or drink room-temperature bitter in the village pubs.

Nine days into the new year, the Patricias began their training on English soil; they started with a route march. In England, as in Canada, they marched and marched and marched some more. Jock Mackie would later recall: "It was terrible . . . we marched all over England . . . I think I did about three thousand miles."[10]

The weather was cold and damp. Each morning dozens of men showed up at sick parade with colds and flu. By mid-January, an eighth of the regiment was bedridden.

The training went on as well as it could in the bad weather. At first, the battalion moved about in civilian buses. Later, the battalion transport began to arrive. It consisted of various sizes of trucks, Jeeps, and Universal (or Bren Gun) Carriers to carry supplies and men when the battalion was on the move. At that stage of the war, though, large-scale manoeuvres (battalion-size or larger) were rare. Before battalions, brigades, or divisions could take to the field, men had to be trained to fight in sections, platoons, and companies.

All training was done according to a training syllabus. There was a syllabus for just about every individual task an infantryman might have to carry out, from firing his rifle to throwing a grenade, to setting up and firing the battalion two-inch mortars. Bren gunners, signalmen, engineers, and other types of combat arms had their own syllabuses. Some of the soldiers had to learn how to handle, or strip and clean, several basic weapons at the same time. As soldiers completed each basic syllabus, they took Tests of Elementary Training. Felix Carriere later recalled the process: "We were very keen on reaching a specific degree of efficiency as soldiers. [In] tests of elementary training . . . you had to have so much speed and so much skill and it was all timed, so many seconds to do certain things . . . if you didn't pass, you had to do it over and over again until you were there. That was it. No failures."[11]

Thus, the Patricias learned how to use the weapons that would keep them alive in combat. Their basic tool was the Lee-Enfield No. 1 Mk III rifle. Later in the war, they would receive the Lee-Enfield No. 4 Mk I. First designed and manufactured before the First World War, the Lee-Enfield was sturdy, reliable, and could take lots of punishment and still fire accurately. It weighed 4.17 kilograms and was just over a metre in length. It had a ten-round magazine and an effective range of between 500 and 900 metres.

The average infantryman was trained to aim and fire one round every twelve seconds when ordered to produce "deliberate" fire, and one round every four seconds in "rapid" or "snap" fire. The men thought it "a very strong, solid weapon [that could] take all kinds of abuse."[12]

In early March 1940, the Patricias moved to the nearby Delville Barracks as their training continued. They and the other infantry regiments were still being trained to defend or assault First World War–era trench systems, a fact that speaks volumes about the state of Canadian military thinking at that time. The PPCLI spent two days in early April on a trench warfare exercise not far from Aldershot. Even as they trained how to fight the previous war, however, the war they were in was about to begin in earnest. On 9 April 1940, Germany invaded Norway and occupied Denmark; eight days later, Colquhoun informed the Patricias that they and the Edmonton Regiment had been selected for "a special task in Norway."

P.P.C.L.I.

Norway and Denmark were strategically important to the Allied war effort. The Danish government surrendered within hours of the German invasion, giving Hitler control over the passage from the North Sea to the Baltic Sea. With Norway fully occupied, Germany could ensure an uninterrupted flow by sea or rail of high-grade iron ore from Sweden to German steel plants and arms factories. Germany would also dominate the Norwegian Sea, and be able to send bombers or reconnaissance aircraft over a wide arc from Spitzbergen to Scotland.

The German attack caught the British napping. Winston Churchill, First Lord of the Admiralty, rushed preparations for a counterattack at Trondheim to split the German forces in Norway and keep hold of this key port. The British army approached Canadian Military Headquarters in London with a request to send parts of two Canadian battalions, about 800 men in all, to accompany the British force attacking German-held forts at the head of Trondheim fjord. McNaughton agreed, gave the job to his 2nd Brigade, and appointed Acting Brigade Commander Colonel E.W. Sansom (who had replaced Pearkes) to command the Canadian portion of the operation.

On 18 April, 1,300 men of the Edmonton Regiment and the PPCLI left Aldershot by rail for the Scottish port of Dunfermline. The troop trains pulled out of Farnborough Station at 2255, and wound their way slowly towards Dunfermline on the east coast of Scotland. Morale was high. Before leaving, the men had drawn a full mobilization kit, including new webbing, a harness worn by infantry to carry basic equipment; they were excited by the prospect of facing the enemy. First, however, they had to survive the British rail system. "Our train was simply an English troop train," one Patricia officer later wrote:

> To those who have experienced these horrible arrangements, that conjures up visions of wash basins grimy from months of dirt . . . empty water containers, complete lack of toilet paper and uncomfortable seats on which it was next to impossible to sleep. As usual, the troops were packed in like sardines, and the officers were in little better shape. But we were off on our job at last, and such conditions could not depress us for long.[13]

The Patricias arrived at their destination at mid-afternoon on 19 April. They disembarked, unloaded their regimental baggage, and began to march to camp. Gilbert Hyde recalled: "They marched us out of the station. We had gone ten minutes before it started to rain. We marched fifteen miles to where they got this camp set up . . . The PPCLI were on the side of a hill . . . about a 45-degree angle, and it rained. We were there for eight days and it rained the whole eight days."[14] As the cold Scottish rain came down, rivulets gathered on the hillside and became streams meandering through the camp, sometimes right under the tents. The men lugged ammunition boxes through the camp and built dams and canals with them to divert the streams away from sleeping and eating areas, but with little result. One Patricia later wrote: "Gradually the grassy slopes disappeared in a film of mud. The film spread and deepened until the whole camp area was a quagmire."[15] It wasn't long before the Patricias dubbed their encampment "sheep shit hill."[16]

Day after day, the men lined up at the quartermaster tent to pick up additional gear for their Arctic foray. They received sheepskin coats, bathing jerkins, sleeping bags, rubber boots, cold-weather gun oil, and mittens with trigger-finger cut-outs. The cooks slaved through the downpour and the chilling wind to keep the stoves and ovens hot, and served up some of the best food the men would ever remember having, with piping hot coffee and tea always available. When the men were not picking up cold-weather gear, or trying to keep tents and equipment from washing down the hillside, they practiced how to land on a rocky shore from small boats.

In the end, however, the Patricias never left for Norway. The operation had been considered risky from the very start. Since the first hours of the German invasion, *Luftwaffe* fighters and bombers had been pouring onto captured Norwegian airfields. British aircraft carrier strength off the Norwegian coast was insufficient to give the Canadians adequate protection; in addition, British troops to the north and south of Trondheim seemed to be doing well. On 21 April, therefore, the Trondheim operation was cancelled. The Eddies, as the Edmonton Regiment was called, and the Patricias boarded trains for Farnborough on the twenty-fifth, and the Patricias arrived back at Delville Barracks the next morning. "There was a lot of disappointment," one officer later recalled, "but the operation in Norway turned out to be a dismal failure. If we had gone in that would have been the end of the war for us because we'd either be killed or captured."[17] The British and French troops already in Norway fought on in a losing cause for another month. By the end of the first week in June, however, all the survivors were evacuated.

Norway capitulated to Germany on 9 June 1940, and was occupied until the end of the war.

The last three weeks of the Norwegian campaign were overshadowed by the momentous events taking place along the German border with Holland, Belgium, and France. On 10 May, Hitler struck west, into the Low Countries and France. German paratroopers seized key airfields, canal crossings, and road junctions in Holland, as glider troops quickly captured the important Belgian fort of Eben Emael. German bombers burned much of Rotterdam to the ground. German *panzer* (armoured) divisions wound their way through the thick, and supposedly impassable, Ardennes forest in southwest Belgium, then bypassed the French Maginot line and won a quick and decisive victory at Sedan in eastern France. As German spearheads, closely supported by *Luftwaffe* ground-attack aircraft, sliced deep into France, the French armies began to collapse in confusion. Then the Germans swung north, toward the English Channel coast, cutting off the bulk of the French army from its Belgian and British allies. The Belgians retreated into Belgium, then quickly surrendered. As German troops enveloped France from the Belgian border to the Pyrenees, the situation of the 300,000-man British Expeditionary Force, originally positioned to guard the French northern flank, grew extremely precarious. The BEF fell back on the Channel coast at Dunkirk and, in what has become known to history as the Miracle at Dunkirk, was pulled off the beaches at the last moment by Royal Navy destroyers and civilian vessels of every size and shape. On the morning of 4 June, the Germans fought their way through the town of Dunkirk, to the beaches, and captured the few remaining soldiers there. But more than 338,000 British and French troops had already escaped. Paris fell on 14 June. France officially surrendered to Germany just over a week later.

In forty-two decisive days, the entire course of the war had changed. But the Canadian soldiers in Britain were bystanders.

On 3 June, just as the last British and French troops were being taken off the Dunkirk beaches, the British had decided to throw a second BEF into the Battle of France. This force was to land at Brest, and then move eastward in the direction of Paris. Canadian Military Headquarters agreed to include 1st Canadian Division in the initiative, and the Patricias received their warning order on 13 June, a day after the lead elements of the division began to disembark at Brest. Those first troops were transported east by rail, reaching a concentration area near Laval on the morning of the fifteenth. There, they learned that the armoured spearheads of German Field Marshal Fedor von Bock's powerful Army Group B, racing westward, were only sixty kilometres away. The expedition was hurriedly called off; the Canadians quickly withdrew to Brest with the Germans hot on their heels. Although some of the Canadian equipment had to be burned and abandoned near the Brest docks, almost all the Canadians returned safely to Britain. At Delville Barracks, Colquhoun received word that the move to France was "temporarily" cancelled. For the second time in two months, the PPCLI narrowly escaped disaster.

On 23 June 1940, the PPCLI left Delville Barracks for good. McNaughton's new assignment was to prepare his division for what everyone thought would be an imminent German invasion. The division was still largely untrained in the ways of modern war, especially the war of *blitzkrieg,* or lightning war, with which the *Wehrmacht* had overwhelmed half of Europe. But the BEF had left virtually all its trucks, guns, signals, and communications equipment, even mobile field kitchens and bath units, on the Dunkirk beaches. Although the Canadian division was not well equipped compared to a German division, it was rich in trucks and guns compared to most British divisions. Thus, McNaughton was ordered to deploy his division south of London to act as a mobile reserve that could rush to the beaches of East or West Sussex, or Kent, to back up the beach defenders if the Germans struck.

"Canadian Force," as it was called, consisted of four mobile formations, each based on an infantry battalion, with ample trucks and other vehicles to allow rapid movement by road. It had attached formations of engineers, gunners, medium machine-gun and heavy-mortar companies, medical companies, and signals troops.

Godstone gave the Patricias a ringside seat for the Battle of Britain and the London Blitz. It was directly under one of the main *Luftwaffe* flyways from France to London. Although the main German bombing force had more important targets to hit, lone bombers, stragglers, or damaged aircraft often dropped their loads on one of the many army camps that ringed London. Sometimes German fighters swooped low as they escorted the bombers to London and back on missions to strafe the countryside — especially the British and Canadian army installations. By the end of July 1940, as the Battle of Britain began in earnest, bombing became a daily occurrence. Don Parrott later recalled: "We got raided, air raided, every day . . . we could hear the guns starting down on Beachy Head or somewhere on the coast. We could tell they were coming. [Someone would yell] 'Man the machine guns!' and as they went over we would fire at them." Once Parrott saw a German bomber being chased by British Spitfires. The bomber was damaged and had its wheels down: "The Spits were on top of them and [the Germans] were wounded and they couldn't get away. The Spitfires were right behind them in a tight circle. [The Germans] lifted their wheels up and landed and skidded on a plowed field so they wouldn't tip over."[18] Parrott and a number of other Patricias rushed over to take the three-man crew prisoner as soon as they climbed out of the wreckage.

In early September, the *Luftwaffe* began to switch its daylight attacks on British aircraft factories and RAF fighter fields to attacks on London and other British cities. They also began, with growing frequency, to target London at night. This was the start of the London Blitz. By the end of September, the air raids came nightly.

The attacks dragged on into the spring of 1941. Each twilight, the German bombers gathered over their French airfields and headed up the Thames Estuary toward the British capital. Each night, just before the wails of the air-raid sirens started up, the Patricias heard the dim roar of the approaching bomber formations. As the bombers drew nearer, the booms of the British anti-aircraft guns opening fire into the night sky punctuated the drones of hundreds of aircraft engines. The flashes of the guns could be seen for miles but rarely did anyone see a flash from an exploding German bomber. Few of those bombers were hit, either by anti-aircraft guns or by the British night fighters, which hunted by eyesight in the days before airborne radar. Sometimes the Patricias would gather outside their tents or billets and watch London under attack. They were close enough to see the flashes of the anti-aircraft guns and the stroboscopic effect of the exploding bombs. They heard the drones of the bombers, the crash of the guns, and the sharp cracks of the exploding bombs over the wails of the air-raid sirens and the bells of the emergency vehicles. London burned night after night; the men from far-away Canada, who had come to Britain to fight a war, were helpless to do anything about it.

P.P.C.L.I.

On 9 September 1940, "Shorty" Colquhoun, the last of the Original officers, said goodbye to the Patricias and left for Canada to assume command of the 7th Canadian Infantry Brigade in the newly forming 3rd Canadian Infantry Division. Major J.N. Edgar, MC (soon to be promoted to Lieutenant-Colonel), who had joined the Patricias as a private in late August 1914, took his place. Edgar had displayed both verve and courage under fire in the First World War. Commissioned in 1916, he was twice wounded, awarded the Military Cross, and had assumed command of the regiment in the thick of the bitter and costly fighting at Tilloy in the late fall of 1918. He had stayed in the PF after the war and had accompanied the PPCLI overseas as second-in-command. In May 1940, he was given command of the Hastings and Prince Edward Regiment in the 1st Brigade, and held this post until he succeeded Colquhoun as Commanding Officer of the PPCLI on 15 September.

Both Colquhoun and Edgar were ideal officers for placing the Patricias on a war footing and settling them into their training routine in the United Kingdom. Both men, however, were simply too old for the rigorous duty of leading a modern infantry battalion in war. In terms of age, they differed little from most of the Canadian Army officers commanding the 1st and 2nd Infantry Division battalions and brigades at the start of the war. In the spring of 1939, the PF officer corps had numbered just 446 men; Chris Vokes, who commanded the PPCLI in an acting capacity for five weeks in the fall of 1941, thought that more than half of them were too old, too sick, or too stupid to command. Born in 1904, Vokes was considerably younger than Colquhoun, Edgar, and most of the PF battalion commanders in the summer and fall of 1941.

Vokes's harsh opinion of the PF officers was echoed in the views of none other than British General Bernard L. "Monty" Montgomery. Born in 1887, Monty had seen action in France in the First World War and had emerged as one of the British army's top field commanders at the start of the Battle of France in 1940. He had been among the last British officers off the beaches of Dunkirk and, as commander of the 3rd British Division, had distinguished himself as an offensively minded tactician and thus a favourite of Churchill. He was also a superb trainer of soldiers, with a good eye for potential weaknesses in commanders. Monty reviewed Canadian units and their commanders in the spring of 1942, and, after several weeks of observing them, he decided that most of the Canadian battalion commanders were totally unsuited to the job of training their men or leading them in combat. As a result of Monty's evaluation, a wholesale housecleaning of officers took place, right up to the divisional level.

The rapid growth of the Canadian Army, and the weeding out of those officers too old or set in their ways to fight this new style of war, brought rapid turnover to the officer ranks, and quick promotion for men such as Vokes, who showed even a modicum of command skills. Edgar left the PPCLI on 18 June 1941, and returned to Canada to assume a staff position. Rodney F.L. Keller, an RMC graduate who had joined the Patricias in 1920, succeeded him for all of eight weeks. Born in the United Kingdom in 1900, Keller was too old for an active field command and moved on at the end of July 1941 to take command of a brigade. He, in turn, was succeeded by R.A. Lindsay on 31 July. Lindsay was a militia officer who had transferred to the Patricias from the South Alberta Regiment in November 1939. Lindsay would command the regiment for two years, train it for action, and lead it in the fight for Sicily, only to lose command under very controversial circumstances in August 1943.

P.P.C.L.I.

The surrender of France had a profound effect on the overall course of the war, and a decided impact on the Canadian role in it. With France neutralized and the United States and USSR not yet in, Canada was suddenly Britain's main ally. Since the people of Canada were strongly pro-British and fully committed to the war, the Canadian government was forced to reevaluate its original intentions of severely limiting the size of the Canadian Army while focusing most of the Canadian war effort on war production, the training of air crew in the British Commonwealth Air Training Plan, and the air war. The government now moved quickly to rush the mobilization of the recently announced 3rd Canadian Infantry Division, and to recruit and train enough troops for two more full divisions and two additional armoured brigades. The size of the First Canadian Army was set at three infantry divisions; two armoured divisions; and two independent armoured brigades, organized into

I and II Canadian Corps. A.G.L. McNaughton was Commander, First Canadian Army.

McNaughton had come to prominence as a Canadian Corps artillery officer in the First World War under Arthur Currie. Like his mentor, McNaughton strongly believed in the necessity of keeping the brigades, divisions, and corps of the Canadian Army together in a single fighting formation. He strenuously opposed all efforts to commit the Canadian divisions to battle in piecemeal fashion under British command. Such unity had helped Currie work a miracle in the First World War; the vaunted fighting ability of the Canadian Corps had been founded, in part, on corps unity. But whereas the First World War battlefields contested by the British and Canadians were located in one relatively small sector in eastern France and western Belgium, the Second World War was truly global. Canadian troops could have been used alongside the British, Australians, New Zealanders, Indians, and other Commonwealth troops battling the Italians and Germans in the Balkans, the Mediterranean, the Middle East, and North Africa. Britain, however, simply had not enough shipping power to transport the entire Canadian Army to any of those global theatres in one go, as McNaughton insisted. So the Canadian Army, the Patricias with them, sat in Britain while the war went on without them, and trained and trained and trained some more.

In August 1941, the PPCLI and other Canadian troops entrained for northern Scotland to practice mountain climbing and beach landings as part of Exercise Heather, the attack on Spitzbergen. After four days, they returned to southern England only to learn that, once again, they had *almost* gone into action. They had been destined to be part of a landing force attacking the German-occupied Island of Spitzbergen, but the attack had been scaled down, and the PPCLI had been dropped from the order of battle. In September 1941, the Patricias took part in Exercise Bumper, then settled in in November for a long stint guarding the beaches of southern England. Early in the new year, they began to practice "battle drill," a battle-inoculation type of training using live ammunition over realistic terrain, designed to teach sections, platoons, and companies the basic steps of fire and movement warfare.

Battle drill was exciting at first, with the men advancing against a pretend enemy through wooded terrain or across rolling fields, while machine guns fired live ammunition alongside them on fixed lines, and shells exploded along their line of advance. But it was still training, not the real thing. As the months dragged by, the Canadian Army in England grew increasingly restless. Long-time Patricia Sydney Frost would later write:

> At that stage in the War the Canadian Army had been sitting in England almost two years. The troops, eager to get into battle, had been buggered about on endless exercises and concentrations all over the south coast on England. For the troops, all these great exercises meant only marching and more marching . . . there was a huge discipline problem throughout the Canadian Army. The troops were browned off and some went AWOL [Absent Without Leave] to vent their frustrations. The Patricias no doubt experienced the same problems as all the other units.[19]

No doubt. Problems such as brawls, crime, drunkenness, and trouble with both the civilian population and the police grew endemic. The need to get the Canadians into action somewhere, anywhere, grew by the month. In August 1942, that need was the chief reason for Canadian participation in the ill-conceived, badly planned, hasty, and poorly executed Dieppe operation.

The Patricias fortunately missed the raid on Dieppe, mounted by the 2nd Canadian Infantry Division. Two-thirds of that division stormed ashore on the morning of 19 August 1942, with little air or naval support. They had orders to capture the French port town of Dieppe and hold it for a day. The Germans were waiting for them. Canadian tanks were destroyed on the shale beaches and

Canadian infantry were slaughtered, often at the water's edge. The attack was called off at 1100 and a difficult evacuation under fire began. Out of the more than 5,000 Canadian attackers that morning, 907 were killed in action and 1,946 were taken prisoner, many of them wounded. Many of the 2,211 who made it back to the UK were also wounded. It was the worst single day for the Canadian military in the entire war.

After Dieppe, the pressure grew on the Canadian government to send Canadian soldiers into battle even if the entire Canadian Army could not be committed to action at once. In March 1943, Ottawa notified London that Canada was now ready to send a division or two of the Canadian Army into battle wherever they might be needed, with the understanding that those troops would be returned to the United Kingdom in time for the opening of the second front in France. Shortly after, the British asked Ottawa if they might use a Canadian infantry division and a Canadian armoured brigade in "operations based on Tunisia." In fact, those Canadians were not wanted for action in North Africa, but to take part in the forthcoming Allied invasion of Sicily. Ottawa readily agreed.

The 1st Canadian Infantry Division and the 1st Canadian Army Tank Brigade were chosen to take part in the forthcoming landing in Sicily because no other Canadian division was ready to take on the task. A good part of 2nd Division had been mauled on the beaches in front of Dieppe, and the 3rd Division was a full year behind 1st Division in training and organization. Commanded by Major General H.L.N. Salmon, the 1st Canadian Infantry Division and 1st Canadian Army Tank Brigade (later 1st Canadian Armoured Brigade) were attached to the 30th Corps of the British Eighth Army under Montgomery. Salmon never got the chance to command the division in battle however; on 29 April, he and much of his staff were killed when the plane carrying them to Tunis crashed within minutes of take-off. He was succeeded by Guy Granville Simonds. The rest of the Sicily invading force consisted of the United States Seventh Army, under US General George S. Patton. British General Sir Harold Alexander was overall ground commander, while the overall theatre commander was US General Dwight David Eisenhower.

The Patricias were encamped at Eastbourne, on the south coast of England, in early May 1943, when Lindsay received a warning order that the regiment would soon be on the move to Scotland for "combined operations" (amphibious) training. Back in February, Salmon had promised the officers of 2nd Brigade that they would surely see action in 1943, but all they had seen thus far was more of the cold, wet Scottish highlands and coast, the scene of much of their training over the last two years. In fact, the PPCLI had gone north to Scotland in mid-February to march, practice beach landings, and scramble over rocks and heather for almost three weeks before returning south to Eastbourne. Now they were going back again. They left on 5 May and reached Inveraray, Scotland, four days later. Instead of falling into their old training routine, however, they embarked aboard the HMT *Llangibby Castle,* an LSI, or Landing Ship, Infantry. Something different was definitely in the air.

For the balance of May and the first four weeks of June, the Patricias trained hard in the art of assault landing, one of the most dangerous and difficult operations in warfare. When they were not learning how to descend rope ladders — carrying full packs, weapons, and equipment — from the decks of the *Llangibby Castle* into pitching landing craft moored alongside, they trained in mountain warfare. The rumours began to fly: they were going into action; they were training to assault Norway; someone had seen crates full of tropical gear at a troop concentration centre near Glasgow. Felix Carriere would later recall: "Once in Scotland we painted great circles on the top of vehicles . . . identification marks . . . so all of a sudden, this is a bit more than an exercise . . . you load up a truck with five hundred or more radio batteries, nothing but radio batteries . . . so we knew things were happening."[20]

On 22 May, the practice landings ended and the regiment entrained for Hamilton, near Glasgow, where they began to load assault gear into transports. Trucks, radio equipment, rations, ammunition, Jeeps, and medical supplies all had to be loaded in such a way that the first items needed would come first out of the assault transports when they hit the beaches. The men's woolen battledress was taken away and replaced with khaki shirts and shorts. "It was obvious that we were going to a fairly warm climate," Sydney McKay later recalled. "Of course that just made us all try to guess where."[21] Finally, the men were issued malaria tablets, one a day for eight days as a starting dose.

The overall plan for the capture of Sicily called for Montgomery's Eighth Army to attack the island's southeast coast on a sixty-kilometre front while the American Seventh Army, under George S. Patton, attacked the south coast further to the west of the Canadians and British. Both armies were to advance northward, roughly to the centre of the island, before swinging eastward to trap the Germans north of Syracuse. The 1st Canadian Infantry Division was allotted a beachhead on the extreme British left, at the southernmost tip of Sicily. Its initial assignment after securing the beach was to take the town and airfield of Pacino. D-Day was set for 10 July 1943.

On 14 June, the Patricias re-embarked the *Llangibby Castle* to continue last-minute amphibious training. They stowed their gear and lived aboard ship in Greenock Harbour for two weeks while a large convoy gathered around them. On 28 June, Brigadier Chris Vokes, who had been in command of 2nd Brigade since May of 1942, came aboard along with Guy Simonds for a visit and inspection. Ever the dramatist, Vokes charged his officers to "fight to the death" in the forthcoming operation.[22] Then, at 2130, with the sun still hanging in the northwestern sky, the convoy weighed anchor and steamed into the open ocean. Operation Husky — the assault on Sicily — was about to begin, with the Patricias in the first wave.

Chapter 8

FROM PACINO TO THE MORO

AT 0145 ON 10 JULY 1943, TEN KILOMETRES OFF "SUGAR" beach, on a stretch of coastline code-named Bark West, Andy Schaen crouched low in the landing craft as it pitched and rolled its way through the dark night. Jammed full of nervous men, the landing craft headed toward the assault beach assigned to the PPCLI, some five kilometres from the whitewashed Sicilian town of Pacino. Some men prayed quietly; some grimly hung on as the boat smashed through the heavy surf; some retched and vomited from fear, seasickness, and the heavy mutton stew they had been served just a few hours earlier aboard the *Llangibby Castle.* Several kilometres inland, they could see the flashes and hear the explosions of bomb bursts as US medium bombers plastered not only Pacino, but the small airfield a kilometre west of it, and enemy beach defences. Tracer bullets hosed through the night sky, and flares popped in the dark as the bombers passed low over the landing craft and headed inland. Then the fifteen-inch guns from the monitor ship HMS *Roberts* opened fire; Schaen and his buddies heard the express-train rumble of the shells passing overhead and saw the huge explosions on the beach.

None of the men in that assault boat, or in the dozens of other landing craft racing to shore around them, had ever experienced such sights and sounds. As the *Roberts* opened up, one of the men crouching close to Schaen began to blabber about being blown to bits. At that moment, however, Schaen had no sympathy for the fearful man. He later recalled, "We'd never been shot at before . . . and I remember [thinking] that I better get this guy quieted down otherwise he's going to have everybody really windy." Fear could be very contagious at moments like this one, just before the ramp went down and the men were exposed to their first incoming fire of the war. Schaen turned to the man and shouted, "Look, you know, they're not coming at us, they're coming off the Roberts . . . If you don't stop talking, I'll shush you myself."[1]

P.P.C.L.I.

Only hours before, aboard the *Llangibby Castle,* the Patricias had started to prepare for war. The convoy had been ravaged by a storm earlier in the day; the ship still rolled and pitched in the swell as the men whiled away their time gambling, sharpening knives, oiling and cleaning rifles and pistols, writing letters, or just lying on their bunks, staring at the overhead deck. Felix Carriere and some others sang their hearts out — popular songs, folk songs, the Ric-a-Dam-Doo: "I played a guitar until my fingers were bleeding," remembered Carriere, "and we sang songs until silence was demanded: quarter-hour dress, half-hour dress, then silence. I recall everybody was singing and all of a sudden, not another sound until we were heading for . . . the beach."[2]

As the ship's loudspeakers issued orders to prepare for disembarkation, some of the men dressed for war in the gilt-and-gold-decorated saloon of the *Llangibby Castle.* Colin M. McDougall, a platoon commander in C Company, would later describe the scene in his Governor-General's-Award-winning novel, *Execution:*

> They were weighted down with extra loads of grenades, mortar bombs, [small-arms ammunition], bandoleers, Bren magazines . . . they helped each other dress, like athletes or actors backstage. They carried more on their bodies than could have been expended in the most desperate firefight, but they did not know this yet because they did not know the actuality of war.[3]

"Each man was given a condom," Sydney McKay recalled, "not for the purpose for which it was designed, [but] to put your wallet, wristwatch and valuables into and then you put this into your helmet before you put it back on your head."[4]

The transports had dropped anchor about ten kilometres southwest of the beach at half-past midnight; the loudspeakers had called the heavily laden men forward one serial, or landing craft group, at a time. They clambered aboard, then sat quietly. At about 0100, the landing craft had been lowered down the sides of the transports into the sea. The boats banged loudly against the hull; one was damaged and started to take in water almost immediately. Major R.P. "Slug" Clark was aboard the damaged craft: "It was quite a sea running and it was pitch black . . . the naval rating [non-commissioned seaman] who was supposed to unshackle the front of the boat . . . failed to do so. The next craft coming down . . . hit the front end of [our] boat and damaged the landing ramp. We couldn't go forward because we would take on water." Somehow, Clark's boat had been able to manoeuvre back to the ship's cranes; the men were lifted aboard, transferred to another landing craft, and sent on their way.[5]

At 0134, the landing craft had started to nose toward shore. As they pushed forward, some of the men were seasick; others had the runs. For Jock Mackie, the discomfort was worse than his fear of getting shot: "All I wanted to do was get on the land and die, that's all. We . . . got in the landing craft. [It was] bouncing. One had tipped over. It was a mess."[6]

Felix Carriere was too wound up to be sick: "There had been a storm . . . when we did land on the water, the water was rough . . . I wasn't [sick] because it was very exciting. We were all hidden, low down, whispering and the two diesel motors were going *wa-wa-wa-wa-wa.*"[7]

The landing craft circled offshore until the two assault battalions had been lowered into the sea. On this, the first morning of war for the 1st Canadian Division, the 2nd Brigade, which included the PPCLI and the Seaforth Highlanders of Canada, had been chosen to attack "Sugar" beach on the left. The 1st Brigade had been selected to assault "Roger" beach on the right. The Edmonton Regiment was the 2nd Brigade's floating reserve, set to come ashore after the Seaforths and Patricias had secured the beach. In the dark and the confusion, the navy men guiding the Seaforths' landing craft got lost and headed for an empty stretch of beach to the right of the Patricias. PPCLI Captain Donald Brain, in command of B Company, later wrote:

> As we approached the shore flares could be seen . . . Machine gun tracer made attractive patterns against the sky. On shore every once in a while there would appear a bright flash followed by a loud report . . . the shore gradually became clearly defined and the order was given for the landing craft to deploy. On touchdown the doors were dropped and the men disembarked in water well above their waists. In a few instances they had to swim for it.[8]

Chester Hendricks was one of those Patricias who started the war with a good soaking: "Chester . . . was carrying a Bren gun and stepped off the end of the gangway and down he went," Andy Schaen later recalled. "He disappeared. He came up, but the Bren gun didn't."[9]

Had the Italian defenders of Bark West been alert, and determined to defend their homeland against the invaders, casualties might have been heavy as men loaded with equipment floundered toward shore. But the Italians, members of the low-grade 122nd Regiment of the 206th Coastal Division, were neither ready nor eager to die for their *patria.* As the landing craft closed the beach, "there were a few bursts of machine-gun fire from the shore," recalled Lou Holten, "but then there was nothing more. When we got to [the machine-gun nest] the goddamned gun had jammed on the guy and whoever was firing it took off hell bent."[10]

"We were lucky," Felix Carriere remembered. "We got there and broke through a bunch of barbed wire. There was very little resistance. We captured a bunch of prisoners and we captured some horses from an artillery group."[11]

Captain Brain's men had a similar experience. A few grenades were tossed their way, but that was all. "We replied with a couple of . . . grenades . . . we cut through the wire and made our way forward, bumping into a machine-gun post with two sentries, whom we wiped out."[12]

"There was almost no opposition . . . no resistance really," Captain "Bucko" Watson, the battalion adjutant, recalled: "The defenders . . . had no will to fight whatsoever. Their main aim seemed to be to surrender and get out of the war."[13] Conscripts all, badly treated by their officers, poorly equipped, hungry, sick, and deprived of even basic comforts, the Italian defenders would surrender by the hundreds over the next few days.

"I recall seeing on day two, maybe even on day one, a whole bunch of them, let's say fifty or sixty, in the PPCLI area," Carriere remembered. "They had their water bottles filled with wine . . . they were cheerful and to them the war was over and they weren't frightened of us. They were laughing and chuckling and telling stories in Italian."[14] The hastily constructed barbed-wire POW cages filled up quickly. The Italian prisoners were hustled aboard transports to be taken to prison camps in North Africa.

Once ashore, the Patricias found few beach defences. The land was poor and strewn with rocks, with bits of grass and shrubs and many patches of swampy ground just behind the sandy beaches. The two assault companies spread out, pushed to the end of the landing area, and secured the ground for the rest of the battalion, which began to come ashore almost immediately. As Colin McDougall later wrote, the PPCLI crossed "a mile of the undulating coastal plain, past vineyards and olive groves, through gardens of aloe and cypress. Their boots crushed and released the scents of rosemary and thyme. There were flowering olive trees, distant orange groves — but no sign of the enemy."[15] Further up the beach, to the right of their intended position, the Seaforths also came ashore with virtually no opposition. Before dawn, they were joined by the Edmonton Regiment and Major-General Chris Vokes's 2nd Brigade Headquarters. Lieutenant-Colonel R.A. "Bob" Lindsay began to send out patrols to scout the ground between the landing ground and the narrow beach road that connected Pacino with the hamlet of Ispica, some fifteen kilometres to the northwest. Ispica was the first PPCLI objective after leaving the assault beach. By 1000, the Patricias had reached their first-phase objectives. They dug in, pried open their compo packs, and began to brew tea, make coffee, and eat their hardtack and bully-beef rations. The occasional incoming shell threw up a cloud of sand and pebbles, but the worst discomfort came from the heat, the stink, and the rising clouds of malaria-bearing mosquitoes.

Even in these first few hours, the Patricias began to get a taste of what fighting in Sicily was going to be like. The island is about 290 kilometres at its widest and 180 kilometres from Pacino to the north coast. The dominant geographical feature is the active volcano Mount Etna, about midway up the island's east coast. South of Mount Etna lies Catania, the island's second-largest city; the ancient port town of Syracuse; and the marshy Catania plain.

Sicily's interior is mountainous, with deep ravines, many kilometres of ridgelines, high peaks, and long, narrow valleys. Most of the stone- and brick-walled villages are at higher elevations, reached by twisting, climbing roads. These roads were easily defended where they ran over ravines or across mountain streams; the Germans invariably blew up the bridges.

Sicily is always dry and, in the summer, very hot, with sanitation that left much to be desired. For much of the Sicily campaign, the heat, flies, dust, rocky ground, and steep terrain posed almost as much challenge to the Allied troops as did the enemy. That enemy — a mixed force of approximately 40,000 German and 230,000 Italian troops — had only to utilize the natural defences of the mountainous interior to hold back large numbers of attackers. Small groups of defenders used explosives to build roadblocks by demolishing bridges, trees, and rocks; mortars and machine guns were used to set ambushes.

"It was very very hot, very dry, and . . . very sparse vegetation," "Bucko" Watson recalled. "There were olive trees [and] huge cactus bushes, and the people lived in abject poverty. The dust on the roads was so fine it was almost like flour."[16] Vokes found the heat oppressive: "Even at that early morning hour . . . the smells on the beach seemed exactly like those of Cairo."[17]

"The heat at that time was intense," Slug Clark remembered. "Our condition was poor because we'd been four weeks aboard a ship with no exercise." At one point in the next few days, Clark lost eighteen men from his company to heat exhaustion, just as an attack was about to begin. "We'd been sitting on a hillside from early morning . . . There was no shade and very little water and they'd forgotten to supply us with salt tablets."[18] After a single day under the hot Mediterranean sun, necks, faces, arms, and knees were bright red from sunburn.

Nights were not much better. Canadian Broadcasting Corporation (CBC) war correspondent Peter Stursberg, who came ashore in the second wave, never forgot those sultry Sicilian nights: "The German planes that let us alone in the daytime made several raids when it was dark . . . when the raiders were not around, there were unseen marauders in the sandy soil to keep me awake . . . between the fleas and the flak, and the fleas were worse, I got no sleep. The next morning my waist was as red as raw beefsteak."[19]

But nothing was as bad as the mosquitoes, and the malaria they brought. "Right to Mount Etna . . . there were mosquitoes all over," Jock Mackie recalled. He was afflicted with the dread disease virtually overnight. "I thought my head was going to blow off . . . two weeks I was [in hospital] with quinine . . . and when I got back I was [still] weak."[20] In the course of the Sicily campaign, the Patricias suffered as many casualties from malaria as they did from enemy bullets.

As their first day ashore drew to a close, the brigade began to move inland. The Patricias' A Company, leading the battalion toward Ispica, came under fire after dark and launched a quick attack on an Italian defensive position. The Italian soldiers threw down their weapons almost immediately, and the PPCLI captured four field guns. Then they pushed ahead through the scrub, feeling their way through the darkness with the ground occasionally lit by explosions to their rear. The PPCLI war diarist wrote: "During this advance the sky was aglow with flak and tracer as enemy planes carried out an attack on our ships which were still unloading on the beaches."[21] Even at the landing beaches, however, the casualties were surprisingly light. On the first day in action, only seven were killed and twenty-five wounded in the entire 1st Canadian Division; the PPCLI suffered four wounded on the first day and one more on the second. The first Patricia killed in action in Sicily fell on 12 July 1943; he was Company Quartermaster Sergeant John Frank Stevens, the son of John Slade Stevens and Mary Stevens of Victoria, British Columbia. Stevens is buried in the Agira Canadian War Cemetery alongside the twenty-nine other Patricias killed in action in Sicily.

P.P.C.L.I.

The Second World War was supposed to be a new kind war: a war of movement, with infantry travelling by trucks to save their strength for fighting. But this was not the case for the Canadians in the first weeks of the Sicilian campaign. Most of the division's vehicles had been lost at sea prior to the landings, when U-boats had torpedoed three ships from one of the support convoys. More than fifty Canadian soldiers had been killed and more than 500 vehicles lost. Now the men would have to walk through Sicily, trudging up steep, narrow mountain roads in the heat and dust, keeping to both sides while passing trucks, tanks, and Jeeps threw up thick clouds of dust that caked the soldiers' arms and faces, sifted beneath their uniforms, and lodged on their skin to mix with the sweat pouring off their bodies. Those who could grabbed farmers' carts or "requisitioned" horses or mules to form makeshift pack teams. Later, they would hire local muleskinners, who would become more essential to the war in Sicily than roadbound vehicles: mules, unlike vehicles, could carry supplies, radios — anything heavy — anywhere in the mountainous terrain. As was the custom in an infantry advance, Vokes shuffled his battalions, giving each a chance to lead while the other two followed along behind in line of march.

Built on a small ridge, Ispica dominated the island as far as the beaches. The Canadians encountered no resistance there, took more Italian prisoners, and then continued to follow the retreating enemy towards Modica, another twenty kilometres to the northwest along Highway No. 115. They had not yet encountered any German troops. Before they left Ispica, Sydney Frost, age twenty-one, was pressed into service by the Allied Military Government (AMG) to serve as the chief magistrate of the town until a more permanent representative of the AMG could be brought in. He ran the town for nineteen days: "Right after we took the city, I became its mayor. I was confused at first, everything was in shambles.

There was no water, no food, no electricity. We had many wounded . . . the people, worn out by years of fascist domination and stricken by the war, received us as liberators, cooperating with us for the reconstruction."[22]

No good commander ever gives a retreating enemy time to rest, and 1st Canadian Infantry Division Commander G.G. "Guy" Simonds was no exception. The Canadians pressed on through the night of 11/12 July. The Patricia war diarist wrote, "This advance was carried out under very hot and dusty conditions and the troops, though tired from the previous activities, carried on magnificently. At mid-night we were still marching, having met little opposition."[23] Just before dawn the next morning, they moved into positions on the heights east of Modica, a town of 40,000 people and the site of the headquarters of Italian General Achilles d'Havet's 206th Italian Coastal Division. Lindsay sent patrols into the town to determine whether any Germans were there; they, unlike the Italians, would put up stiff resistance. Andy Schaen was one of the first Patricias to enter Modica: "Away we went into this town," he later recalled, "and on the way in we were creeping along in this ditch which was about four or five feet deep and this voice says, 'What the hell are you doing down there?' I look up and it's Brigadier Vokes and he says, 'There's nothing here . . . get out of there . . .' "[24]

At Modica, the PPCLI captured General d'Havet and most of his staff. The general insisted on surrendering to an officer of equivalent rank, so Brigade Major R.S. Malone conducted d'Havet to Simonds's HQ. Once again, the Canadians found themselves with scores of Italian POWs. CBC war correspondent Peter Stursberg entered Modica not long after it was secured: "We passed columns of Italian prisoners, who had fallen into our hands with the capture of General d'Havet's headquarters at Modica. There were thousands of them, and they were only too willing to cheer and raise their fingers in the V sign for the photographers."[25]

On the morning of 13 July 1943, the PPCLI took up positions on the high ground near Modica. Here, the PPCLI captured two Italian men carrying rifles. Vokes later recorded the event in his memoirs: "Lindsay . . . got on the blower. 'We got sniped at' he reported to me . . . and we caught three [*sic*] of them. What will I do with them?'" Apparently believing (or knowing) that the men were in civilian clothes and thus subject to immediate execution according to the Geneva Convention rules, Vokes decided the men ought to be shot. But since he and Lindsay were conversing over the radio in the clear, Vokes did not want to order Lindsay outright to shoot the prisoners. He replied: "Use your head." Lindsay wouldn't take the bait. "What will I do with them?" he asked again. Again, Vokes told him, "Use your bloody head." After a minute or two of futile conversation, Vokes ordered the prisoners brought back to Brigade HQ. Just after they arrived, Simonds came up. Vokes explained that he was going to have the men shot. Simonds at first agreed. Then, according to Vokes's account, he changed his mind, and the captured Italians were given a good beating instead.[26]

Despite Vokes's account, there is substantial evidence that Lindsay did in fact order the execution. The shooting was the central event of Colin McDougall's 1958 novel *Execution.*[27] Other Patricias confirm McDougall's version of events. According to Major "Slug" Clark:

> The [Italians] were obviously deserters because they had army boots on. They were carrying a suitcase with all their army identification in the suitcase. They were very pleasant little fellows and the lads used them as flunkeys . . . brigade headquarters heard about these two men and they got on the blower and said that they had to be executed. The CO objected . . . but anyways the order had to be carried out, much to my regret.[28]

Sydney McKay remembered, "Colonel Lindsay at the time sentenced them to death and was going to have them shot in the town square in Modica to set an example. He chose not to, and had them taken out to the field, had them dig their own graves and they were shot."[29] Given the conflicting accounts of this incident, no one can say for certain whether or not Vokes had the two men executed, and, if he did, whether that execution was either legal or moral. But the incident does throw some light on the growing friction between Vokes and Lindsay, a friction that would soon have significant consequences for the Patricias.

P.P.C.L.I.

The 1st Canadian Infantry Division remained near Modica for two days as the Americans battled German *panzer* troops just a few kilometres to the west and the British fought their way north along the eastern coastal plain. General Bernard L. Montgomery now changed the original plans for the capture of Sicily. Running into stiffening opposition, he decided to attack to the west of Mount Etna, directly to Messina, to cut off the German and Italian escape route to the mainland. He lobbied to have the Americans play the entirely secondary role of protecting the British left flank. In this new plan, the Canadian division would switch its axis of attack to the north, toward the town of Enna in the centre of the island. In so doing, the Canadians were fated to run into major concentrations of German troops along the main German line of resistance, which straddled the island from east to west along Highway No. 121. The change in plan raised several major problems for the Canadians, as one history of the Sicily campaign would later note:

> The outermost blow of Monty's left hook was to be delivered by his least motorized division and the only one in his army not yet fully acclimated to the semitropical conditions of the Mediterranean summer. It was also committed to an axis of advance along a single highway in a mountainous area, where all the advantages of the terrain accrued to the defenders.[30]

Monty visited the Canadians on 14 July; the troops gave him a hearty welcome before moving off the next morning for Ragusa, about seven kilometres to the north of Modica. By now the division was pushing deeply into the most mountainous areas in central Sicily with deep, narrow defiles; switchback roads; and long climbs under observation that were easily defended by only a handful of men and a few hundred kilograms of explosives. The German aim was to slow, rather than stop, the Canadian advance, using the terrain to set up ambushes manned by rearguards under orders to withdraw as soon as their positions were in danger of being outflanked or overrun. Day after day, the brigade pushed deeper and higher into central Sicily. Most of the time, the men marched. Sometimes, trucks could be spared for a few hours to leapfrog one battalion or another a few kilometres along the road. Always, it was very hot.

Grammichele is about sixty-five kilometres northwest of Pacino. There, 1st Brigade had its first firefight with the retreating Germans when it ran into a German rear guard on 15 July. The fight lasted only a few hours: the Germans quickly pulled back and Grammichele was taken by noon. The 1st Brigade suffered twenty-five casualties in the encounter.

The Patricias passed through Grammichele several hours after the Germans had withdrawn. Then, with the Edmonton Regiment leading 2nd Brigade, they began the climb up the twisting, dust-choked road to Caltagirone and Piazza Armerina, a hilltop market town that dominated the road to Enna. The brigade reached Piazza Armerina on 17 July just a week after the Pacino landings.

In that first week, only two Patricias had been killed and ten wounded; the battalion had seen very little fighting, a situation that was about to change quickly. On the Canadian right, the British advance to Messina had stalled as the Germans put up fierce resistance at the Primosole Bridge, which spanned the Simeto River near Sicily's east coast. The Americans, meanwhile, under General

George S. Patton, were enveloping the entire western part of the island, bent on capturing Palermo, then driving east on the north coast to Messina. Since the Americans were now closing in on Enna, Simonds decided to bypass that town and begin his swing eastwards. The 1st Canadian Division would leave Highway No. 117 to move up a narrow secondary road to Valguarnera, and then head north to Leonforte. At Leonforte they would swing eastward to attack along Highway No. 121.

Simonds chose the 1st Brigade to lead off on the night of 17 July. After initial resistance, the Germans withdrew once again. The 2nd Brigade went into action only after the initial German resistance died out; the PPCLI hit the road at nightfall on the nineteenth, transported by truck through Piazza Armerina and deposited in the mountains south of Valguarnera as dawn broke. They marched upward through Valguarnera in the searing heat. The Seaforths, who were leading the brigade, ran into a formidable German defensive position on 19 July, and were stopped dead by heavy shelling and mortaring. The Patricias continued to struggle up the road until they encountered the stalled Seaforths. Vokes then ordered Lindsay to mount an immediate flanking attack to the heights of Mount Rossi, a few kilometres to the west of the road. Backed by heavy machine-gun fire and tanks, the PPCLI secured their objectives by 2000, with two wounded. Once again, the Germans had pulled back when they were in danger of being outflanked. The Patricias occupied their positions and prepared for the push to Leonforte. They had finally met the Germans in action.

P.P.C.L.I.

The sun-baked town of Leonforte, with 20,000 residents, clung to the western side of a cluster of peaks that dominated the countryside to the north and west. It was jammed against an escarpment below craggy peaks that reached up to 720 metres and higher. From the south, the road to Leonforte ran from Valguarnera until it reached a point just 800 metres from the southernmost buildings of the town. It then swung right, down a series of switchbacks, and across a deep ravine. From there, the road turned sharply left and climbed steeply alongside the escarpment until it entered the town. Vokes's plan was simple: the Seaforth Highlanders would attack up that road at dawn on 20 July and take Leonforte. He thought (or hoped) the Germans might withdraw as soon as the attack began.[31]

Early on the twentieth, the Seaforths moved down the road toward the ravine. As they approached, they came under intense German fire from machine guns, mortars, and anti-tank guns. The Seaforths discovered that German sappers had blown the bridge across the ravine. Under fire, they could not hope to scale the ravine; CO Bert Hoffmeister ordered them back. Vokes came forward to see what was happening and decided not to send Hoffmeister's men back into action without artillery support. When Divisional HQ told him that no artillery could be turned his way until the following afternoon, he postponed the attack until then.

The next day, as the Seaforths prepared at their start line to follow the barrage down the road and across the ravine, the Canadian artillery opened up. At least four rounds fell short, among the Seaforths and near battalion HQ. Hoffmeister was miraculously unhurt but badly shaken up. Vokes ordered the barrage stopped. He scheduled a new attack for 2100 and directed the Edmonton Regiment to make it. At zero hour, two companies of the Eddies, along with their CO and his forward HQ, followed the barrage, crossed the ravine, and penetrated into the town. Then the Germans counterattacked. By midnight, the Eddies were cut off, maybe lost altogether: "I felt the despair of failure," Vokes later wrote. "I considered I had lost most of a fine battalion."[32]

He hadn't. Cut off and surrounded by German troops, tanks, anti-tank guns, and self-propelled guns, the Eddies and their CO, Lieutenant-Colonel J.C. Jefferson, held out. With their radios inoperable, Jefferson scribbled a short note seeking help and gave it to a young Italian lad who made his way back to the Canadian lines. Vokes read it and quickly ordered a relief effort. Down in the ravine, Canadian engineers working under Major K.J. Southern struggled in the darkness and under fire to span the gap with a Bailey bridge. Lindsay was ordered to select a company of Patricias to accompany a quick attack across that bridge, up the road, and into town to reach the Eddies before it was too late. He assigned C Company, commanded by Major Rowan Coleman. As the first streaks of dawn began to colour the sky on the twenty-third, Vokes's attack force was in position. It consisted of four Sherman tanks from the Three Rivers Regiment; self-propelled, quadruple-mounted, twenty-millimetre guns; anti-tank guns; and Coleman's hundred or so men.

Coleman's infantry mounted the idling vehicles and waited. Men smoked, spoke softly, or laughed loudly. Everyone was nervous. Slowly, the darkness turned to pre-dawn grey, just enough light to see. Then the hills were bathed in sunlight. It was almost time to go. Suddenly, the men heard the Canadians' shells rocketing overhead. Explosions blossomed across the ravine and up the approaches to Leonforte. Someone gave the signal to go. The column gunned its engines. They roared off down the road, raced across the just-completed bridge, swung left at the end of the bridge, and charged up the approach road and into Leonforte. As the Germans awoke to the threat, heavy machine-gun fire broke out. But it was too late to stop the Canadians. The PPCLI halted in the centre of town, near a wine cellar where Jefferson and some of his staff were taking refuge at the Eddies' tactical HQ. They rescued Jefferson, then fanned out, some following a Sherman up the main street. A German Mark IV tank poked its barrel around a corner. The Sherman let loose at ten metres; the German tank blew up and blazed like a blowtorch as the PPCLI riflemen inched past. They worked their way to the railway station and up the tracks beyond. A small group of Germans toting automatic weapons and grenades mounted a counterattack. The Patricias beat the Germans back but then stopped, exhausted and too far forward with exposed flanks to continue. House-to-house fighting raged between Eddies and Germans in the centre of town, while tanks sniped each other amidst the periodic crack of anti-tank guns.

For almost all the Patricias, this was the first real taste of the confusion and the terror of combat. Felix Carriere became a veteran that day: "All of a sudden, ZAP . . . everyone was involved. You know, you're in the centre of a street and there's nothing but fireflies running by, and these are tracer bullets, these fireflies."[33]

As the fighting raged, Lindsay sent B Company under Captain Donald Brain and A Company under Major J.R.G. Sutherland into Leonforte. Andrew Donaldson was one of the reinforcing Patricia infantrymen: "We went through the town and the Germans were holding a line through a couple of olive orchards . . . their guns were well situated . . . to really cover the roads, but we came in."[34] The three Patricia company commanders then held a quick conference under fire in the centre of town. If they could push through to the north and hold the high ground, the Germans would have to withdraw. Sutherland's men drew the short straw. At 1520, they charged toward the heights with mortars and machine guns giving cover. They reached the crest, but the Germans stood fast. Along the rim of hill overlooking Leonforte, small knots of Patricias shot, grenaded, and bayoneted the Germans out of their firing pits. Lieutenant Rex Carey, commanding No. 7 Platoon, and Private W. Reilly, from the same platoon, destroyed three German machine-gun positions in quick succession. Carey was later awarded the Military Cross and Reilly the Military Medal. Private S.J. Cousins single-handedly knocked out two German positions. Lindsay put him up for the Victoria Cross, but he was instead awarded a "Mention-in-Dispatches." He never knew it; he was killed in action later that day. The Germans began to withdraw from Leonforte in late afternoon; Lindsay sent D Company to secure the rest of the town, which they did by nightfall.

Thirteen Patricias were killed and nine wounded in the fight for Leonforte. Jock Mackie was a stretcher-bearer that day: "I'll never forget it," he later recalled. "My first casualty was just shelled and it took both legs off this chap and you know you can't do anything with both legs. There's nothing but a mess. You can't tourniquet or anything like that. You can bleed to death in a minute with both the main arteries gone. And it's just as well because what man wants to live with no legs?"[35]

With Leonforte secured, the 1st Canadian Division now swung to the east, toward Adrano, twenty-five kilometres away along Highway No. 121. Adrano was the key to the German defences around Mount Etna; if the Canadians could take it, the Germans would have to pull back, releasing Monty's troops for their drive to Messina. Ahead of Simonds's men lay forty hard kilometres of twisting mountain road, dominated on the north side by peaks and ridges. Ahead also lay the towns of Nissoria, Agira, and Regalbuto, and the determined German troops of the Hermann Goering Panzer Division, commanded by Lieutenant General Paul Conrath. Conrath was well aware of Adrano's importance to both sides, and was determined to delay the Canadians as long as possible.[36] If the Germans were not enough to plague the Canadians, the temperature soared to over forty degrees Celsius each day. Men constantly dropped out along the line of march with the first symptoms of malaria, dysentery, or heat exhaustion.

The 1st Brigade attacked Nissoria on the night of 24/25 July. The Canadians were driven back at first, and the Royal Canadian Regiment suffered heavy losses in one company. The fight continued for a day and a half before the Germans pulled back to Agira, seven kilometres to the east. On the twenty-sixth, 2nd Brigade took the lead from 1st Brigade; Vokes ordered Lindsay to take and hold two German defensive lines, code-named "Lion" and "Tiger," that straddled the highway west of Agira. The Canadian artillery opened up at 2000 and the PPCLI moved forward, with C and D Companies in the lead followed by A and B Companies. After the first two companies secured the first line, some 500 metres up the road from their start line, the second two were supposed to pass through them and continue to the second objective, a thousand metres beyond. D Company took considerable German fire, but both the lead companies reached their objectives. With poor maps to guide them in the dark, radios that failed often in the mountains, and the usual confusion of battle, A and B Companies got lost. Vokes sent the Seaforths to bolster the advance and the troops broke through by dawn.

Next came Agira. At noon on 28 July, the Patricias were trucked up the road to within 2,000 metres of the hilltop town. A creeping barrage had been scheduled, but patrols reported Agira clear. The barrage was called off and the Patricias' A and B Companies advanced cautiously into the town. As the two companies approached the first buildings, civilians appeared from nowhere to give the troops a rousing welcome. The companies moved cautiously into the town and were also welcomed by well-hidden German snipers and machine gunners. "Bucko" Watson was in command: "We entered the town and thought it was free of the enemy because the town square was at the bottom of the hill and the local population came out to welcome us, but as soon as we left the square we came under fire. The enemy was in very small numbers up there but they put up a determined resistance."[37]

The streets were narrow and wound uphill; the layout gave rooftop snipers perfect cover and forced the Patricias to advance slowly from street corner to street corner, eyes raised toward the roofline, Bren gunners providing covering fire for the riflemen. After several hours of this sporadic fighting, Agira was secured; the Patricias established defensive positions to the east of it in the event that the Germans counterattacked. On the twenty-ninth,

1st Brigade and the Edmonton Regiment pushed through the PPCLI's positions and continued to pursue the fleeing enemy toward Regalbuto. It rained that day for the first time since the campaign began three weeks earlier. A cloudburst swept the dry countryside, cooled the air, and revitalized the Canadian infantry.[38]

The Canadians continued their drive toward Regalbuto. The village was strongly held by the Hermann Goering division, and Simonds chose 1st Brigade to take it. The Germans drove back the initial attacks of 31 July. The following day, the Royal Canadian Regiment managed to get as far as a small bridge to the southeast of the town before the Germans stopped them again. Throughout the daylight hours, the RCR clung to their positions in the heat, baked by the sun and exposed to German machine-gun fire from two directions. Simonds decided it would be useless to continue and pulled the RCR back after dark. The Germans, however, also withdrew, as they had so many times, and 1st Brigade took Regalbuto on 3 August.

Vokes's brigade was given a different assignment: to move north off the highway into the badlands and capture three peaks that dominated Highway 21 between Regalbuto and Adrano. The Patricias were assigned to take the most easterly of these peaks, Monte Seggio, to which they closed up on 4 August under cover of a heavy artillery barrage. Brigade orders called for the Patricia attack on Monte Seggio to begin at nightfall on the fifth, with all four rifle companies accompanied by tanks. But Lindsay worried that the Eddies would run into severe problems in their own attack on Monte Revisotto, some four kilometres to the east of Monte Seggio, and decided to go forward with only A and B Companies, accompanied by armour, and leaving C and D Companies behind to support the Edmonton Regiment. His attacking companies got lost in the dark. The two PPCLI company commanders, out of touch with Lindsay due to radio failure, decided on their own to postpone the attack until dawn.

The attack began on 6 August at 1100 after a heavy bombardment. Sydney Frost took part as a platoon commander, his first time in action:

> Under cover of this massive bombardment, we struggled up the rugged slopes of Monte Seggio and assaulted our first objective, a suspected German strongpoint. Luck was with us. The enemy had decamped in haste, leaving behind a damaged heavy machine gun, tools, "potato mashers" (grenades), ammunition belts, and a dead officer — a paratroop lieutenant. It was my first view of a dead German soldier. He had been caught in our barrage and his lower body was a horrible mess of bone, flesh, guts and torn uniform . . . "The poor misguided bastard," I mumbled to myself. "Thousands of miles from home, his shattered body lies abandoned by his comrades on a barren Sicilian mountainside. Soon the peasants will steal his boots; the follow-up troops will take his watch and iron cross . . ." I [wondered] if fate would be so unkind to me.[39]

But Frost and the other Patricias had an easy time of it that day; once again the Germans faded away, and the position was secured in two hours. The only PPCLI casualties came when the Germans shelled an advancing reinforcement column, killing one and wounding seven others.

Vokes, however, was furious. He blamed Lindsay for postponing the attack on Monte Seggio, claiming that the Germans had been given a gift of an entire night to make their escape. As he later wrote, "I felt they had missed an opportunity to deal the enemy a telling blow . . . I blamed Lindsay, as commanding officer, and the two company commanders for the cancellation of the operation without my permission and I made up my mind really to houseclean the regiment's officers when the battle cooled. And I did."[40] Three days later, Vokes called Lindsay to a conference and fired him. He did not, as he claimed in his 1985 memoirs, fire anyone else. Was he correct in removing Lindsay? Sydney Frost, for one, thought not: "[Lieutenant-Colonel] Lindsay was unjustly blamed and fired for postponing the attack," Frost wrote in his memoirs. Frost believes that poor maps and bad radio communications often caused men to get lost in the dark and that the company commanders' decision to delay the attack was "an inevitable, sensible decision." Frost also points out that the attack was not cancelled, as Vokes claimed, but delayed, and that Vokes had no real knowledge of whether Lindsay had condoned the delay.[41] In fact, the episode showed Vokes in a very bad light. He was many kilometres from the scene of battle, and unaware of the conditions prevailing near Monte Seggio that night. His dismissal of Lindsay was an error of judgment that reveals him as a martinet rather than a good commander. Vokes's actions were also undoubtedly influenced by Lindsay's reluctance to carry out the execution order he had given at Modica several days earlier.

Lindsay was immediately succeeded by the second-in-command, Major Cameron B. Ware. Born in 1913, Ware epitomized the newest generation of bright, energetic, and imaginative young officers coming to the fore within the division. A graduate of Royal Military College, Ware had joined the PPCLI in 1935. He had been sent overseas to serve on attachment with the British army prior to the outbreak of war, had rejoined the PPCLI in 1940, and had been appointed second-in-command in 1941. Of medium build with thinning hair and a moustache, Ware bore himself with a confidence that inspired confidence in his men. He possessed that rare combination of charisma and quiet self-assurance that reassured his soldiers that their CO would keep them alive and get them through, or at least ensure that their sacrifices would not be in vain.

Monte Seggio was the last action in Sicily for the PPCLI. In the northeast sector of the island, the curtain was falling on the battle as the Americans and the British pushed through to Messina and the Germans withdrew. Italian dictator Benito Mussolini's government had been toppled on 25 July and Mussolini himself replaced by Marshal Pietro Badoglio, whose secret intentions were to strike a peace agreement with the Allies and switch sides in the war. Though openly still committed to their Axis partnership, most Italian soldiers simply melted back into the civilian population after Mussolini fell. The Germans continued fighting, conducted a skillful defence, and withdrew both men and equipment back toward Messina. There, an elaborate shuttle operation brought them quickly over the Strait of Messina to the Italian mainland. As the battle wound down, Montgomery pulled the Canadians out of the line for a well-deserved rest. The PPCLI encamped at Militello, near Catania on 11 August, and remained there while preparing to cross the strait to begin the drive up the Italian mainland. The 1st Canadian Division suffered 562 killed in action or dead on active service in the Sicilian campaign, with 1,664 wounded and 84 taken prisoner. The Patricias lost 30 dead and 108 wounded.

P.P.C.L.I.

Although the Americans and the British were at odds over the strategy to follow after Sicily was taken, it was virtually inevitable that some sort of campaign to drive the Germans out of Italy would follow almost immediately. It was decided that two Allied armies would fight the campaign under the overall command of British Field Marshal Sir Harold Alexander. Those armies were the US Fifth Army under General Mark W. Clark, which would fight on the western slopes of the Apennine Mountains, and the British Eighth Army under Montgomery on the eastern slopes. When Monty returned to the United Kingdom to prepare for D-Day, Oliver Leese took command. The 1st Canadian Division, to be joined shortly by the 5th Canadian Armoured Division and 1st Canadian Corps Headquarters, would fight with the British.

Italy is a bad place to fight a modern war. It is a defenders' paradise, and poses severe challenges to an attacker. The Apennine range divides the peninsula from north to south; the natural flow of water is from the centre of the peninsula to the Mediterranean on the west and the Adriatic on the east. Moving north up either Italian coast entails constant river crossings using bridges or culverts easily blown by defenders. Marching troops must repeatedly descend into small valleys — some dry, some with rivers — climb up to the next headland, then descend into the next valley. Headlands sometimes reach all the way to the sea. The old coastal roads are narrow, twisty, easily covered by shellfire, and easily blocked by explosives. There is almost no open country suitable for tank warfare anywhere on the peninsula. The many small villages nestling in the valleys or perched atop hills are built of stone or masonry. Their tall, multi-storeyed, houses shade the narrow streets and alleyways from the strong Mediterranean sun, making movement especially dangerous for advancing infantry and armour. The summers are hot and dry, as in Sicily; unlike Sicily, winters are cold and rainy, with heavy snow in the mountains.

Field Marshal Albert Kesselring coordinated the German defence. He intended to withdraw virtually all his troops from Calabria, the southernmost province of Italy, to allow the Allies to advance rapidly north through most of southern Italy up to the Sangro River. Along the Sangro, and in succeeding defensive lines anchored in the mountains to the north, his troops would fight for every centimetre. At his disposal were the German Tenth Army and other veteran units, including most of the troops who had escaped from Sicily, along with a number of elite parachute regiments. The most important of his major defensive positions, comprising several fortified lines strung across the peninsula about 120 kilometres southeast of Rome, was known collectively as the Gustav Line. Alexander planned two invasions of the Italian peninsula. The first, to be carried out by Montgomery's Eighth Army across the Strait of Messina, would take place on 3 September. Dubbed Operation Baytown, it was intended not only to secure a toehold on the Italian mainland but also to draw German and Italian defenders to the south and away from the second landing — Operation Avalanche — to be carried out by the US Fifth Army at the Bay of Salerno on 9 September. Simonds's 1st Canadian Division was chosen to take part in the initial Baytown landing along with the 5th British Infantry Division. The attack went forward in the pre-dawn hours of 3 September under a massive artillery bombardment against a mostly deserted shore.

The PPCLI crossed the strait along with the rest of 2nd Brigade on 4 September. After occupying Reggio di Calabria, the capital of Calabria, just on the coast, the Patricias followed the leading 3rd Brigade up the centre of the peninsula. In the meantime, 1st Brigade moved straight into the mountains and pushed over the high Aspromonte range toward the small town of Locri, on the other side of the Italian "toe." The weak Italian opposition caused few delays; blown bridges and blocked roads accounted for most of the wasted time. As Sydney McKay remembered: "We never ever got too far without finding blown bridges and these bridges were over ravines, more than over water but they still had to be bridged before we could move on."[42]

As the Canadians drove north toward Potenza, they passed through a countryside mostly untouched by war. The rapid German withdrawal had preserved the small villages and the picturesque vineyards that covered almost every flat bit of terrain and grew up the hillsides. Canadian war artist Charles Comfort later described the scene: "The grape harvest was going on everywhere. The principal native traffic of the road was concerned with the harvest and with wine. The grapes were contained in large tubs, carried on low wagons. As we passed, bunches were thrown at us, sweet and lush."[43]

The Italians were poor and desperate after the German seizure of their crops. They were also suffering from the ravages of war. Despite their losses, they were remarkably friendly and, for the most part, the Canadians formed strong bonds with them. One night in the mountains of Reggio di Calabria, an old man approached a PPCLI platoon commanded by Lieutenant Gerald Richards:

> We were just sitting on the hill waiting for orders to move in the morning and an old Italian man who spoke some English came and sat down amongst my men and started talking to them. He was talking about the history of warfare in Italy, about the many invasions that had occurred. My men all listened to him . . . he was obviously a very pleasant old fellow. And then he went back into the village.[44]

Later, Richards's men heard singing and celebrating from the village. In the morning, they learned that the Italian government under Marshal Badoglio had surrendered. That was good news, of course, but the Patricias soon learned that the surrender hardly counted; the Germans had always been the real opposition in Italy and, as yet, they were nowhere to be found.

Within a week of landing, the Canadians had reached Catanzaro, about 120 kilometres from Reggio di Calabria as the crow flies. After Clark's Fifth Army fought its way off the beaches at Salerno, Simonds took the 1st Division inland to seize Potenza, a crucial road junction about ninety kilometres east of Salerno. From there, the division pushed north toward Campobasso, eight kilometres southeast of the Biferno River and fifty-one kilometres southeast of the Adriatic coastal town of Termoli. The drive for Campobasso began on 1 October; it took the Canadians two weeks to cover the sixty-five kilometres of broken plateau that lay ahead. They entered Campobasso unopposed on the fourteenth. Although Vokes assigned the PPCLI to mount patrols on the north bank of the Biferno, the battalion moved into billets in the hamlet of Busso, eight kilometres west of Campobasso, on 27 October.

A small city of some 17,000 people high in the mountains, Campobasso became one of the Canadian Army's most famous (or notorious) leave centres of the war. The troops billeted there, and in the small towns nearby, called it Maple Leaf City. In his memoirs, Vokes described Campobasso as a kind of sin city, no doubt revelling in the oft-repeated rumour that he had somehow established an unofficial Canadian Army brothel there. "The personal view of a private soldier in war is 'I'm here today and gone tomorrow,'" Vokes wrote. "So, the mentality of a soldier in the field is that he wants to get drunk and he wants to get laid, because these are pleasant things he may perhaps never experience again."[45] Patricia Jerry Richards had a very different recollection of Campobasso:

> One building [was] a dance floor for the soldiers and I recall going in there and dancing with a few Italian girls but we had the most imposing ring of *duennas* around the room. You wouldn't dare touch [the girls] because none of us spoke much Italian and what we did speak was exceedingly crude . . . it was really more torment than anything else because we couldn't be too familiar with them, which of course was not the thing which was in most soldiers' minds back then.[46]

The 1st and 2nd Brigades stayed in position near Campobasso throughout November. The division began to withdraw from the Campobasso area on 29 November. Bound for the Adriatic coast, they were to replace a British division that had been badly mauled in the crossing of the lower Sangro River. The Canadians were assigned the far right flank of the Eighth Army, on the coast, and given the task of driving northward to capture the small port town of Ortona. Before they could do that, however, they would have to cross the heavily defended Moro River, about three kilometres south of Ortona. After several days of winding slowly down steep mountain roads at the onset of the wet Italian winter, the Patricias fetched up in positions on a ridge overlooking the south bank of the Moro.

Chapter 9

FROM ORTONA TO VICTORY

AT TEN MINUTES TO MIDNIGHT ON 5 DECEMBER 1943, Lieutenant-Colonel Cameron Ware peered through his field glasses at the silent cluster of houses of Villa Rogatti, about two kilometres away. The town was just visible in the darkness. Ware, his intelligence officer, and his radio operator crouched in their slit trenches[1] just above the Moro River, a small stream that meandered from the hills in the west to the Adriatic, some nine kilometres to the east. About ten kilometres north of Ware's position was the Canadians' objective, the small coastal town of Ortona. The 1st Canadian Infantry Division would have to cross the valley of the Moro, a significant obstacle, before launching an attack to take the town. Perched on a low plateau on just the other side of the Moro, Villa Rogatti dominated the left flank of the division's line of march; the hamlet of San Leonardo, four kilometres to the northeast, dominated the centre. At midnight, the Patricias would begin crossing the Moro just below Ware's position. The Seaforths would cross downstream, near San Leonardo.

Ware had made certain that the battalion was well prepared for the advance. Reconnaissance patrols and a careful study of maps and aerial photographs had revealed that the Germans had blown up a small bridge across the Moro, below Villa Rogatti. The river, however, was shallow and fordable by infantry and armour about a third of the way between that town and San Leonardo. Ware's plan called for B Company, under Captain R.F.S. Robertson, to move down into the valley and downstream to the ford before climbing up a narrow path to advance on Villa Rogatti from the east. A Company, under Major "Bucko" Watson, would follow closely behind. The two rifle companies were to take the town and hold it until dawn, when a troop of Sherman tanks from the British 44th Royal Tank Regiment would work its way across the Moro and then climb a slippery, twisting mule path to the plateau to reinforce the Patricias.

Ortona, which dated back to the ancient Trojans, was dominated by a cathedral and two massive defensive towers standing on a promontory alongside a small harbour. The town was not important in itself; its harbour was of almost no consequence as a resupply port. But Ortona anchored the Adriatic end of a road that ran inland to the key German defensive positions in and around Orsogna, about twenty kilometres to the southwest. If Ortona was taken, Orsogna would be outflanked and thus untenable, and the Germans would have to pull back to the north. Ortona was virtually unapproachable from the southeast, neither along the sea front nor from the rugged country to the west. To reach — and capture — it, the Canadians would have to cross first the Moro, then a deep, narrow gully that ran parallel to and about two kilometres beyond it. They would then have to gain the junction of the Orsogna-Ortona highway — No. 538 — and a narrow secondary road that ran roughly parallel to the coast. Finally, they would have to wheel to the right, and advance northeast along Highway No. 538 into the town.

Major-General Chris Vokes had ordered his 1st and 2nd Brigades to attack across the Moro at three points. Along the coast road, the Hastings and Prince Edward Regiment from the 1st Brigade would cross the river near its mouth and set up a defensive bridgehead just atop the bluffs on the west bank of the river. This thrust was intended as a diversion from the main attack, conducted about one-and-a-half kilometres upriver by the Seaforth Highlanders of the 2nd Brigade. Their task was to drive up a narrow, twisting road from the river to San Leonardo, which they then would hold in preparation for a second attack by the Royal Canadian Regiment. The RCR would move through the hamlet to take the key crossroads. The PPCLI attack on Villa Rogatti was also meant as a diversion, though Vokes always had the option of switching his main axis of attack from San Leonardo to Villa Rogatti if things did not go well for the Seaforths or the RCR.

The advance across the Moro was supposed to proceed behind the usual curtain of artillery from the division's field guns. B Company had readied itself to cross the river as soon as the shells lifted, at one minute to midnight. Unbeknownst to Ware, however, Brigade HQ had allocated the artillery elsewhere. As the second hand on Ware's watch swept the minute hand closer to midnight, however, he heard no shells. No explosions blossomed across the river. Five minutes passed; four minutes remained until the start of the attack. Ware stole quick glances at his wristwatch. Still no shells. He worried more as each second passed. Was the artillery delayed? Should he hold Robertson back until the shelling began? What if the brigade commander, Brigadier Bert Hoffmeister, had called off the shelling? And if B Company did go ahead, what if the shelling began just as the men reached the outskirts of the town? Then Patricias would die by friendly fire. The second hand swept around to twelve. Ware could hear firing downstream as the Seaforths went ahead. He ordered Robertson to go. B Company moved off into the darkness. They would try to take the Germans in Villa Rogatti by surprise.[2] The riflemen moved slowly, feeling their way down the steep embankment in the darkness, trying not to make any noise. Signalman Jack Haley accompanied two mules chained together, one with a radio strapped to its back, the other with the radio battery. "At the top of the valley, as we were starting out, it was pitch dark," he recalled, "but as you're entering the valley, there's always what you call 'harassing fire,' . . . [when] the Germans open up and they sometimes fire on fixed lines . . . as we came into the valley there were a few Schmeissers [German sub–machine guns] and also the odd sniper."[3]

Unlike the riflemen, the mules saw no special reason for undue caution. As they plodded along, they broke twigs, hee-hawed in complaint, and splashed across the shallow stream. Robertson decided to leave them behind until the village was secured. He'd rely on runners to communicate with battalion HQ. Most of the Germans in Villa Rogatti slept through the commotion; sleep was too important for the average infantryman in a battle zone to worry about sporadic fire unless a specific alarm was given. None was. "There was a good deal of firing," Cameron Ware later recalled, "but I think they probably thought that there were patrols coming because we'd been patrolling fairly actively from the day or so before."[4]

Robertson's men crept up the far slope toward Villa Rogatti, taking the right of two paths that ran from about halfway up the embankment to each end of the town. Suddenly, the flashes and hammering of two German machine guns, one on each flank of the advancing Patricias, split the night. Luckily, the fire was high, probably from guns set to shoot on fixed lines. The Patricia riflemen hit the dirt. Robertson ordered them back to the junction of the two paths and sent two platoons up the other one. Riflemen and Bren gunners fired at the Germans to hold them in place while the Patricias executed the flanking manoeuvre. Private H.C. Nixon held his two-inch mortar nearly parallel to the ground as he fired, scoring hits close to one of the German guns. Other Patricias, armed with rifles and Tommy guns, crept around to the German flanks, only to come under fire from other machine guns. But after four hours of close-in fighting, the Patricias machine-gunned and grenaded their way through the German defences into the centre of the town.

In the pre-dawn twilight, the PPCLI riflemen hunted down the Germans in Villa Rogatti. In building after building, they kicked in doors; sleepy Germans were shot or rousted out and taken prisoner. In some of the buildings, hot rations sat on tables, ready to be eaten. At first, "Bucko" Watson's A Company followed closely behind Robertson's men. They soon moved to the north edge of the town to cut off the road to Villa Jubatti, about two kilometres away. B Company, meanwhile, dug in just to the west of Villa Rogatti to block a German counterattack from the direction of Villa Caldari, also about two kilometres away. The Germans withdrew into the olive groves and brush around Villa Rogatti and awaited reinforcements. Ware brought forward his tactical HQ, leaving D Company at the Moro and C Company to cover the ground from the river to the town.

At first light on the sixth of December, the Patricias began to improve their defences. They dug slit trenches in the town and on the approach to it, cleaned and readied their weapons, and laid out their grenades for the inevitable German counterattack. The roads from Villa Rogatti to Villa Caldari and Villa Jubatti were still wide open, making it doubly important, Ware knew, to guide the British Shermans into the town as quickly as possible. As the sky brightened, and the weather turned surprisingly warm and pleasant, German fire on Villa Rogatti increased. Snipers took potshots at Patricias moving among the buildings; occasional bursts of machine-gun fire sent them headlong into the dirt. Mortar rounds began to explode. Then the Germans opened up with field guns and the six-barrelled mortar they called *Nebelwerfer* — the Allied infantry dubbed it the "moaning Minnie." Below the lip of the escarpment above the Moro, the Patricias could hear the British tanks grinding up the narrow, muddy path from the river, but the tanks were still nowhere in sight. Ware sent Lieutenant W. Riddell, his signals officer, back down the path to guide the tanks in. It was obvious that the increased German shelling was preliminary to a counterattack. Who would arrive first: the Germans or the tanks?

At mid-morning, Ware, Robertson, Watson, and the Patricia riflemen took cover as the German fire intensified into a full barrage. Shells blew in walls, punched through roofs, and tore up the dirt streets and alleyways. Machine-gun fire ricocheted off bricks and stone. Mortar blew mules to bits as men crouched low in their slit trenches, holding their helmets tight on their heads and gripping their weapons. The German infantry began to move into the town. They ran from building to building as their machine gunners gave covering fire. The Patricias fired back. The Germans manhandled an anti-tank gun into position on the north side of the town and began to fire over open sights into the A Company positions. The Patricia war diarist later wrote: "Things began to get critical . . . as ammunition was running short and the Germans were working in closer." One Bren gunner in A Company refused to fire at Germans in groups less than twenty so as to save ammunition. Then, suddenly, the British Shermans ground their way over the edge of the escarpment and began to take up positions in aid of the beleaguered rifle companies. Tank commanders stood in their open hatches with German bullets buzzing around them as Patricia riflemen emerged from their slit trenches to point out the positions of the German infantry. "The bullets were flying so thick it didn't make any difference whether one was laying down, standing up, or running," Ware later told his intelligence officer. But the tank machine guns and 75-millimetre main guns soon made short work of the German attackers. "It was touch and go for a while," Andrew Gault Donaldson later recalled. "We got our tanks up just in time . . . it would have been pretty sticky if we hadn't . . . Once we got the tanks up . . . that was the end of that . . . [they] just decimated their attacking infantry."[5] Those Germans who were still standing retreated when a green flare shot up from their lines at about 1130, but they were not yet done with Villa Rogatti.

Ware's men had a respite of about ninety minutes after the German retreat. A mule train arrived with fresh supplies and ammunition. Lieutenant Jerry Richards was one of the Patricias who accompanied the mules:

> When I went into battalion headquarters I found that Colonel Ware had finally managed to get some sleep . . . of course I had to go in and wake him up to give him some message . . . he seemed to have aged overnight. I thought he looked terribly tired and worn out and I even began to wonder if he wasn't too old for the job. I learned in later years that he was twenty-eight. I was twenty-one at the time.[6]

In the ruins of Villa Rogatti, Patricias broke open their ration packs and ate quickly. It got noticeably cooler as clouds rolled in. It began to rain, a steady downpour that soaked the men to the bone and made it difficult to see and hear. But at about 1330, the men in the forward positions west of the town heard the unmistakable grinding of tank treads and the low rumble of tank engines echoing through the olive trees. The sound grew louder as the German armour came down the road from the direction of Villa Caldari. The men of B Company braced themselves. Suddenly, German tanks and infantry — nine Mark IV tanks and about seventy riflemen — burst from the trees and rolled through the rain toward the Patricias. Despite Patricia rifle and machine-gun fire, the Germans rolled on, across the open ground between the olive groves and the town, into the buildings occupied by B Company. One Patricia platoon was forced to pull back under tank and rifle fire. The Patricias crouched in the rubble and readied their anti-tank weapons as the British Shermans ground forward. They waited for German tanks to draw close. "It was a fair massacre," Ware recalled. "We allowed them to come . . . within fifty metres before anti-tank fire was opened."[7] Three German tanks exploded almost immediately, and another two by the end of the action. Two Shermans were lost as well. But the momentum had shifted to the Patricias, who drove the Germans back yet a second time that day under heavy shell and mortar fire. By 1530, the German attack was broken. Ware ordered defences improved, prisoners and wounded evacuated, and more British tanks brought forward to strengthen the defences. The next day, the battalion prepared to pull out, to be replaced by the 8th Indian Division. The PPCLI war diarist noted: "After nearly sixty hours of fighting and 'standing to' the troops are beginning to look tired. The strain and excitement has keyed them to a pitch higher than . . . any previous battle during the Italian campaign."[8] Since crossing the Moro, the PPCLI had suffered eight killed in action, fifty-two wounded, and had lost seven men as prisoners. Much worse was yet to come.

P.P.C.L.I.

By noon on 7 December, the 1st Canadian Division's initial attack towards Ortona had petered out. At the mouth of the Moro, the Hastings and Prince Edward Regiment held a small, precarious foothold on the north bank. The 8th Indian Division had relieved the PPCLI at Villa Rogatti, and the Seaforths had been driven back from San Leonardo. At neither Division nor Corps headquarters could anyone think of an attack strategy more original than just forging ahead in the true style of the First World War's Battle of the Somme. Vokes launched his plan: while 2nd New Zealand Division was ordered to attack toward Orsogna on the left flank, and the Indian Division was ordered to assault northwest from Villa Rogatti, the 1st Canadian Brigade was sent to capture San Leonardo. It attacked with two battalions on 8 December: the 48th Highlanders from Toronto managed to work their way into the town, but the RCR, attacking out of the Hastings and Prince Edward bridgehead, suffered heavy casualties. They did not link up with the 48th Highlanders until nightfall on the ninth. San Leonardo was finally in Canadian hands. With the north bank of the Moro virtually secure from Villa Rogatti to the sea, it was time for the 2nd Brigade to re-enter the fight, secure the all-important crossroads northwest of San Leonardo, then advance into Ortona.

The gully, however, was in the way. Like a malevolent snake, it lay across the 2nd Brigade's path of attack. The gully's head opened on the Adriatic about a kilometre south of Ortona, where it ran deep and narrow. As it wound back about six kilometres, it gradually rose to meet the surrounding ground. Strewn with garbage and overgrown with bushes, brush, and old vineyards, it offered an excellent German defence. Not only was it a natural tank trap, but it also had a perfect reverse slope that gave the Germans ample cover for weapons pits and firing trenches. These they laid out so as to catch advancing infantry silhouetted against the sky — that is, if the enemy even got near the gully's edge. The Canadian artillery could not be elevated high enough to destroy the German positions dug in on the south bank of the gully. Before the Canadians could get to the gully, they would have to cross a rise, known as Vino Ridge, that ran on its south edge. Worse, they would have to do that over open ground and in the teeth of German fire.

Brigade Commander Hoffmeister planned his attack in three stages: the Seaforths would secure about half the length of the road from San Leonardo to the crossroads. The Loyal Edmonton Regiment (they had received the "Loyal" designation in November) were then to attack through the Seaforths to capture the crossroads. When they had secured the crossroads, the Patricias were to follow the Eddies up the road to the south side of the gully, then turn right to advance up the length of Vino Ridge, and secure it. The attack began on 10 December; it started well, but the Loyal Eddies came up short under German fire and mistakenly signalled that they had reached the crossroads. At PPCLI tactical HQ, Ware was under tremendous pressure. San Leonardo was being heavily shelled; he had barely escaped with his life when a shell had exploded next to a parked tank in which he and "Bucko" Watson had taken refuge. Watson had been wounded. Major Donald Brain, crouching outside the tank, had been killed. Now, Ware had to decide about the message from the Loyal Eddies. Was it accurate? He did not believe it was. There was no way they could have got that far so quickly under such heavy shelling. But he had no choice. The Patricia advance would have to begin. D Company began to move up Vino Ridge under command of Major P.D. Crofton.

The gully lit up with German fire. Crofton was hit almost immediately. The tanks accompanying the Patricias fell behind the infantry, and were pulled back as the Germans began to work their way around D Company. As darkness fell, no one was quite certain where they were, but they knew Vino Ridge lay ahead of them, untaken, and that the Germans would not soon yield. It stayed cold the next day and began to rain again as C Company tried to assault the ridge. "Going was very difficult," the war diarist recorded, "fighting through low olive groves all the way. Shelling increased in intensity throughout the day."[9] The Canadians made no progress.

The battalion licked its wounds on the twelfth. On the thirteenth, B Company tried once more to advance upon Vino Ridge. It was clear and cold as they crossed the start line and began to ascend the ridge. Canadian shells plastered the gully ahead of the advancing infantry. Surely, reasoned B Company, no one was left alive in that smoking hell! But the German gunners were waiting. Scrambling out of their holes to meet the Patricias, they opened withering fire with machine guns, sub-machine guns, and rifles. The previous night, unbeknownst to the Patricias, the worn-out *Panzergrenadier* defenders had pulled out and had been replaced by crack parachute troops, the *Fallschirmjaeger,* who never retreated. Heavy artillery and mortar fire fell among the B Company riflemen and at battalion tactical HQ. Ware's radio was smashed. There was no way B Company could advance over open ground with such fire. The Patricias pulled back. Vokes ordered Hoffmeister to try again the following day. He insisted his brigade commanders throw their battalions straight at the gully, that there was no way around it. The butcher's bill was high for this sort of bull-headed approach to war: the PPCLI had suffered nine killed in action and sixty-nine wounded since 10 December. They had had no time to bring up reinforcements after Villa Rogatti, but they went at it again on the fourteenth.

This time, the Patricias attacked with two companies. Their immediate objective was a house on Vino Ridge that the Germans were using as an outpost, or OP. "They had mortars in this house," Patricia Andy Schaen recalled. "They could fire them and there would be no muzzle flash or anything because they were sitting down maybe fifteen, twenty feet below the rooftop."[10] One of the Patricia companies called for mortar fire, but the fire went awry and began to land in the other company area. Captain J.B. Hunt, an acting company commander, was killed and the PPCLI attack beaten back. Shermans came up to support the attack, but ran into a German anti-tank minefield; one tank blew up. The others tried to give covering fire from the edge of the minefield but were too far away to be effective. It was another disaster in the making. With six dead and sixteen wounded since dawn, the attackers pulled back. At nightfall, the German paratroopers began to patrol forward, infiltrating between the PPCLI company positions and ambushing a patrol.

It was the First World War all over again. Jerry Richards never forgot the intensity of the German shelling in those few fateful days on Vino Ridge: "The amount of heavy shell fire that was coming down . . . was really quite intimidating and the noise of the shell fire was enormous." Eventually, Richards himself was hit by a shell from an 88:

> I was face down in the mud with blood pouring out in front of my eyes, in excruciating pain in my belly and my right hip. I rather suspected that both of my legs had been torn off and I thought I'd been killed. I thought very sorrowfully of my mother and how she would react when she got yet another telegram from Ottawa telling her that I had been doing something I shouldn't have.[11]

Richards, however, was lucky; he survived — and so did his legs.

Jack Haley would later describe Vino Ridge in words reminiscent of Passchendaele:

> As time went on you looked out at the battlefield and the scene on those cold, wet, sort of drizzly days, and it was bleak. The shell holes were everywhere . . . There was broken houses, rubble and splintered trees and worst of all there was the mud. We were bogged down many times and the ground was all churned up and it really slowed us down. I remember an old man standing in front of this house which was now just a pile of rubble. He was saying something about his whole life. He looked so forlorn and sad . . . On another occasion we were in San Leonardo, we could hear somebody crying. It sounded like a girl crying somewhere and we checked it out and we found her in a cave. She was in there alone. She'd been wounded in the thigh and she sort of crawled in there for safety. We got her to our own doctor.[12]

The Patricias could not go on, at least not until their depleted ranks were reinforced and the men given some rest and hot food. But over on the division's left flank, the only battalion Vokes had not yet committed on the north bank of the Moro went into action. The objective was Casa Berardi, a cluster of walled farm buildings on the west side of the gully, about three kilometres cross-country from San Leonardo. The job of securing Casa Berardi was given to the Royal 22e Régiment, the Van Doos. On 14 December, C Company, courageously led by Captain Paul Triquet and supported by the Sherman tanks of the Ontario Tank Regiment, battled their way through German paratroopers and armour across the gully to Casa Berardi. They took it. The gully was quickly outflanked. Five days later, the 3rd Brigade took the vital crossroads southwest of Ortona after heavy fighting and brutal casualties. In the words of the RCR regimental history, "the slaughter was terrible." The RCR attacked on 18 December and was forced to pull up short of the crossroads. The next morning, the advance resumed and the crossroads were taken. The battle for Ortona itself began the following day.

A few days before Christmas, Cameron Ware grabbed a moment to write a short letter to Hamilton Gault, telling him about the state of the regiment: "I have not been out of my clothes for three weeks," Ware wrote:

> Guess you know all about that feeling! The fighting has been pretty bitter and a different proposition from the early days of Italy and Sicily. The Hun is stubborn and has lots of guts and skill. Have lost many fine men and officers but it's been a grand show . . . we have not changed from the time of 1914 and we are never stopped and we never give any ground . . . they are so proud of being Patricias and I am so proud of them and I hate losing any of them.[13]

Despite Ware's reluctance to lose any of his men, December 1943 had been the worst month yet for the Patricias. The regiment had suffered 38 killed in action, 195 wounded, and 8 taken prisoner by the Germans.

The PPCLI stayed on Vino Ridge while the Loyal Edmonton Regiment and the Seaforth Highlanders took on the long and very costly job of rooting out the German paratroopers from Ortona. The Germans fought for every metre of ground. This was the worst type of street fighting: house by house and block by block.

The battle was fought at close quarters with grenades, rifles, machine guns, sub-machine guns, satchel charges — even pistols and bayonets. The Germans had set up killing zones by using rubble to force the Canadians up certain streets into deadly ambushes. Tanks were easily blocked and extremely vulnerable to anti-tank fire, Molotov cocktails, and explosives. The Canadians blasted their way through the walls of the row houses to avoid the rifle and machine-gun fire in the streets.

The battle raged through Christmas Day, as the Canadians inched painfully towards the Piazza Municipale, the centremost of the town's three large, open squares. A Christmas dinner was laid on as close to the fighting as possible. As the battle was waged a block or so away, men were brought back a few at a time, fed, given Christmas sweets and cigarettes, then returned to action. Eventually Vokes's troops outflanked the Germans in Ortona and cut off the German escape and supply routes. The German position in Ortona became untenable. On 27 December, the survivors began to pull out of the town. By the twenty-eighth, Ortona was secure.

On New Year's Eve, 1943, the 48th Highlanders captured San Tommaso and San Nicola, a little more than three kilometres west of Ortona. An assault on Point 59, a small hill on the coast about three kilometres northwest of the town, was less successful: more than fifty Canadians were killed, wounded, or captured. The Carleton and York Regiment finally secured Point 59 on 4 January 1944, and the Canadian front on the Adriatic fell quiet.

The Italian winter made fighting all but impossible in the high mountains and the mountain passes that dominated the terrain of the peninsula's interior. The winter months gave the Allied commanders time to rethink and rework their strategies for vanquishing what Winston Churchill had once called "the soft underbelly of Europe." There was no point in trying to push north up the Adriatic coast at that stage of the war, with a major Allied blow about to land in Normandy. The next major objective had to be Rome, but the Eternal City could only be reached through the Liri Valley, after overcoming the formidable defences of the Gustav and Hitler lines.

P.P.C.L.I.

The Allies had once believed they might be in Rome by Christmas, 1943. German Field Marshal Albert Kesselring's Tenth Army, however, had other ideas. Using the Italian terrain to best effect, they had built two major defensive lines southeast of Rome in a bid to deny the Allies entry to the Liri Valley. This broad valley formed a corridor running southeast to northwest through a fold in the Apennines, almost from the direction of Naples to the doorstep of Rome. The first line the Allies would have to penetrate was the Gustav Line, anchored on Monte Cassino and running almost nine kilometres due south to the Liri River. The second line, dubbed the Adolf Hitler Line by the Allies, ran from the village of Piedmont, on the western slopes of Monte Cassino, west to Highway No. 6, then southwest to the hamlet of Sant Oliva. In constructing both lines, Kesselring's troops used ravines, small streambeds, farmhouses, woods, and open fields to good effect. They dug deep anti-tank ditches. The Germans armed themselves with self-propelled anti-tank guns. They sited their machine guns with interlocking fields of fire. Some pillboxes had machine guns mounted in cupolas; others were equipped with Panther tank turrets. There were dug-in, hull-down, tanks. Hundreds of snipers and infantry were armed with the new and deadly *Panzerfaust,* a personal anti-tank weapon. Thick barbed wire was hung everywhere. And mortars and field guns were sited on all possible approach routes.

Since the German defences at the entrance to the Liri Valley seemed impenetrable, the Allies decided to outflank them with a landing at Anzio (dubbed Operation Shingle), about fifty kilometres due south of Rome, on 22 January 1944. American and British troops, accompanied by the Canada-US First Special Service Force, took part. The landings went off with few problems and little opposition. Instead of seizing the opportunity to surprise the Germans by driving directly from the Anzio beaches to Rome, however, the timid Allied commander, Major-General J.P. Lucas of the 6th US Corps, decided to consolidate his position before moving. By the time he did move, the approximately fourteen thousand German troops already in the Anzio area, and another twenty thousand or so from the vicinity of Rome, were ready and waiting. They blocked any breakout attack from the beachhead and left the troops bottled up there, under constant fire, for months.

Allied attention shifted back to the Liri Valley. There, British Lieutenant-General Sir John Harding, a skilled staff officer with extensive combat experience, conceived Operation Diadem. This was a daring plan to secretly transfer the bulk of the British Eighth Army from the Adriatic side of Italy to the Cassino area, to join with US General Mark Clark's Fifth Army in a concerted plan to capture Monte Cassino, the hinge of the German defences. The two armies would then mount a massive armoured assault westward, from the area east of the Gari River. Sir Oliver Leese, GOC-in-C of the Eighth Army, would command three corps for Diadem: 13th British, 2nd Polish, and 1st Canadian. They attacked on 11 May 1944. In three days of heavy fighting, the 8th Indian Infantry Division, assisted by the 1st Canadian Armoured Brigade, penetrated the initial Gustav Line defences and established a number of bridgeheads across the Gari River. Then the tanks and troops of the British 78th Division moved through and began to advance to the Hitler Line. On the left flank, the skilled Moroccan mountain troops of the French Expeditionary Corps made a wide, sweeping advance through the rugged terrain south of the Liri. The Germans were forced to abandon the Gustav Line and retreat to the Hitler Line, some thirteen kilometres west of the Gari.

The 1st Canadian Infantry Division had spent the winter months along the Adriatic, probing enemy defences and patrolling along the general line of the Riccio River, just north of Ortona. There was no point in trying to launch any new offensives on this front; the cold weather, the almost constant rain, and the swollen, rushing streams flowing from the mountains made even patrolling difficult and costly. The number of casualties mounted; some inflicted by the enemy, many due to illness and a growing phenomenon known as battle exhaustion. This condition, known as "shell shock" in the First World War, was as old as soldiering and war itself. It arose as men saw the hopelessness of their situation, the unlikelihood of their survival. Battle exhaustion usually accompanied long spells at the front, with little chance of relief, when bad weather, dirty living conditions, enemy fire, and illness took a constant toll of friends and comrades-in-arms. It became particularly serious in Italy over the cold winter months of 1943/44, when men were told to go out day after day and night after night to patrol for reasons that may have been apparent to their commanders, but not to them. After a time, the mud, rain, lack of clean uniforms or hot food, and apparent purposeless existence of the infantry took a heavy toll. No one was sorry when, in the last ten days of April 1944, Indian troops began to replace the Canadians, who were trucked over the mountains to the east of the Gari River and deployed at the entrance to the Liri Valley. The Canadians had been bystanders in the first phase of the fighting, the breakthrough of the Gustav Line. It was their turn now.

Canadian Corps commander Lieutenant-General E.L.M. Burns prepared for a set-piece attack against the Hitler Line with heavy artillery support. The 1st Division infantry would lead, followed by the tanks of the recently arrived 5th Canadian Armoured Division, under command of former Seaforth CO Bert Hoffmeister. In the initial attack, which began in the early-morning hours of 17 May, 3rd Canadian Infantry Brigade was on the right or northern flank, 1st Brigade on the left or southern flank, and 2nd Brigade was held in reserve. The Germans resisted the Canadian advance throughout the day, but pulled back completely at nightfall. The two Canadian brigades failed to make contact with them on the eighteenth. When they reached the Hitler Line, however, on the nineteenth, they ran into a stone wall of resistance. The Ontario Regiment lost thirteen tanks, and many others were damaged supporting an attack by the British 78th Infantry Division. The Van Doos, meanwhile, suffered heavy casualties in a direct assault on the line's barbed wire. The initial Canadian attack ran out of steam. Rome remained unassailable.

As part of a renewed Allied offensive to break out from the Anzio beachhead and, at the same time, open Highway No. 6 through the Liri Valley to Rome, Burns prepared for another set-piece attack to begin in the pre-dawn hours of 23 May. He planned to punch through the Hitler Line at a point about two kilometres southwest of the hamlet of Aquino, then continue to push northwest to take the junction of Highway No. 6 and the Aquino-Pontecorvo road. The latter ran to the west of, and parallel to, the Hitler Line defences. The attack would begin with a concentrated bombardment over a front of some 2,000 metres at dawn on the twenty-third. Then, 2nd Brigade would attack on the right, or northern, flank and 3rd Brigade on the left. If the infantry got through the Hitler Line, Hoffmeister's armour would exploit toward the Melfa River, cross it, and proceed westward on Highway No. 6 toward Rome.

Ware's plan for the attack was simple in conception and constructed to fit the small piece of ground the PPCLI was ordered to take. The main objective lay at the top corner of a triangle bounded by a small stream and gully on the right, the Aquino-Pontecorvo highway on the left, and the start line as the base. Before reaching that objective, the infantry would have to move rapidly behind a rolling artillery barrage over dry, dusty, and uneven ground, through a wooded area, and then out into the open and across an uneven field in front of the main German defences. At the end of the field, the Germans had laid several thick belts of barbed wire. Behind the wire they had sited their forward machine-gun positions. Both the PPCLI infantry and the Churchill tanks of the supporting armoured regiment, the North Irish Horse, faced significant obstacles. The Germans had laid anti-personnel and anti-tank mines throughout the area. They had positioned snipers in the woods. The barbed wire in front of their machine guns was hung with anti-personnel explosives, and the narrow ground between the gully and the road was well covered by dozens of 75- and 88-millimetre anti-tank guns positioned to support the Hitler Line's pillboxes and other man-killing defences. The Irish tanks would have little room to manoeuvre to avoid their own destruction, let alone provide the infantry with fire support.

Into that kill zone Ware decided to send A Company, under command of Major "Bucko" Watson, up the left side of the triangle, and C Company, under Major R.B. Hobson, up the right side. When these two companies achieved their initial objectives, B Company, under Captain A.M. Campbell, would move in behind them and secure the battalion's final objective on the Aquino-Pontecorvo road. Then the Loyal Eddies, now commanded by former Patricia company commander Rowan Coleman, would attack through the PPCLI towards the final brigade objective, the road junction. The attack would begin with about 500 guns firing 1,500 rounds per minute on a 2,000-metre front. The barrage would be timed to lift one hundred yards every five minutes, which, under most circumstances, was not an unreasonable pace for an infantry advance.[14]

On the night before the attack, thousands of Allied troops facing the Hitler Line, or along the Anzio perimeter, prepared for the dawn. Everyone knew the final push was about to begin; no one was under any illusion of the high price that would be paid. It was unusually cool in the Liri Valley for that late in the spring. Word passed that there would be mist hugging the ground at dawn, which would aid the defenders. Along the front, the infantry checked and cleaned their weapons, wired their grenades to prevent accidental removal of the arming pins, ate a bite or two of dry rations, and smoked. Some tried to sleep; some even succeeded. Others spoke in low voices, or wrote those last letters that were always stuffed in the front pockets of their battledress tunics. They could hear the armour move up in the dark night behind them, but saw little until the sky began to lighten. Then the dark forms of tanks, trucks, anti-tank guns, Jeeps, and other vehicles, drivers and mechanics clustered around them, began to emerge from the gloom. Patricia Jim Reid of 7 Section, No. 7 Platoon, A Company, was one of the thousands of Allied infantry waiting for the dawn: "We spent the night of May the twenty-second in slit trenches as close to the enemy lines as possible. At 0400 h[ou]rs we were up and around after a sleepless night. We had a quick breakfast and moved back to our deployment area, about a hundred yards back from the slit trenches."[15]

The Canadian guns opened up at 0557. The men began to rise from their slit trenches to follow the barrage. The German counter-barrage exploded only moments later. German field guns, mortars, "moaning Minnies," and direct-fire guns shooting into the trees sent jagged chunks of steel shrapnel and large deadly wooden splinters into the advancing infantry. The Irish tanks slewed crazily as tracks were shot off, or "brewed up" as armour-piercing shells punched through to kill or maim the tank crews and set the interiors ablaze. Patricias began to fall by the dozens. Back at battalion tactical HQ, Ware knew almost from the beginning that the attack was in trouble: "We were attacking through woods and trees and groves and then there'd be an open space . . . we were doing stupid things like we were following a barrage through a wood, well geeze . . . suddenly you emerged into the open and then you hit the wire . . ."[16]

There was only one way to get through a thick barbed wire

barrier like that — it had to be blown apart with Bangalore Torpedoes. These were long tubes filled with explosives screwed together to form a pipe-like device with a cap and a fuse; ideally, they were inserted under the wire, then detonated. On the right flank of the PPCLI attack, George Quartly, a farm boy from Innisfail, Alberta, had been randomly selected by an Engineer NCO just prior to the attack to carry one of the C Company's ten Bangalore Torpedoes. His job, and that of the other men chosen to carry the Bangalores, was to somehow get up to the wire and blow it, so the rest of the company could get through. Quartly wore a brand-new wristwatch that he had just received from home. Private Elmer Davis, who carried a rifle and a radio, accompanied Quartly and the others as they approached the German wire under heavy fire.

"They were to go up near enough to the wire entanglements to throw the torpedoes out on the wire and light the fuse," Davis recalled. "Half walking and crouching [I] went forward on the extreme right of them. I was outside man, George was next to me." As they came within about twenty-five yards of the wire, the men rose up to throw the torpedoes. At that moment, the German machine gunners opened fire. "I was over [approximately ten yards] still on [Quartly's] right hand side when those dirty b[astards] cut loose on us . . . and instantly killed them all but me." Davis found a big rock, took cover, and stayed there as bullets kicked up the dirt around him. Not long after, some Patricia infantry came up and cleaned out two of the German machine-gun nests. The Germans manning the third position tried to run for it. "I shot one in the back, killed him," recalled Davis. "One rifleman nailed the other one. The third one came back with his hands up but we riddled him." When Davis finally made it over to George Quartly's body, the watch was gone.[17]

Somehow, A and C Companies made it to the wire. Somehow, some of the men, including Watson and Campbell, made it through. But by the time they did so, their radios were out, effective communications with Ware's tactical HQ were cut, and their strength had dwindled to perhaps several dozen out of the more than two hundred who had started out. Jim Reid was one of the wounded: "By the time we reached the barbed wire . . . there were only a handful of men left. I was hit in the leg with shrapnel and dove into the nearest shell hole. I had lots of company as there were six others as well as Sergeant Arbour, our platoon sergeant."[18] Andy Schaen lost his helmet in the early going; he had no trouble finding a replacement: "I was looking for a helmet to put on . . . I was trying helmets on. There were quite a number of them laying there . . . one of the rifle companies had gone through there and they had casualties . . . it was a very poor thing up here you know."[19]

The only word filtering through from the front came from walking wounded who somehow made it back. Ware moved forward to try to maintain contact; he would later admit that he moved too far: "I made the fatal error as a Commanding Officer that I was too far forward. I was caught up virtually with the forward companies and this big fight, and fire, and barrage."[20] Lieutenant Donald A. Gower, in command of the PPCLI's anti-tank platoon, lost contact with Ware: "I tried to link up with him again. Eventually I reached the edge of the wooded area, ahead lay the barbed wire and fortifications. I began to retrace my steps, passing knocked-out tanks and small groups of men." Whenever German shells rumbled in, he would take cover behind one of the knocked-out tanks: "On one of these occasions I questioned the man I was lying beside but got no answer. I shook him — no response. He was dead — probably having been struck by flying shrapnel with instantaneous results as his buddy, who was pressed up against him, was unaware of his fate."[21]

The slaughter was indescribable. The North Irish Horse suffered as greatly as the Patricias. Tanks blew up on mines and were blown up by anti-tank and self-propelled guns. Or, they slithered and twisted to get away from the murderous fire but were trapped by the gully on one side of the triangle and the raised road on the other. The North Irish lost twenty-five Churchills that day. Their CO was distraught over the failure of his men to protect the infantry. His distress was gallant; his men were not even able to protect themselves. Ware was similarly distressed. After moving forward, he found himself out of contact and unable to direct his men. He moved several times looking for a radio in working order to at least put him in touch with brigade. He knew that his two forward companies were on their own, would have to fend for themselves, and were a virtual write-off as tactical units as far as the battalion was concerned. At about 1500 hours, he also learned that B Company was stalled at the wire, taking casualties, and that the Loyal Eddies were in similar circumstances. Their CO, Lieutenant-Colonel Rowan Coleman, had been hit and was directing his battalion from a ditch. Ware and Coleman had last seen each other as the attack pushed off that morning. Coleman, wearing a soft hat instead of a helmet, had been puffing placidly on his pipe with a "happy smile on his face," according to the PPCLI War Diary. Ware would later recall: "It became apparent we were not going to get on to this objective with enough people to be able to do anything . . . In other words, the right flank [attack] was not a success. A glorious failure if you want to call it because there wasn't anybody left."[22]

When Ware finally did locate a radio, he was surprised to learn that the attack was actually going well on the other fronts. To his left, the infantry battalions of 3rd Brigade had moved quickly through the German defences and over the Aquino-Pontecorvo road. Vokes had thrown his divisional reserve into the battle behind them. The follow-up advance started late in the afternoon in a heavy rain, and caught the Germans in the open, preparing to counterattack. They were slaughtered. So when Ware told Brigadier T.G. Gibson over the radio that his battalion was in desperate shape, Gibson replied, "Hold on. Good work. Will do all we can for you and send up more t[an]ks. Looking at the broader picture the news is excellent. German [transport] is streaming up the road north westwards and the Adolf Hitler line has been breached all along its length."[23]

Ware also learned that the troops in the Anzio bridgehead had broken through. That was good news, of course, but small consolation to a man whose battalion was being shattered around him. Sydney McKay never forgot the sight of Cammie Ware clutching dozens of identity disks, one of two worn by every Canadian infantryman.[24] One of the disks was always left with the body; the other was collected for graves registration.

At 1700, Patricia second-in-command Major D.H. Rosser received a surprise signal from Brigade HQ, ordering Ware to return to the battalion's rear area headquarters, known in military parlance as "B" Echelon: "Bde Comd has ordered you to relieve Col Ware tonight. He is to return to 'B' ech as an LOB [left out of battle] no nonsense."[25] The order was not a rebuke of Ware, nor of the battalion's performance on this bloody day. In fact, it was standard practice to pull a commanding officer out of the front lines after a battle went badly, in order to give him a chance to rest and recuperate. Ware resumed command the very next day. Brigadier Gibson also gave Rosser command of C Company of the Loyal Eddies to bolster Patricia defences overnight.

The battle on the Patricia front petered out by nightfall. Those who could make it back from the shattered forward companies dragged themselves to a small perimeter around the B Company position near the wire, waiting for the inevitable German counterattack. The PPCLI had been beaten up: 59 killed in action, 118 wounded, and 17 prisoners lost — or nearly half of its effective fighting strength — in about twelve hours. Only 77 men remained in the B Company perimeter, though stragglers continued to rejoin the regiment all night and into the next day. One of those men was Donald Gower, whose father had been one of the few Originals who survived the Battle of Frezenberg twenty-eight years earlier. Now Gower had survived the Hitler Line. He would later write: "One has to wonder if there is such a thing as luck or fate that might run families."[26]

The twenty-third of May was the worst day for the PPCLI in all of the Second World War; the next day the regiment began the solemn task of finding its dead and burying them. "That was the first time I really saw our own Canadian boys really massacred, especially PPCLI," Gilbert Hyde remembered. "I had seen other ones before but not in the numbers that there were there."[27] "I buried my best chum in that field," Robert Eddy later recalled. "Kind of left me wondering, 'Whoa, do I want to be here or what?'"[28] "The Hitler Line is better forgotten," Wallace Smith would always believe: "It was dirty, it was rough, I lost a memory . . . Any Patricia that was there knows all about it. It was bad."[29]

The Patricia sacrifice was heavy, but it was not in vain; the Hitler Line was broken, the road to Rome open. The Allies entered Rome on 4 June, the Canadians of the First Special Service Force among them. Two days later, the other three divisions of First Canadian Army and about ninety thousand other British, American, and Allied troops began the Normandy invasion. The real "second front" was finally open; most supplies, reinforcements, and public attention shifted from Italy to Normandy and the subsequent costly struggle to drive a final stake through the heart of the Third Reich. The Patricias and all the other Canadian and Allied troops who continued to fight their way up the Italian peninsula against Kesselring's skilled defensive troops, mostly in obscurity, became known to history as the "D-Day Dodgers." At first, most of them resented the epithet. Later, they wore it proudly. They composed and sang a song, to the tune of the German popular hit "Lili Marlene," that reflected their wry and self-deprecating humour. Each verse of the song concluded: "We are the D-Day Dodgers, in sunny Italy."

P.P.C.L.I.

By the end of the first week of June 1944, Italy had become a sideshow in the grand theatre of the Second World War. Sideshow or not, Churchill and British Field Marshal Sir Harold Alexander were determined to push ahead with the conquest of Italy — and that meant an assault on the Gothic Line. The Gothic Line was yet another of Kesselring's defence lines, stretching from south of Pesaro on the Adriatic coast to Luca on the Mediterranean. It was not nearly as well laid out or defended as the Hitler Line had been, but the mere fact that Kesselring was responsible for it gave any Allied commander pause at that stage of the war in Italy.

The 1st Canadian Corps enjoyed a two-month hiatus after the Liri Valley, spending much of that time encamped south of Cassino. After the hard fighting at Ortona and the Hitler Line, Cameron Ware was overdue for a long leave and release from the heavy burden of command. On 29 June, he left the Patricias and was replaced by Major Rosser. Not long after, the Patricias left the Liri Valley for good, heading north through sunny Tuscany, its luxuriant vineyards untouched by war. They and the rest of the 1st Canadian Corps initially advanced to the south bank of the Arno River, near Florence, in a feint to fool the Germans that a major Eighth Army attack would begin shortly on that front. In fact, Leese had decided to return to the Adriatic coast for his next major push. His aim was to cross the Metauro River and drive north into the Po River Valley, beyond the Gothic Line, clearing the Germans from the northern Apennines. Ahead lay a hundred miles of undulating coastal plain, hemmed in by the eastern foothills of the mountain range, crossed by a dozen or so eastward-flowing rivers, dominated by hilltop towns, with ample dead ground and reverse slopes for defenders. In some places, the plain was barely wide enough for a full division, let alone three corps.

No one was happy to return to the Adriatic coast. In the

mountains near Cassino, the cool nights and clear air had given soothing relief from the heat of the Italian midday sun. Clear streams and green forests were balm for the soul after the hell of the Hitler Line. There had been time for the Canadians to rest, eat good food, get steady mail from home, and absorb what few reinforcements came their way. Most of the new men coming from Canada were not going to Italy, but were sent to the Canadian Army in Normandy. Eventually, there would be too few new men to replace those killed or taken from their units for long periods of recuperation. But that problem was not apparent as long as the Patricias and the other Canadian formations remained far from the front. When they returned to the heat and humidity of the coastal plain in late August, however, the lack of sanitation, the mosquitoes, the bad water, and the sheer heat of the midday sun began to take a high toll in sick and exhausted men. And once they entered combat again, as they would shortly do, the lack of reinforcements meant that wounded men would return to their combat units again and again, increasing further the risk of battle exhaustion.

Leese's attack on the Adriatic front, one part of a two-pronged assault dubbed "Operation Olive," began on 25 August 1944. His objective was to smash the right anchor of the Gothic Line. Leese had placed 2nd Polish Corps along the coast, 1st Canadian Corps in the centre, and 5th British Corps on the left flank of the attack. The 2nd Canadian Infantry Brigade spearheaded the drive on the left of the Canadian front. The Loyal Eddies led on the left of the Brigade front, and the PPCLI on the right. The assault began at one minute to midnight on 25 August with the usual massive bombardment. Miraculously, the Patricia assault companies made it across the Metauro and on to their objectives by 0400, suffering only three casualties from *Schu* mines. For the next four days, the attack went forward smoothly. Though the Germans had detected the gathering storm, they had neither the time — nor the men — to mount a quick defence. Leese's forces reached the Foglia River by 29 August. That river, really a small stream in late summer, meandered lazily through lush, hilly farmland with broad fields on its south bank and a small ridge to the north. It would have been an idyllic scene but for the fact that the Gothic Line lay hidden in the trees and brush atop the ridge on the north bank.

The Metauro River crossing had been easy; although seven Patricias had been killed, thirty wounded, and one taken prisoner in the subsequent advance to the Foglia, they had also covered close to twenty kilometres in just four days. No one had expected such progress at so little cost. Now, they believed, the easy time would end. On the morning of 30 August, Rosser received his orders for the next phase of the attack and was given a map with the most recently detected German defences overprinted on it. As the war diary summary noted, "Def[ence] overprint maps of the Foglia R[iver] and the country to the north fairly bristled with red printed enemy strongpoints; the real thing had been reached."[30]

The assault on the Gothic Line had begun. The immediate Patricia objective was the ruined town of Osteria Nuova, situated on the line just below the ridge overlooking the Foglia, and behind an anti-tank ditch. Canadian field guns provided the usual rolling barrage to clear the way for the infantry. As the Patricias began their advance at five minutes past midnight on 1 September — the Perth Regiment to their immediate left and West Nova Scotia Regiment to their right — Canadian self-propelled guns and anti-tank guns blasted away at the top of the ridge. Once again the Germans were caught by surprise; the Patricia assaulting companies were dug in in the ruins of Osteria Nuova by 0600. Casualties were very light, and the PPCLI took an astonishing 231 German prisoners. But one of the men they lost that day was the very popular PPCLI Padre H/Captain K.E. Eaton. Ken Eaton had started the war as an "other ranks," an ordinary soldier, a corporal who had decided his true calling was to minister to his comrades-in-arms. He had returned to Canada to attend divinity school before rejoining the

Canada goes to war under the flag of the United Nations. Here, Australian UN delegate J. Plimsoll presents the UN flag to Lieutenant-Colonel J.R. Stone, DSO, MC, Commanding Officer 2 PPCLI, Miryang, Korea, 11 January 1951.

A soldier, with mess tins in hand, pauses on his way to lunch to watch a Korean woman, dressed in rags, walk by.

In February 1951, Major George Flint, OC A Company 2 PPCLI, points out the objective to his officers. Sergeant Tommy Prince, the most decorated native soldier, is second from the left. Lieutenants John Deegan and Jack Regan with CSM Doug Acton are at the rear.

In March 1951, Brigadier Basil Coad, Commander 27 British Commonwealth Brigade, briefs Lieutenant-Colonel Jim Stone on a new offensive.

(Right) A Chinese mortar bomb explodes near two soldiers caught in the open — a near miss.

Sergeant James McGhee, 12 Platoon D Company 2 PPCLI, wounded during an attack on Hill 532, is escorted to the rear by Captain Andy Foulds and Sergeant "Red" Pennell, 7 March 1951.

With yet another hill to take, soldiers of 2 PPCLI advance in line, March 1951.

Lieutenant-Colonel Norman Wilson-Smith, Commanding Officer 1 PPCLI, briefs his company commanders on a new sector of operations, January 1952.

B Company 3 PPCLI leave their front line positions, 1953.

1 PPCLI Company Quarter Master Sergeant Joe Devlin issues C-7 ration packs to a Korean Army Service Corps porter. Porter trains provided excellent service to the Canadians, moving rations, ammunition, water, and even beer to front-line troops.

Thanks to the porters, two soldiers of 1 PPCLI receive C Ration packs, and most welcome Asahi beer.

Assault Pioneers of 1 PPCLI with signs bearing greetings from the Chinese People's Volunteer Army. Clockwise, from top left: Glen Mathews, Russ Piche, Ron Kirby, Glen Palmer.

Captain Arthur Kemsley reads the ceasefire order to soldiers of 3 PPCLI in their front-line bunkers, 27 July 1953.

3 PPCLI Sergeant Don Ardelian and Private Eager dig in platoon Command Post on Line WYOMING, March 1953.

Soldiers of 3 PPCLI with a KATCOM (Korean Augmentation Troops attached Commonwealth Division) soldier. Integrated with the Canadians, these Koreans reinforced rifle companies.

4 Platoon, B Company, 2 PPCLI, winning a Forced March Competition on NATO duty in West Germany, 23 January 1956. Note the Second World War pattern dress and vehicles.

The founder, Brigadier A. Hamilton Gault, DSO, ED, CD, returns to Frezenberg in Belgium, scene of the 8 May 1915 battle, to plant a memorial Canadian maple, 1 October 1957. From the left: Lieutenant David Snowball, ADC; Lieutenant-Colonel Tom deFaye, MBE, CD, Commanding Officer 1 PPCLI; Guard Commander Major E.D. McPhail, CD; the Founder; WOII Roy Appleton, MM, CD.

2 PPCLI Para Company prepare to move out after landing on a northern lake. Note the dog sleds and local native guides.

Private D.R. Barnes, 1 PPCLI, on sentry duty in Cyprus in 1968.

Sergeant D.R. Weathers (right) and Private M.L. Deschamps, 3 PPCLI, check out the buffer zone in the old city of Nicosia, Cyprus, in 1988. Both soldiers are carrying the new C7 rifle.

A first for the Regiment — the Colonel-in-Chief, accompanied by Colonel of the regiment, Major-General H.C. Pitts, MC, CD, present new Queen's and Regimental Colours to 3 PPCLI in an operational theatre, at Pakrac, Croatia, 9 March 1993.

In Croatia in 1994, soldiers of 1 PPCLI occupy Observation Post DeCoste, named in honour of Captain Jim DeCoste, killed on a previous tour of duty with 2 PPCLI.

MCpl. Flemming briefs the Colonel-in-Chief on arrival at C Company 1 PPCLI compound in Croatia in June 1994. From the left: Major Mike English; Colonel of the Regiment Major General C.W. Hewson; and Lord John Brabourne, husband of Countess Mountbatten.

3 PPCLI patrolling the Serb sector, Pakrac, Croatia, 1993.

B Company 1 PPCLI anti-armour detachments establish a roadblock at Martin Brod, Bosnia, with Armoured Personnel Carriers equipped with TOW (**T**ube launched, **O**ptically guided, **W**ire controlled) missiles, autumn 1997.

The Colonel-in-Chief presents the Stabilization Force (SFOR) Medal to Corporal T.R. Woods of 3 PPCLI at Camp Maple Leaf, Zgon, Bosnia, in July 2000.

army. After the capture of Osteria Nuova, Eaton had gone forward to help with the wounded. He knelt on a *Schu* mine; his leg was blown off and he died shortly after. Coming from the ranks, Eaton had had a way with the men. He spoke their language; he knew their concerns. He left an indelible impression on the Patricias who knew him. Wallace Smith was one of those men: "I can't remember the next Padre . . . I met a lot of Padres in my day, over the years in military service . . . but I have no recollection of a Padre after Kenny."[31] "That was the worst of everything," Robert Eddy would recall, "when we lost him."[32]

P.P.C.L.I.

On 4 September, the Patricias were withdrawn to the small, rear-area coastal town of Cattolica for a ten-day rest. After the break-through of the Gothic Line, the Germans had quickly put into place the Rimini Line. As the remainder of the Eighth Army prepared to storm this secondary defence line, the battle-weary men of the PPCLI enjoyed the warm September sun on the beaches of the Adriatic. Billeted in small seaside resort hotels, private homes, and *pensions* in the town, they drank the good local wines and ate fresh vegetables and seafood while they slept to the sound of the surf. The *Luftwaffe* tried hard to disturb the warm evenings by sending an occasional bomber or two to ruin their sleep, but Cattolica was a heaven compared to much of the rest of the country the Patricias had been through. Their vacation could not last, of course: on 14 September the battalion was put on notice to be ready to move within two hours. They were due to go into action to relieve the Van Doos, who had tried, unsuccessfully, to capture the small village of San Martino, five kilometres due south of Rimini.

San Martino stood atop a low, north-south ridge that dominated a rail line running southwest from Rimini and the Ausa River, which ran parallel to the line and a few hundred metres to the north of it. The Patricias had to cross both railway and river before they reached Highway No. 72 and the Rimini defensive line on the other side of the narrow Ausa valley. The initial attack on San Martino had been launched by 1st Brigade on 15 September and had stalled near the crest of the ridge. The Patricias were ordered first to take over the positions gained by the Van Doos in the centre of the ridge, then outflank the ridge to the west and try to cut the German line of retreat to the Ausa River beyond.

On the afternoon of 16 September, Rosser was at his tactical headquarters when German shells began to explode around it. One of those shells made a direct hit: Rosser was wounded. He was rushed to the rear while his second in command, Major R.P. Clarke, quickly came forward to take over the battalion prior to the attack. Rosser never returned, but Clarke was well versed in the brigade and battalion objectives and carried right on. The main attack was postponed because of heavy German shelling, but a Patricia patrol went forward to feel its way towards a ford over the Ausa. The patrol, however, was stopped cold about 200 metres from its start line, and well short of the river. The main attack did not begin until 0530 on the eighteenth. When it did, German artillery and anti-tank guns took a heavy toll. Major P.D. Crofton, in command of C Company, was wounded, forcing Major Colin McDougall of B Company to take over both companies. They reached the rail line, still short of the river, with about half their effective strength intact.

On the Adriatic coast in the late summer and fall of 1944, the German defence lines — the Gothic Line, the Rimini Line, and others — were not nearly as formidable as the Gustav and Hitler lines on the approaches to Rome. But the Allied casualties were still heavy as the Germans used mines, booby traps, mortars, "moaning Minnies," artillery, and direct-fire weapons to good effect. The German defence was easy in a land of constant rivers, where the mountains of the interior and the high foothills to the west of the coastal plain funnelled the attackers into the few small areas that were relatively flat. On 18 September alone the Patricias suffered seven killed and fifty-two wounded, mostly from shells and mortars. Robert Eddy was one of the wounded: "I got hit at about seven o'clock in the morning and about fifteen more of us were in an old building all day . . . that night we heard an ambulance coming . . . you could see the big red cross coming but so much dust . . . all of a sudden there was a bang and he was gone. There were just pieces flying everywhere."[33] Eddy and his wounded comrades were forced to stay another night before being evacuated the next morning. San Martino was finally taken on the nineteenth and the river crossed.

The small village of San Fortunato, and the ridge it sat on, dominated the route from the river to the north. The attack against the ridge began on 19 September; the PPCLI went into action the following day with orders to take the ground from the ridge to the Marecchia River. Sydney Frost was a platoon commander in D Company; on the afternoon of 20 September he watched as three Churchill tanks moved across a ridge line in support of the attack. German tanks were waiting:

> Three Churchills churn over the crest and head along the trail to [the village of] Bovey, in full sight of the waiting Tigers. We see the Tigers elevate the barrels of their 88s. In a second we hear the sickening sound of steel through steel and then a tremendous explosion. The rear Churchill blows up. Instantly the lead Churchill meets the same fate. The middle tank is now a sitting duck for the expert German gunners. They calmly dispatch it with one round.[34]

Frost and his men were forced to go on without armour protection.

After a second day of advancing into the teeth of German shell, tank, small-arms, and mortar fire, the Patricias' B and C Companies approached the Marecchia. Frost's platoon was one of the first across: "Ahead, a wooden bridge ha[d] been thoughtfully left for our use," he recalled. "We pour[ed] over it and reached[ed] the far bank, unscathed by the air bursts. We burrow[ed] into the hard, rocky soil with a will, scarcely believing our good fortune."[35] The Patricias' final objective was to cut the main road running west from Rimini. They achieved it, and pulled back on 22 September, to be replaced by a New Zealand battalion. On the twenty-third, they returned to Cattolica once more for rest and recuperation. In a month of hard slogging, not unlike the attrition warfare of the First World War, the PPCLI suffered 62 men killed in action or dead of wounds, 6 missing, and 235 wounded.

In northwest Europe, the Battle of Normandy had ended in October 1944; the Allies had won it decisively, but at heavy cost. Then the American, British, and Canadian armies had driven the Germans from France into the Low Countries. The battle to open the Scheldt Estuary had begun as Montgomery's great gamble at Arnhem, operation Market-Garden, concluded. Far to the east, the Soviet armies were crushing the *Wehrmacht,* chasing the Germans from the Soviet Union into Poland, toppling the Nazi satellite states in the Balkans, and preparing for the last major push to Berlin. Allied bombers by the thousands visited massive destruction on German cities, factories, rail yards, bridges, roads, power systems, and canals, destroying German life and national infrastructure day by day. There was no point in continuing the dead end of the war in Italy; it would never lead to victory. The decisive blows would come from the Allied armies now closing up to the borders of Germany east and west.

And yet the war in Italy dragged on, past Rimini, into the Romagna plains, towards the Po River Valley. From 20 to 23 October, the Patricias and the rest of 1st Canadian Corps forced a crossing of the Savio River as they drove toward Bologna. Nine Patricias were killed, forty-nine wounded, fourteen taken prisoner. Then it was on to the Ronco River, the Naviglio Canal, and finally the River Senio, the Canadian winter line. There they patrolled, enduring the cold and wet until 25 February 1945, when they were relieved by a British battalion and began the long journey to join the rest of the Canadian Army in Holland for the last major Canadian battle of the war. The December fighting had cost the Patricias nineteen killed, seventy wounded, and two lost as prisoners. While they had fought and bled, the attention of Canadians at home was focused not on the Romagna plains, but on the final stages of the Battle of the Scheldt Estuary, the Battle of the Bulge, and the first stages of the Battle of the Rhineland, which began with a Canadian attack from southeast Holland towards Wesel on 8 February 1945.

P.P.C.L.I.

In February 1945, the Combined Chiefs of Staff, the American and British generals responsible for the overall military direction of the war, met in Malta and decided to shift more Allied troops from Italy to northwest Germany. Long separated from the rest of First Canadian Army, the two divisions of 1st Canadian Corps, now under command of Lieutenant-General C.G. Foulkes, were among those troops selected to go. The entire Canadian Army — five divisions and two independent armoured brigades — would be reunited for the last weeks of the war. On 27 February, the Patricias pulled out of the front lines along the Adriatic and began their journey to Livorno, also known as Leghorn, on the Mediterranean coast. There, they boarded transports for the port of Marseilles in southern France. They landed on 15 March and immediately started out for the front, travelling by road up the Rhone Valley, through Burgundy, and past Paris, Compiègne, and the last battlefields of the First World War into Belgium. There, they rested and regrouped while Montgomery and his generals planned the last major battles of the war.

Harry Crerar's First Canadian Army was assigned to cross the Rhine into southeastern Holland. It would drive the Germans out of eastern Holland as far as the North Sea, and then swing eastward into north Germany. At the same time, 1st Canadian Division, along with the 49th British Division, was to attack westward across the IJssel River in a bid to liberate west-central Holland, including the major cities of Amsterdam, Rotterdam, The Hague, and Utrecht, which were still under German occupation. The Allies had bypassed that region of Holland; no food supplies had been able to get through and its population was now near starvation. On 3 April, the Patricias left Belgium and moved into the Reichswald, south of Nijmegen, to prepare for the attack. It was cold and wet; the forest bivouac amid the detritus of the recent bitter fighting provided a fitting backdrop for the impending action. Everyone knew the war was almost over, that victory was no more than weeks away. Everyone shared the same thought: "Have I survived this far only to be killed at the end?" But there was no faltering, no slackness, as the Patricias squared themselves for the final push. On 7 April they boarded their trucks and were driven to the hamlet of Baak, in Holland, some eleven kilometres east of the town of Zutphen on the IJssel.

The battle opened on the afternoon of 11 April with the 3rd Canadian Division forcing a crossing near Deventer. When that was accomplished and the right flank of 1st Canadian Division secured, the Patricias and the Seaforths led their division across the IJssel, some five kilometres south of Deventer, attacking on a two-company front. British Buffaloes, large tracked amphibious vehicles, carried them across the river. Sydney Frost, in command of D Company, later recorded the moment:

> April 11 — 1430 hours. Dog Company quickly loads on the Buffaloes. We've practised this so many times we can do it blindfolded. I speak to the platoon commanders and wish them luck. The Buffaloes roar into life and fill the woods with their heavy fumes. The great beasts snort and lurch forward to the river. I look at my watch — 1530 hours. In [thirty] minutes the smoke

> screen will start. It's a fine day for smoke, just a light breeze. Ten minutes to smoke — five minutes. We emerge from the woods. The artillery opens up. Shells whine over our heads and land on the far bank of the river. Smoke drifts across the whole front, completely shielding us from enemy observation.[36]

The Buffaloes were into the water and across the river in minutes. The Germans, who had not expected an attack from across the IJssel, were taken by surprise. C Company avoided German fire completely. D Company was not so fortunate, but the opposition was light. The Germans did not make a showing of any significance until 0300 the next morning, when three tanks and a company of German infantry tried to drive the Patricias back to the river. All three tanks were destroyed by PIAT bombs — squash charges fired by an ungainly spring-loaded, shoulder-fired mechanism that looked like a stovepipe. Virtually all the German infantry was killed, wounded, or captured in the wild melee in the dark.

Organized German opposition was beginning to collapse. None of the tanks facing the Patricias were the newer, fearsome Tigers (Mark Vs) or Panthers (Mark VIs), and the soldiers were poorly led, and unusually young and badly trained. But their mortars and artillery could still kill, as platoon commander George Grant found out shortly after the crossing when he and his driver were caught in a prolonged shelling: "I said to Harry, my runner and driver . . . 'You know this stuff's been going over, these shells been going over, for a long time, some hours. I think we should do something.'" Grant quickly found a shell hole and took cover. His driver was not quick enough: "[A] shell hit, blew him to pieces. The main body landed on me, the torso. The rest of him was up in the trees . . . Holey moley, that was fairly quick. There he was. So I pushed this torso off of me and I was red, top to bottom."[37]

The PPCLI attacked southwest from their bridgehead on 13 April; two days later, their division linked up with the 49th Division, trapping hundreds of Germans west of the IJssel. They cleared the enemy for three days before pushing west again to a separation-of-forces line about fifty-five kilometres west of the IJssel. There, they stopped in accordance with an agreement worked out between the Allied high command and the Nazi occupation authorities to allow food and supplies to flow into west-central Holland in return for Allied restraint in attacking the Germans. The Allies agreed to these terms to alleviate the suffering of the Dutch population; the war was clearly within days of ending and there was no point in risking further civilian casualties to gain ground that would soon be theirs anyway.

As Soviet troops fought their way into the heart of Berlin, Hitler killed himself on the afternoon of 30 April. Then, at 2000 on 4 May, Sydney Frost heard the news he had been waiting for for nearly six years: his signaller recorded a message from battalion headquarters that read, "CEASE FIRE tomorrow, May 5th at 0800 hours." The German forces in Italy had already surrendered; those facing the British and Canadian armies now appeared ready to do the same. Frost didn't trust them. He feared the Germans "would now make a final insane attack to avenge their dead Führer." He and his men manned their defences all night and waited while the Dutch population began to celebrate in the hamlets and villages all around them. At 0800 the next morning, the hour of ceasefire finally came. Frost would later write: "Maj[or] 'Snuffy' Smith [another Patricia company commander] and I quietly clasped hands. No words passed between us. We knew, without saying, what each of us had endured on that long, hard road to victory. We were thankful to have survived."[38]

Thus did the Second World War pass into regimental history. Because of that war, more honours were added to the regimental Colour, and more tradition spun into regimental lore. Hamilton Gault wired Lieutenant-Colonel R.P. Clarke just after the fighting ended: "You have magnificently maintained the traditions of your Regiment on the battle fields of Sicily, Italy and Germany and have added proud laurels to your Colours. God Bless you all." Those were stirring words, but the battle honours were won at a high price: 264 Patricias were killed in action or died on active service, 1,118 were wounded, and 47 had been taken prisoner in the greatest war in history.

For the second time in a half-century, Gault's vision of fielding a fighting regiment with a tradition rooted in the long history of the British army had been fulfilled. No doubt there were some Patricias who thought of Gault, and of their regimental family, as they gazed on the now silent battlefield of central Holland. No doubt also that the vast majority of the battle-worn regiment were thinking of home, wives, children, parents, sweethearts, and of the very sweetness of allowing themselves once again to think about a future. It may well be, however, that at the moment the guns fell silent in Europe for the second time in a half-century, their uppermost thoughts were of comrades who had not made it. In his final personal message of the war, Monty put it best: "I would ask you all to remember those of our comrades who fell in the struggle. They gave their lives that others might have freedom, and no man can do more than that. I believe that He would say to each one of them: *'Well done, thou good and faithful servant.'*"

Chapter 10

KOREA

THE FIRST CANADIAN ARMY OF THE SECOND WORLD WAR was one of Canada's most epic creations. When Canada had declared war in September 1939, the Permanent Force had consisted of fewer than 4,200 soldiers, scattered across the country in formations badly under strength. By July 1944, the overseas army had expanded to some half a million soldiers, fighting in Italy and France in five full divisions and two independent armoured brigades. Though small in comparison to the Soviet, American, and British armies, the Canadian Army made significant contributions to Allied victories in Normandy, Italy, the Low Countries, and the Battle of the Rhineland. The Canadian Army suffered 75,596 casualties overall; 22,917 were killed in action or died on active service.

In the summer and fall of 1945, the great majority of Canadian soldiers wanted nothing more to do with war or military life. They returned to Canada by the tens of thousands to find jobs in newly expanding industries, attend schools under the government's new veteran benefits plans, open businesses, and start — or take over — family farms. They also got married in record numbers and began to raise families. Canadians demanded basic social security, government-guaranteed housing loans, family allowances, and better schools, roads, and cities. They had sacrificed for six years in a common struggle to defeat fascism and Nazism; they now wanted a safer and better Canada. Fulfilling those demands would cost money. Moreover, the nation had incurred the largest debt in its history in financing the war. That debt had to be paid.

Almost immediately after the end of the fighting, the Canadian government began to make huge cuts in its defence budget. When post-war plans for a new military were announced in 1946, the size of the Permanent or Active Force army was set at 25,000 overall, with just 7,000 in the combat arms. Once again, mirroring the inter-war years, the infantry would revert to just three battalions — Princess Patricia's Canadian Light Infantry, the Royal Canadian Regiment, and the Royal 22e Régiment. Lieutenant-Colonel Cameron Ware, DSO, resumed command of the peacetime Patricias on 3 January 1946. He prepared them for their move from Manitoba to Currie Barracks, on the southwest edge of Calgary, in the spring of that year.

Ware was determined not to let his battalion fall into the doldrums of peacetime barracks life. Instead, he focused on Arctic and cold-weather training. Learning how to fight in the North, he reasoned, would not only allow his soldiers to contribute to the potential defence of the nation, but also provide them with tough physical and mental challenges. In late August 1946, for example, he took the battalion up the Alaska Highway for an experience that combined scouting out the North with living and training in remote country. As Ware later recorded, "[the exercise] was worth its weight in gold; from it stemmed both winter and summer training policies in the Northwest which became part of Regimental training in the years to come."[1]

The unique challenges of northern soldiering further distinguished the PPCLI from its other Active Force counterparts. It was thus fitting that the PPCLI Regimental Association was established in the fall of 1947, with the specific purpose of protecting Patricia heritage and traditions. Hamilton Gault travelled to Calgary to preside at the founding of the association at Currie Barracks on 25 October 1947, which followed a ceremonial parade in his honour.

The post-war Active Force was supposed to defend Canada, prepare alongside the country's allies for possible overseas operations to keep or enforce the peace, and train the Army Reserves, as the militia was henceforth called. The army, however, lacked sufficient money, equipment, or manpower to do any of those things tolerably well. In barracks across Canada in the first years after the war, soldiers were poorly paid, base housing was bad, opportunities for promotion were few, and training was cut to the bone. Many lower-rank soldiers were forced to work part-time at jobs off base in order to make ends meet. Lieutenant-General Charles Foulkes, the Chief of the General Staff, told the Cabinet Defence Committee in the fall of 1947 that the combat arms were more than 50 percent below authorized strength. He did not bother to mention that they were still equipped with Second (and sometimes First) World War–era rifles, machine guns, grenades, anti-tank weapons, radios, uniforms, helmets, and mortars.

Ware left at the end of September 1947 to attend Staff College. He was succeeded by Lieutenant-Colonel N.M. Gemmell, DSO, who commanded the Patricias from 1 October 1947 to 6 October 1948. Lieutenant-Colonel D.C. Cameron, DSO, ED, succeeded Gemmell on 7 October 1948. Under these leaders, the Patricias did the best they could to keep morale high and the men well trained. They returned to the North whenever circumstances permitted. The northern operations were not simply opportunities for "toughening up" the soldiers; it was now obvious that the defence of Canada in the Cold War era required a thorough knowledge of how men and gear would stand up to the Arctic environment. The only realistic threat to Canada in the late 1940s came from the Soviet Union over the North Pole, and stemmed from the possibility that the USSR might someday test Canada's ability to defend its vast North by sending small raiding parties into select northern areas.

These fears, coupled with the need to defend as much of the remote North as possible with the few troops available on the Department of National Defence's starvation budget, gave rise in 1948 to the creation of the Mobile Striking Force (MSF). The MSF would consist of the three Active Force infantry regiments — all to be trained as parachutists — and a large enough contingent of transport aircraft to drop them and their equipment wherever a Soviet force might attack in the north. The MSF's mission would be to hold such an attacking force down while reinforcements arrived overland from southern Canada or the United States. In early August 1948, Major-General C.C. Mann, CBE, DSO, Vice Chief of the General Staff, visited the Patricias at Currie Barracks to explain this development and to announce that the PPCLI had been selected as the first of the three Active Force regiments to convert to the airborne role. In accord with the already entrenched tradition that a soldier might become a paratrooper only by specifically volunteering for that assignment, Mann asked the officers, then the warrant officers, and finally the "other ranks" if they were willing to volunteer. Every single one replied, "I volunteer to be a jumper, sir."[2]

Parachute training at the Canadian Joint Air Training Centre at Rivers, Manitoba, began shortly thereafter. The conversion from infantry to airborne paratroopers was not easy. It called for thorough retraining of the men, both as individuals and as members of a fighting team. But the parachute wings that successful volunteers — and most were successful — sported on their uniforms brought added allure to service with the PPCLI. That, and the increased pay and better living conditions that came with the first post-war increase in the defence budget, brought more and higher-quality recruits into Patricia ranks. At the same time, everyone bent to the task of creating a viable airborne battalion; all were determined to qualify for the jump wings and pass the initiation together. Thus, another distinctive element was added to the Patricia tradition.

By the spring of 1949, the PPCLI had completed its transformation to an airborne battalion. The new concept was first tested in Exercise Eagle, held in the Fort St. John area of northern British Columbia in early August of that year. The culminating parachute drop was a success, but the overall exercise produced less-than-spectacular results because of a shortage of transport aircraft. Nevertheless, a much larger and more complex exercise, dubbed "Sweetbriar," was mounted in conjunction with the US Army in Alaska and the Yukon in January and February 1950. With some 5,000 troops involved, Sweetbriar was "the first attempt to reproduce battle conditions on a major scale in the far north."[3]

Sweetbriar was the site of an occasion long remembered in the lore of the new Active Force Patricias. There is a tradition in northern operations, especially those conducted by paratroopers, that all the men in a tent are treated equally in the performance of basic duties such as tending the stove or carrying water and provisions. Bill Davies of A Company shared a tent with a crusty old Patricia veteran known as Gulka, as well as Major W.J. Saul, father of well-known Canadian author (and husband of Governor General Adrienne Clarkson) John Ralston Saul. On one cold early morning during the exercise, Major Saul ordered Gulka to light the lamp and get the stove going. Davies would later recall: "Old Gulka turned around and said, 'Sir, with all due respect, it's your turn. Now get out of that sleeping bag and do it.'"[4]

In Sweetbriar, most of the Patricias were roadbound alongside the US troops; only one PPCLI company took part in the culminating parachute mock-attack. But that company, and paratroopers in general, were special, as Barclay "BAJ" Franklin found in the US Army mess hall just after the exercise ended:

> We were all lined up for our meal . . . and we were a scruffy-looking bunch of troops . . . being on the trail and being on the road with our so-called white camouflage uniforms . . . they were pretty grungy looking. And in comes Charlie Company, the jumpers, with their pure white mukluks and their white smocks and the American cook says, "[T]he paratroopers eat first." Boy, this really choked us all up. We were booing and hooting and hollering and it was all in fun, of course [but] we were a little cheesed off . . . [the parachute company] only had about an hour on the exercise and we were on the trail for days.[5]

Sweetbriar was a difficult test of soldiers in an arctic environment, but it was only a test, nothing more. Though the Patricias of early 1950 were as well trained a professional peacetime military force as Canada had ever had, they were not yet ready for the real thing; the nation itself was complacent and unready. While Canada and its American comrades were conducting winter exercises in the Yukon and Alaska in early 1950, the soldiers of Communist North Korea were training for war.

Liberated from Japanese occupation at the end of the Second World War, Korea had been divided into a northern zone of occupation, controlled by Soviet forces, and a southern zone, controlled by the United States. The 38th parallel divided the two zones. In time, the Americans decided to establish an anti-communist republic in the south, headed by Syngman Rhee, elected in 1948. The Communists, meanwhile, installed Kim Il Sung to head their republic in the north. Gradually, the US withdrew virtually all its troops from the south, leaving a small military mission and a handful of instructors. Washington was uncertain that South Korea — or the Republic of Korea, as it was officially known — constituted a vital American interest. Soviet leader Josef Stalin had no such qualms about where the USSR's interests lay. When Kim Il Sung decided to launch a war to conquer South Korea and unify the Korean peninsula by force, Stalin eventually gave the project his blessing. His blessing was much more than mere sanction: Soviet tanks, artillery, aircraft, advisors, and instructors were made available to the North Koreans, who could also rely on the backing of the new Communist government in Beijing. While the Patricias played at war, the North Korean Peoples' Army (NKPA) made ready for it.

P.P.C.L.I.

At 0400 on 25 June 1950, 135,000 NKPA troops, led by Soviet-supplied tanks, swept across the 38th parallel to launch the Korean War. American President Harry Truman was determined to help the South Koreans throw back the aggressors. The Kremlin, he believed, was testing the resolve of the West — especially the newly created North Atlantic Treaty Organization (NATO). To be sure, Europe and NATO were far from the hills of Korea, but if the West failed to respond to Communist aggression in Korea, Truman reasoned, western Europe would also be in danger of Communist attack. Truman quickly got United Nations Secretary General Trygve Lie on side. The USSR was boycotting the UN Security Council in an argument over Communist Chinese membership; the boycott allowed the US to sponsor a series of successful resolutions calling on UN member states to come to the aid of South Korea. American General Douglas MacArthur was named Commander of the UN forces. Britain and Australia were quick to respond, and backroom discussions aimed at forming a division of Commonwealth troops began.

Having cut its military to the bone in the late 1940s, Canada had little to contribute to the defence of South Korea. The government first dispatched three destroyers to Korean waters, then committed a squadron of four engine transports to help the US fly men and supplies to Japan from the west coast of the United States. It was not until 7 August 1950, however, that Prime Minister Louis St. Laurent announced that Canada would send a brigade group to Korea.

The Canadian brigade group was essentially an infantry brigade with field artillery, armour, engineer regiments, and support troops attached. It was to consist of the newly formed 2nd Battalions of the three Active Force infantry regiments and their combat arms counterparts, and would be a formation specifically recruited for Korean service. Though initially known as the Canadian Army Special Force, it was officially designated the 25th Canadian Infantry Brigade Group. General C.G. Foulkes, Chief of the General Staff, had at first mooted the idea of a Special Force for service only in Korea; the Active Force was the only standing army Canada had, he reasoned, and the nation's defences could not be denuded by sending Active Force troops to Korea. In an effort to shorten training time, the government hoped to attract as many army reservists and Second World War veterans as possible to the Special Force. The men would use old, Second World War–era British pattern equipment. Where special Korea volunteers were not available for specific jobs, Active Force soldiers would be selected to fill the positions. For the most part, however, the government did not want the ranks of the Active Force depleted. The Special Force was initially intended as just that — a Special Force — created to serve the needs of a moment. Eventually, it would be replaced by an expanded Active Force.

Minister of National Defence Brooke Claxton personally selected the commander of the Special Force. He was Brigadier John Meredith Rockingham, an Australian by birth who had immigrated to Canada in 1930, joined the militia, and gone overseas with the Victoria-based Canadian Scottish Regiment. By the end of the war he had amassed a distinguished record as a brigade commander. Claxton wanted Rockingham not only for his war record, but because he was a reserve officer; the minister hoped that Rockingham's leadership of the Special Force might draw other reservists to enlist.

Rockingham selected another reserve officer, Lieutenant-Colonel Jim Stone from Edmonton, to command the new 2nd Battalion of the Patricias. Stone was almost forty-one years old. He might have been thought too old for an active battalion command, but he was physically and mentally tough, had commanded the Loyal Edmonton Regiment with great distinction in the Second World War, and was a born warrior leader. In August 1950, Stone was bald, sported a full moustache, and had thick, muscular arms and broad shoulders. He had been awarded a Military Cross and a Distinguished Service Order even before taking command of the Loyal Eddies in Italy; he was awarded a bar to the DSO after taking command. He knew mountain warfare and he knew the Patricias, who had fought alongside the Loyal Eddies in the 2nd Brigade. Though Canadian regiments generally saw themselves as rivals, Stone took to the Patricias easily, as Patricia Jean Pariseau would later recall. At the mess hall at Currie Barracks, Pariseau once commented on the good war record of the Loyal Edmonton Regiment. Despite his career as a Loyal Eddie, Stone clapped Pariseau on the shoulder and told him, "'You're a Patricia now and don't ever forget it.'"[6]

Across the country, potential Special Force recruits lined up at recruiting offices. At first, recruiting officers followed the usual procedures of checking the men's backgrounds, health, and mental and physical fitness before attesting or swearing them in, and sending them off for training. The procedural checks took too long, however; Claxton ordered the recruiters to cut corners wherever possible. As a result, a number of men who were lame, sick, or elderly, or who had jail records, were taken in. The training centres were left with the burden of weeding them out; Stone would continue to send unfit men home from Korea for months after his battalion arrived there in December 1950.

Men enlisted in 2 PPCLI in the summer of 1950 for many of the same reasons that other men had enlisted in the First and Second World Wars: they were bored; they sought adventure and travel; they didn't want to miss a war (especially if they had just missed the last one); they wanted to stay with buddies who were joining; because they believed in a cause. Donald Dickin was working on a construction site in Preston, Ontario, when he heard about the Special Force. He and a friend decided to join up: "We drove down to London [Ontario] on a motorcycle," he recalled. They saw the recruiting officer at 4 p.m. one day and were told to report the next morning for transfer to Camp Petawawa, where their training would begin: "So we were both sworn in, in London . . . we came back home and got everything straightened away, whatever we had . . . not much, and the next day we were off to Petawawa." Not long after, they were sent by train to Calgary: "When we got to Calgary, we were in the Patricias then. They gave us a lecture; who you were going to be and who you had to be."[7]

Calgarian Rod Middleton had been a member of the Calgary Highlanders militia regiment, but he knew the Patricias well because they had been based in Calgary since the end of the war: "I was told at the end of my interview [with an Officer Selection Board] that I was now a member of Princess Patricia's Canadian Light Infantry . . . I was very proud to be selected to join this illustrious regiment."[8]

John Stuber was working in an oilfield when the call for volunteers went out: "I had one brother that was in the service during World War Two and it sounded very adventurous to me and I decided I was going to join the service myself."[9]

Ken Umpherville was working as a labourer on a job site in Calgary when he heard about the Special Force. At first he was undecided about what to do: "I went for a load of gravel and came back . . . and had a smoke, as I had nothing else to do. So the boss came over and he says, 'Uh, you're too young to smoke.' I said, 'If I'm too young to smoke I'm too damned young to work for you.' So I walked off the job and joined the army."[10]

At Calgary's Currie Barracks and at Camp Wainwright, northeast of Edmonton, the tough paratroopers of the 1st Battalion trained the volunteers of the 2nd Battalion, a job the paratroopers weren't particularly fond of. Mel Canfield enlisted in Vancouver on 13 August and was soon shipped to Calgary to begin training. There he met the smartly uniformed soldiers of the 1st Battalion: "They were all so magnificent; jump boots and pressed trousers and pressed shirts and they were angry because we were going to be trained to go to Korea and they were going to have to stay behind. So we didn't get treated too well to start with."[11] On one occasion, Charles Scot-Brown watched a soldier from 1st Battalion try to prepare a small knot of Second World War veterans for their required Tests of Elementary Training. As Scot-Brown recalled, one of the veterans piped up, "'Never mind all that shit, Corporal, we know all about that. Just show us where we got to go and we're all ready to go.'" The Corporal stopped his demonstration and told the men, "'Well, soldier, I'm quite sure you do know it, but I'm being paid to make sure you do know it, so I'm going to make sure that you're going to pass your [tests], or you're going to get the training, because I don't want to be responsible for your deaths.'"[12]

Through August and September 1950, the recruiting continued. Training began at army camps and barracks across the country. Rockingham chose another reservist, the dashing and highly decorated former CO of the Fusiliers Mont Royal, Lieutenant-Colonel Jacques Dextraze, to command the 2nd Battalion of the Van Doos. No reserve officer with credentials comparable to Stone's and Dextraze's could be found to command the 2RCR, so Rockingham selected Lieutenant-Colonel Robert A. Keane from the Directorate of Plans and Operations at Army HQ in Ottawa. Keane had less command experience than his two counterparts, but his leadership skills had been well and truly tested during the Battle of the Scheldt Estuary in the fall of 1944.

P.P.C.L.I.

The North Koreans had no intention of waiting for the small contingent from Canada; as Ottawa had dithered over its ground contribution through June and July, the Communist juggernaut had rolled southwards. Much better trained and armed than the Republic of Korea (ROK) forces, they also overran the handful of US Army troops rushed to Korea from occupation duties in Japan. Other national contingents — notably the British, Australians, and Turks — arrived to help out, while US forces, including a strong contingent of US Marines, prepared to ship out from Hawaii and the US mainland. American fighter-bombers from Japan and US Navy and Royal Navy aircraft also tried to stop the North Koreans. For almost three months, however, the NKPA seemed unstoppable as it drove the ROK Army and their American and UN allies to a small perimeter around the southern port city of Pusan.

Foulkes and Claxton were anxious to concentrate the Special Force in one place as quickly as possible; no single base in Canada, however, was large enough to effectively train an entire brigade group and remain free of ice and snow over the winter. So the government arranged with the Americans to use Fort Lewis, a sprawling US army base located near Seattle, Washington. The components of the Special Force made ready to transfer to Fort Lewis from bases across Canada before the end of November 1950. At about the same time, those men surplus to the 2nd Battalions were formed into 3rd Battalions. Before they did, the war in Korea took a dramatic and sudden turn, to the benefit of the UN. On 15 September 1950, the 1st US Marine Division made a daring landing at the small port of Inchon, southwest of the occupied South Korean capital of Seoul. Inchon was quickly taken, the Marines advanced on Seoul, and the long North Korean supply lines from the 38th parallel to the Pusan perimeter were cut. The North Korean army virtually melted away. United Nations forces, led by the US Army and Marines, crossed the 38th parallel and drove north to the Yalu River — the border between North Korea and China. It suddenly seemed as if a UN victory was just a month or so away.

For several weeks after the virtual collapse of the North Korean forces, the Canadian government tried to back out of its commitment to supply ground troops for the war. At the time, Canada was obligated to raise a brigade group for service in Europe as part of its contribution to the new NATO alliance. It tried to convince the US to give its blessing for Canada to send the Special Force to Europe instead of Korea. The Americans, however, insisted that Canada send at least one battalion for what was increasingly likely to be occupation duty in Korea. On Rockingham's advice, Foulkes chose to send the 2nd Battalion of the PPCLI. As Rocky put it, "their training was as well advanced as any other unit in the Brigade and . . . they were closest to the West Coast."[13]

Thus, while the rest of the Special Force concentrated at Fort Lewis and prepared for several months of training, 2 PPCLI got ready to depart for Korea. The battalion was only partially trained, and was certainly not ready for the kind of war, nor the type of enemy, it would encounter. Many men unfit for combat operations still remained in the battalion, and some of the equipment they brought with them to Korea would prove totally unsuitable for war. But then, the UN was winning the war in Korea in mid-November 1950, and 2 PPCLI would not likely be called upon to fight. Reports circulated about a clandestine but massive infiltration of Chinese "volunteers" making its way across the Yalu River from Manchuria into the frozen, tree-covered hills of North Korea. But UN Commander General Douglas MacArthur and the US military did not appear to be alarmed. If they weren't worried, why should Ottawa be concerned?

P.P.C.L.I.

On 25 November 1950, the 2nd Battalion, Princess Patricia's Canadian Light Infantry, along with several hundred US soldiers, boarded the US Navy transport *Private Joe P. Martinez* at Seattle and left the US West Coast for a twenty-four-day voyage to Pusan, Korea. They made short stops at Pearl Harbor, Yokohama, and Kobe. The *Martinez* was a Second World War Liberty Ship of 7,500 tons displacement. Small and overcrowded, it was no luxury cruise ship. "It was just a little thing," Ken Gawthorne would later recall. "You can tell how damn small it is when they name it after a private."[14] "They put us in like sardines," Donald Hibbs remembered. "It was the worst trip I ever had. I got on the boat I weighed 210. I got off I weighed 168." The food was awful, the quarters close, and the below decks stunk from unwashed bodies and seasick men. Then there were the late-fall Pacific storms. William J. Chrysler rarely suffered from seasickness; as a result, he was ordered to clean the toilets:

> We had one hell of a storm and that ship was being tossed all over the place. They had to batten down all the hatches. Even the sailors were sick. I got a pretty cast-iron stomach. I can pretty well take it all. One of the sergeants came to me he says, "Bill, you look pretty good, go up to the heads [ship's toilets] and help clean up that mess." I went up to those heads, took one look and I started to get sick. I took off. He wouldn't know who I was. He was sick too.[15]

The *Martinez* stopped briefly at Pearl Harbor, then crossed to Yokohama, arriving on 13 December. After a brief stopover there and at Kobe, they crossed the Straits of Tsushima and arrived in Pusan on the afternoon of the eighteenth. Most of the men were shocked by the sights, smells, and sounds of grinding poverty, overcrowding, filth, and pollution everywhere in the busy harbour.

Koreans in rags jammed the narrow streets; soldiers and army vehicles were everywhere; the air stank of raw sewage. Rod Middleton would later recall:

> As our troop ship . . . neared the southern shore of Korea on a dreary, drizzly day we stood lining the rails, wondering what lay ahead of us . . . The mystique was soon to disappear when we got our first whiff of the place. A strong smell of sewage struck our nostrils. Welcome to the land of "Honey Wagons," night soil, soft coal fires and the stench of too many people crammed into the refugee-filled and overcrowded city.[16]

But there was also a small welcoming party — the mayor of Pusan and a ragged group of Korean schoolgirls waving Union Jacks. The mayor welcomed Stone on behalf of the Korean people while a military band blared out, "If I Knew You Were Coming I'd Have Baked a Cake," which they played for every arriving troopship. After four hours of unloading men and supplies, the battalion was trucked to the small island of Mok-to at the entrance to Pusan harbour. This was to be their base and quarters until they could move north of Pusan to finish their combat training.

Stone had seen plenty of poverty amidst war in the Italian campaign, but he had never seen anything like Korea in December 1950. Only a few days after he arrived he wrote Rockingham:

> Korea is a land of filth and poverty. Social amenities of a desirable type are lacking . . . Lack of buildings will preclude the showing of movies, particularly in the winter. Beer is in fair supply but the alcoholics in the battalion are already drinking the very poor liquor brewed in local bathtubs. Diseases, except venereal ones probably will not be a problem during the winter but as all fertilizing of fields is done with human excreta there is no doubt that there will be a health problem in the spring and summer.[17]

Stone was prophetic. Korea was a breeding ground for diseases, especially hemorrhagic fever, malaria, and cholera. It was hot and muggy in the summer but extremely cold in the winter; the men had their hands full just trying to survive the weather, let alone the enemy.

When the Patricias had set out from Seattle, the UN had appeared to be winning the war in Korea. The men had expected little worse than boring and prolonged occupation duty. By the time they arrived, however, the military picture had changed drastically. On 25 November, advanced UN units nearing the Yalu River came under heavy and sustained attack by Chinese troops who had crossed the frozen Yalu by the hundreds of thousands and then regrouped in the thick coniferous forests south of the river. The UN forces began to fall back, first in orderly retreat, then in a rout. The green draftees of the US Army panicked and ran. The US Marines and the British troops withdrew in a more orderly fashion, but withdraw they did. By mid-December, the Chinese drive was nearing the 38th parallel and threatening to recapture Seoul. The prospect of UN defeat loomed again. Virtually as soon as the PPCLI arrived, US Lieutenant-General Walton H. Walker, commanding general of the US Eighth Army, and responsible to MacArthur for the overall UN ground forces in Korea, called on the PPCLI to move quickly to the front near Seoul. Stone knew his Patricias were not yet ready for battle. He had brought instructions from Ottawa giving him permission to refuse any assignment he might deem overly dangerous to his battalion, and he was prepared to confront Walker with them. On 21 December, he met Walker, described the state of the battalion, and gained Walker's commitment not to send the Patricias to the front until Stone believed them to be ready.

For most of the next week, Stone and his company commanders worked the men hard. After a long ocean voyage, they needed toughening up with route marches, plenty of physical training, and frequent climbs in the hills around Pusan. Stone knew the Patricias would need to be in top physical condition to master the steep hills of central Korea. As they trained, Stone sent some men back to Canada. These were the final remnants of the hurried recruitment conducted back in August and September. During this period of intense physical activity, Stone later wrote, "bad legs, wheezy lungs and faint and weak hearts were exposed . . . many sorry specimens of manhood were returned to Canada."[18]

On 27 December, the Patricias moved north to Miryang, where they spent an additional month adjusting to the new American equipment they had acquired in Korea to replace some of the obsolete British pattern kit they had used in the Second World War. American 2.36-inch "Bazooka" rocket launchers, useless against the T-34 tanks that the Russians had given to the North Koreans, but good against bunkers, replaced the PPCLI's venerable PIAT anti-tank weapons. Later, these early-model Bazookas would be replaced with the superior 3.5-inch models. The Patricias practiced with their now venerable 17-pounder anti-tank guns (later replaced with 75-millimetre recoilless rifles) and their new 60- and 81-millimetre mortars. Their brand-new American SCR 300 radio sets had much better range and reception in mountain country than the radios they brought from Canada. But they kept their basic personal weapons, the First World War–era Lee-Enfield bolt-action rifle and the British Sten gun, a Second World War improvisation that was far less reliable and had less hitting power than the US "Tommy guns."

On 15 February 1951, the PPCLI joined the 27th British Commonwealth Infantry Brigade (27 BCIB) under command of Brigadier Basil Aubrey Coad, who was replaced in late March by Brigadier B.A. Burke. The Commonwealth Brigade consisted of 2 PPCLI, 3rd Battalion Royal Australian Regiment (3 RAR), 1st Battalion Middlesex Regiment (British army), 1st Battalion Argyll and Sutherland Highlanders (British army), 16th Field Regiment Royal New Zealand Artillery, and 60th Indian Field Ambulance.

It fought as part of IX Corps, US Eighth Army, under commanding general Matthew Ridgway, who had replaced Walker after the latter had been killed in a road accident. The PPCLI would eventually split away from the Commonwealth Brigade to join the rest of the Canadian troops when the 25th Canadian Infantry Brigade arrived from Fort Lewis. Eventually, the Canadian Brigade would join with the British, Australians, New Zealanders, and Indians to form 1st Commonwealth Division.

On 21 February 1951, Ridgway launched a major UN counterattack, dubbed "Operation Killer." Using their complete command of the skies and overwhelming superiority in artillery, UN troops pushed back the Chinese with heavy casualties. The 27th British Commonwealth Brigade fought in the midst of the battle from the very beginning; the Patricias came under enemy fire on 21 February as the brigade's van advanced north from the small village of Sangsok. In the next few weeks, the PPCLI learned how to fight in the Korean hills: never advance on a ridgeline, never use roads on valley floors unless the hills were cleared first, never underestimate the Chinese and their ability to set ambushes or to hold up entire companies with a few well-positioned riflemen or machine gunners. The Chinese were retreating and regrouping, aiming for one last try at driving the UN out of the Korean peninsula and winning the war. Like the Germans in Sicily and Italy, they were determined to make their enemies pay for every metre of ground.

The Chinese were excellent at siting automatic weapons along possible approach lines, and at using the terrain to conceal their defensive positions. They built dummy defensive positions on hilltops to attract enemy fire, but put their main defences just below the summits of the hills. They defended reverse slopes to pick off enemy troops who showed themselves above the ridgelines. They patrolled aggressively, and they almost always fought at night and at close quarters to neutralize the UN's superiority in air and fire power and crew-served weapons such as heavy mortars and heavy machine guns. Corporal Kerry Dunphy told Canadian war correspondent Pierre Berton that the Chinese were "sporting soldiers"; he was personally convinced that if they wanted to, they could "[hold] the hills of Korea indefinitely."[19]

The final major Chinese offensive of the Korean War began on the night of 21/22 April 1951, with a two-pronged attack aimed at splitting the UN front. The Chinese intended to punch a hole in the UN lines northeast of Seoul, pour through the gap, and outflank the city. In the sector where 27 BCIB was in reserve, the main Chinese assault fell on the 6th Republic of Korea Division, some twenty-five kilometres to the north of the Patricias. The South Koreans broke, and began to stream southward through the Kap'yong River valley. To the west, the Chinese hit the 29th British Infantry Brigade, virtually wiping out the 1st Battalion of the Gloucestershire Regiment. Suddenly, the Commonwealth Brigade was the UN's only real hope to stem the Chinese advance. At 0400 on 23 April, the New Zealand gunners who had been assigned to the 6th ROK Division withdrew from the remnants of that smashed formation and drove south towards Kap'yong to rejoin the Commonwealth Brigade.

Just north of the village, the Kap'yong River, not much larger than a stream, joined a small stream known as the Somok-tong. The junction of the two created a Y-shaped depression in the rugged, scrub-covered hills that dominated the country all around. From the valley floor to the highest peaks, the ground rose by some 600 metres. The terrain, and the direction from which the Chinese advance was expected, dictated Brigadier Burke's battle plan.

Burke ordered the 3 RAR, backed by C Company of the US 72nd Heavy Tank Battalion, to dig in on the peak and forward slopes of Hill 504, the highest position to the east of the Y-shaped valley. He positioned Stone's Patricias on Hill 677, to the west of the Y, about three kilometres from the Australians. When Jim Stone received Burke's order to place his battalion on Hill 677, he organized a complete reconnaissance of possible Chinese attack approaches. Brian Munro accompanied Stone:

> It was a very large recce [reconnaissance] party. There was virtually almost every line officer in the battalion on it. We went up in Jeeps . . . went forward of [the hill] looked back to see how it would look from the enemy's point of view and by that method [Stone] decided where his companies would be and the company commanders decided where their platoons would be.[20]

Stone placed his companies in a rough semicircle, with A Company on the lower slopes of the hill, facing the Australians; C Company on the north side of the hill; B Company just to the west of C Company; and D Company southwest of B Company. The rugged terrain of the hill made it virtually impossible for the companies to fire in direct support of each other, so Stone ordered each company commander to ensure that he positioned his platoons where they could support each other. The men sited their artillery, heavy mortars, and medium machine guns to rake areas between the companies should the Chinese begin to infiltrate. A and B Companies were given two medium machine guns each, while D Company was given a single gun. The mortar platoon, with its half tracks mounting Browning .30 and .50 machine guns, and Stone's tactical HQ, were dug in on a low rise south of the battalion position. Brigadier Burke also assigned a company each of the 2nd Chemical Heavy Mortar Battalion, with twelve 4.2-inch mortars, to the 3 RAR and the Patricias. The defenders of Kap'yong could also call in fire from two batteries of the US Army's 105-millimetre self-propelled guns, and a battery of the 213th Medium Artillery Regiment, firing US 155-millimetre "Long Toms."

It was hot and dry as the Patricias climbed the long slopes of the hill, hauled up weapons, ammunition, food and water, and communications equipment, dug their gun pits and slit trenches, and sited their weapons. Donald Dickin was there: "I can remember it took us all day to get to the top of the hill. We walked our asses off up there, [when] we got to the top we were tired and they said that we had to hold these positions."[21] On the road below the Patricias, the remnants of the shattered ROK division and thousands of Korean refugees streamed past to the rear. As he tried to dig his slit trench, Brian Munro watched the flood of humanity: "It was very difficult to dig there. We never really got properly dug in. The slits were shallow . . . We could see ROK soldiers retreating and they were all mixed up with civilians and undoubtedly there were infiltrators . . . but there really wasn't much we could do about it. These were long lines of people wandering through the valley."[22]

Just after midnight on 23 April 1951, the Chinese hit the Australians on Hill 504. Blowing whistles and bugles, swarms of Chinese infantry surged forward and rushed the RAR slit trenches behind a shower of mortar rounds and grenades. Many were carrying Bangalore torpedoes. The Australian CO managed to call for defensive artillery fire before communications with Brigade HQ broke down. Then the Chinese infiltrated into the New Zealanders' gun lines, firing on the gun crews and forcing Burke to pull the gunners back to the rear of his HQ.

Stone's men could hear the fire of the automatic weapons and the exploding mortar and artillery shells. The sky lit up with tracer fire and explosions. But no one had any idea of the intensity of the hand-to-hand battle that raged just three kilometres away. Chinese troops climbed onto the American tanks in an attempt to fire into their viewing slits or force grenades down their hatches; Chinese and Australians killed each other with grenades, rifles, and automatic weapons at close range. Daylight brought no respite for the defenders; by mid-afternoon, Burke ordered them to withdraw. The Australians pulled back under mortar and machine-gun fire, their vehicles protected by the US tanks. The Aussies had suffered thirty-one killed, fifty-eight wounded, and had lost three men as prisoners.

Watching and listening through the night, Stone decided on

the morning of the twenty-fourth that an attack on his battalion would most likely come against the eastern slope of Hill 677. He ordered the Patricias' B Company to move to the south of A Company to protect the "back door to the battalion area," as he put it. Just as B Company was digging in, the men saw large numbers of Chinese infantry moving in and around the hamlet of Naechon, about 300 metres below their positions. Then, at 2130, just as the Australian withdrawal was completed, about 400 Chinese infantry were spotted in a valley near B Company. Company commander Major C.V. Lilley called for artillery and mortar fire, but the Chinese attacked immediately.

One sergeant later described the initial assault to Canadian war correspondent Bill Boss:

> They were on top of our positions before we knew it. They're quiet as mice with those rubber shoes of theirs and then there's a whistle. They get up with a shout about [ten] feet from our positions and come in. The first wave throws its grenades, fires its weapons and goes to the ground. It is followed by a second[,] which does the same, and then a third comes up. They just keep coming.[23]

The sergeant threw his bayoneted rifle at the attackers like a spear when his ammunition ran out.

Within minutes, the forward platoon, No. 6 Platoon, commanded by Lieutenant H. Ross, was in danger of being overrun. Ross ordered his men back. By the light of flares, tracers, and exploding grenades, they worked their way back to the B Company area. Bren gunner Private W.R. Mitchell had been wounded in the first moment of the attack, but he stayed at his post and poured a withering fire at several waves of advancing Chinese troops. His actions allowed his comrades to withdraw and brought him an immediate Distinguished Conduct Medal for bravery under fire. Clarence Ruttan was in No. 5 Platoon as the stragglers came in:

"They fell back on us, on 5 Platoon, but Corporal Evans was wounded . . . in both legs. He asked them to leave him behind and get out themselves. There was two, three come through that were wounded." Then the survivors of No. 6 Platoon regrouped, asked for volunteers from Ruttan's platoon, and fought their way back. "We found Corporal Evans shot through the head," recalled Ruttan. "He was shot right through the hat badge . . . they could have taken him prisoner but they didn't. They shot him."[24]

The other B Company platoons fought on. Donald Hibbs was with one of them: "It was dusty, dirty, noisy, scary. This is the first time you can really see your enemy. Really up close . . . they were really close." He took some comfort in the knowledge that his company commander, Major Lilley, was an experienced infantryman: "Lilley was an old war vet from the Second World War and he knew his things backwards and I believe that he probably helped us save our lives because nobody would disappoint the major."[25]

In the D Company area, Bren gunners Ken Barwise, Jim Waniandy, and several riflemen found themselves in front of a large group of Chinese grenadiers. "We opened up with our Brens," Waniandy later recalled. They started "falling all over."[26] Barwise killed at least six Chinese in one of the attacks directed at D Company. "They kept coming in waves," he remembered.[27]

While B Company was under attack, some 500 Chinese soldiers tried to infiltrate behind Stone's tactical headquarters. The Chinese were silhouetted against the Kap'yong River as they approached. Stone later described what happened: "The mortar platoon, located with HQ, was mounted for travelling on twelve half tracks. Each vehicle was equipped with one .50- and one .30-calibre machine gun . . . Fire was held until the Chinese had broken through the trees about two hundred metres away. Eight machine guns[28] cut loose together."[29] The Chinese were cut down.

The main Chinese assaults after midnight on the twenty-fifth focused on D Company's No. 10 and No. 12 platoons. At 0130 they hit No. 10 Platoon, commanded by Lieutenant Mike Levy, on the western tip of Hill 677. About 200 Chinese infantry came rushing in from the west and poured heavy rifle and machine-gun fire into the Patricias' position. Then they attacked a No. 12 Platoon machine gun supporting Levy's men, killing Bruce MacDonald and Maurice Carr with a fusillade of Burp (submachine) gun fire. Waniandy was in the thick of the fighting:

> The charging Chinese make one hell of a lot of noise, banging bamboo sticks together, rattling noise makers and shouting . . . As they come forward our booby traps are exploding. Our Vickers machine gun begins to fire but does not last long. Mortars rain down in front of us and there is one hell of a lot of noise. I am scared. The Chinese . . . begin to infiltrate right into our position. I remember looking at Private Lessard, at the Bren gun. He takes a direct hit in the head. His face is smashed to hell, contorted blood and mashed flesh — it literally disintegrates in front of my face. I can't remember anything after that.[30]

By 0300, No. 12 Platoon had been overrun, opening a gaping hole in the company's defence perimeter. Lieutenant Mike Levy's No. 10 Platoon was engaged on three sides and just hanging on. If they were driven out, D Company would be lost. At D Company HQ, acting company commander Captain J.G.W. "Wally" Mills asked Stone over the radio if he could pull D Company back. Stone refused: "I told him to stay there, that nobody could pull out."[31] Stone knew that if the enemy took the D Company positions, they would break into the battalion's perimeter, overrun the hill, and wipe out the Patricias. Levy called for fire support to within twenty yards of his own positions and warned his men to stay deep in their slit trenches. A torrent of fire exploded all around Levy's platoon; New Zealand and American gunners worked like fiends to fire more than 4,000 shells at the hill. According to the Patricia war diary, "most of this fire was concentrated on [No. 10

Platoon], the most heavily engaged platoon of the [Company]." Many of the shells burst just below treetop height, shredding the Chinese ranks while the Canadians hunkered down in their slit trenches. The shelling stopped the Chinese cold. Their immediate attack was broken up; Levy's platoon emerged from its slit trenches and fought on. The 27 BCIB war diary recorded that the shelling "was completely successful inflicting heavy enemy casualties and daylight found the Canadian company still in position and holding their ground."[32]

The Chinese pulled back as dawn approached. The Patricias still held Hill 677, but they were cut off, almost out of ammunition, short of almost everything else, and dead tired. Levy's platoon suffered harassing fire all day. Stone radioed for an airdrop; six hours later, a flight of United States Air Force C-119 Flying Boxcars flew low over the Canadian positions as loadmasters kicked containers of food, ammunition, and water down onto Hill 677. Virtually all of it fell within the Patricia positions. The battle for Hill 677 — the Battle of Kap'yong — was over; the next day the Patricias pulled out, relieved by troops of the 1st US Cavalry Division. They had lost ten killed and 23 wounded. Ken Barwise, Wally Mills, and many others were decorated for bravery.

One American chronicler of the Korean War has written: "The holding action of the Commonwealth Brigade at Kapyong [*sic*] had been decisive. It plugged the hole left by the ROK 6th Division and blocked the [Chinese] long enough for the 24th [US Infantry] Division to withdraw."[33] The holding action also allowed the UN Command to bring up reinforcements from the 1st US Cavalry Division and deploy them to the south of the village to block any further Chinese advance. Kap'yong gave the new Eighth Army Commander, James A. Van Fleet, time to set up a new defensive line north of Seoul, withdraw his units to that line in good order, save the capital, and prepare his counterattack. (Van Fleet had succeeded Matthew Ridgway, who became overall UN Commander after President Truman fired General Douglas MacArthur for insubordination on 11 April.) For imaginative and gutsy leadership, Stone received a second bar to his DSO. For the forty-eight hours they had bought the UN at Kap'yong, 2 PPCLI, 3 RAR, and A Company of the US 72nd Heavy Tank Battalion were awarded a US Presidential Unit Citation. Battle honours were traditionally approved by the Crown; because the Americans gave the PPCLI the citation outright, the Canadian Army did not let the Patricias display that honour on the Regimental Colour until June 1956, when the blue streamer representing the citation was affixed to it. To this day, the PPCLI is the only regiment in Canadian history to have been so honoured. Almost fifty years later, Chuck Jones summed up Kap'yong: "They told us we made a good stand at Kap'yong. We stayed in our positions and returned the fire . . . the experience of the Second World War vets, from the CO on down [made the difference]. Stay in your positions . . . keep your head down, the safest place to be is in your trench, don't get up on top of the ground and move around."[34]

P.P.C.L.I.

After Kap'yong, Van Fleet organized a new UN offensive, dubbed "Operation Piledriver." The offensive began on 22 May and lasted until 8 July, during which time it pushed the enemy back some seventy kilometres, killing tens of thousands of Chinese soldiers in the process. The Patricias took part in the advance under command of 27 BCIB, then joined the newly created 28 BCIB when it assumed the mantle of 27 BCIB in May; the British component of 27 BCIB, meanwhile, was transferred out of Korea on rotation. In the meantime, Rockingham and the rest of the 25th Canadian Infantry Brigade had arrived in Korea in early May. On 10 June, Stone and his 2 PPCLI rejoined their Canadian comrades for the first time since sailing from Seattle the previous November. On 19 June, the Canadian Brigade moved to the area known as the "iron triangle" to begin patrolling the Chorwon Plain, a vital Chinese staging area in Central Korea. The weather was unusually hot and muggy; many soldiers were laid low by heat exhaustion and illness. The stench of the rice paddies in the lowlands and the swarms of insects made life even more unpleasant than usual.

On 30 June, General Ridgway was authorized by Washington to make a radio broadcast inviting the Communists to begin cease-fire talks. Under the intense pressure of Operation Piledriver, the Chinese and North Koreans agreed; the talks began on 10 July at the small central Korean village of Kaesong, two days after Piledriver ended. The negotiations progressed in fits and starts until 22 August, when the Communists called them off on the pretext that UN aircraft had violated the airspace over Kaesong. In fact, the end of Operation Piledriver had eased the pressure on the Communists, who then saw no need to continue the discussions.

The Patricias and the rest of the Canadian brigade were in corps reserve towards the end of July. It was a good time for them to join the rest of the Commonwealth contingent to form the new Commonwealth Division. The Commonwealth formations gathered near the town of Tokchong, and, in a brief ceremony on 28 July, the division was born. British Major-General A.J.H. Cassels was the General Officer Commanding. His divisional staff were drawn from the participating units — the 25th Canadian Infantry Brigade, the 28th British Commonwealth Infantry Brigade (consisting of British, Australian, and New Zealand troops), the 29th British Infantry Brigade, a battalion from Belgium, and a number of attached artillery, armour, anti-aircraft, engineer, and medical formations. The Commonwealth Division was assigned a ten-kilometre section of the UN front along the Imjin River. The 1st ROK Division was on their left, and the 25th US Infantry Division on their right.

At the end of August, Van Fleet launched the first of a new series of attacks. On 3 October, the 1st Commonwealth Division, along with four other divisions under the command of the 1st US Corps, drove across the Imjin River in Operation Commando. They established a new UN defensive front line — the Jamestown Line — that ran northeast-southwest to the west of Hill 355. Because of its resemblance to the Rock of Gibraltar, the troops called this hill Little Gibraltar. The Jamestown Line, intended more as a trip-wire than a strong defensive position, stayed the UN front line for the rest of the war. Henceforth, both sides patrolled no-man's land, raided each other's positions, and sometimes even wrested a hilltop or a portion of a ridge from the enemy. The Korean War, however, became a war of waiting and attrition, especially after armistice talks resumed at Panmunjŏm on 25 October 1951.

When the Canadian Brigade was allotted its place in the Jamestown Line in the fall of 1951, the men got down to the task of building the positions in which they would eat and sleep — and defend at the cost of their lives — for the balance of the war. The line snaked over a sea of hills, along a ridgeline overlooking the Samichon creek, and across a valley from the Communist front line. Unlike the western front of the First World War, there was no practical way to build continuous trench lines in these mountains. Instead, select hilltops were fortified with circular defensive trenches, barbed wire, minefields, and pre-sited firing lines for machine guns. The valleys between these hills were strewn with barbed wire and minefields, and were zeroed in by field artillery batteries and heavy mortars. Searchlights were installed at fixed locations to enable no-man's land to be flooded with light in the event the men heard enemy patrols. Tanks were dug in at strategic positions to give the infantry extra firepower in the defence or to add their guns to the field artillery when needed. Bunkers were dug on reverse slopes for sleeping and eating, and roads were pushed forward as far as possible to bring in supplies. Korean porters usually carried the supplies the last few kilometres up the hills. To the rear, an elaborate system of medical facilities was constructed, from small Regimental Aid Posts to mobile surgical facilities. Casualties were evacuated overland by porters and Jeeps or flown out by US helicopters. Eventually, rear-area recreation facilities were constructed, a leave policy was put into place based on time in the line, and a rotation policy was adopted in which battalions (or regiments) would serve a year at the front, then be rotated back to Canada as a unit and replaced with another battalion from the same regiment.

The peace talks at Panmunjŏm dragged on for nearly two years. One reason why the Communists dragged their feet for so long may well have been the UN's policy of restricting front-line commanders from engaging in any sort of extended offensive operations. As far as the UN Command was concerned, the Jamestown Line was the farthest forward that UN troops would go. This was in line with the policy — no doubt the best policy under the circumstances — that Korea was to be a limited war fought not to obtain a "victory" but only to restore the status quo that had existed before the Communist invasion. The restriction, however, had the effect of taking the pressure off the Communists, forcing the UN troops to fight a strictly defensive war along their front lines. The Chinese took advantage of the respite by bringing in vast numbers of artillery pieces and self-propelled guns — greatly increasing their firepower — and by launching frequent night attacks against the UN front lines. In these continuing night actions, the overwhelming UN strength in artillery and air power was cancelled by the darkness. The UN troops were forced to fight the war according to Chinese terms for the balance of the fighting in Korea. More Canadians were killed in action in Korea after the start of the peace talks at Panmunjŏm than in the first phases of the war.

P.P.C.L.I.

For the Patricias, as for the rest of the Canadians, the Korean War after October 1951 was a war of patrolling no-man's land and defending against company-size attacks at night, and occasional forays against the enemy's lines. It was also a war of boredom, extreme cold in the winter, extreme heat in the summer, illness, and irrelevance. Most of the original Special Force volunteers in 2 PPCLI missed the later phases of the Korean War; they were rotated back to Canada beginning in mid-October 1951 and replaced by the 1st Battalion. The men of 1 PPCLI were the trained paratroopers of the Mobile Striking Force who had given 2 PPCLI its initial training in Canada in the late summer and fall of 1950. They remained in Korea under the command of Lieutenant-Colonel Norman Wilson-Smith, DSO, MBE, and Lieutenant-Colonel J.R. Cameron, OBE, until they were relieved by 3 PPCLI in November 1952. Wilson-Smith and Cameron were both experienced officers who had served in command and staff appointments and who had been in action in Europe in the Second World War.

In the final Patricia rotation of the war, completed on 3 November 1952, 3 PPCLI took over the 1st Battalion's positions on the Jamestown Line. They would hold them until after the armistice on 27 July 1953, when they were sent back to Canada. Commanded at first by Lieutenant-Colonel H.F. Wood, CD, then by Lieutenant-Colonel M.F. Maclachlan, OBE, MC, CD, the 3rd Battalions of the three Active Force infantry regiments had been formed in the fall of 1950 from the surplus of volunteers left over after the 2nd Battalions took shape. Active Force volunteers, and others, such as platoon commanders recently graduated from Royal Military College, supplemented their ranks. In each rotation, battalion members who had served in Korea for only a short time stayed on to be transferred to the newly arriving battalion when their original units went back to Canada.

In static warfare of the type fought on the Jamestown Line from October 1951 to July 1953, soldiers need to maintain constant guard against the enemy drawing near to their defences, whether to snatch a prisoner for information, reconnoiter for weaknesses, or launch a surprise attack, especially at night. The best way to guard against such eventualities has always been to try to dominate "no man's land," particularly during the hours of darkness, by patrolling as far forward as possible. Soldiers of all command ranks in Korea hotly debated issues of the amount and frequency of patrolling necessary, the size of forces to be sent, and what kind of special training, if any, they should receive. Many of these issues were decided not by an established patrol doctrine, but by the personal views of corps or division commanders. Rockingham and his two successors, Brigadier M.P. Bogert and Brigadier J.V. Allard, had no say in the matter; neither did any of the battalion commanders. They just took orders from their superiors. Until Allard took command of the Canadian Brigade in early 1953, however, not one of the senior Canadian commanders saw the need for specialized training in the craft of mounting infantry patrols by night.

Night after night, patrols went out from the UN and Communist lines. The Chinese usually sent larger parties than the Canadians, but the Canadians could often rely on pre-sited artillery or tank fire for support if they ran into difficulties. Sometimes there were no clashes between the opposing forces. At other times, the fighting in the dark, somewhere near the Samichon, was both vicious and deadly. On the night of 15/16 October 1952, Sergeant John Richardson was leading a twenty-five-man fighting patrol mounted by No. 12 Platoon, D Company of 1 PPCLI. The patrol mission was to capture a prisoner and to determine enemy dispositions. Richardson heard Chinese digging and decided to call down artillery fire on the approximate position of the noise. He reached for his signaller's microphone. "Just then," he later recalled, "a shadowy form came towards us and I reckoned it was one of ours. 'Where the hell do you think you're going?'" Richardson called out. That was a mistake. "It turned out he was a scout for the . . . enemy patrol and he couldn't get his Burp gun in action."[35] Shooting broke out immediately. The signaller's radio was shot off his back as the enemy scout disappeared into the night. The patrol Bren gunner, Private C.H. Chute from the Maritimes, hammered away with his weapon. He shot down many Chinese, but Lance Corporal Johnstone was killed by small-arms fire.

The Patricia patrol was outnumbered and outgunned. Richardson and two other men, Sergeant Rocky Prentice and Corporal D.P. Hastings, were armed with two US rapid-fire carbines and a Tommy gun. They provided covering fire for the rest of the patrol as Chute led them into a defensive circle on a nearby knoll. Then, Hastings was killed, Prentice took a bullet in the hip, and Richardson, already shot in the stomach, was hit with grenade fragments; Richardson and Prentice were barely able to crawl toward the other men. Led by Corporal Pahall, the survivors edged slowly out of the area as friendly artillery fire began to explode in the vicinity of the Chinese. Eventually, the patrol survivors met a rescue party that had come forward from the line.[36] For his bravery and leadership in trying to cover the withdrawal of his men that night, Richardson was awarded a Distinguished Conduct Medal.

The Patricias were not properly equipped for a war of patrolling and defending against Chinese mass night attacks. Their basic weapons stemmed from another era. The problem began with the Lee-Enfield No. 4 Mk I, a bolt-action rifle. In the hands of an expert marksman, the Lee-Enfield was effective between about 500 and 900 metres; in the two world wars, it had proved itself the equal to any bolt-action rifle in the world. But no bolt-action rifle in Korea could throw enough lead at the enemy, quickly enough, to defend against the sudden night attacks from just outside the defensive perimeter that the Chinese favoured. The problem was compounded by the fact that large numbers of the Chinese were armed with submachine guns. Canadian riflemen were at a serious disadvantage in the close-in fighting of a Chinese night assault, as Donald Hibbs found out: "We were up against Chinese that had machine guns, like burp guns . . . and hand guns that were automatic. You had no chance. You [had to] hit them with your first round . . . our guys were good shots because those guys were all [equipped with] automatic weapons and it was scary."[37] Hibbs was not alone in his views. Lieutenant-Colonel K.L. Campbell, sent from Ottawa to evaluate field conditions in Korea, reported that the Lee-Enfield was "almost useless . . . except as a personal weapon for troops not manning the defensive positions, for example, troops in the echelons." What was needed, Campbell urged, was "a fully automatic short range weapon of short overall length and with light magazines of a shape easy to carry."[38]

The troops didn't have to be told that there were better weapons available to help keep them alive on patrol or during Chinese attacks. For most of their time on the Jamestown Line, those weapons were readily available from their neighbours, the US 25th Infantry Division, and later the 1st US Marine Division. There were three weapons of choice: the M1 Garand, a .30-calibre, gas-operated, semi-automatic rifle; the M2 Carbine, also a .30-calibre weapon, but shorter and lighter with full automatic capability; and the venerable Tommy gun, a .45-calibre submachine gun.

Colonel Roger Rowley, the Director of Infantry for the Canadian Army, thought the US M1 was a much better rifle for Korea than the Lee-Enfield. He wrote to Ottawa that the Lee-Enfield did not "produce an adequate rate of fire," while the American rifle, "carefully maintained and nursed," would put out "a much more adequate volume of fire."[39] Given an easy availability of whiskey and beer in the Canadian lines — and the virtually dry conditions the US Army imposed in its areas — it wasn't long before a thriving trade began in arms for booze. "There were a lot of guys who wanted to get their hands on US equipment, especially the automatics," Stanley Carmichael of 1 PPCLI would later recall.[40] Don Bateman of 3 PPCLI remembers that it was "common in Korea for the members of [my] platoon to . . . bargain with the Americans to get access to their weapons."[41] On orders from Ottawa, Stone and his successors discouraged this unofficial upgrading of weapons, but it was virtually unstoppable. Lieutenant Ken Robertson of 1 PPCLI was one of the many officers who made sure he had the best weapon available. He carried the M2: "The Carbine that I had originally got had only a ten round mag in it. So I got two 30 round mags and taped them back to back so there were 60 rounds in the weapon at all times." This particular carbine (unlike most) was not designed to fire on full automatic, and its low muzzle velocity reduced its hitting power. But Robertson found a way to address that problem: "The solution to the lighter hitting weight was neatly solved by taking my trusty American bayonet and notching the head of every slug, which we were not supposed to do but that's what we did. If I did shoot somebody, he would stay shot."[42]

Problems with outmoded, ineffective, even dangerous kit were not limited to the Lee-Enfield. The men despised their Sten guns. The Sten was a cheap, mass-produced stopgap weapon, made by the British in the Second World War. When Lieutenant-Colonel D.A.G. Waldock, Deputy Director of Armament Development for the Canadian Army, visited Korea to check weapons performance in the field in 1952, he reported: "Almost without exception, personnel complained that [the Sten] was generally unreliable . . . the mere appearance of the weapon had a poor psychological effect on the men and the men had no confidence in it." As one officer put it: "this was a cheap 'backs to the wall' weapon produced to meet an emergency situation, so let's put it away until we have our backs to the wall again."[43] The troops also refused to wear their First World War–era "tin hat" helmets, almost useless in Korea. Eventually, the officers gave up trying to force them to do so. Even the basic winter jacket and pants were deficient. Made of nylon, they "swished" in cold weather and produced sparks from static electricity build-up — both dead giveaways on night patrol. They also burned easily from cigarette ash or campfire sparks.

Many of these equipment deficiencies added to the discomfort of living on the Jamestown Line; some added to the risk. After the fall of 1951, however, the worst problem for these men was that they were increasingly ignored by the folks back home. Once the war lost its dramatic quality — large, sweeping, Communist attacks down the peninsula and equally sweeping UN attacks back up — and settled into a humdrum series of raids and patrols, the media lost interest. Korea became "the forgotten war." When Lieutenant Robert Frost eventually returned to Canada, he and his wife went to church the first Sunday back. When the service was over, the minister said to Frost: "'Oh, we haven't seen you here for a long time, Mr. Frost. Your wife has been in from time to time . . . Where have you been?'" Frost answered: "'Well, sir, I've been in Korea.'" The minister responded: "'Did you have a nice holiday?'"[44]

P.P.C.L.I.

The forgotten war dragged on through the spring and into the summer of 1953. The last major action fought by Canadians on the Jamestown Line was the vicious fight for control of Hill 123, a not-very-important piece of real estate, on 2/3 May 1953. The battle cost twenty-six Canadian dead, twenty-seven wounded, and eight taken prisoner, all from the 3rd Battalion of the Royal Canadian Regiment, which had had the bad luck to be on the hill when the Chinese decided to attack it. The killing did not stop until the ceasefire; eighteen more Canadians lost their lives from 3 May to 27 July 1953, when the armistice finally ended the active phase of the Korean War. With the death of Josef Stalin earlier in the year, the constant bleeding away of Chinese lives, and threats that new US President Dwight D. Eisenhower would use nuclear weapons to end the war, the Communists finally agreed to stop the shooting. By then, the PPCLI had sent an estimated 3,800 soldiers to Korea, of whom 537 had become casualties according to the PPCLI official history (107 killed in action, 429 wounded, and one taken prisoner). In total, 21,940 Canadian soldiers served in

Korea. Of these, 309 were killed in action, died of wounds or are still missing and presumed to have been killed; 1,251 were wounded; and 32 became prisoners of war. An additional 93 soldiers and sailors were dead from non-battle causes.

Korea remains divided. Cynics might say that the deaths of all those Patricias — and those of the many, many other UN soldiers from the Republic of Korea, the United States, Britain, Australia, and the dozens of other countries that came to South Korea's aid — were in vain. It is an irrefutable fact, however, that Korea was the first and last time that a Communist nation, backed by the USSR, made an open effort to conquer a western-aligned neighbour. If the North Korean invasion of South Korea was intended by the Soviets to be a test of the resolve of the western democracies to meet force with force, Canada and its allies passed that test with flying colours when they held the line in Korea. With the Communists thwarted, the long Cold War standoff — and the eventual deterioration of Communism — began. In one way, then, the West's victory in the Cold War began in the frozen hills of Korea. And, once again, Hamilton Gault's regiment played a proud and honourable part.

Chapter 11

KEEPING THE PEACE

PRINCESS PATRICIA'S CANADIAN LIGHT INFANTRY CAME home from the Korean War in the fall of 1953. The previous two generations of Patricias had returned from war to a nation that yearned only for peace and disarmament. In late 1953, however, Canada and its western allies were in the throes of the earliest — and scariest — stages of the Cold War. In Washington, London, Paris, Bonn, and Ottawa, fears ran rampant of a new kind of war, the most terrible in history. At best, citizens and their governments feared a war between the mass armies of NATO and the Warsaw Pact, wreaking havoc and destruction throughout central Europe. At worst, they feared total annihilation in a war fought with nuclear weapons. When the Patricias returned from Korea, therefore, they came back to a nation undergoing the largest peacetime mobilization in Canadian history. For the first time in the history of the regiment, the end of war brought not the tranquility of barracks life lived out in the backwater of the nation, but constant preparation for a new war with the Soviet Union and its allies.

The Canadian government had cut its defence budget to the bone in the two years after the Axis surrender that ended the Second World War. The three branches of Canada's armed services had shrunk drastically and dramatically. Tensions had risen between the West and the Soviet Union in the late 1940s, however, a result of a series of incidents in Europe: the Soviet takeover of central and eastern Europe, the Communist coup in Czechoslovakia in February 1948, the Berlin Blockade in the summer of 1949, and the explosion of the USSR's first atomic bomb in 1949. Canada and the other western nations gradually began to restore their defence budgets, increase the size of their armed forces, and purchase modern weapons and equipment. It was not until the Chinese intervened directly in the Korean War, however, and appeared in the late fall of 1950 to be on the verge of winning that war, that western capitals opened the budget floodgates. Toward the end of December 1950, Canada's minister of national defence, Brooke Claxton, and minister of foreign affairs, Lester Pearson, presented their cabinet colleagues with a jointly signed memorandum warning that a period of great danger was upon them. Communist attacks "on other parts of Asia, the Middle East and Eastern Europe" could be expected. Indeed, "the whole of Asia and Europe, apart from the United Kingdom, Spain and Portugal, might fall rapidly under Soviet domination."[1] In January 1951, 53 percent of Canadians told pollsters that the threat of a global war was their greatest fear (up from 4 percent a year earlier).

The only course of action for Canada and its allies was to build up their armed forces as rapidly as possible so as to meet Soviet and Chinese threats with western strength and resolve. The Canadian government added $1.2 billion to the original 1950/51 defence budget of $700 million. The Canadian military was increased from about 40,000 Active Force members in 1950 to more than 140,000 Active Force personnel by 1955.

As one of the three Active Force infantry regiments, the PPCLI was directly affected by this increase in Canadian defence capabilities. Although the 3rd Battalion PPCLI had been reduced to nil strength (meaning it was temporarily disbanded), on 8 January 1954 when it returned from Korea, the 2nd Battalion was kept in existence and sent for airborne training. For the first time since Gault established the regiment in 1914, the PPCLI had two battalions during peacetime. In the fall of 1953, 2 PPCLI left Canada for a two-year posting in Germany as part of the 27th Canadian Infantry Brigade Group, Canada's contribution to the NATO standing forces in Europe. The brigade was located in the area of responsibility of the I British Corps, British Army of the Rhine, and would have fought under command of the British in the event of a Soviet attack.

At first, the Patricias were based at Fort Macleod, in Hemer, Westphalia, part of the German Bundesrepublik. The Patricias' 1st Battalion relieved 2 PPCLI in the fall of 1955, by which time the 27th Canadian Infantry Brigade Group had been transformed into the 1st Canadian Infantry Brigade Group. The 1st Battalion, in turn, stayed in Germany for two years, returning to Canada in 1957. Other Canadian regiments provided the infantry component for the evolving Canadian Infantry Brigade Group (CIBG). When 1 PPCLI returned to Germany in 1963, it joined the newly designated 4th Canadian Infantry Brigade Group (4CIBG), which later became the 4th Canadian Mechanized Brigade Group (4CMBG), a highly mobile formation of infantry in tracked vehicles and tanks. The PPCLI's 2nd Battalion relieved the 1st in 1966, and remained until 1970. They made up almost half of the newly formed 3rd Mechanized Commando that moved to Canadian Forces Base Baden/Soellingen in southwestern Germany. It was to this base that the Patricias' 2nd Battalion would return fourteen years later, for a four-year tour of duty, from 1984 to 1988. By then, 4CMBG was no longer equipped with first-generation weapons and equipment, and the size of Canada's NATO contingent had been slashed. Thus, after years of front-line duty with the British Army of the Rhine from their base at Hemer, the Patricias found themselves in south-western Germany, acting as Corps reserve in a downsized 4CMBG with the United States Army 7th Corps.

Germany and NATO were plum assignments for Canadian soldiers. For most of the time Canada kept troops in Europe, rotations were long — from two to four years — and soldiers' families accompanied them to live in communities that were very much like the bases they had lived in — or near — in Canada. From midget hockey to Little League baseball, Canadian radio and TV, and Canadian elementary and high schools, it was just like home for the families as the soldiers, mostly men, prepared for the awful possibility of all-out war with the Warsaw Pact. Especially in the early years, the strength of the Canadian dollar against the German mark, coupled with the increased pay the soldiers received for the overseas posting, was a real bonus to them and their families. Goods and services were cheap, they could buy everything from appliances to cars duty free, and all of western Europe was within a day's drive. Ken Villiger of 1 PPCLI went to Germany in 1955: "It was a good chance for our wives and families to get over there and see the other side of the world. Our leave periods over there were quite good and you could travel in no time to all kinds of darn countries."[2]

Life in Germany was good for the Patricias as they prepared for a war that would never be fought. From the late fall of 1951, when the Canadian NATO contingent arrived in Europe, until the early 1970s, Canadian infantry regiments in Europe were equipped with the best weapons and equipment available to any of the NATO allies. The Canadians trained constantly in mechanized and armoured warfare, and mounted major training exercises in conjunction with other NATO countries. The soldiers got a chance to practice for the full-fledged, all-out ground war they all hoped would never come. They knew that if it did, chances were good that the vastly outnumbered NATO forces would have to absorb the first blow and try to hang on until reinforcements arrived from the UK and North America — or until the conflict went nuclear.

To prepare for the fateful day that never came, the Canadian Army in Europe trained to operate with a full range of modern equipment, including tactical nuclear weapons mounted on "Honest John" short-range missiles. The British-built Centurion tanks of the Royal Canadian Armoured Corps were first-class equipment. So were the US-built M-113 armoured personnel carriers, which the Canadian Army first deployed in Europe in 1965. The M-113s were designed to carry infantry into battle alongside the armour — the essence of the infantry's new "mechanized" role. Major Charles "Chic" Goodman commanded the first Patricia company to be equipped with these new vehicles. He later recalled:

> It was a real treat to train with these and have them on the exercise . . . We drove them up the Autobahn, from Fort Macleod in Germany, in Hemer, to the training area at Saltau. It must have terrified every German on the Autobahn as these things came hurtling down. We didn't know enough at the time not to drive them flat out . . . that it was going to shorten the track life of these things.[3]

From then on, the M-113s, like the tanks, were moved from the base to the training area by rail. There, a squadron of tanks and a company of mechanized infantry would train together.

Don Ardelian, who had served as a platoon sergeant in the Korean War with 3 PPCLI, thought the Canadian Army in Europe was as good as any in the world when he took part in Exercise Rob Roy in the fall of 1968. With the British, Germans, and Dutch, Ardelian's company practiced helicopter operations and armoured tactics. They learned how to fight in both rural and "built-up," or urban, areas. When the exercise ended, Ardelian was confident about the ability of NATO troops from different countries to fight alongside each other. He believed that the Canadian Army was at the peak of its profession: "Our tails were up. We had absolute confidence and really, I think we knew our job very, very well."[4]

The happy situation, however, did not last. Deep defence budget cuts in the late 1960s and early 1970s eroded the Canadian Army's capacity to fight a front-line battle. By the time the Patricias returned to Europe in 1984, their role had been reduced to dying gloriously in the first few hours of a Warsaw Pact attack, while the rest of the NATO forces tried to hang on. Brigadier General Pat Grieve, who commanded the Canadian Brigade from 1972 to 1974, wrote: "Delay operations could only have lasted about three days. After that it was clearly NATO policy to employ nuclear weapons to halt the Warsaw Pact forces . . . I used to wonder what the Canadian people and Trudeau in particular would have thought had they been aware of the script."[5] Still, NATO service was the only chance the Patricias ever had to practice mechanized warfare on a large scale alongside their NATO comrades. When Canada pulled out of its NATO standing-force commitment in 1993, that chance was lost forever. Many a Patricia looks back on NATO service in Germany with nostalgia, not only for the uniqueness of the living experiences, but for the loss of the chance to train for war with the best against the best.

P.P.C.L.I.

On 1 October 1957, Hamilton Gault visited with his beloved regiment on the old battlefields that had early on shaped the destiny of the PPCLI. The Patricias' 1st Battalion was stationed in Germany, providing a perfect opportunity for the Founder and the battalion to return to Frezenberg. Gault flew to Germany, picked up a PPCLI guard of honour, and, with a handful of First World War veterans, was driven to Bellewaerde Ridge. There, he planted a maple tree on the right of what had once been the line the Originals had defended to the death. Colonel Hugh Niven, who had taken command of the few survivors on that eighth of May in 1915, accompanied Gault, as did Colonel A.G. Pearson and Sergeant H.F. O'Connor.

Gault was seventy-five. He had been seriously wounded in the First World War. Now, after a full life of riding, flying his own aircraft, swimming, and exploring rough country all over the world, his age showed. In the PPCLI Archives there is a photo of Gault taken at the 1957 ceremonies. He is impeccably dressed in a dark business suit, with a large row of medals attached, his homburg at a jaunty angle. He wears thick gloves to better use his two canes as he proceeds between two ranks of his regiment's guard of honour. On his face are the unmistakable signs of both pride in his regiment and determination that his age and his physical troubles will not deter him. Gault's official biographer noted that he and the other Originals "found it difficult to recognize the battlefield of 1915 in the green, softly undulating Bellewaerde and Frezenberg ridges. It was easier to sense the link between the immaculate guard of honour from the Regiment and the battle-worn Patricias who fought there [forty-two] years before."[6]

Despite his many business, recreational, and private activities, Gault remained deeply interested in the affairs of the regiment; Patricia COs wrote him regularly with reports of the Patricias' doings. On 17 December 1948, Gault had been appointed the PPCLI's first Honorary Lieutenant-Colonel of the Regiment, with duties that included helping to safeguard regimental heritage, aiding the governance of the Regimental Association, and raising funds for regimental activities and requirements. A decade later, on 25 September 1958, he was appointed the PPCLI's first Colonel of the Regiment, also an honorary position, but a very important one in that the person holding it is supposed to embody the spirit of the regiment and act as the chief guardian of regimental tradition. By then, however, Gault was dying of cancer; he passed away on 28 November 1958 and was buried in Montreal. He was seventy-six.

Major-General (Ret'd) C.B. "Cammie" Ware succeeded Gault as Colonel of the Regiment; he was appointed to the position on 13 September 1959 and served the Patricias faithfully in that office until 21 April 1977. Ware had twice commanded the Patricias, in both war and peace and, like Gault, maintained a deep interest in regimental affairs. After his death, all his papers were deposited in the PPCLI Archives in the Museum of the Regiments in Calgary. There have been six Colonels of the Regiment since Ware: Major-General George Brown, OStJ, CD (1977–1983); Colonel William Sutherland, CD (1983–1987); Brigadier-General Stuart Graham, CD (1987–1990); Major-General Herbert Pitts, MC, CD (1990–1994); Major General William Hewson, CMM, CD (1994–1999); and General John de Chastelain, OC, CMM, CD, CH. Brown, Hewson, and de Chastelain all served as Patricia battalion commanding officers.

P.P.C.L.I.

When young J.H. Stewart, one of the first Ottawa-area officers to volunteer for Gault's new regiment, first saw Princess Patricia of Connaught, he thought of her as "the most beautiful one of her sex I have ever seen."[7] The ties that bound the princess to the Patricias, and they to her, were forever established on that solemn day in August 1914 at Ottawa's Lansdowne Park at the start of the First World War. There, she presented the camp colour she had made to her regiment. Those ties grew stronger over the course of the war; at its end, the princess attached her wreath of laurel to the very same colour at Bramshott, England. Officially recognized as "Colonel-in-Chief" of the regiment on 22 February 1918, Lady Patricia Ramsay, as she became after her marriage to Sir Alexander Ramsay in early 1919, continued to inspire the regiment and participate in important regimental occasions.

The first, unofficial camp colour presented by Princess Patricia in 1914 was retired in a formal ceremony at Minto Barracks in

Winnipeg in 1934. At that time, a replica of that colour, and a replica King's colour, both presented to the Patricias by Governor General Viscount Byng in 1922, were also retired. To replace them, Governor General the Earl of Bessborough presented the Patricias with their first official colours in 1934. These were a King's colour and a regimental colour bearing the regiment's First World War battle honours. In September 1953, Lady Patricia Ramsay visited her 2nd Battalion at Currie Barracks to present the Queen's and regimental colours. The regimental colour carried, for the first time, the Patricias' Second World War and Korean War battle honours. On the fiftieth anniversary of the regiment in 1964, Lady Patricia visited her 1st Battalion in Germany, and her 2nd in Edmonton, to repeat the ceremonies she had first performed at Bramshott in 1919, placing a silver gilt wreath of laurel on the regimental colour. She was still Colonel-in-Chief of the Patricias when she died on 12 January 1974.

Before her death, Lady Patricia Ramsay had discussed her succession with the regiment and with her cousin, Patricia Edwina Victoria Mountbatten — Lady Mountbatten, currently the Right Honourable Countess Mountbatten of Burma, CBE, CD, JP, DL. Lady Mountbatten was the daughter of Lord Louis, Earl of Mountbatten, who had served as the Allied forces Chief of Combined Operations from 1942 to 1943 and Commander-in-Chief of the South East Asia Command from 1943 until the end of the Second World War. Though Lady Mountbatten was somewhat intimidated by the prospect of filling Lady Patricia's shoes, she soon accepted the position. On 15 June 1974, she was appointed on the recommendation of the regiment to succeed Lady Patricia as Colonel-in-Chief of the regiment. Lady Mountbatten has visited her regiment often over the past quarter-century, not only on ceremonial occasions, but also in the field, and particularly in the war-ravaged Balkans.

When 3rd Battalion had been reduced to nil strength in early 1954, many of the officers and men were rebadged (transferred) to the 2nd Battalion of the newly created Canadian Guards. The army was expanding in the early 1950s, and the government was anxious to ensure that newly established formations would have a core of experienced soldiers from the start. By the late 1960s, the government's attitude to the Canadian military had cooled considerably. The early Trudeau years were an era of deep cutbacks, neglect, and consolidation. In the late 1960s, the newly unified Canadian Armed Forces actively considered disbanding a number of Regular Force regiments in Mobile Command, as the army was then referred to.

Whether it was the beginning of an open governmental attack on the regimental system, or simply the result of budget cutbacks, the outcome was the same. In September 1969, the minister of national defence, Marcel Cadieux, disbanded the Regular Force battalions of the Queen's Own Rifles of Canada (QORofC), the Royal Highland Regiment (Black Watch) of Canada, the Fort Garry Horse, the Canadian Guards, and the 4th Regiment of the Royal Canadian Horse Artillery. The QORofC was the oldest of these regiments, with its own distinct battle history and regimental traditions. Founded in Toronto in 1860 from six independent militia rifle companies, the Queen's Own had sent battalions to fight with the Canadian Expeditionary Force in the First World War and with the Canadian Army Overseas in the Second World War. It had contributed the 1st and 2nd Canadian Rifle battalions to Canada's first NATO brigade. In October 1953, these two formations had been redesignated 1st and 2nd battalions of the Queen's Own Rifles. Now they were gone. The QORofC continues to this day to raise a militia battalion, but the two Regular Force battalions were rebadged; 2nd Battalion QORofC, based in Calgary, was disbanded, while 1st Battalion QORofC, based at Victoria, BC, became the newly reactivated 3rd Battalion of the PPCLI.

Given the great strength of the regimental tradition in the Canadian army, such rebadging was both rare and apt to be fraught with difficulties. But the transition went smoothly. One of the former 2 QORofC officers who made the shift was Major-General Lewis MacKenzie:

> When it was announced that the Queen's Own was reduced to no strength, as were the Black Watch and the Guards, there was no hesitation whatsoever in all of the [2nd Battalion of the] Queen's Own . . . that we would rebadge PPCLI, being sort of the Army of the West, and knowing members of the regiment very well . . . nobody but nobody could ever say anything other than that the Patricias welcomed the Queen's Own with open arms. It was an unbelievably successful amalgamation.[8]

Thus the PPCLI once again had three battalions in the Regular Force. The Loyal Edmonton Regiment, which had fought alongside the PPCLI in the 2nd Canadian Infantry Brigade in the Second World War, had been affiliated with the PPCLI as its 3rd Battalion in October 1954. As a militia regiment, the Loyal Eddies were supposed to supplement the PPCLI in the event of war or national emergency. When 1 QORofC became 3 PPCLI in 1970, the Loyal Eddies became 4th Battalion, PPCLI.

The regimental colours also evolved to reflect changing times in the regiment. In June 1956, Livingstone T. Merchant, US Ambassador to Canada, attached the streamer of the United States Presidential Unit Citation to the Colour of 2 PPCLI. In 1959, Elizabeth II, Queen of Canada, presented 1st Battalion with its new colours. The PPCLI's 3rd Battalion received its first colours from Governor General Roland Mitchener on 20 November 1971. In 1993, Colonel-in-Chief Lady Mountbatten, accompanied by Colonel of the Regiment Major-General Herb Pitts, presented 3 PPCLI with new colours in Pakrac, Croatia — the first time such a ceremony ever took place in an operational theatre. The most recent presentation of colours was held in Edmonton on 24 June 2000, when the Colonel-in-Chief presented new colours to 1st Battalion. Present at the ceremony were outgoing Colonel of the Regiment, Major General C. W. Hewson, and the newly appointed Colonel of the Regiment, General A.J.G. de Chastelain. All retired colours are now in the care of the PPCLI Gallery at the Museum of the Regiments in Calgary.

P.P.C.L.I.

In 1957, Canadian Minister of Foreign Affairs Lester B. Pearson won the Nobel Peace Prize for his invention of UN peacekeeping during the 1956 Sinai/Suez crisis. The concept of a lightly armed, neutral force grew from the need to separate Egyptian from Israeli forces in the Sinai Peninsula and Gaza strip after the war of October/November 1956. As well, peacekeeping troops were needed to separate Egyptian forces from the British and French troops who had used the excuse of the Israeli attack to invade and seize Port Said and much of the Suez Canal from Egypt. Pearson's belief was that, in conflicts where the parties wished to stop fighting and start talking, but did not trust each other, the Blue Helmets of a UN peacekeeping force could serve a useful function as a trip-wire. These UN forces, with their blue helmets and berets, who travelled in white vehicles with "UN" on them, were always lightly armed, but only for self-protection. They could not shoot unless fired upon and even then, only at the immediate source of the threat. They took their orders from UN headquarters in New York and relied totally on the voluntary contributions of member countries. By convention, none of the five permanent members of the Security Council ever contributed troops to these forces. Further, the presence of troops from western nations such as Canada was always balanced by troops from Communist countries such as Poland.

Since Canada took great pride in its alleged invention of peacekeeping, it became a matter of standing Canadian defence and foreign policy that Canada always volunteered to participate in some way for all UN peacekeeping operations. That was how the 1st Battalion of the Patricias first came to Cyprus in April 1968.

In December 1963, communal violence broke out in the newly independent island nation of the Republic of Cyprus. Cyprus is home to two major ethnic/linguistic groups: Turkish and Greek Cypriot. Between them stands a long history of distrust and violence, brought about in part by the efforts on the part of some members of the Greek Cypriot community to bring about a political union with Greece. In late 1963 and early 1964, the Greek and Turkish Cypriots began to kill each other anew. At first, British troops based in southern Cyprus tried to stand between the two communities to keep the peace. Then, Turkey threatened to invade the island and partition it by force if the international community did not take quick action to end the fighting. Since the USSR warned that it would veto any Security Council move to send NATO troops to Cyprus, a UN peacekeeping force seemed the only answer. On 4 March 1964, the UN Security Council authorized the United Nations Force in Cyprus (UNFICYP) as a "temporary" force to stand between the warring communities until a political solution could be found to the island's troubles. That "temporary" force is still there, although Canada withdrew its main contribution in 1993. For much of the time between 1964 and 1993, an average of 1,120 Canadian soldiers were stationed in Cyprus, helping the UN keep the peace between Greek and Turkish Cypriots on the island. They were given responsibility for peacekeeping in the north-central sector of the island; HQ was in the mountains south of the port of Kyrenia and northwest of the capital, Nicosia. Lewis MacKenzie served his first of three tours on Cyprus while still with the Queen's Own Rifles in 1965, three years before the 1st Battalion of the PPCLI arrived:

> My first impression of Cyprus was that the place was absolutely magnificent . . . As we drove from Nicosia airport

> north to our headquarters . . . we saw our first evidence of the ethnic tension that was tearing the island apart. Windows of houses were sandbagged; and along some streets, manned defensive positions squared off against each other as close as twenty metres apart.[9]

Cyprus baked most of the year in the Mediterranean sun, under blue skies from May until October. Thick forests covered much of the island's centre. But Canadian soldiers soon learned that the beauty of Cyprus hid a recent past of murder and atrocity. They also learned that the island's warring communities were on a hair trigger, literally metres, or seconds, away from renewing their bloody vendetta.

All three Patricia Regular Force battalions served six-month tours of duty in the Canadian-monitored sector of Cyprus, from April 1968 until March 1973. After the first tour, the Canadian HQ moved to Nicosia. Then, in July of 1974, mounting tensions on the island, caused by a military coup in Greece, sparked a full-scale invasion of northern Cyprus by the Turkish armed forces. Turkish paratroopers quickly brushed aside the UN peacekeepers to effectively partition the island, with the Turkish community forming a self-declared independent republic on the island's northern half. The partition, or Green Line, meandered from Larnaca Bay on the island's southeast coast to Morphou Bay on the northwest coast, and cut through the capital. From that point on, the various UN contingents took responsibility for patrolling different sections of the Green Line, trying to defuse the many minor — and sometimes not so minor — incidents that threatened the UN-brokered ceasefire, and reporting those ceasefire violations that did occur to the UN. The Canadians were responsible for the part of the line that divided Nicosia.

Duty on Cyprus could be described as sun, sand, and cold beer punctuated by moments of sheer terror. Most of the time, the Patricias donned their blue helmets and flak jackets and patrolled the Green Line on foot or in white Jeeps. Or, they sat tight in observation posts for long hours in the hot sun, and dreamed of waterskiing, jet-boating, and suntanning, beer in hand, on the nearby beaches. Any commotion along the Green Line was generally nothing more dangerous than one side or the other mounting a political demonstration over some incident, real or imagined. Warrant Officer Rob Dearing of 2 PPCLI was present for one such incident in 1990: "All the [Greek Cypriot] mothers that had sons captured by the Turks marched onto the Turk's side in protest . . . So we tried to keep them from having conflict with the Turks. We put up a barrier and separated them so the Turks wouldn't beat them up or take them away."[10]

On another occasion, Major Wayne Eyre of 2 PPCLI found himself playing the role of Good Shepherd under somewhat strange circumstances:

> A herd of Turkish sheep somehow disappeared . . . in the neighbourhood of fifty sheep and the Turkish farmer went to my . . . OP [observation post] . . . and he was all concerned about the sheep . . . I was out there with two Australian civilian police and we decided to look into this. So we spent about eight hours tracking sheep droppings. We finally found where they went. They were about five kilometres on the Greek side . . . found them about seven o'clock at night. It was just getting dark. So we ended up herding these sheep back through the buffer zone. We finished about ten o'clock or so, getting fairly dark. Herding these sheep by radio antennae, ten-foot whips, moving them in. We finally got them linked up with their owner.[11]

At other times, Patricias had to handle far more serious situations, as Warrant Officer Rick Dumas of 3 PPCLI found out on the morning of 31 July 1988. Dumas had just completed a three-hour patrol: "[It was a] nice, hot sunny day," he remembered. "Greeks and Turks alike [were] nodding off [at] their OPs."[12] One group of Greek soldiers were so intent on napping that they removed the barrier at their checkpoint and leaned it up against a building wall so that they would not have to rouse themselves to leave their OP and check vehicles passing through. Dumas got out of his vehicle, took off his gunbelt — with a 9-millimetre pistol in the holster — and was about to re-heat the previous evening's supper for his breakfast when a private came running into the bunker to tell him that there had been a shooting; a man lay wounded in the buffer zone. Two Patricia privates had been in the vicinity when the shot rang out. They stood guard near the stricken man to try to prevent any further outbreaks. Dumas rushed to the spot where the shooting had occurred and radioed for soldiers from three nearby OPs to join him to cordon off the area.

Dumas and one or two other soldiers used bandages from their medical kits, supplemented by bedsheets, and applied first aid to the fallen man, a Greek Cypriot national guardsman. He was lying face down in the dirt when Dumas reached him: "He had a hole in his forearm and a bullet hole into his lower back," Dumas recalled. "Of course he was in shock and talking [but] not making much sense."[13] Shortly thereafter, an ambulance with a doctor arrived from Nicosia. The Patricias escorted the doctor into the buffer zone and then brought him back with the wounded man. The ambulance took the man away. Dumas never learned his fate. Then, Dumas went to call on the senior officers on both the Greek and Turkish sides to try to stop the situation from escalating. On that particular day, as on most, they succeeded.

Cyprus demonstrated both the strengths and the weaknesses of the traditional type of UN "Blue Helmet" peacekeeping operations. In the thirteen rotations that Patricia battalions spent on Cyprus from April 1968 to August 1991, many individual shooting incidents took place between Greek and Turkish Cypriots. Some shots were even directed at the Canadians. Canadians also helped unearth evidence of mass atrocities that had taken place in the earliest days of the inter-communal conflict. For the most part, however, both communities, as well as the Turks who occupied northern Cyprus from July 1974 on, had no intention of breaking the military status quo and launching all-out war on each other. That was why lightly armed UN peacekeepers proved so effective in helping to keep the lid on. On the other hand, neither side was especially willing to break the political deadlock; the same peacekeeping presence that kept a lid on the violence relieved the pressure for a settlement. Eventually, Canada decided that there was no end in sight to their Cyprus commitment and withdrew. There was no point keeping more than a thousand Canadian troops, doing relatively little, on Cyprus when the need for Canadian troops elsewhere suddenly and dramatically increased with the collapse of the Federal Republic of Yugoslavia, which began in June 1991.

P.P.C.L.I.

The breakup of the Federal Republic of Yugoslavia was precipitated by the successive secessions of Slovenia, Croatia, and Bosnia from Serbia and Montenegro in the latter half of 1991. The secessions sparked off intense ethnic and religious conflict in Croatia and Bosnia among Yugoslavia's three dominant groups, the Croatian Roman Catholics, Bosnian Moslems, and Serbian Orthodox. Slovenia was barely affected by the fighting, but large numbers of Serbs lived in the Krajina region of eastern Croatia, and all three groups live in significant numbers throughout much of Bosnia. After a thousand years of hatred, atrocity, and oppression of each group by one or both of the others, none was prepared to live as a minority in a nation controlled by someone else. Civil wars raged within civil wars as Croatians, for example, battled the Serb-controlled armed forces of Yugoslavia to wrest their independence from Belgrade. Meanwhile, Serbs living in Croatia, especially in the Krajina, battled to wrestle their independence from Croatia. In January 1992, the UN brokered a ceasefire between Serbs and Croatians in Croatia and established the United Nations Protection Force (UNPROFOR) to police that ceasefire. Canada agreed to participate in UNPROFOR by sending a "battle group" — a strengthened infantry battalion or armoured regiment — to police one of a number of United Nations' Protected Areas.

No one expected service with UNPROFOR to be much different from other "Blue Helmet" UN peacekeeping operations. After all, there was a ceasefire in place, as there had been in Cyprus, and the UN had been invited in. What no one reckoned on was the depth of the hatred and mistrust in the region, which far surpassed the intense feelings on Cyprus. Lieutenant Colonel Glenn W. Nordick commanded the 3rd Battalion of the PPCLI in 1992/93. It was the first Patricia battalion to serve in Croatia, and formed the core of what the UN designated as "CANBAT 1" — the Canadian battalion serving with UNPROFOR. Nordick's area of operations was known as "Sector West," in the central Krajina. His formation consisted of 876 soldiers, organized into four rifle companies mounted in M-113 armoured personnel carriers, and a full complement of combat engineer, supply, administration, signals, and reconnaissance troops. His battalion was also equipped with TOW — wire-guided, anti-tank missiles mounted on a number of the armoured personnel carriers — and medium (81-millimetre) mortars. CANBAT 1 was augmented by regular soldiers from 2 PPCLI and reserve soldiers from militia units across Canada, but especially in the west.

Despite many years of soldiering with the PPCLI, at home in Canada and overseas with NATO and on peacekeeping missions, Nordick was not prepared for the Balkans. Six years after he commanded 3 PPCLI there, he composed a "personal experience monograph" for the United States Army War College at Carlisle Barracks, Pennsylvania:

> As a Westerner, a Canadian, and a practising Roman Catholic I had a great deal of difficulty understanding and accepting the depth of hatred and total disregard for human life that was prevalent among the leaders of both sides of this dispute at both the local and national levels. Violations of international law surrounded us (the ethnically cleansed villages, the mass graves, the systematically destroyed churches, and the ongoing and deliberate terrorizing and targeting of civilians). Yet, for all that, there was no sense of shame, guilt or remorse among the local population. Instead, a defiant, one-sided view of history and historical events prevailed, centered on World War Two, but often reaching into centuries past. This history was deemed sufficient justification for illegal acts and brutality in the present — a seemingly never[-]ending cycle of violence.[14]

As CANBAT 1, 3 PPCLI under Nordick's command carried out three major types of assignments: missions associated with enforcing the UNPROFOR mandate, training or assisting other UN contingents in Sector West, and missions assigned from Canada. Many obstacles stood in their way, from the primitive road system that was ice- and snowbound through mountainous country for most of the winter to the refusal of local militias to respect UN jurisdiction or authority. The peacekeepers were often targeted by snipers, or caught, deliberately or otherwise, in crossfire shootings between Serbs and Croatians. In late January 1993, the ceasefire broke down in the Sector South area of the Krajina. Only one serious incident threatened the overall tranquility of Sector West, however: local Serbs broke into a weapons storage area in the city of Pakrac, intending to arm themselves against a possible Croatian attack. The Patricias and a group of peacekeepers from Argentina blocked the Serbs and forced them to withdraw.

On 4 April 1993, the 3 PPCLI battle group was replaced in Sector West by 2 PPCLI battle group. This group was similar in composition to 3 PPCLI, but approximately 40 percent of the troops were reserve soldiers, added as augmentees. Lieutenant-Colonel Jim Calvin commanded the battle group. At first, it operated under very much the same conditions and in the same area as its predecessor. Until late July, the Patricias carried on with their basic tasks of patrolling the area on foot and vehicles, manning checkpoints, and confiscating illegally held weapons. In late July 1993, however, Calvin led the bulk of the battle group into Sector South in the Krajina region of southern Croatia, near the Peruca Dam, the scene of heavy fighting earlier in the year between local Serbs and the Croatian Army. About six weeks later, the rest of the battle group joined Calvin. The new CANBAT 1 area of responsibility encompassed some 2,000 square kilometres astride the Velebit Mountains. Calvin's HQ was in Gračac, about thirty-five kilometres by road from the Serb town of Medak. His four rifle companies, his engineer troops, and his administrative company were positioned in towns and villages in the area. This was the region of the Krajina known as the Medak Pocket.

The Patricias were now smack in the middle of one of the most fought-over regions in Croatia, with well-armed Croatian and Serb forces entrenched in the high mountains and armed soldiers at virtually every roadblock and in every village. PPCLI patrols were regularly fired upon, despite the high visibility of their white vehicles, the "UN" letters, and the blue helmets and banners. Captain Brian Flynn was second in command of D Company one night when a report came in that two of his soldiers were pinned down by sniper fire:

> We could actually hear the shots being fired. I never really thought about being a 2IC [second-in-command], that you'd all of a sudden be in command, until [Sergeant-Major] Mike [Spellum] looked at me and said, "Well, what do you want to do sir?" It all of a sudden dawned on me, I got two guys that are being shot at. They're pinned down and . . . I had to react.[15]

Flynn and his Sergeant Major grabbed every paraflare they had in the company, then ran to a hilltop and started to fire them off into the darkness. The sniper stopped shooting.

On 9 September 1993, the Croatian Army launched an all-out offensive in the Medak Pocket, aimed at driving the Serb forces — and every Serb man, woman, and child living in the area — out of the Krajina. There was intense shelling throughout the Patricia battle-group area, but especially in the town of Medak itself, where a Serb HQ — and a Patricia platoon house — were located. A reservist, Lieutenant Tyrone Green of the Seaforth Highlanders of Canada, commanded the Patricia platoon house. The soldiers under his command sat in the basement of the small house while shells rained down on their position. During periodic stoppages in the shellfire, Warrant Officer Greg Trenholme and his men patrolled the town in their armoured personnel carriers, searching for civilian casualties and taking them to Serb bunkers. When the Croatian shelling finally began to tail off, Croatian troops, backed by tanks, began to push down the road towards Medak from their headquarters in the town of Gospič, fifteen kilometres to the northwest. When the Croats began to penetrate into Medak, tank fire struck near the Patricia platoon house. Four of Calvin's men were under continuous mortar and artillery fire for twelve hours; four were wounded in this stage of the fighting.[16]

Serb forces retaliated against the Croats by firing a missile at the Croatian capital of Zagreb and shelling the city of Karlovac. The Croatians then agreed to a UN-brokered ceasefire and a return to the positions they had occupied on 9 September before their offensive had started. Calvin's job, to be carried out by CANBAT 1 augmented by two French infantry companies, was to monitor the withdrawal and occupy a buffer zone between the Serb lines west of Medak and the Croatians. The initial stages of the operation went smoothly until the early afternoon of 15 September, when C Company of the Patricias and one of the French companies moved between Serb and Croatian forces. As Calvin later reported:

> On numerous occasions shortly after . . . Croatian forces directly engaged these UNPROFOR soldiers with small arms, heavy machine gun and in some instances 20-[millimetre] cannon fire. The CANBAT 1 returned fire when it was obvious it was directed at them. Fire was responded to in kind . . . Numerous firefights occurred some lasting up to ninety minutes between Croatians and CANBAT 1 troops over the following [fifteen-]hour period.[17]

Calvin was unsure why the Croatians opened fire, and guessed that some Croatian troops may not have been informed about the UN ceasefire. By 2000 hours, an uneasy calm had been restored and the Croatians agreed to resume their pullback by noon the next day, 16 September.

The Medak Pocket operation was not much of a battle as Patricia battles went. It stretched out barely more than half a day, and the PPCLI took no casualties, though Croatian media reports indicated that as many as twenty-seven Croatian soldiers may have been killed. And yet it signalled that the Patricias were ready to meet force with force in this most difficult peacekeeping environment. The Canadian government recognized that readiness by awarding Calvin the Meritorious Service Cross, and Mentions-in-Dispatches to eight other members of the Patricia battle group for their steadfastness under fire on 15 September, or for bravery during other operations in the Medak Pocket. Two of those awards went to reservists. The 2nd Battalion received the UNPROFOR Force Commander's Unit Commendation for turning back the Croatian attack on 15 September and diligently enforcing the UN mandate. For the time being, Calvin's troops had saved the UN mission in the Medak Pocket.

At daybreak on 16 September, the Patricias awoke "to the sounds of gunfire and explosions."[18] Jim Seggie was there:

> All we could hear was explosions in the Medak pocket. You could see the smoke rising and you knew darned well what was

> going on. Somebody asked, "What the hell are they doing anyways?" People would just look at him. "Can't you tell? Think a little. All the [Serb] people don't live there anymore. They're probably dead or ran away. They're [the Croats] just blowing the houses up."[19]

Calvin knew what was happening, but when his D Company tried to push into the buffer zone — as the original ceasefire agreement and the agreement of the previous night had provided for — Croatian troops backed by tanks stood in their path. For an hour and a half, the Canadians and the Croatians faced off at ranges of from fifty to one hundred metres in full combat readiness. The Patricias had no tanks, but every one of the Croatian tanks was in the crosshairs of their TOW anti-tank missiles.

Then Calvin got an idea. He called forward a TV crew accompanying his column and, in front of the Croatian troops, he gave them an interview in which he charged that the Croatian soldiers were deliberately delaying the Canadian advance to give their own forces time to erase evidence of "ethnic cleansing." On orders from above, the Croatian troops relented. The Patricias began to move into the buffer zone as night fell. They found their worst fears realized, as Calvin later wrote:

> The Croatians had systematically destroyed every building, poisoned every well, killed all the animals and purged the inhabitants. Sixteen bodies were found; some burned, some shot. Most bodies were civilian, both men and women. Highly suspicious was the surgical gloves littered on the ground . . . leading to the belief that even more individuals had been murdered, cleaned up, and transported out of the pocket.[20]

One Patricia platoon was ordered to form a "sweep team" to help identify and remove bodies and work with a forensics team composed of UN officials and members of the RCMP to investigate war crimes scenes. Warrant Officer Geof Crossman commanded the sweep team when it was called to a farm where it had been reported that two women had been burned:

> We went to this area. It was the basement of a house. It was levelled but the basement was still there. I kicked the door in. There were 9-[millimetre] rounds outside the door so we could only hope that they shot these two women before they burned them. I went inside to get this big smell of . . . burnt pork roast, which I still can't eat. If somebody burns any pork on a barbecue, I'll throw up. I looked. There were two bodies sitting there . . . you could tell they had been attached to a chair and set on fire.[21]

In the Medak Pocket, far from home, the Patricias came face to face with modern, post–Cold War war. In Canada, people and press still spoke of "peacekeeping," under the illusion that Canada's blue-helmeted soldiers were continuing to do in the disintegrating nation of Yugoslavia what they had done in the Sinai Peninsula, or on the Golan Heights, or on Cyprus: maintaining ceasefires between people who were tired of fighting each other. But that was not so. There was no peace to keep in the Balkans. The Patricias and the rest of UNPROFOR — and the two battalions that Canada eventually contributed to UNPROFOR — were in fact in the middle of a war, hated by all sides, often attacked, and taking casualties. The Patricias contributed one more battle group to UNPROFOR, in Croatia in 1994, with one company going to Bosnia. By the time 2 PPCLI returned to the Balkans in January 1997, however, they formed part of NATO's SFOR, or Stabilization Force. SFOR was heavily armed, and had a strong mandate to maintain the ceasefire and political arrangements as laid out in the Dayton Peace Accords. Canada continues to maintain troops in its own Canadian-run area of responsibility in northwestern Bosnia; no doubt future Patricia battle groups will rotate into Bosnia for six-month stretches.

The world is a far different place at the dawn of the twenty-first century than it was in August 1914, when Hamilton Gault first thought of raising a regiment for war. It is no coincidence, however, that members of the regiment he founded helped to bring a sort of peace to the Balkans and now serve there whenever their turn comes. The war the Patricias were raised to fight, after all, started in Sarajevo, capital of Bosnia, not very far from the Canadian area of responsibility in Bosnia today. War today is a much more technical phenomenon than it was in 1914, and some would argue that it is far deadlier and more destructive. That may be so, but war is still war and the primary job of all soldiers — killing others and offering themselves up to be killed — has not changed since the dawn of time. The same attributes of courage, steadfastness, loyalty, dedication to a higher cause, and a love for comrades in arms that exceeds love of self, motivated and sustained the Patricias in those first days in the Ypres Salient, at Bellewaerde Ridge, at the Hitler Line, at Kap'yong, and at the Medak Pocket. They sustain the regiment today. If they were still here to see their regiment, Hamilton Gault, Princess Patricia, and Francis Farquhar would be as proud of their Patricias as they were on that day in August 1914 when they gathered at Lansdowne Park. Perhaps, from somewhere, they still watch over the Princess Patricia's Canadian Light Infantry.

Epilogue

KOSOVO, 1999

CLARKE STADIUM, EDMONTON: 2 JULY 1999. MORE THAN 7,000 people huddled under the lights in the cool, wet weather, waiting for the tattoo/sunset ceremony that marked the eighty-fifth anniversary of the Princess Patricia's Canadian Light Infantry to begin. At the same time, A Company, 1 PPCLI was arriving in the Balkans to prepare the ground for the remainder of the battalion, and the battle group that would form around it, as part of Canada's contribution to KFOR — NATO's Kosovo Force. The Canadian government had announced Canada's participation in KFOR on 27 April 1999, while NATO's bombing campaign against the Serbs in Kosovo, Serbia, and Montenegro continued. Canadian fighter-bombers were part of those NATO strike forces, marking the first time that Canada had actively participated in an air war on an ongoing basis since 1945. When Canada initially agreed to provide at least 800 troops for KFOR, no one knew for sure whether those troops would enter Kosovo after a ceasefire or fight their way in. In either event, the Patricias would be ready.

As part of the 1st Canadian Mechanized Brigade Group, based at CFB Edmonton, 1 PPCLI had been preparing for war in the Balkans for many months.

P.P.C.L.I.

NATO's bombing campaign ended before KFOR fought its way into Kosovo. The Patricias moved rapidly to send the rest of the battle group to the area as quickly as possible. The Canadian battle group would eventually consist of 1 PPCLI, an engineer troop, and a troop of Leopard 1A tanks from Lord Strathcona's Horse (Royal Canadians). The Canadian Forces also deployed a reconnaissance squadron with brand new, state-of-the-art Coyote vehicles and a tactical helicopter squadron. The PPCLI battle group was deployed in the area of responsibility of 4 UK Brigade. Within their zone, the Patricias policed the ceasefire, aided forensics teams investigating Serbian war crimes, uncovered illegal weapons caches, and helped rebuild bridges, roads, water supply systems, and even a playground destroyed by the Serbs or wrecked in collateral damage by NATO bombs. Canadian medical staff worked at British 22nd Field Hospital and 2nd Armoured Field Hospital to provide medical support to the NATO soldiers and emergency services to the local population.

The Canadian presence in Kosovo could not be sustained beyond a year because of the deep defence budget cuts of previous years and the continuing Canadian commitment in Bosnia. The Patricias left Kosovo in December 1999. When they had deployed, however, they may well have been the best-prepared Canadian soldiers in the nation's history to be sent overseas by their government for a possible mission of war.

There will never again be wars like the First and Second World Wars. Nuclear weapons alone guarantee that. So does the new awareness among most of the technologically advanced nations of the world that sustained conflict for abstract political goals is just too costly in treasure or lives to sustain. Since the end of the Cold War in 1989, however, the world has not seen the end of war, just its transformation. Today, wars are likely to be local, even though they may well have global implications. A new international consciousness that democracy and human rights are not divisible prompts the people of Canada and other democratic nations to demand that men and women not be led to slaughter like cattle at the whim of their own governments in the name of national sovereignty. In the three major international conflicts that Canada engaged in in the twentieth century, Canadians learned that a peace broken in Sarajevo, or on the German-Polish border, or across Korea's 38th parallel, could cost hundreds, if not thousands, of Canadian lives. They also learned that tyrants who terrorize their own people inevitably turn to terrorizing others.

There is a new awakening in the nation of the idea that a free and prosperous Canada is nurtured by an international system resting both on the free flow of people, goods, services, and ideas across boundaries, and on the rights of individuals everywhere to live peaceful, secure lives. Such a system does not just happen. It must be built and defended. And Canada must play a part in both processes to stake any rightful claim to the fruits of that system. That is why Canada and its allied nations will continue to maintain effective military forces well into the foreseeable future. It is also the reason why proud regiments with fighting traditions, such as the PPCLI, will always be needed to guard the nation and its interests and to challenge those who would strip us of our heritage. Thus the regiment that Hamilton Gault founded almost a century ago will no doubt proudly continue to nurture its heritage, increase its strength, deepen its traditions, and prepare its fighting skills in preparation for the time when its country will need it once again.

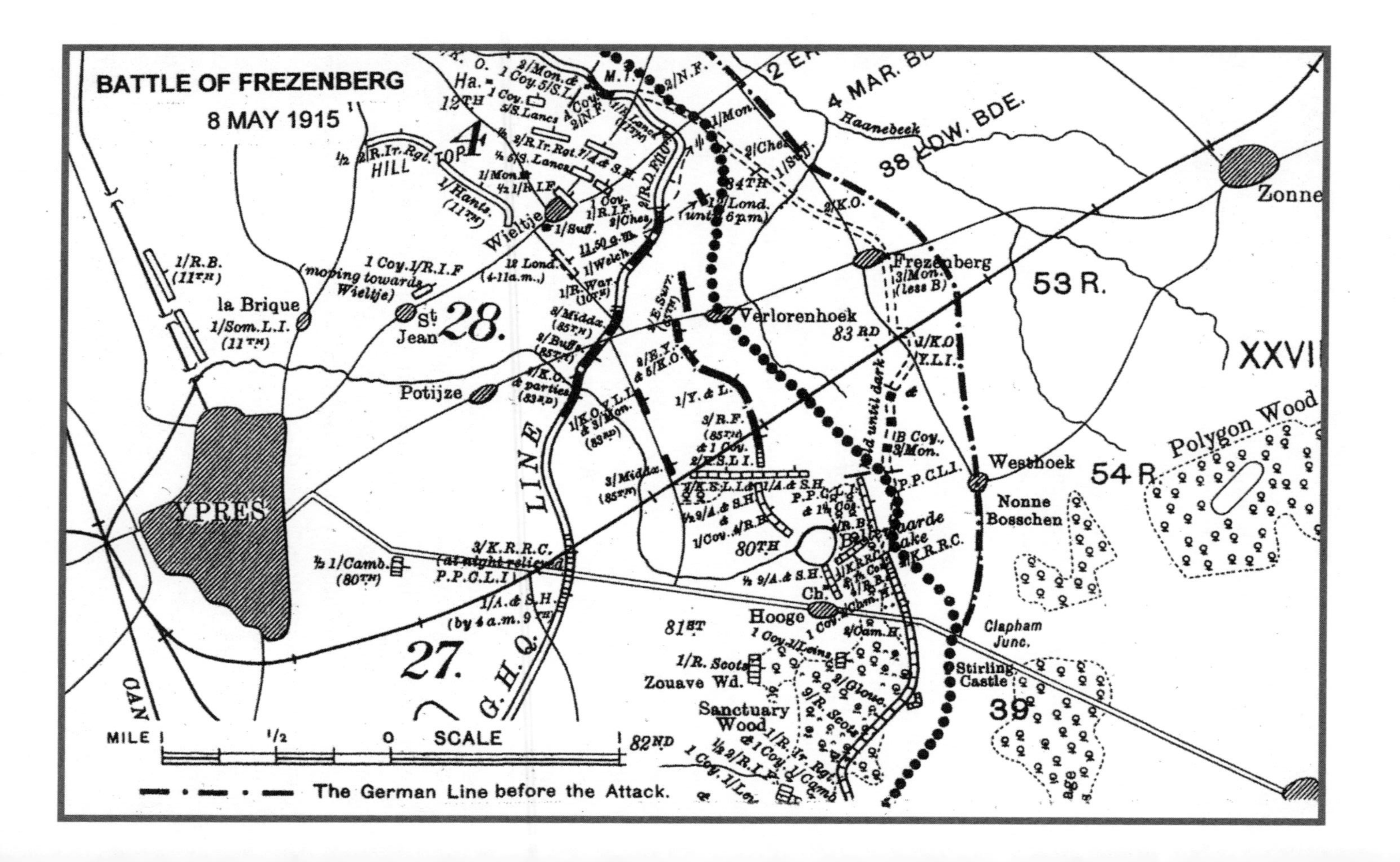
BATTLE OF FREZENBERG
8 MAY 1915
HILL
Wieltje
la Brique
1/Som.L.I.
(11TH)
1/R.B.
(11TH)
St. Jean
28.
Potijze
YPRES
27.
G.H.Q.
LINE
Verlorenhoek
Frezenberg
Westhoek
Zonne
Haanebeek
4 MAR. BDE.
38 LOW. BDE.
53 R.
54 R.
XXVI
Polygon Wood
Nonne Bosschen
Hooge
Zouave Wd.
Sanctuary Wood
Clapham Junc.
Stirling Castle
39
80TH
81ST
82ND
83RD
84TH
1 Coy.1/R.I.F
(moving towards Wieltje)
1/Y.&L.
3/K.R.R.C.
P.P.C.L.I.
1/A.&S.H.
MILE
1/2
0
SCALE
The German Line before the Attack.

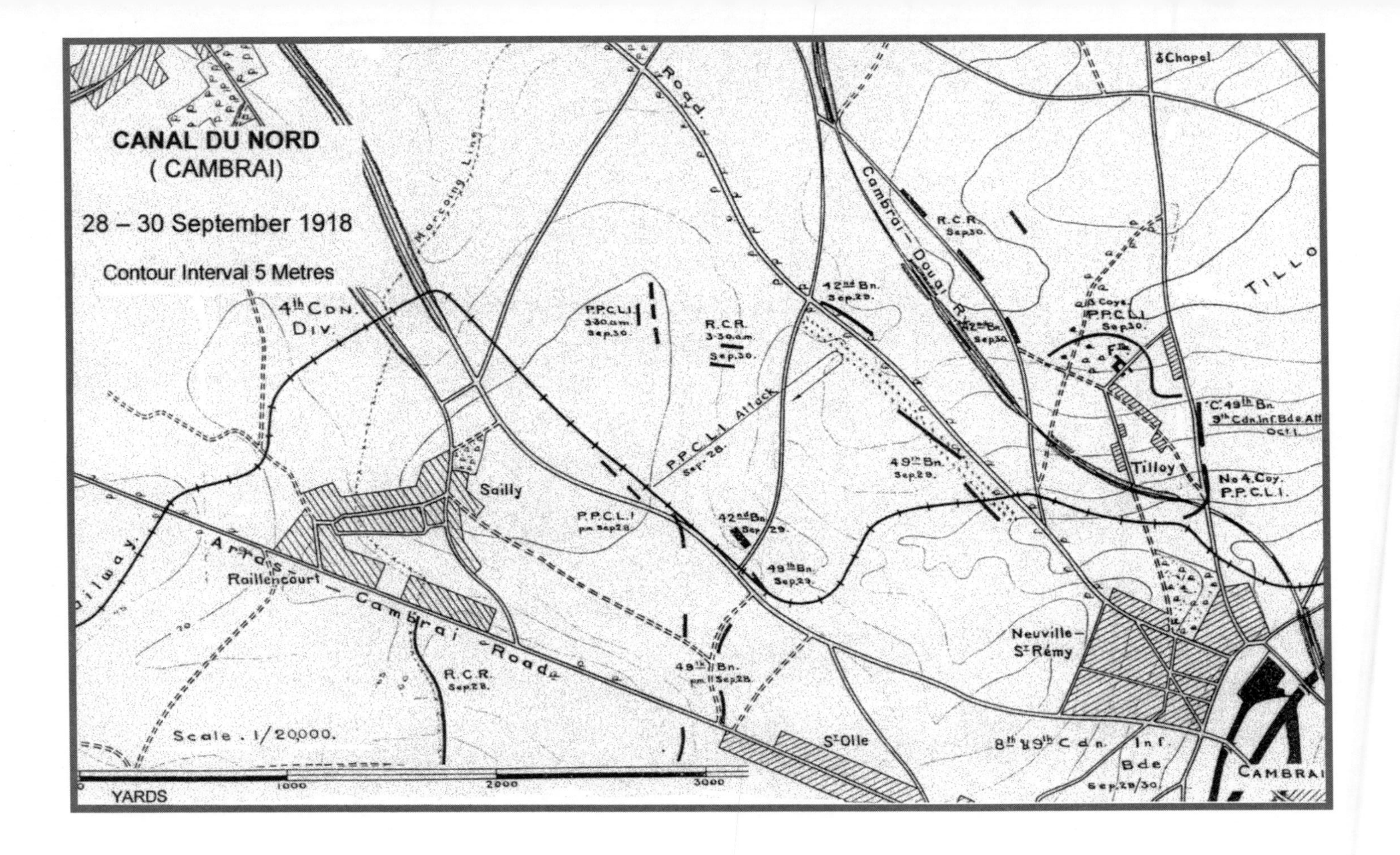
CANAL DU NORD
(CAMBRAI)
28 – 30 September 1918
Contour Interval 5 Metres
4th Cdn. Div.
Marcoing Line
Road
Cambrai – Douai R.
R.C.R. Sep.30.
42nd Bn. Sep.29.
42nd Bn. Sep.30.
a & B Coys. P.P.C.L.I. Sep.30.
Tilloy
'C' 49th Bn. 9th Cdn.Inf.Bde.Att. Oct.1.
No.4.Coy. P.P.C.L.I.
P.P.C.L.I. 3.30.a.m. Sep.30.
R.C.R. 3-30.a.m. Sep.30.
P.P.C.L.I. Attack Sep.28.
49th Bn. Sep.29.
Sailly
P.P.C.L.I. p.m. Sep.28.
42nd Bn. Sep.29.
49th Bn. Sep.29.
Arras – Cambrai – Road
Raillencourt
Railway
R.C.R. Sep.28.
49th Bn. p.m. Sep.28.
Neuville-St Rémy
St Olle
8th & 9th Cdn. Inf. Bde. Sep.28/30.
Cambrai
Scale . 1/20,000.
1000
2000
3000
YARDS

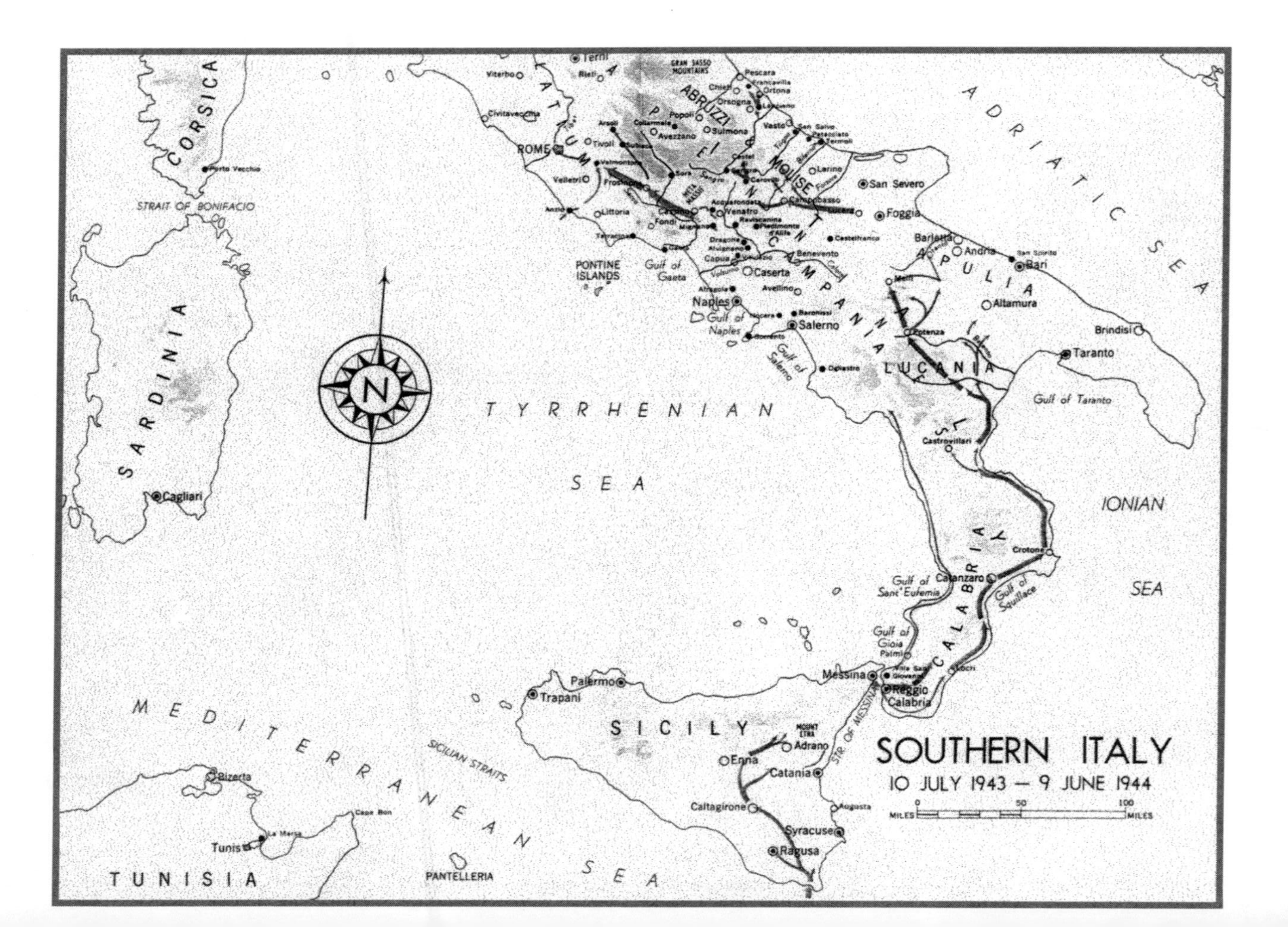
SOUTHERN ITALY
10 JULY 1943 — 9 JUNE 1944
MILES 0 50 100 MILES
ADRIATIC SEA
TYRRHENIAN SEA
IONIAN SEA
MEDITERRANEAN SEA
CORSICA
SARDINIA
SICILY
TUNISIA
STRAIT OF BONIFACIO
SICILIAN STRAITS
STR. OF MESSINA
PONTINE ISLANDS
PANTELLERIA
LATIUM
ABRUZZI
MOLISE
CAMPANIA
APULIA
LUCANIA
CALABRIA
Rome
Naples
Salerno
Foggia
San Severo
Bari
Altamura
Brindisi
Taranto
Gulf of Taranto
Gulf of Gaeta
Gulf of Naples
Gulf of Salerno
Gulf of Sant' Eufemia
Gulf of Gioia
Gulf of Squillace
Castrovillari
Crotone
Catanzaro
Reggio Calabria
Messina
Palermo
Trapani
Enna
Adrano
Catania
Caltagirone
Syracuse
Ragusa
Augusta
Cagliari
Bizerta
Tunis
Cape Bon
Terni
Viterbo
Civitavecchia
Tivoli
Velletri
Pescara
Ortona
Vasto
Termoli
Sulmona
Popoli
Avezzano
Cassino
Fondi
Caserta
Benevento
Avellino
Campobasso
Lucera
Barletta
Andria
Potenza
Melfi

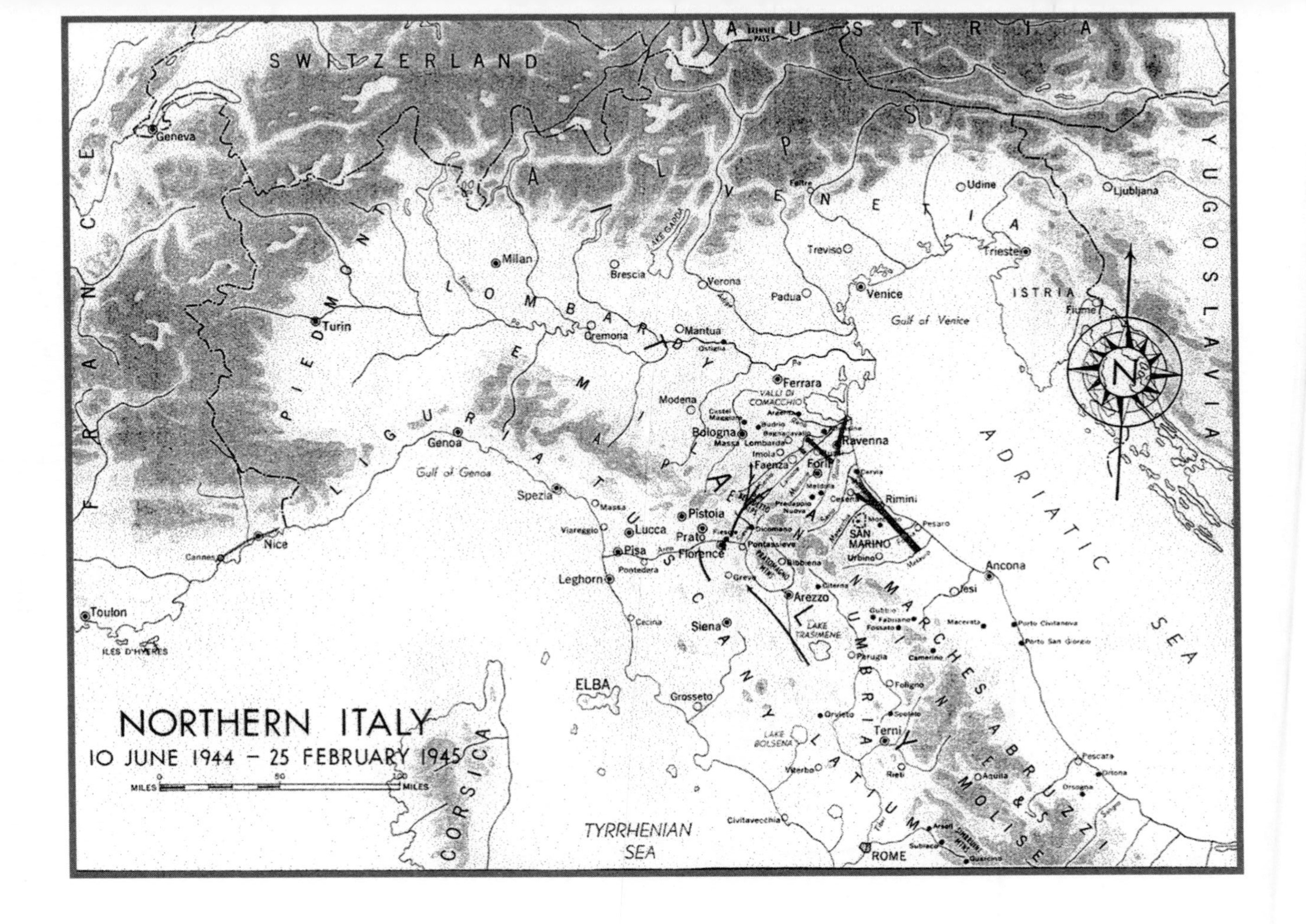
NORTHERN ITALY
10 JUNE 1944 – 25 FEBRUARY 1945
MILES 0 50 100 MILES
SWITZERLAND
AUSTRIA
YUGOSLAVIA
FRANCE
ALPS
VENETIA
LOMBARDY
PIEDMONT
LIGURIA
EMILIA
TUSCANY
UMBRIA
MARCHES
LATIUM
ABRUZZI & MOLISE
ISTRIA
CORSICA
ELBA
ADRIATIC SEA
TYRRHENIAN SEA
Gulf of Venice
Gulf of Genoa
LAKE TRASIMENE
LAKE BOLSENA
BRENNER PASS
Geneva
Turin
Milan
Brescia
Verona
Mantua
Cremona
Padua
Treviso
Venice
Udine
Trieste
Ljubljana
Fiume
Ferrara
Modena
Bologna
VALLI DI COMACCHIO
Massa Lombarda
Imola
Faenza
Forli
Ravenna
Cervia
Rimini
Pesaro
SAN MARINO
Urbino
Genoa
Spezia
Massa
Viareggio
Lucca
Pistoia
Prato
Pisa
Florence
Pontassieve
Dicomano
Bibbiena
Pontedera
Leghorn
Greve
Arezzo
Cecina
Siena
Grosseto
Perugia
Orvieto
Spoleto
Foligno
Terni
Rieti
Viterbo
Civitavecchia
ROME
Ancona
Iesi
Macerata
Camerino
Porto Civitanova
Porto San Giorgio
Aquila
Pescara
Ortona
Orsogna
Nice
Cannes
Toulon
ILES D'HYERES

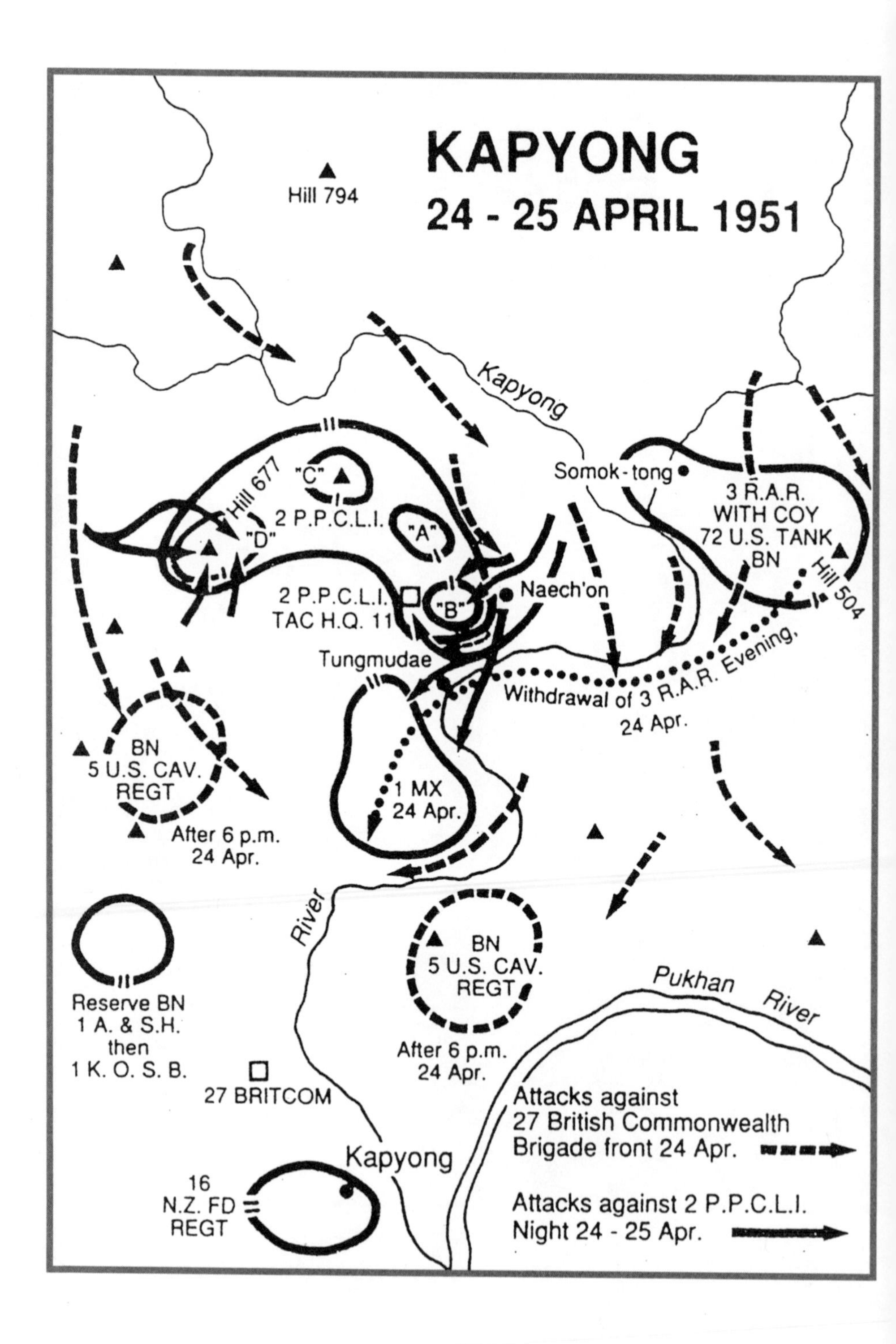
KAPYONG
24 - 25 APRIL 1951
Hill 794
Kapyong
Hill 677
"C"
"D"
2 P.P.C.L.I.
"A"
"B"
2 P.P.C.L.I.
TAC H.Q. 11
Somok-tong
Naech'on
3 R.A.R.
WITH COY
72 U.S. TANK
BN
Hill 504
Tungmudae
Withdrawal of 3 R.A.R. Evening,
24 Apr.
BN
5 U.S. CAV.
REGT
After 6 p.m.
24 Apr.
1 MX
24 Apr.
River
BN
5 U.S. CAV.
REGT
After 6 p.m.
24 Apr.
Pukhan River
Reserve BN
1 A. & S.H.
then
1 K. O. S. B.
27 BRITCOM
Kapyong
16
N.Z. FD
REGT
Attacks against
27 British Commonwealth
Brigade front 24 Apr.
Attacks against 2 P.P.C.L.I.
Night 24 - 25 Apr.

PPCLI OPERATIONS IN THE FORMER YUGOSLAVIA

UNIT	DATE	AREA	FORCE
3 PPCLI	Nov '92 - Apr '93	Croatia	UNPROFOR
2 PPCLI	Apr '93 - Oct '93	Croatia	UNPROFOR
1 PPCLI	Apr '94 - Oct '94	Croatia	UNPROFOR
B Coy 1 PPCLI	Apr '94 - Oct '94	Bosnia	UNPROFOR
2 PPCLI	Jan '97 - Jun '97	Bosnia	SFOR
A Coy, 3 PPCLI	Jan '97 - Jun '97	Bosnia	SFOR
B Coys 1 & 3 PPCLI	Jul '97 - Jan '98	Bosnia	SFOR
1 PPCLI	Jul '99 - Dec '99	Kosovo	KFOR
3 PPCLI	Mar '00 - Sept '00	Bosnia	SFOR
2 PPCLI	Oct '00 - Mar '01	Bosnia	SFOR

KFOR - KOSOVO FORCE (NATO)
SFOR - STABILIZATION FORCE (NATO)
UNPROFOR - UNITED NATIONS PROTECTION FORCE

PRINCESS PATRICIA'S CANADIAN LIGHT INFANTRY ROLL OF HONOUR

FIRST WORLD WAR 1914–1918

For a common cause they gave their lives, for themselves they won the crown that never fades.

Pte. J.J. Abbott
Pte. J.A. Adam
Pte. C.F. Adams
Pte. G.L. Adams
Pte. G.R. Adams
Lt. H.E. Agar
Pte. R. Aitken
Pte. A. Albrow
Sgt. F. Alderson
L/Cpl. E.H. Aldwinckle
Pte. P. Allan
Pte. W.A. Allan
Pte. S.J. Allanson
Pte. B. Allen
Pte. T.W. Allen
Lt. J.E. Almon
Pte. G.L. Amell
Pte. A.S. Anderson
Pte. C.L. Anderson
Pte. D. Anderson
L/Cpl. F.J. Anderson
Pte. J. Anderson
Pte. J.E. Anderson
Pte. J.W. Anderson
Pte. S.M. Anderson
Pte. W. Anderson
Pte. W.F. Angell
Pte. J.C. Anglin
Pte. R.B. Annan
Pte. J. Archer
Pte. J. Armour
Pte. C.J. Armstrong
Cpl. P. Armstrong
Sgt. W. Arnold
Pte. G.E. Arthur
Pte. A.J. Ascott
Pte. D. Atkinson
Pte. E.C. Baddeley
Pte. S. Badley
Pte. H.E. Bagsley
L/Cpl. A. Bailey
L/Cpl. G.W. Bailey
Pte. J. Bain
Pte. G.L. Baker
L/Cpl. J. Baker
Pte. J.R. Baker
Pte. S.R. Baker
Pte. S.J. Bale
Pte. J. Balfour
Cpl. C.H. Ball
Pte. G. Ball
Pte. H.J. Ball
Sgt. R.E. Bandur
Pte. F. Barker
Pte. W. Barkley
Pte. R. Barley
Pte. C.R. Barnes
Pte. C. Barnicoat
Pte. W.A. Bassett
Pte. H.J. Bastable
L/Cpl. G. Batchelor
L/Cpl. A. Batten
Pte. G. Battershill
Pte. S. Beatie
Pte. W.D. Beaton
Pte. G.G. Beatson
Pte. R.M. Beaumont
Pte. A. Beazley

Pte. C.I. Beck
Lieut. H.T. Beecroft
Pte. H.D. Belding
Pte. E.C. Bell
L/Cpl. E.S. Bell
Pte. J. Bell
L/Cpl. H.G. Bellinger
Pte. A. Bendek
Pte. J.R. Benette
Pte. W.D. Benger
Sgt. J. Benham
Pte. A.E. Bennett
Pte. R.W. Bennett
L/Cpl. W.H. Bennett
Pte. A. Benvie
Pte. E. Berry
Pte. C.W. Bethune
Pte. S. Betts
Pte. W. Betts
Pte. F. Beuthch-Millar
Pte. G.T. Bickell
L/Cpl. E.H. Bicker
Lt. C.F.H. Biddulph
Pte. R.H. Biddulph
Pte. G. Bielby
Pte. P.A. Bieler
Pte. W.C. Biffin
L/Sgt. R.K. Bigland
Pte. C.B. Birt
Pte. D.R. Bishop
Pte. A. Blachford
Pte. P.N. Blacklock
Pte. J. Blackman
L/Cpl. G. Blake
Pte. V. Blaker
Pte. O.S. Blakstad
Pte. W.J. Blane
Cpl. H. Blatch
Pte. J. Bleakley
Pte. J. Blees
Pte. T. Bliss
Pte. A. Blitch
Sgt. D. Boag
Pte. F. Bob
Pte. H. Body
Pte. E.J. Boland
Pte. J.R.D. Bole
Pte. S.J. Bond
Pte. F. Bondar
Pte. R. Boulter
Sgt. E. Bourbonnais
Pte. T. Bourget
Pte. A. Bourque
Pte. J. Bowe
L/Cpl. T. Bowlt
Pte. G.C. Bowness
L/Cpl. J. Bowness
Pte. W. Box
Pte. T.B. Boyd
Pte. C. Bradbury
L/Cpl. R.C. Bradford
L/Cpl. C.A. Bradley
Pte. T. Bradley
L/Cpl. A. Bramley-Moore
Pte. S.J. Braund
Sgt. H.M.S. Bredin
Pte. G.E. Brewer, MM
Pte. E.A. Brigden
Pte. D.H. Briggs
Pte. G. Briggs
Pte. L.F. Britton
Pte. B.D.S. Broad
Pte. H. Brockbank
Pte. G. Bronquest, DCM
Pte. R. Broom
Pte. A. Brown
Pte. B.B. Brown
Pte. C.E. Brown
Sgt. F.S. Brown
Pte. G. Brown
Pte. J. Brown
Pte. W.H. Bryant
Pte. H. Buchan
Pte. M. Buck
Pte. R.T. Bullen
L/Cpl. W. Bullen
Lt. Col. H.C. Buller, DSO
Pte. O.H. Bulmer
Pte. J.H. Bulpitt
Pte. R.S. Bunn
Pte. F. Burdett
Sgt. G.J. Burgess
Pte. W.H. Burgess
Pte. A.J. Burnard
Pte. A. Burns
Cpl. S.W. Burns
Pte. W. Burns
Pte. C.R. Burrows
Pte. G. Burrows
L/Cpl. E.F. Burton
Pte. F. Burton
Pte. J.H. Burton
Pte. E.A. Burwash
Pte. E. Butler
Pte. J.H. Butler
Pte. C.B. Buxton
Cpl. T. Caldwell
Pte. H.M. Callaghan
Pte. A. Callan
Pte. A.F. Cameron
Lt. D.E. Cameron
Pte. G. Cameron
Pte. J.S. Cameron
Pte. D. Campbell
Pte. F. Campbell
L/Cpl. T. Campbell
Pte. J. Canavan
Pte. H.N. Canning
Pte. J.G. Carlaw
Pte. L.G. Carleton
Cpl. P.W. Carleton
Pte. T.E. Carr
Pte. G.V. Carroll
Sgt. G.A. Carson
Pte. J.B.C. Carson
Pte. J.M. Carson
Pte. T.J. Carson
Pte. F.C. Carter
Pte. J.A. Carter
Pte. M. Carter
Pte. W.F. Cartwright, MM
L/Cpl. E.H. Case
L/Cpl. A.H. Casewell
Pte. W.J. Casey
Pte. R.E. Caspell
Pte. M.R. Caughren
L/Cpl. W.J. Causton
L/Cpl. F. Cavanagh
Pte. J. Chadwick
Pte. J.R. Chalmers
Pte. T.C. Chalmers
L/Cpl. G.M. Channell
Pte. R.F. Chant
Pte. W.C. Chapman
Pte. A.W. Chestnut
Pte. J.W. Chisholm
Sgt. H.F. Christie, DCM

Pte. M. Chrystal
Pte. R. Claney
Pte. J.H. Clare
Pte. L.V. Clare
Pte. E.B. Clark
Pte. G.A. Clark
Pte. J.F. Clark
Pte. S.J. Clark
Pte. W.J. Clark
Pte. A.R. Clarke
Pte. G.F. Clarke
Pte. S. Clarke
Pte. A. Clarson
Sgt. T.R. Clason, MM
Pte. A.G. Clayton
Pte. R.H.F. Cleary
Pte. G. Clementson
Pte. R.T. Coates
Pte. H.A. Cochran
Pte. J. Coetzee
Pte. H.A. Coit
L/Cpl. C. Coke
Pte. F.B. Cole
Pte. J.E. Cole
Pte. R. Colin
Pte. J.H. Collacott
Pte. P.S. Collett
Pte. W.B. Collings
Sgt. J.D. Collins
Sgt. H. Connor
Pte. W. Connor
Pte. R.B. Conquest
CSM J. Conway
Sgt. E.H. Cook, MM
Pte. F.F. Cook
Pte. T.H. Cook
Pte. F. Cooper
CSM A. Cordery
L/Sgt. A.B. Cork
Pte. A.E. Cork
Capt. P.V. Cornish
Pte. H. Cosh
Sgt. P.E. Cote
Pte. F.G.W. Coulson
Pte. W. Courtney
Pte. F. Cox
Pte. H.G. Cox
Pte. R. Cox
Pte. H. Crabtree
Pte. W. Crabtree
Pte. L. Craig
Pte. W.K. Craighead
Pte. G. Cram
Pte. R. Craven
Pte. L.H. Crawford
Lt. R.G. Crawford
Pte. S.J. Creighton
Pte. D. Crichton
Pte. A.G. Crisfield
Pte. F.J. Crofts
Pte. C. Crook
L/Cpl. P. Cross
Pte. R.A. Cross
Pte. T. Crosthwaite
Pte. J.F. Crozier
Pte. G. Cryer
Pte. E.P. Cunningham
Pte. G.J. Cunningham
Pte. J.C. Cunningham
L/Cpl. R. Cushman
Pte. A. Daffern
Pte. T. Daley
MM J.W. Dames
Pte. F. Danore
Pte. C.S. Darby
L/Cpl. C.T. Darling
Pte. O.G. Darling
Pte. J.M. Davey
Pte. M.L. Davey
L/Cpl. E.L. Davey-Thomas
Pte. N. David
Pte. A.P. Davidson
Pte. G. Davidson
Pte. W. Davies
Pte. A.E. Davis
Pte. A.S. Davis
Pte. E. Davis
Pte. F.L. Davis
Pte. G.E. Davis
Pte. R.M. Davis
Pte. E.A. Davison
Pte. J. Davison
Pte. C. Dawson
L/Cpl. R.J. Dawson
Pte. S.P. Deayton
Lt. M.S. de Bay
Sgt. W. Dedman
Pte. V.L. Defoe
Pte. A.W. Deitz
Pte. W.H. De Line
Pte. A. Dempster
Capt. H.S. Dennison
Pte. H.A. Denniss
Pte. A. Deschamps
Pte. W.P. Detlor
Pte. J.H. Devoo
Pte. H.B. De Wolfe
Pte. D. Dibbs
Pte. C.F. Dick
Pte. W.J. Dicker
Pte. A.E. Dight
Pte. H.H. Dinning
Pte. W. Dinning
Pte. J. Dixon
Pte. S.J. Dixon
L/Cpl. F. Dobie
Cpl. E.W. Dodson
Pte. C.H. Dodwell
Pte. W.J. Dolan
Pte. W. Dolby
Pte. H.W.W. Donaldson
Cpl. D.E. Donnelly
Pte. M.J. Donovan
Pte. R. Dougall
Pte. W.H. Douglas
Pte. D. Doull
Cpl. A.A. Dove
Cpl. C. Dover
Pte. H. Dowling
Pte. J. Doyle
Pte. M. Driscoll
Maj. L.V. Drummond-Hay, MC
Pte. W. Dubois
Pte. S.E. Dudley
Pte. J.R. Duff
Pte. G. Duncan
Pte. W.B. Dunham
Capt. St. C. Dunn (CAMC)
Pte. J. Dunning
Pte. W. Dursley
Lt. E.W. Duval
Pte. G. Dwyer
Pte. G.E.G. Eales
Lt. F.L. Eardley-Wilmot
Pte. W.R. Earls

Pte. A.E. Eason
Pte. S. Edmondson
Lt. N.A. Edwards
A/Cpl. P.S. Edwards
Pte. H. Egar
Pte. W.A. Elderkin
L/Cpl. A. Elliott
Pte. J.H. Elliott
Pte. G.C. Ellis
Pte. H. Ellis
L/Cpl. P.E. Ellis
Pte. T.G. Ellis
Pte. N.V.M. Emery
Pte. E.W. Empey
L/Cpl. N.R. English
L/Cpl. F.A. Evans
Pte. R. Evans
L/Cpl. W.J. Evans
Pte. R.B. Everest
Pte. W. Everett
Pte. A.C. Ewing
Pte. A.E. Exall
Lt. Col. F. D. Farquhar, DSO
Cpl. A.B. Farrell
Pte. H. Farrer
Pte. G. Fayeta
Pte. J.C. Feeney
Pte. C.F. Fenn
Pte. C.L. Fenton
Pte. W.R. Fenton
Cpl. N. Ferguson
Pte. R.M. Ferguson
Pte. V.A. Ferrier
Lt. G.S. Fife
L/Cpl. H.A. Finlayson
Pte. J.K. Fisk
Pte. E.J. Fitzgerald
Capt. F. Fitzgerald
Pte. R.F. Fitzgerald
Pte. N. Fleming
L/Cpl. T. Flintoft
Pte. E.A. Ford
Pte. J.H. Ford
Cpl. W.D. Ford
Cpl. C.I. Forman
CSM H. Forman
Pte. J. Forrest
Pte. L. Forrest
Pte. O. Forrester
Pte. A.N. Forsberg
Pte. J.C. Forster
Pte. R.E. Forster
Pte. A.H. Foster
Pte. H. Foster
Pte. H.V. Foster
Pte. L.C. Foster
Pte. O.W.P. Fournaise
Pte. W.B. Fowler
Sgt. A. Fox
Sgt. G.R. Fox
Pte. T. Fox
Pte. G.E. Franklin
L/Sgt. A. Franks
RSM A. Fraser
A/Cpl. L.D. French
Cpl. R.C. Fruen
L/Cpl. N. Fry
Pte. W. Fry
Pte. F.W. Fullarton
Pte. L. Fuller
Pte. W.B. Gaffikin
Pte. B. Gallagher
Pte. F. Gallagher
A/Cpl. J. Gallagher
Lt. N.F. Gammel
Pte. G. Gardiner
Pte. D. Gardner
Pte. W.J. Garrow
Pte. J. Garscadden
Pte. D.S. Gay
Pte. D. Geekie
Pte. J.D. Gibson
L/Cpl. R.M. Gibson
Pte. N.W. Gilbert
Pte. W.E. Gilbert
Pte. A. Giles
Cpl. C. Gillen
Pte. P. Gillen
Pte. J.H. Gillespie
Pte. V.A. Gillespie
Pte. M. Gillett
Pte. G. Gleed
RSM S. Godfrey
Cpl. F.E. Godwin
Pte. J.F. Goldie
Pte. W. Gomme
Lt. A.E. Goodeve
Pte. W.A. Goodger
Pte. A.B. Goodwin
Pte. C. Goodwin
Pte. C.W. Gordon
Cpl. J. Gordon
Pte. J.A. Gordon
L/Sgt. J.D. Graham, MM
Pte. R. Graham
L/Cpl. W.H. Grainger
Lt. C.A. Grant
Pte. E.F. Grant
Pte. R. Grant
Pte. R.C. Grant
Pte. J. Gray
L/Cpl. J.E. Gray
Pte. P.H. Green
L/Cpl. A.W.H. Greene
Pte. H. Greenhill
Pte. E.W. Greenhow
Pte. H.G. Grenkie
Sgt. L.J. Griffith
Pte. W.L. Griffith
Pte. C.D. Griffiths
Pte. M. Grimes
Pte. C. Grundy
CQMS J.W. Guerin
Pte. G.J. Guy
Pte. T.E. Hackett
Pte. C.A. Hackshaw
Pte. T.B. Haddock
Lt. D.G. Hagarty
Capt. R.L. Haggard
Pte. G.R. Hales
Pte. E.C. Haley
L/Cpl. A. Hall
Pte. H.W. Hall
Pte. A.R. Hamilton
Pte. R.H. Hamilton
Cpl. H.L. Hammond
Pte. A. Harbridge
Pte. C.N. Hardie
Pte. C. Harding
Sgt. J.T. Harflett
L/Cpl. W. Harkness
Pte. C. Harrington
L/Sgt. C.T. Harris
Pte. R. Harris
Pte. W. Harris
Pte. C. Harrison
Pte. J. Harrison

Pte. I. Hart
L/Cpl. E. Hartley
Pte. N.J. Harvey
L/Cpl. W. Harvey
Pte. C.S. Haskell
Pte. T. Hasted
Cpl. J.L. Hastings
Pte. J. Hatchman
A/Sgt. H. Hawke
Pte. F.G. Hawkes
Pte. E.H. Hawthorn
Pte. T.R. Hay
Pte. M.D. Hayes
Cpl. J.S. Hays
Pte. W.J. Hazell
Pte. C.E. Heath
Pte. G. Heath
Pte. D. Heaslip
Pte. H.B. Heather
Pte. A.C. Henderson
Pte. J.H. Henderson
Pte. A.L. Hendry
Pte. E.D. Henry
Cpl. R.E.G. Henry
Pte. S.G. Henry
Pte. W.G. Herbert
Pte. L.A. Herdman
Pte. W.R. Herraghty
Pte. R.H. Hess
Pte. A. Heward
Pte. R.E. Hewitt
Pte. A.H. Hickey
Pte. J.S. Hiddleston
Pte. W. Higgins
Pte. J.W. Hildred
Pte. H.R. Hill
Pte. W.E. Hill (123010)
Pte. W.E. Hill
Pte. T. Hinton
Pte. J. Hobbs
Pte. G.M. Hodgson
Lt. J.E. Hodgson
Pte. J.S. Hodgson
Pte. W.B. Hodgson
Pte. H.B. Hodson
Pte. G. Hogg
Pte. O.M. Hogg
Pte. J. Hoile
Pte. W. Holder
Pte. F.D. Holland
L/Cpl. R.V. Holland
Pte. G. Holleron
Pte. J.S. Hollies
Pte. L. Holmes
Pte. W.H. Holmes
Pte. L. Homer
Pte. T.G. Homersham
Pte. W.H. Honeychurch
Pte. A. Hookey
L/Cpl. W. Hope
Pte. G.C. Hopkins
Lt. A.H. Horner
L/Cpl. C.E. Horner
Pte. G.S.W. Hough
Pte. A. Howie
Sgt. F. Hubbard
Pte. C. Hudson
Pte. I.H. Huehn
Pte. H.S. Hughes
Pte. J. Hughes
Pte. W. Hughes
Pte. W.T. Hughes
Pte. A. Hummel
Pte. E. Huntbach
L/Cpl. W.J. Huston
L/Cpl. A. Hutchinson
Pte. P.A. Hyder
Pte. F. Illingsworth
Pte. W. Imrie
Pte. F.W. Inch
Pte. G. Ingraham
Pte. G. Inkster, DCM
Pte. E.H. Ireland
L/Sgt. C.F. Irwin
Pte. J.C. Irwin
Cpl. A.C.D. Jackman
Pte. J. Jacks
L/Cpl. H. Jackson
CSM J.R. Jacques
Pte. E.A. James
Pte. G. Jameson
Pte. J. Jardine
Pte. L.J.E. Jarvis
Pte. E. Jauvin
Pte. P. Jeandron
Pte. F.N. Jeffrey
Pte. A.C.W. Jeffs
Pte. W.J. Jeffs
Pte. H. Jenkins
L/Cpl. M.J. Jenkins
Pte. E.S. Jennings
Pte. A.H. Jephson
L/Sgt. S. Jerred
Pte. E.H. Johnson
Pte. F. Johnson
Pte. R.G. Johnson
Pte. A.A. Johnston
Pte. J. Johnston
Pte. M.S. Johnston
Pte. R.N. Johnston
Sgt. W. Johnston
L/Cpl. G. Johnstone
Cpl. P.E. Joiner
L/Cpl. G.J.C. Joliffe
A/Cpl. A.E. Jones
Pte. H.J. Jones
Pte. I. Jones
Sgt. J. Jones
Pte. J.E. Jones
Pte. S. Jones
Pte. S.L. Jones
Pte. W.N. Jones
Pte. W.H. Joyce
Pte. A. Kane
Pte. A. Kay
Cpl. J.H.B. Kayss, MM
Pte. A. Keats
Pte. W.M. Kedey
Pte. F.M. Keffer
Pte. G.M. Kehoe
CSM J.R. Keith
L/Sgt. J.F.T. Kelley, MM
Pte. J. Kelly (1601)
Pte. J. Kelly
Pte. M. Kelly
Pte. J. Kelso
Pte. J.S. Kerr
Pte. W. Kerr
Pte. L. Key
Pte. H.L. Kidd
Pte. J.R. Kilgour
Cpl. E.C. King
Pte. F.W. King
Pte. G.T. King
Pte. J.C. King
L/Cpl. J.D. King
Pte. W.H. King

Pte. W. Kirby
L/Cpl. P.D. Kisbey
L/Cpl. H.R. Kissack
Pte. R. Klees
Pte. R. Knight
Lt. A.J. Knowling
Pte. J. Knox
Pte. F. Lablanche
Pte. C.H. Ladler
Pte. H.D. Laidlaw
Pte. J.P. Laidlaw
Pte. F.A. Lake
Pte. R.L. Laking
Pte. S. Lancaster
Lt. P.E. Lane
Pte. H.D. Lang
Pte. M.R. Lank
Pte. A. Laplante
Pte. G.F. Large
Pte. R. Larmour
Pte. G.E. Latimer
Pte. G.M. Lavell
A/Sgt. R. Lavers, MM
L/Cpl. A.H. Law
Pte. J.E. Law
Pte. A. Lawrence
Pte. F.D. Lawrence
Pte. W.R. Lawrence
Pte. J. Lawrie
Cpl. W.G. Lawson
Pte. P.C. Lea
Pte. D. Leach
Pte. J. Leach
Pte. J.H. Leary
Pte. J.T. Leatherby
Pte. F.E. Lee
Pte. R. Lee
Pte. W. Leib
Pte. R.C. Leitch
Pte. J.F. Leslie
Pte. W.R. Lester
Pte. A.F. Levangie
Pte. W.F. Lewin
Pte. A.H. Lewis
Pte. C. Lewis
Pte. M.W.F. Lewis
Pte. S. Lewis
Pte. W. Lewis
Pte. P.F. Light
Lt. C.J. Lightbody
Pte. J. Lightbody
Pte. M.B. Lilly
L/Cpl. W. Lindsay
Pte. S.A. Linington
Sgt. A. Linnington
Pte. G. Lister
Pte. J.E. Livett, MM
CSM C. Lloyd
Pte. L.J. Lloyd
Pte. D. Logan
Cpl. T.W. Lognon
Pte. A. Lomax
Lt. S. Loptson, MC, MM
Pte. J. Lorette
Pte. H.R. Love
Pte. S.J. Luck
Pte. R. MacCrimmon
Pte. A.A. MacDonald
Pte. J. MacDonald
Sgt. J. Macdonald, DCM
Lt. J. MacKay
Lt. M. MacKay
Pte. T. MacKay
Pte. C.H. MacKenzie
CSM C.J.M. MacKenzie
Pte. K. MacKenzie
Pte. W.D. MacKenzie
Pte. R. MacKinnon
Pte. T.N. MacKinnon
Pte. A. Maclachlan
Pte. G.A. Maclaren
L/Cpl. W. MacLurg
Maj. J.R. MacPherson, DSO
Pte. J. MacRitchie
Pte. R.H. Magee
L/Cpl. J.P. Mahoney
Pte. E. Maidment
Pte. G.H. Main
Pte. F. Mangin
Pte. C.C. Manning
Pte. G. Manser
Sgt. R.J. Mansfield
Pte. J. Manson
Pte. I. Maracle
Pte. H.G. Marchant
Sgt. G. Marsh
Pte. A.M. Marshall
Pte. J.G. Marshall
Pte. A.J. Martin
Pte. C. Martin
Pte. M. Martin
Maj. S.F.A. Martin
Pte. T.J. Martin
Pte. J. Martindale
L/Cpl. F.G. Martyn
Pte. C.W. Mason
Pte. W.J. Mathers
Pte. W.W. Mathers
Pte. A. Mathews
L/Cpl. G. Matthews
Pte. J.L. Matthews
Pte A.W. McAllister
CSM L. McAllum
Pte. A. McAlpine
Pte. T.E. McAndless
Pte. A. McArthur
Pte. N. McArthur
Pte. R.J. McAvoy
Pte. C.L. McBride
Pte. J. McBride
Pte. M.J. McCallum
Pte. W. McCallum
Pte. J. McCarthy
Lt. D.H. McCartney
Pte. J. McCauley
Pte. G. McCoach
Pte. W. McConnell
Pte. R.P. McCordick
Pte. J.J. McCormack
Sgt. J.H. McCormick
Sgt. T. McDermott
Cpl. R. McCullough
Sgt. D. McDonald
Cpl. G. McDonald
Pte. J. McDonald
Pte. M. McDonald
Pte. N. McDonald
Pte. P. McDonald
Pte. J.E. McDougall
Pte. J.L. McEwen
Pte. L.J. McEwen
Pte. C. McGeary
Pte. M.L. McGihon
Pte. J.B. McGill
Pte. J.J. McGill
Pte. A.D. McGillivray

Pte. D. McGillivray
Pte. G.A. McGillivray
Pte. W.B. McGillivray
Pte. J. McGonigal
Pte. F.W. McGowan
Pte. S.E.T. McGreer
Pte. W. McGregor
Pte. J. McGuirk
Pte. J.D. McInnes
Sgt. J.E. McInnes, MM
Pte. C. McInnis
Cpl. J.W. McInnis
Cpl. D. McIntosh
Pte. R.W. McIntosh
Pte. J. McIntyre
Pte. N. McIvor
Pte. T. McKennell
Pte. F.L. McKenzie
Pte. F.M. McKenzie
Lt. H. McKenzie, VC, DCM
L/Cpl. W. McKenzie
Pte. W.D. McKenzie
Pte. R.L. McKiel
Pte. T.A. McKinlay
Pte. F.A. McKinnon
Lt. I.L. McKinnon
Pte. J. McLaughlin (1517)
Pte. J. McLaughlin
Pte. P. McLaughlin (475968)
Pte. P. McLaughlin
Lt. D. McLean
Pte. D. McLean
Pte. J.A. McLean
L/Cpl. T.G. McLean
Pte. A. McLellan
Pte. W.J. McLellan
Pte. A.A. McLeod
Pte. C.H. McLeod
Pte. H. McLeod
A/Cpl. J.M. McLeod
Pte. N. McLeod
Pte. E.G. McMahon
Pte. J.V. McMahon
Pte. T. McMahon
Pte. D. McMillan
Pte. H. McMillan
Pte. J. McNamara
Pte. C. McNaught
Pte. W.A.K. McNaughton
Pte. J. McNish
Pte. N. McNiven
Pte. E.E. McNulty
Pte. C.B. McPhail
Pte. A. McPhee
L/Cpl. A.R. McQueen
Pte. J. MacRitchie
Pte. J.F. McVeaty
L/Cpl. J. Meadowcroft
Pte. J.D. Meehan
Pte. E.S. Meeres
Pte. J. Meiklejohn
Pte. G.L. Mellott
Pte. C. Methven
Pte. C. Meti
Pte. W.J. Metivier
L/Cpl. P. Michael
Sgt. T. Michaud
Pte. J. Middleton
Pte. M. Milatovich
Pte. W.H. Mildon
Pte. A.A. Miles
Pte. N.F. Millar, MM
Cpl. J.F.L. Millen
Pte. F.G. Miller
Pte. F.R. Miller
Pte. J.F. Miller
Pte. J.H. Miller
Pte. J.J. Miller
Pte. J.M. Miller
Pte. F.E. Mills
Pte. F.L. Mills
Pte. J.S. Mills
Lt. R.D. Millyard
Pte. A.G. Mitchell
Pte. G. Mitchell
L/Cpl. R.A.B. Mitchell
Pte. W.B. Mitchell
Lt. J.R. Mitchener
Pte. T. Mochrie
Capt. P. Molson, MC
Pte. J. Moneypenny
Pte. W. Mooney
Pte. L.C. Moore
Pte. E. Morgan
Pte. H. Morgan
Pte. M.A. Morgan
Pte. C. Morphy
Pte. A.R. Morris
Capt. W.H. Morris
Pte. G. Morrison
Pte. P. Morrison
Pte. S. Mortimer
Pte. A. Mould
Cpl. J.A. Mowat
Cpl. A. Muir
Pte. J. Muir
Cpl. J. Mulheron
Pte. R.T. Mullin
Sgt. W.G. Mundell
Pte. M.J. Munroe
Pte. J. Murdoch
Pte. W.C.B. Murdoch
L/Cpl. J.H. Murphy
Pte. T.F. Murphy
Pte. G. Murray
L/Cpl. H.M. Murray
Pte. K.F. Murray
Sgt. A.R. Mutton
Pte. J.H. Myatt
Pte. C. Naum
Pte. J. Nedon
Pte. F.V. Nelson
Pte. W. Nelson
A/Sgt. H.W. Nesbitt
Pte. M. Nesbitt
Pte. A.O.W. Newbury
L/Cpl. J.R. Newell
Pte. A.F. Newton
Capt. D.O.C. Newton
Pte. H. Newton
Pte. J.E. Newton
Pte. J.L. Nicholls
Pte. A. Nicholson
Pte. W. Nicoll
Pte. W. Nightingale
Pte. A.T. Niven
Pte. J. Noble
Pte. J.A. Noble
Pte. J. Noons
Pte. C.A. Nunn
Pte. G. O'Brien
Pte. W. O'Connell
Pte. W.J. O'Connor
Pte. A. O'Keefe
Pte. D. O'Keefe

Pte. R.G. O'Leary
Pte. A. O'Meara
Pte. M.J. Olafson
Pte. W.J. Oliver
Pte. K. Olsen
Pte. A.R. Ostrom
Pte. G.E. Otis
Pte. J.M. Otley
Pte. T.G. Owen
Pte. G. Page
Pte. A.T. Paige
Pte. H. Palmer
Pte. E.E. Pannabaker
Maj. T.M. Papineau, MC
Pte. C. Parent
Pte. C.W. Parke
Pte. E.F. Parke
Pte. A.E.L. Parlett
Pte. R.E. Parrott
Pte. O. Parry
L/Cpl. E.H. Parsons
Pte. C.G. Partridge
Pte. F.W. Paterson
Pte. T. Patten
Pte. E.G. Patterson
Pte. N.E. Patton
Pte. A. Paxton
Pte. J. Pearcey
Pte. H. Peck
Pte. D.R. Peel
Pte. A.H. Penny
Pte. E.M. Peoples
L/Cpl. R.C. Pepler
Pte. W.C. Perkin
Pte. J.B. Perkins
Pte. P.C. Perry
Pte. A.J. Peters
Pte. E.C. Peters
Pte. W.E. Peters
Pte. H. Phelps
L/Cpl. C.A. Philion
Pte. E.M. Phillips
Pte. J. Phillips
Pte. A. Phillipson
Pte. J. Philpotts
Pte. F.R. Pickford
Pte. G. Pickles
Pte. N.J. Pilon
Pte. R.J. Poast

Pte. W.J. Pollock
Lt. C.A. Pope
Pte. C. Porter, MM
Pte. F. Pregent
Pte. A.W. Price
Lt. C.H. Price
Pte. J. Price
Pte. G.H. Pryke
Pte. A.E. Quigley
Pte. J. Ralph
L/Cpl. A. Ramage
Lt. W.T. Ramsay
Sgt. J. Ramsey
Pte. D.H. Rankin
Pte. T. Rankin
Pte. E.J. Rawe
CSM W.W. Ray
Pte. W.L. Raynes
Pte. D.G. Read
Cpl. F.N. Read
Pte. S.T. Read
Pte. W. Read
Pte. E. Reading
Pte. E.C. Reed
Pte. H. Reekie
Pte. D. Rees
Pte. T. Regan
Pte. E.J. Reid
Pte. S.J. Reid
Pte. W. Reid
Pte. J. Rennie
Pte. D.B. Rennoldson
Pte. J.G. Reymond
Pte. H.A. Riach
Pte. A.S. Richards
Pte. C.A. Richards
Pte. J.S. Richards
L/Cpl. C.D. Richardson
Pte. D. Richardson
A/Cpl. G.A. Richardson
Pte. E.R. Riches
Lt. J.R. Riddell
Sgt. S.J. Ridley, MM
Pte. D.T. Riekie
Pte. T. Rigg
Pte. T. Ritchie
Sgt. H.W. Rittenhouse
Pte. C.J.W. Ritter
Pte. W. Roach

Pte. J. Roberts
Pte. J.G. Roberts
Sgt. J.L.A. Robertson
Pte. R. Robertson
Pte. S.G. Robertson
Pte. W.M. Robertson
Pte. W.T. Robertson
Lt. A.J. Robins
Pte. A.E.F. Robinson
Pte. C. Robinson
Pte. J. Robinson
Pte. M.A. Robinson
L/Cpl. P. Robson
Pte. F.R. Rock
Pte. M.T. Roett
Pte. E. Roper
Lt. A.G. Rosamond
L/Cpl. J.H. Rosher
Cpl. D. Ross
Pte. H. Ross
Pte. J. Ross
Pte. E. Rossiter
Pte. J. Rothschild
L/Cpl. D.S. Rough
Pte. J. Routledge
Pte. J.A. Rowe
Pte. J. Rowley
Pte. W.M. Roys
Sgt. T. Ruddigan
Pte. W.L. Ruddy
Pte. J. Russell
Pte. S. Ruston
Pte. W.F. Ryan
Pte. W. Sabean
Pte. L. Salsbury
Pte. W. Savell
Sgt. M.D. Schell, DCM
Pte. D. Scott
Pte. J. Scott (51423)
Pte. J. Scott
Pte. J.A. Scott
Pte. J.J. Scott
Pte. J.W. Scotting
Pte. W.H. Screen
Pte. G. Seguin
Pte. G. Selley
Pte. R. Sero
Sgt. J.F. Sexton
Pte. D.C. Seymour

Pte. O. Sharp
Pte. R.W. Sharpe
Pte. A.J. Shaver
Pte. H.S. Shaver
Pte. H. Shaw
Pte. H.R. Shearer
Pte. J.D. Shearer
Pte. A.J. Sheppard
Pte. G. Sheppard
Pte. G. Sheppherd
Pte. L. Sherriff
L/Cpl. J.C. Shipton
Pte. A.H. Shute
Pte. H.R.S. Shuter
Pte. R.E. Shuttleworth, MM
Pte. C.J. Sibary
Pte. E. Silcox
Pte. T. Sillence
Pte. G.R. Silson
Pte. G.B. Simmons
Lt. R.H. Simonds
Pte. P.A. Simons
Pte. H. Simpson
Pte. P.M. Simpson
Pte. R. Simpson
Pte. A.J. Sinclair
Pte. C. Singer
L/Cpl. H.A. Skene
Lt. R.L. Sladen
Pte. B. Slater
Pte. J.P. Sloan
Pte. J. Slonemsky
Pte. A.G. Small
Pte. W. Smedley
Pte. A. Smith
Pte. C. Smith (McG173)
Pte. C. Smith
Pte. C.K. Smith
Pte. E.J. Smith
Pte. H. Smith
CSM H.G.L. Smith
Sgt. J. Smith
Pte. J.A. Smith
Pte. L.R. Smith
Pte. R. Smith (487283)
Pte. R. Smith
Pte. F.G. Snare
Pte. F.G. Sniderhon
Pte. R.D. Snow
Pte. C.W. Snyder
Pte. W.E. Sollars
L/Cpl. W. Sowden
Sgt. R. Spall, VC
Pte. J. Spanswick
Pte. A.J. Sparks
Pte. A. Splicer
Pte. T.A. Spoor
Pte. E. St. Amour
Sgt. W. Stanborough, DCM
Pte. R.A. Stanbury
Pte. F.W. Standish
Pte. R.R. Staveley
L/Cpl. G. Stayman
Pte. J.H. Steele
Pte. J.E. Stender
Pte. A. Stephen
Pte. W.J. Stephens
Pte. S.S. Sterns
Pte. J. Steven
Pte. A.E. Stevens
L/Sgt. A.W. Stevens
L/Cpl. O. Stevenson
Lt. Col. C.J.T. Stewart, DSO
Pte. E.M. Stewart
L/Cpl. G.B. Stewart
Lt. J. Stewart
Pte. J. Stewart
Pte. W. Stewart
Cpl. A.T. Stoner
Pte. F. Storey
Pte. A. Strachan
Lt. G.S. Stratford
Pte. F.H. Striker
Pte. A.J. Stripp
Pte. H.E.J. Strong
Pte. F. Stuwart
Pte. E.P. Sullivan
Maj. H.E. Sullivan
Pte. P. Sullivan
Pte. F. Summers
Pte. J. Sutton
L/Cpl. C.J. Swan
Pte. J.E. Sweeney
Pte. J.A. Sweet
Pte. G. Sweetland
Pte. J. Tabor
Pte. W. Tallamy
Pte. J.W. Tate
L/Cpl. F.I. Taylor
Pte. G. Taylor
Pte. G.W. Taylor
Pte. J. Taylor
Pte. O.B. Taylor
Pte. S. Taylor
Pte. W.E. Taylor
Pte. W.J. Taylor
Pte. J.H. Telfer
L/Cpl. W.S. Telfer
Pte. A. Templeton
Pte. E.W. Thackray
Pte. C.D. Thomas
Pte. F.W. Thompson
Sgt. G.R. Thompson
Cpl. H.E. Thompson
Pte. W.E. Thompson
Pte. A. Thomson
Pte. A.M. Thomson
A/Sgt. J.B. Thomson
Lt. W.D. Thomson
Pte. W. Thorburn
Pte. S.A. Thorne
Pte. S.T. Thornley
Pte. M. Thorpe
Pte. J. Tilton
Pte. R.J. Tisdale
Pte. D.P. Tobin
Pte. G.H. Townshend
L/Cpl. S. Trezise
Lt. G. Triggs
Pte. A.S. Trow
Pte. A.E. Tucker
Pte. H. Tucker
Pte. P.W. Tucker
Pte. T. Tully
Sgt. F.W. Turner
Pte. J.H. Turner
Pte. R.S. Turiff
Pte. H. Tyldesley
Pte. F. Tyo
Pte. R. Tyrer
Pte. J. Underwood
Cpl. A. Unicume
Pte. E.H. Utley
Pte. C.B. Vanluven
Pte. W.H. Vaughan

Pte. C. Vellenzer
Pte. H.J. Venn
Pte. W.G. Vincent
Pte. H. Vitler
L/Cpl. A. Volker
Pte. W. Wade
Lt. A.F. Wagner
L/Cpl. J. Waldron
Pte. P.V. Waldron
Sgt. A. Walker
Pte. J. Wallbridge
Pte. H.E. Waller
Pte. R. Walsh
Pte. W.G. Walsh
Pte. W.L. Walsh
Lt. A.A. Wanklyn
Pte. J.J. Ward
Maj. J.S. Ward
Pte. H.J. Warin
Pte. L.A. Wark
L/Cpl. F. Warner
Pte. T. Waterfield
Pte. J. Waters
Pte. J. Waterson
Sgt. D.M. Watkins
Pte. A. Watson
Pte. R.W. Watts
Pte. E.A. Webb
L/Cpl. G.E. Welbourn
L/Cpl. T. Welch
Pte. W. Welch
Pte. W.H. Welch
Cpl. S.C. Westgate
Pte. E.S. Weston
Pte. J. Wheatley
Pte. J. Whelan
Pte. P. Whitaker
Pte. E.G. White
Pte. H. White
Pte. H.W. White
Pte. J.W. White
Sgt. A.W. Whitehead
Pte. H. Whiting
Pte. A.G. Wiffen
Pte. A.E. Wiggens
Pte. E.G. Wilbur
Pte. H.J. Wildman
Pte. E.W. Wilkes
Pte. G. Wilkie
Pte. A. Wilkinson
Pte. J.W. Wilkinson
Pte. A. Willey
Pte. C. Williams
L/Sgt. C.H. Williams
Lt. M.W. Williams
Pte. T.A. Williams
Pte. A. Williamson
Pte. F.A. Williamson, MM
Pte. A. Wilson
Pte. A.A. Wilson
Pte. C.B. Wilson
Pte. C.J. Wilson
L/Cpl. D.D. Wilson
L/Cpl. E.D. Wilson
A/Cpl. G.T. Wilson
Cpl. W.G. Wilson
Sgt. W.M. Wilson
Pte. G. Wood
Pte. J.N. Wood
L/Cpl. H. Woodcock
Cpl. E.J. Woodgate
Pte. G. Woods
Pte. L.D. Woods
Pte. C.H. Wright
Lt. D.A. Wright
Pte. F.F. Wright
Pte. G. Wright
Pte. J.H. Wylie
Pte. R. Wylie
Cpl. H.M. Yeats
Pte. D. Young
Pte. W. Young (1709)
Pte. W. Young
Pte. A.E. Yuill

SECOND WORLD WAR 1939–1945

Lt. V.S. Allan
L/Cpl. G. Amos
Pte. V. Anderson
A/L/Cpl. J.A. Andros
Sgt. E. Arbour
Cpl. J.F. Archer
A/L/Cpl. R.G. Argue
Pte. H. Badleck
Pte. A.J. Baker
Pte. L.P. Baker
L/Cpl. C.F. Bangle
Pte. E.R. Barnes
Pte. M. Bazzlo
Pte. B.G. Beaton
Pte. F. Beitz
Pte. R.R. Bennett
Pte. F. Bernath
Pte. R.G. Birch
Pte. J.T. Bjornson
Pte. D.A. Black
Pte. R.R. Blair
Pte. W. Boak
Pte. C.R. Botham
Pte. W.R. Boulton
Pte. J.L. Bowen
Pte. F.V. Bradshaw
A/Maj. D. Brain
Pte. R.R. Brogden
Pte. A. Brown
Pte. E.H. Brown
Pte. G.D. Brown
Pte. W.S. Brown
Cpl. J. Buck
Lt. Col. K.C. Burness, MC
Capt. L.G. Burton
Pte. R. Butterfield
CSM V.E. Cahill
Pte. C.A. Calder
Pte. W. Camelon
L/Cpl. G.I. Carleton
Sgt. R. Carter
Pte. J.A. Cassells
Pte. P. Charney
Pte. W.H. Cherry
Cpl. P. Child
Sgt. C.E. Christie
Pte. A. Clark
Pte. A.G. Clark
Pte. R.G. Clark
Pte. N.F. Clarke
Pte. L.J. Cleunion
Pte. A. Clifton
Pte. A.C. Collins
Pte. J.E. Connolly
Capt. G. Corkett
Pte. O. Cormier
Pte. R.T. Cornwall
Pte. W.L. Cory

Pte. J.A. Cousens
Pte. S.J. Cousins
Pte. R. Cowie
Pte. W.J. Cox
Lt. J.C. Crabtree
Pte. G.R. Crane
Pte. A.L. Crassman
A/L/Cpl. C.H. Currie
L/Cpl. G.B. Daniel
CSM W.D. Davidson
Pte. W.T. Davis
Pte. R.H. Dearle
Lt. J. deBalinhard
Pte. J.S. Dell
Cpl. W.G. Denman
A/Cpl. W. Dobson
Pte. C.A. Dodd
Pte. A.J. Donohue
Pte. J. Dool
Pte. J.H. Driedger
Cpl. S.C. Duncan
Pte. D.F. Durant
Pte. J.A. Durr
Pte. J. Eastland
H/Capt. K.E. Eaton
Pte. L.M. Egerton
Pte. F. Ehinger
Pte. G.H. Elefson
Pte. A.D. Ellis
A/L/Sgt. E.H. Ellis
Pte. A.M. Falardeau
Pte. W.J. Fennell
Cpl. P. Fidiadis
Pte. F. Firth
L/Cpl. H.J. Fleming
Pte. A. Foulsham
A/L/Sgt. J.E. Fox
Pte. L.L. Francis
A/L/Cpl. P. Furey
Pte. D. Garneau
Lt. M.E. Garritty
Pte. G. Gascoyne
Cpl. J. Gates
Pte. J.P. Gattinger
Pte. M. Gayoway
Pte. L. Genaille
Pte. F. Gensorick
Pte. C. Gerrassimou
A/Cpl. B. Gill
Sgt. W. Goodburn
Pte. A.J.C. Gosselin
Pte. R. Gosselin
A/Sgt. C.C. Graham
Pte. J.J. Graham
Pte. T.C. Gravelle
Pte. B. Green
Capt. E.P.T. Green
Pte. M. Griffin
Pte. J.E. Griffiths
Pte. W. Grimes
Sgt. W. Grimshaw
Lt. W.A. Groomes
Pte. G. Groves
Pte. G.H. Groves
Pte. C.R. Haight
Pte. J.E. Hanishewski
Pte. W.J. Harford
Maj. J.T. Harper
Pte. R. Harrison
Pte. H. Hayes
Pte. W.A. Hayward
Lt. J.R. Heppell
L/Sgt. W.H. Hickey
Pte. A.E. Hill
A/Cpl. H.J.E. Hill
Lt. J.D. Horn
Pte. J. Hossay
A/Sgt. W.R. Howard, MM
Pte. M. Hudson
A/Capt. J.R. Hunt
Pte. G.L. Hurford
Cpl. J. Hutchinson
Pte. D.J. Hutson
A/Cpl. H. Ilasevich
L/Cpl. S. Jackson
Pte. C.G. Jacobs
Pte. L.J. Jankulak
Pte. R.E. Johns
Pte. O.E. Johnson
Pte. W. Johnson
Pte. R.N. Jones
Pte. J.A.J. Joyal
Pte. J.E. Kennard
Pte. P. Kivi
Pte. D.V. Klassen
Pte. P. Kolcun
A/L/Cpl. R.B. Kotchorek
Pte. L.E. Kramer
A/Cpl. W. Krasny
Pte. S. Krysowaty
Pte. L.F. Kucy
Pte. R.W. Kyler
Pte. N.E. Lamke
Pte. S.J. Landry
PSM M.L. Larson
Pte. R.L. LaRue
A/Sgt. F.J. Leguee
Pte. D.E. Lewis
L/Cpl. G.A. Lincoln
Pte. L.V. Longney
L/Sgt. C.G. Lord
Pte. B.W. Loree
Pte. C. Low
Pte. D.M. Low
Sgt. C.J. Lowson
Pte. E.G. Ludwig
Lt. W.J. MacNeil
Pte. C.L. Madigan
Cpl. L.C. Manness
Pte. M.H. Marks
Pte. R.M. Marquette
Pte. F. Marty
Pte. S.R. Maxwell
Pte. P. Maynard
Pte. R.H. McAuley
Pte. J.H. McCourt
Pte. S. McFee
Pte. E.E. McGhee
L/Cpl. J.F. McGowan
Pte. W. McIvor
A/L/Cpl. E.J. McKay
A/L/Sgt. W.L. McKay
A/L/Sgt. W.G. McKee
Pte. P. McLean
A/Cpl. A.D. McLeod
Pte. L.N. McQuitty
Pte. A.H. McRae
Pte. L.D. Mencini
Pte. M. Menzoski
Pte. E.R. Miller
Pte. O.E. Miller
Pte. J. Milliken
Pte. A.L. Milne
Pte. E. Milne
Pte. H.R. Monson
A/CSM G.S. Moore
Pte. C.E. Morris

Pte. W. Mowatt
Pte. J.R. Muir
Lt. C.S. Munro
Pte. C. Murray
Pte. P. Musquash
Pte. H.T. Nelson
Pte. L. Nelson
Pte. L.W. Nelson
Pte. R.W. Newman
Pte. A.H. Nicholson
Pte. K. Nicholson
Pte. J. Nicol
A/Sgt. J. Nile
A/L/Cpl. H.C. Nixon
Pte. J. Norgang
Pte. J.A. North
Cpl. L. O'Connor
Pte. H. Oddy
Cpl. D.P. O'Keefe
Pte. J.E. Oslund
Pte. L. Palmer
Pte. E.C. Parker
L/Cpl. B.H. Parmeter
Pte. J. Parrish
Pte. P. Pasowysty
Pte. E.O. Paulson
Pte. A. Pavelick
Pte. R.F. Pearos
Pte. L.G. Pearson
A/L/Cpl. T. Pearson
Pte. F. Penner
Pte. F. Perepelitz
Pte. L.R. Peters
Pte. A. Pietrasz
Pte. L.S. Pinkerton
L/Cpl. J.E. Potter
Pte. A. Poulain
Pte. E. Poulin
Pte. S. Prescott
Pte. N.L. Pretty
Pte. H. Prince
Sgt. G.T. Prior
Pte. A. Proulx
Pte. G. Pugh
Pte. A. Pulford
Pte. J.W. Purvis
Pte. G.C. Quartly
A/Cpl. H.D. Rathert
Pte. K.R. Ray
Pte. A.J. Rebbeck
Pte. H.C. Rees
Pte. J.H. Reid
Pte. R.F. Reid
Pte. H.S.E. Renaud
Pte. A. Renz
Pte. E.P. Ries
Pte. H.B. Robinson
Pte. H. Roth
Cpl. P.A.D. Routh
Pte. H. Rudko
Pte. A.J. Saddleman
A/Cpl. J.H. Saunders
Pte. W.G. Saunders
Pte. J.R. Scholey
Pte. W. Scott
Pte. J.E. Seivewright
Pte. M. Seman
Pte. D. Serhon
Pte. B.Z.B. Shanas
Pte. H.R. Sharp
Lt. C.N. Shea
Pte. C. Sherb
Pte. D. Sinclair
L/Cpl. A.R. Skinner
Pte. M. Slemmons
Pte. D. Sloan
Pte. J. Slyzuk
Pte. E.V. Smallpiece
Pte. I.D. Smith
Pte. J.M. Sowerby
Cpl. M.P.J. St. Denis
Pte. G.S. Stefanson
Pte. W. Steinke
L/Cpl. F.G. Stephenson
A/CQMS J.F. Stevens
Pte. J.G.W. Stinson
Pte. R.J. Strachan
Pte. J. Talbot
Pte. H. Taralson
Pte. J.J. Tarnausky
Pte. S. Taylor
L/Cpl. H.J. Thacker
Pte. L. Theberge
L/Cpl. L.R. Thompson
Pte. C. Thorne
Pte. J. Tod
Cpl. K.L. Toland
Pte. W.H. Trewolla
L/Cpl. C. Tucker
Cpl. R. Turcotte
Pte. H.D. Turnbull
Pte. W.J. Turnbull
Pte. J. Umpherville
Pte. E.N. Unrow
Pte. L. Urquhart
Pte. R. Vermette
Pte. W.G. Vickery
Pte. G. Vinette
A/Sgt. M.F. Waller
Pte. R.J. Warrington
Pte. G.R. Watson
Pte. E.J. Wearmouth
L/Cpl. H. Weidenhamer
Pte. R.D. Whitlam
Cpl. C.R. Whittaker
Pte. P.D. Wiebe
A/Sgt. A.S. Wood
Sgt. J.D. Wright
Pte. R.H. Wright
L/Cpl. C. Wynne
Pte. J.A. Youngren
Pte. P. Zeglinski
Pte. W.J. Zentner

KOREA
1950–1953

Pte. C.M. Alford
Pte. H. Althouse
Pte. F. Andersen
Pte. R.V. Arnott
Pte. H.A. Barkhouse
Pte. J.W. Batsch
Cpl. W.A. Black
Pte. E.F. Bradshaw
Pte. E.P. Broden
Pte. B.B. Brown
Pte. H.B. Brydon
Pte. E.C. Buchanan
Cpl. J.A. Calkins
Cpl. R.D.M. Campbell
Pte. L.A. Canning
Pte. M.S. Carr
Pte. B. Clements
Lt. H.R. Cleveland
Pte. T.H. Colbourne

Pte. R.L. Colp
Pte. E.R. Copinace
Pte. J.R.I. Cote
Pte. K. Crompton
Sgt. C.J. Currie
Pte. M. Debeck
Pte. G. Ducharme
Pte. M.A. Dunphy
L/Cpl. H.V. Edgley
L/Cpl. R.D. Elliott
Pte. R.C. Enos
Cpl. G.R. Evans
Pte. R.B. Fairservice
Pte. H.J. Farand
Pte. L.T. Fielding
Pte. W.J. Fowler
Pte. J.E.H. Garand
Pte. J.R.Q. Gillan
Pte. L.P. Gladu
Pte. E.H. Goodwin
Pte. A.L. Gray
Lt. J.D. Hamilton
Pte. A.E.R. Hansen
Pte. E.J. Hanspiker
Pte. R.O. Haraldson
Pte. J.F. Harmon
Pte. R. Harrison
Cpl. D.P. Hastings
Pte. C.A. Hayes
Pte. J.W. Hearsey
Pte. C.C. Helm
L/Cpl. H.E. Higgins
Pte. D.G. Hull
Sgt. R.A. Jodrie
L/Cpl. W.E. Johnstone
Pte. D.R. Jones
Pte. J.A. Jordan
L/Cpl. J.W. Kennedy
Pte. R.F. King
Pte. G.G. Knorr
Pte. W. Kostiuk
Pte. W. Lapka
Pte. H.J. Lavallee
Pte. R.C. Leach
Pte. H.D. Legge
Pte. J.M.L. Lessard
L/Cpl. T.N. Letkeman
Lt. J.Y. Levison
Pte. A.C. Lewis
Pte. G.L. Lucas
Cpl. E. MacAskill
Pte. B.M. MacDonald
Pte. E.W. MacDonald
Pte. R. MacDonald
Pte. H.B. MacEachron
Pte. W.J. Marshall
L/Cpl. J.N.J. Maxwell
Pte. G.D. McInnes
Pte. E.A. McIntyre
Pte. E.G. McKay
Pte. D.A. McKinnon
Pte. W.C. McPhail
Pte. R.F. McPhee
L/Cpl. R. Michaud
Pte. K.R. Monague
Pte. M.J. Moreau
Pte. J.H. Morford
Pte. S.R. Mudd
Cpl. F.A. Mullin
Pte. J.R. Murcar
Pte. L.L. Murray
Pte. E. Normand
Pte. K.W. Norton
Pte. K.D. O'Brien
Pte. L.H. Oliver
Pte. J.O. Ouellette
Pte. R.R. Patrick
Pte. E.E. Patterson
Pte. G.L. Patterson
Pte. R.B. Pearson
Pte. L.E. Peters
Pte. R.A. Plumb
Pte. A.E. Polnuk
Pte. A.G. Poupart
Pte. E.J. Power
Pte. G.E. Robinson
Pte. J. Sauve
Cpl. M.H. Schwenneker
L/Cpl. A.E. Scott
Pte. T. Siha
Pte. G.C. Small
L/Cpl. H. Smart
Pte. D.E. Spence
Pte. D.L. Stanley
Pte. R.M. Stenseth
Pte. L.A. Stewart
Pte. A.W. Storey
Pte. R.R. Sweeney
Cpl. H.A. Szlahetka
Pte. L.J. Tellier
Cpl. E.E. Theobald
Pte. T.H. Thoveson
Pte. R.H.G. Tolver
Cpl. J.R. Toole
Pte. G. Tremblay
CSM G.S. Trenter
Pte. W.J. Walch
Pte. D.E. Walker
Pte. R.L. Walker
Pte. J.R. Warren
Pte. V.R. Weatherbee
Pte. F.O. Wells
Pte. F.R. Wood
RSM J.D. Wood, DCM
Cpl. N. Woodcock
Pte. F.G. Works
Pte. T.B. Wotton
Pte. D.E. Wright
Pte. L.K. Wylie

UNITED NATIONS PEACEKEEPING

Palestine 1958
Lt. Col. G.A. Flint, CD

Cyprus 1964–1992
Capt. C.K. Crawford, CFMS
Cpl. P.C. Isenor
Pte. D.R. Krieger
Cpl. J.R. Lessard
MCpl. J.D.G. McInnis
Pte. A.J. Prins
Pte. T.J. Trottier
Pte. M.D. Wilson

Croatia 1992–1995
MCpl. J.M.H. Bechard
Pte. K.D. Cooper
Capt. J.P. DeCoste, CD
MCpl. M.R. Isfeld, 1 CER

Kosovo 1999
Sgt. H.J. Squires, CD

NOTES

Unless otherwise noted, all unpublished documents cited in the footnotes below (war diaries, after-action reports, letters, diaries, etc.) are held by the PPCLI Archives, located at the Museum of the Regiments in Calgary. In some cases, these are copies of documents also on deposit at the National Archives of Canada. All interviews cited below are from audio- or videotapes held by the PPCLI Archives. Some originate with the University of Victoria; others were donated to the PPCLI Archives by Mr. Mark Zuehlke. Those are so noted. Some of the interviews conducted specifically for this project have not been transcribed. Others have been transcribed only in part. Interested readers should check with the PPCLI archivist at the Museum of the Regiments regarding which materials cited below are available and how they may be accessed.

Introduction The Ghosts of Bellewaerde Ridge

1 Ralph Hodder-Williams, *Princess Patricia's Canadian Light Infantry: 1914–1919,* vol. 1 (London: Hodder and Stoughton 1923), 60–76

2 In those armies that are rooted in British military tradition, "regiment" has two meanings. In the infantry, regiments are responsible for recruiting one or a number of infantry battalions and for sustaining their own unique histories and traditions within those battalions. An infantry regiment is not a field formation. In fact, a regiment can form or create several different field formations that carry the same name but with a different battalion number, such as 1st, 2nd, or 3rd Battalion, Princess Patricia's Canadian Light Infantry. In other combat arms, such as armour or engineers, a regiment is a field formation roughly equivalent to the infantry battalion.

3 The corps eventually grew to four divisions and was, in effect, the fighting force of the CEF at the western front. It was the strong desire of the Canadian government that the Canadian Corps be a permanent formation. Thus the Canadian divisions fought together virtually all the time.

4 *The Edmonton Journal,* 4 July 1999

5 *www.1ppcliinkosovo.com/ARTICLES/cosmsg.htm,* "A Message from our CO"

6 *The Western Sentinel,* 15 July 1999

7 Ibid.

8 *The Edmonton Journal,* 1 July 1999

9 *The Western Sentinel,* 15 July 1999
10 *The Edmonton Journal,* 1 July 1999
11 *The Edmonton Sun,* 4 July 1999

Chapter 1 Princess Patricia's Regiment

1 For Gault's background prior to the founding of the PPCLI, see Jeffery Williams, *First in the Field: Gault of the Patricias* (London: L. Cooper 1995), 1–58
2 PPCLI Archives, Box 16–3, File 16–(19)–3, Bastedo to McIntosh, 2 August 1964
3 Williams, *First in the Field,* 19
4 Ralph Hodder-Williams, *Princess Patricia's Canadian Light Infantry: 1914–1919* (London: Hodder and Stoughton 1923), 3
5 Although there is no standardized definition of what constitutes "light" infantry, the term has generally been applied to formations that are both smaller and more lightly armed than standard infantry units. The PPCLI was set up with the same establishment and armament as any other infantry battalion in the Canadian and British armies and was not, therefore, a "light" battalion.
6 Robert Zubkowski, *As Long as Faith and Freedom Last,* (Unpublished manuscript, 2000), 2
7 PPCLI Archives, Gault papers, Box 10–1, File 10–(2)–1, Hughes to Gault, 10 August 1914
8 Ibid.
9 Sandra Gwyn, *Tapestry of War* (Toronto: HarperCollins 1992), 90. Gwyn's excellent portrait of Papineau is on pp. 85–106.
10 PPCLI Archives, Box 31–12, File 31–(8)–12, Papineau, "The War and Its Influences upon Canada"
11 Ibid., Box 23–8, File 31–(23)–8, Keys to Bastedo, 9 June 1964
12 Ibid., Box 33–11, File 31–(33)–11, Niven to MacGregor, 21 April 1965
13 Zubkowski, *As Long as Faith and Freedom Last,* 4
14 Ibid., 4–5
15 PPCLI Archives, Box 31–1, File "R.G. Barclay"; "A Soldier of the Queen"
16 PPCLI Archives, interviews with WWI Veterans, F.G. Young
17 Zubkowski, *As Long as Faith and Freedom Last,* 5
18 Ibid., 8
19 Ibid., 10
20 Ibid., 8
21 Hodder-Williams, *Princess Patricia's Canadian Light Infantry,* 10
22 Zubkowski, *As Long as Faith and Freedom Last,* 11–12
23 *The Globe,* 27 August 1914
24 Zubkowski, *As Long as Faith and Freedom Last,* 11–12
25 PPCLI Archives, interviews with WWI Veterans, Andre Bieler
26 Ibid.

27 Ibid., Sergeant G.W. Candy
28 Ibid., William Roffey
29 Ibid., Box 16–6, File 16–(2)–6
30 Ibid., Box 31–8, File 31–(15)–8, Stanley Jones, "When Patricias Marched into Trenches"
31 Ibid.
32 Ibid.
33 Williams, *First in the Field,* 70–74
34 PPCLI Archives, Box 31–4, File 31–(12)–4, Draycott to Bastedo, 10 January 1964
35 PPCLI Archives, Box 31–8, File 31–(15)–8, Stanley Jones, "When Patricias Marched into Trenches"
36 PPCLI Archives, interview with Sergeant Lewis Scott

Chapter 2 **Wipers**

1 PPCLI Archives, Box 31–5, File 31–(20)–5, Farquhar to Adamson, 13 January 1915
2 Ibid., interview with Private F.G. Young
3 Ibid., interview with Sergeant G.W. Candy
4 Ibid., interview with Lieutenant-Colonel Hugh Niven
5 Ibid., Box 31–6, File 31–(29)–6, Letter of 12 February 1915
6 Ibid., unknown narration, "Life in the Lines"
7 Daniel Dancocks, *Welcome to Flanders Fields: The First Canadian Battle of the Great War: Ypres, 1915* (Toronto: McClelland and Stewart 1988), 87
8 PPCLI Archives, Box 31–2, File 31–(33)–2, "Sniper Extraordinary"
9 Ibid., Box 31–8, File 31–(15)–8, Stanley Jones, "When Patricias Marched into Trenches"
10 Ibid., unknown narration, "Life in the Lines"
11 Ibid., Box 31–4, File 31–(20)–4, "Lt.-Col. Francis Douglas Farquhar . . . A Memorial"
12 Bill Rawling, *Surviving Trench Warfare: Technology and the Canadian Corps, 1914–1918* (Toronto: University of Toronto Press 1992), 48
13 Jeffery Williams, *First in the Field* (London: L. Cooper 1995), 81–82
14 PPCLI Archives, interview with Sergeant Louis Scott
15 Ibid., Box 31–4, File 31–(20)–4, "Lt.-Col. Francis Douglas Farquhar . . . a Memorial"
16 Well-constructed trenches had a firestep on the bottom facing the enemy so that men could stand above the trench-lip to shoot if necessary. Traverses were sections of trench dug at right angles to the main trench line, designed to make it difficult for an enemy to capture more than one section of trench at a time.
17 Quoted in Lyn Macdonald, *1915: The Death of Innocence* (London: Headline 1993), 189–90

18 Robert Zubkowski, "H.P. Maddison," *As Long as Faith and Freedom Last* (Unpublished manuscript) vol. 1, 83
19 Ibid., "F.E. Godwin," 82
20 Ibid., "J.W. Vaughan," 82
21 Ibid., "J.J. Burke," 83
22 PPCLI Archives, 1962 National Archives interview with Sergeant Lewis Scott
23 Ibid., Box 31–7, File 31–(22)–7, Herbert to Bastedo, 25 January 1964
24 Ibid., Box 16, File 16–(1)–1, "The Gassing of Three Company"
25 N.M. Christie, ed., *Letters of Agar Adamson* (Nepean, Ontario: CEF Books 1997), 71
26 Ralph Hodder-Williams, *Princess Patricia's Canadian Light Infantry: 1914–1919,* vol. 1 (London: Hodder and Stoughton 1923), 54
27 Ibid.
28 Zubkowski, "J.J. Burke," *As Long as Faith and Freedom Last,* vol. 1, 89
29 PPCLI Archives, Box 31–12, File 31–(15)–12, Peacock to Bastedo, 27 March 1964
30 Ibid., Box 31–2, File 31–(12)–2, J.E. Brice, "Memories of the 500 Draft"
31 Ibid., Box 31–2, File 31–(22)–2, Diary of J.J. Burke
32 Christie, *Letters of Agar Adamson,* 72
33 Hodder-Williams, *Princess Patricia's Canadian Light Infantry,* vol. 2, 21–22. Entry for 4 May 1915.
34 Christie, *Letters of Agar Adamson,* 72
35 PPCLI Archives, Box 31–2, File 31–(12)–2, J.E. Brice, "Memories of the 500 Draft"
36 Ibid., Box 31–2, File 31–(22)–2, Diary of J.J. Burke

Chapter 3 The Salient

1 PPCLI Archives, Box 31–13, File 31–(3)–13, notes made by W.J. Popey
2 Ibid., CBC interview for "Brothers in Arms," interview with Jimmy Vaughan
3 Ralph Hodder-Williams, *Princess Patricia's Canadian Light Infantry: 1914–1919* (London: Hodder and Stoughton 1923), 60
4 Robert Zubkowski, "T. Richardson," *As Long as Faith and Freedom Last,* vol. 2 (Unpublished manuscript, 2000), 85
5 PPCLI Archives, 1962 National Archives interview with Sergeant Louis Scott
6 Quoted in Lyn Macdonald, *1915: The Death of Innocence,* 287
7 Zubkowski, "J.J. Burke," *As Long as Faith and Freedom Last,* vol. 2, 85
8 PPCLI Archives, 1962 National Archives interview with Lieutenant-Colonel Hugh Niven
9 Ibid., Box 31–13, File 31–(1)–13, notes made by W.J. Popey
10 The Rifle Brigade was the proper name of a British army infantry regiment; it was *not* a brigade in the organizational sense.

11 PPCLI Archives, Box 31–13, File 31–(1)–13, notes made by W.J. Popey

12 Zubkowski, "G.W. Candy," *As Long as Faith and Freedom Last,* vol. 2, 85

13 PPCLI Archives, Box 31–13, File 31–(1)–13, notes made by W.J. Popey

14 Hodder-Williams, *Princess Patricia's Canadian Light Infantry,* 76

15 PPCLI Archives, Box 31–3, File 31–(9)–3, "John Collins," by R.G. Barclay

16 Ibid.

17 *McGill Daily,* 18 November 1915

18 Hodder-Williams, *Princess Patricia's Canadian Light Infantry,* 83

19 PPCLI Archives, interview with Andre Bieler

20 Ibid., Box 31–1, File 31–(15)–1, "Bobby Annan," nd

21 Ibid., Box 16–6, "Two Years with the PPCLI"

22 Ibid., all Livingston quotes

23 Shane B. Schreiber, *The Shock Army of the British Empire* (Westport, Conn.: Praeger, 1997), 18ff

24 Zubkowski, "R.C. Bradford" and "W. Stirling," *As Long as Faith and Freedom Last,* vol. 2, 178

25 PPCLI Archives, Box 31–8, File 31–(23)–8, "The Battle of Sanctuary Wood"

26 Ibid., Box 31–3, File 31–(5)–3, as quoted in M. Baker to Rod Middleton, 13 November 1994

27 Ibid., Box 31–8, File 31–(15)–8

28 Mention-in-Dispatches was a minor honour accorded a soldier, sailor, or airman named in official reports as having acted in a meritorious way while engaged in combat.

29 Ibid., Box 31–9, File 31–(35)–9, "Letter written by Col. A.H. McGreer, Sr. Chaplain to parents of Stanton McGreer," nd

Chapter 4 Vimy Ridge

1 See, for example, Bill Rawling, *Surviving Trench Warfare: Technology and the Canadian Corps* (Toronto: University of Toronto Press 1992) and Shane B. Schreiber, *Shock Army of the British Empire: The Canadian Corps in the Last Hundred Days of the Great War* (Westport, Conn.: Praeger 1997).

2 A.M.J. Hyatt, *General Sir Arthur Currie: A Military Biography* (Toronto: University of Toronto Press 1987); Denis Winter, *Haig's Command: A Reassessment* (London: Viking 1991); Ian M. Brown, "Lieutenant-General Sir Arthur Currie and the Canadian Corps 1917–1918: The Evolution of a Style of Command and Attack" (Unpublished MA thesis, University of Calgary 1991)

3 Quoted in Jeffery Williams, *First in the Field* (London: L. Cooper 1995), 119

4 Ralph Hodder-Williams, *Princess Patricia's Canadian Light Infantry: 1914–1919* (London: Hodder and Stoughton 1923), 145

5 N.M. Christie, ed., *Letters of Agar Adamson* (Nepean, Ontario: CEF Books 1997), 218

6 Ibid.

7 PPCLI Archives, NAC interview of A.E. Potts
8 Robert Zubkowski, "A.L. Potentier," *As Long as Faith and Freedom Last,* vol. 1 (Unpublished manuscript), 253
9 Hodder-Williams, *Princess Patricia's Canadian Light Infantry,* 162
10 Zubkowski, "A.R. Milne," *As Long as Faith and Freedom Last,* vol. 1, 254–5
11 PPCLI Archives, Box 16–1, File 16–(1)–1, "Sweet Memories of Sugar Trench"
12 Ibid., Box 31–13, File 31–(2)–13, selections from the diary of Bert Potentier
13 Ibid., Box 31–12, File 31–(3)–12, Oliver to McGuire, 14 November 1916
14 Hodder-Williams, *Princess Patricia's Canadian Light Infantry,* 174
15 PPCLI Archives, Box 16–3, File 16–(33)–3, Stanley Davis to Kathleen, 5 October 1916
16 Ibid.
17 Christie, *Letters of Agar Adamson,* 223
18 Ibid., 272
19 PPCLI Archives, Box 31–11, File 31–(5)–11, "Remember Vimy"
20 Zubkowski, "F.E. Conley," *As Long as Faith and Freedom Last,* vol. 1, 299
21 PPCLI Archives, Box 31–2, File 31–(3)–2, A.A. Bonar, "On Active Service"
22 Zubkowski, "F.E. Conley," *As Long as Faith and Freedom Last,* vol. 1, 300
23 PPCLI Archives, Box 31–2, File 31–(3)–2, A.A. Bonar, "On Active Service"
24 Ibid., Box 31–11, File 31–(5)–11, "Remember Vimy"
25 Ibid., interview with Andre Bieler
26 Zubkowski, "G.E. Hancox," *As Long as Faith and Freedom Last,* vol. 1, 310
27 PPCLI Archives, Box 31–2, File 31–(3)–2, A.A. Bonar, "On Active Service"
28 Hodder-Williams, *Princess Patricia's Canadian Light Infantry,* 220
29 Christie, *Letters of Agar Adamson,* 274

Chapter 5 The Road to Mons

1 N.M. Christie, ed., *Letters of Agar Adamson* (Nepean, Ontario: CEF Books 1997), 294
2 PPCLI Archives, Box 31–5, File 31–(23)–5, P. Howard Ferguson, "Tales of the Trenches"
3 Robert Zubkowski, "R.W. Wilson," *As Long as Faith and Freedom Last,* vol. 1 (Unpublished manuscript), 330
4 PPCLI Archives, interview with Andre Bieler
5 Jeffery Williams, *Princess Patricia's Canadian Light Infantry* (London: Leo Cooper 1972), 24
6 Daniel Dancocks, *Welcome to Flanders Fields* (Toronto: McClelland and Stewart 1988), 146
7 PPCLI Archives, Box 31–11, H. Mulock to Bastedo, nd
8 Ibid., interview with Andre Bieler

9 Christie, *Letters of Agar Adamson,* 309
10 Quoted in Desmond Morton and J.L. Granatstein, *Marching to Armageddon: Canadians and the Great War 1914–1918* (Toronto: Lester & Orpen Dennys 1982), 204
11 Williams, *Princess Patricia's Canadian Light Infantry,* 25
12 Jeffery Williams, *First in the Field* (London: L. Cooper 1995), 134
13 Ibid., 131
14 PPCLI Archives, Box 31–5, File 31–(5)–5, J.E. Duggan, "Excerpts—letters from France to his mother," letter of 10 May 1918
15 Ralph Hodder-Williams, *Princess Patricia's Canadian Light Infantry: 1914–1919,* vol. 2 (London: Hodder and Stoughton 1923), 40
16 PPCLI Archives, Box 31–5, File 31–(5)–5, J.E. Duggan, "Amiens and Parvillers"
17 Hodder-Williams, *Princess Patricia's Canadian Light Infantry,* vol. 2, 43
18 PPCLI Archives, Box 31–5, File 31–(5)–5, J.E. Duggan, letter to his mother 6 October 1918
19 Hodder-Williams, *Princess Patricia's Canadian Light Infantry,* vol. 2, 45
20 PPCLI Archives, Box 31–13, File 31–(1)– 13, "Bill Popey; His Story"

Chapter 6 From Armistice to War

1 Jeffery Williams, *First in the Field* (London: L. Cooper 1995), 141–142
2 George Roy Stevens, *Princess Patricia's Canadian Light Infantry, 1919–1959* (Griesbacht, Alta.: The Historical Committee of the Regiment), 3
3 Ian McCulloch, "Crisis in Leadership: The Seventh Brigade & the Nivelles 'Mutiny', 1918," in *The Army Doctrine and Training Bulletin,* Summer 2000, 35–45
4 Williams, *First in the Field,* 144
5 Gerald W.L. Nicholson, *Canadian Expeditionary Force, 1914–1919* (Ottawa: Queen's Printer 1964), 532
6 The story of the mutiny at Nivelles is taken from McCulloch, "Crisis in Leadership"; Williams, *First in the Field,* 144–149; PPCLI Archives, Box 31–8, File 31(26)–8, Eric Knight to Hamilton Gault, 2 July 1939.
7 PPCLI Archives, Box 31–8, File 31(26)–8, Knight to Gault, 2 July 1939
8 Ibid.
9 Ibid., and McCulloch, "Crisis in Leadership"
10 Williams, *First in the Field,* 147
11 PPCLI Archives, Box 31–8, File 31(26)–8, Knight to Gault, 2 July 1939
12 Ibid.
13 Ibid., 146
14 PPCLI Archives, Box 31–8, File 31(26)–8, Knight to Gault, 2 July 1939
15 Robert Zubkowski, *As Long as Faith and Freedom Last* (Unpublished manuscript, 2000), extract from a letter from H.W. Niven, nd, 418; Stevens,

Princess Patricia's Canadian Light Infantry, 3–4; R.S. Reid, "The Otter Committee: The Reorganization of the Canadian Militia, 1919–1920" (Royal Military College graduate course paper, 23 April 1970); Jeffery Williams, *Princess Patricia's Canadian Light Infantry* (London: Leo Cooper 1972), 32

16 PPCLI Archives, Box 10–1, File 10(2)–1, "Special Order of the Day by Lieutenant-Colonel A. Hamilton Gault, DSO," 19 March 1919

17 Zubkowski, *As Long as Faith and Freedom Last,* 413

18 University of Victoria Library Archives, Roy Collection, interview with John Cave

19 Stevens, *Princess Patricia's Canadian Light Infantry,* 8

20 Charles Sydney Frost, *Once A Patricia* (St. Catharines: Vanwell Publishing 1988), 59–60

21 PPCLI Archives, interview with Jock Mackie

22 Ibid., interview with Sydney McKay

23 University of Victoria Library Archives, Roy Collection, interview with John Cave

24 C.P. Stacey, *Six Years of War* (Ottawa: Queen's Printer 1966), 13

25 PPCLI Archives, interview with Ken Arril

26 Ibid., interview with Don Parrott

27 Ibid., interview with Gilbert John Hyde

28 D.F. Parrott, *Princess Patricia's Regiment: 1938–1941* (Privately printed 1990), 24

29 PPCLI Archives, interview with Don Parrott

30 Ibid., interview with Gilbert John Hyde

31 Stacey, *Six Years of War,* 42

Chapter 7 **To War Again**

1 D.F. Parrott, *Princess Patricia's Regiment* (Privately printed 1990), 35–36

2 George Roy Stevens, *Princess Patricia's Canadian Light Infantry, 1919–1959* (Griesbacht, Alta.: The Historical Committee of the Regiment), 20

3 PPCLI Archives, interview with George Grant

4 University of Victoria Library Archives, Roy Collection, interview with Felix Carriere

5 PPCLI Archives, interview with Sydney McKay

6 Ibid., interview with Jock Mackie

7 Parrott, *Princess Patricia's Regiment,* 38

8 PPCLI Archives, interview with Lou Holten

9 University of Victoria Library Archives, Roy Collection, interview with Felix Carriere

10 PPCLI Archives, interview with Jock Mackie

11 University of Victoria Library Archives, Roy Collection, interview with Felix Carriere

12 Ibid.
13 PPCLI Archives, Box 16–2, File 16(2)–2, Major Murphy, "The Battle of Sodden Field," nd
14 Ibid., interview with Gilbert John Hyde
15 Ibid., Box 16–2, File 16(2)–2, Major Murphy, "The Battle of Sodden Field," nd
16 Ibid., interview with Lou Holten
17 Ibid., interview with Colonel Clarke
18 Ibid., interview with Don Parrott
19 Charles Sydney Frost, *Once A Patricia* (St. Catharines: Vanwell Publishing 1988), 533
20 University of Victoria Library Archives, Roy Collection, interview with Felix Carriere
21 PPCLI Archives, interview with Sydney McKay
22 Ibid., War Diary (WD) 28 June 1943

Chapter 8 From Pacino to the Moro

1 PPCLI Archives, interview with Andy Schaen
2 University of Victoria Library Archives, Roy Collection, interview with Felix Carierre
3 George Roy Stevens, *Princess Patricia's Canadian Light Infantry, 1919–1959* (Griesbacht, Alta.: The Historical Committee of the Regiment), 72
4 PPCLI Archives, interview with Sydney McKay
5 Ibid., interview with Lieutenant-Colonel R.P. Clark
6 Ibid., interview with Jock Mackie
7 University of Victoria Library Archives, Roy Collection, interview with Felix Carrierre
8 Stevens, *Princess Patricia's Canadian Light Infantry,* 73
9 PPCLI Archives, interview with Andy Schaen
10 Ibid., Lou Holten
11 University of Victoria Archives, Roy Collection, interview with Felix Carierre
12 Stevens, *Princess Patricia's Canadian Light Infantry,* 73
13 PPCLI Archives, interview with Colonel W. de N. "Bucko" Watson
14 University of Victoria Archives, Roy Collection, interview with Felix Carierre
15 Stevens, *Princess Patricia's Canadian Light Infantry,* 75
16 PPCLI Archives, interview with Colonel W. de N. "Bucko" Watson
17 Chris Vokes, *Vokes: My Story* (Ottawa: Gallery Books 1985), 93
18 PPCLI Archives, interview with Lieutenant-Colonel R.P. Clark
19 Peter Stursberg, *The Sound of War: Memoirs of a CBC War Correspondent* (Toronto: University of Toronto Press 1993), 98
20 PPCLI Archives, interview with Jock Mackie

21 PPCLI War Diary (WD) 10 July 1943
22 "The Canadian who became a Sicilian Mayor," *Corriere Canadese,* 3–4 August 1990. Clipping supplied by Charles Sydney Frost
23 War Diary, 11 July 1943
24 PPCLI Archives, interview with Andy Schaen
25 Stursberg, *The Sound of War,* 100
26 Vokes, *Vokes: My Story,* 97
27 Colin McDougall, *Execution* (Toronto: Macmillan paperbacks 1988)
28 PPCLI Archives, interview with Lieutenant-Colonel R.P. Clark
29 Ibid., interview with Sydney McKay
30 Samuel W. Mitcham Jr. and Friedrich von Stauffenberg, *The Battle of Sicily* (New York: Orion Books 1991), 182
31 The battle is reconstructed from Gerald W.L. Nicholson, *Canadian Expeditionary Force, 1914–1919* (Ottawa: Queen's Printer 1964), 107–110, and War Diary PPCLI, 22 July 1943
32 Vokes, *Vokes: My Story,* 111
33 University of Victoria Library Archives, Roy Collection, interview with Felix Carierre
34 PPCLI Archives, interview with Andrew Gault Donaldson
35 PPCLI Archives, interview with Jock Mackie
36 Mitcham and von Stauffenberg, *The Battle of Sicily,* 239
37 PPCLI Archives, interview with "Bucko" Watson
38 Stevens, *Princess Patricia's Canadian Light Infantry,* 87
39 Charles Sydney Frost, *Once a Patricia* (St. Catharines: Vanwell Publishing 1988), 123–124
40 Vokes, 120
41 Frost, 534–535
42 PPCLI Archives, interview with Sydney McKay
43 Charles Comfort, *Artist at War* (Toronto: Ryerson 1956), 21
44 PPCLI Archives, interview with Gerald Richards
45 Vokes, 123
46 PPCLI Archives, interview with Gerald Richards

Chapter 9 **From Ortona to Victory**

1 Slit trenches were pits about five feet by two feet, dug as deep as possible to give cover from enemy shells or bullets. American troops referred to them as "foxholes."
2 The fight for Villa Rogatti is reconstructed from: PPCLI Archives, War Diary 5–7 December 1943; PPCLI Archives, Box 74–1, "The Crossing of the Moro and Capture of V. Roatti [*sic*]," 21 April 1944, "Val Roatti[*sic*]," nd, "The Capture of V. Roatti[*sic*] as Seen from A Coy PPCLI," nd

3 PPCLI Archives, Mark Zuelhke interview with Jack Haley. Interview donated to PPCLI Archives by Mr. Zuelhke.

4 University of Victoria Archives, Roy Collection, interview with Cameron Ware

5 PPCLI Archives, interview with Andrew Gault Donaldson

6 Ibid., interview with Jerry Richards

7 University of Victoria Archives, Roy Collection, interview with Cameron Ware

8 PPCLI Archives, War Diary, 7 December 1943

9 Ibid., 11 December 1943

10 PPCLI Archives, interview with Andy Schaen

11 Ibid., interview with Gerald Richards

12 Ibid., interview with Jack Haley

13 Ibid., Ware collection, Box 12.1–1, Ware to Gault, 21 December 1943

14 The events of 23 May are reconstructed from PPCLI Archives, War Diary, 23 May 1944 and Box 74–1, File 74(5)–1, "Princess Patricia's Light Infantry, Battle of the Hitler Line," nd, unless otherwise cited

15 PPCLI Archives, interview with Jim Reid

16 University of Victoria Archives, Roy Collection, interview with Cameron Ware

17 All quotes in the paragraph are taken from PPCLI Archives, Quartly Collection, Davis to Mrs. F. Quartly, 15 August 1944

18 Ibid., interview with Jim Reid

19 Ibid., interview with Andy Schaen

20 University of Victoria Archives, Roy Collection, interview with Cameron Ware

21 PPCLI Archives, Donald A. Gower, "The Years of My Youth (Recollections of an Old Soldier)"

22 University of Victoria Archives, Roy Collection, interview with Cameron Ware

23 George Roy Stevens, *Princess Patricia's Canadian Light Infantry, 1919–1959* (Griesbacht, Alta.: The Historical Committee of the Regiment), 162–163

24 PPCLI Archives, interview with Sydney McKay

25 Ibid., Box 71–1, 2 CIB HQ to Rosser, 23 May 1944

26 Ibid., Donald A. Gower, "The Years of My Youth (Recollections of an Old Soldier)"

27 Ibid., interview with Gilbert Hyde

28 Ibid., interview with Robert Eddy

29 Ibid., interview with Wallace Smith

30 Ibid., Box 74–1, File 74(9)–1, "Condensed War Diary PPCLI from 24 August 1944 to 23 September 1944"

31 Ibid., interview with Wallace S. Smith

32 PPCLI Archives, interview with Robert B. Eddy
33 Ibid.
34 Charles Sydney Frost, *Once A Patricia* (St. Catharines: Vanwell Publishing 1988), 283
35 Ibid., 287
36 Frost, "Crossing the IJssel River," 2 May 1990
37 PPCLI Archives, interview with George Grant
38 Frost, *Once A Patricia,* 453–454

Chapter 10 **Korea**

1 George Roy Stevens, *Princess Patricia's Canadian Light Infantry, 1919–1959* (Griesbacht, Alta.: The Historical Committee of the Regiment), 258
2 Ibid., 263
3 Ibid., 267
4 PPCLI Archives, interview with William E. "Bill" Davies
5 Ibid., interview with Barclay "BAJ" Franklin
6 Ibid., interview with Jean Pariseau
7 Ibid., interview with Donald Dickin
8 Ibid., interview with Rod Middleton
9 Ibid., interview with John Stuber
10 Ibid., interview with Ken Umpherville
11 Ibid., interview with Mel Canfield
12 Ibid., interview with Charles Scot-Brown
13 Quoted in David J. Bercuson, *Blood on the Hills: The Canadian Army in the Korean War* (Toronto: University of Toronto Press 1999), 58
14 PPCLI Archives, interview with Ken Gawthorne
15 Ibid., interview with William J. Chrysler
16 Rod Middleton, "Pilgrimage to Korea, 1998," *The Patrician,* vol L (Edmonton: PPCLI 1998), 46
17 Quoted in Bercuson, *Blood on the Hills,* 62
18 J.R. Stone and Jacques Castonguay, *Korea 1951: Two Canadian Battles* (Ottawa: Canadian War Museum 1988), 14
19 Pierre Berton, "Corporal Dunphy's War," *Maclean's Magazine,* 1 June 1951, 7
20 PPCLI Archives, interview with Brian Munro
21 Ibid., interview with Donald Dickin
22 Ibid., interview with Brian Munro
23 *Calgary Herald,* 26 April 1951
24 PPCLI Archives, interview with Clarence Ruttan
25 Ibid., interview with Donald Hibbs
26 John Melady, *Korea: Canada's Forgotten War* (Toronto: Macmillan 1983), 77

27 Ibid.

28 According to Hub Gray, there were only four half tracks, thus eight machine guns.

29 Stone and Castonguay, *Korea 1951,* 20–21

30 Hub Gray, unpublished account of the Kap'yong battle in Mr. Gray's possession

31 Quoted in Bercuson, *Blood on the Hills,* 109

32 Public Records Office, Kew, UK, War Diary of the 27th BCIB, 25 April 1951

33 Clay Blair, *The Forgotten War: America in Korea, 1950–1953* (New York: Times Books 1987), 838–839

34 PPCLI Archives, interview with Chuck Jones

35 Ibid., interview with John Richardson

36 Ibid.

37 Ibid., interview with Donald Hibbs

38 Quoted in Bercuson, *Blood on the Hills,* 165

39 Ibid., 166

40 PPCLI Archives, Bruce McIntyre interview with Stanley Carmichael

41 Ibid., Bruce McIntyre interview with Don Bateman

42 Ibid., interview with Lieutenant Ken Robertson

43 Both quotes from Bercuson, *Blood on the Hills,* 168

44 PPCLI Archives, interview with Major Robert "Bob" Frost

Chapter 11 Keeping the Peace

1 Quoted in D.J. Bercuson, *True Patriot: The Life of Brooke Claxton, 1898–1960* (Toronto: University of Toronto Press 1993), 222

2 PPCLI Archives, interview with Ken Villiger

3 Ibid., interview with Charles "Chic" Goodman

4 Ibid., interview with Don Ardelian

5 Quoted in Sean M. Maloney, *War Without Battles: Canada's NATO Brigade in Germany, 1951–1993* (Toronto: McGraw-Hill Ryerson 1997), 289

6 Jeffery Williams, *First in the Field: Gault of the Patricias* (London: L. Cooper 1995), 249

7 Quoted in Robert Zubkowski, *As Long as Faith and Freedom Last,* vol. 1 (Unpublished manuscript, 2000) 2

8 PPCLI Archives, interview with Major General Lewis MacKenzie

9 Lewis MacKenzie, *Peacekeeper: The Road to Sarajevo* (Toronto: Douglas & McIntyre 1993), 29

10 PPCLI Archives, interview with Warrant Officer Rod Dearing

11 Ibid., interview with Major Wayne Eyre

12 Ibid., interview with Warrant Officer Rick Dumas

13 Ibid.

14 Colonel Glenn W. Nordick, "Battalion Command — UNPROFOR (Sector West) Croatia, September 1992 to April 1993," personal experience monograph, U.S. Army War College, Class of 1999, 3

15 PPCLI Archives, interview with Major Brian Flynn

16 This account of the Medak Pocket fighting is taken from "The Medak Pocket Operation — September 1993," by Lieutenant-Colonel Jim Calvin, and Calvin's official post-operations report, "CANBAT 1 Report on Medak Pocket Operations, 15–21 September, 1993," sent to the author by Colonel Calvin.

17 Calvin, "CANBAT 1 Report on Medak Pocket Operations, 15–21 September, 1993"

18 Calvin, "The Medak Pocket Operation — September 1993"

19 PPCLI Archives, interview with Jim Seggie

20 Calvin, "The Medak Pocket Operation — September 1993"

21 PPCLI Archives, interview with Warrant Officer Geof Crossman

INDEX OF DIVISIONS, BRIGADES, BATTALIONS, AND REGIMENTS

80th Brigade, 27th British Division (First World War), 35, 51, 59, 71
1st Canadian Division (First World War), 8, 35, 47, 53–54, 56, 97, 100, 103, 127
2nd Canadian Division (First World War), 8, 88–89, 100, 103, 127
3rd Canadian Division (First World War), 71, 80, 88–89, 93, 97, 100, 103, 105, 106, 114, 116, 121, 127
4th Canadian Division (First World War), 97, 100–101, 103, 105, 106
7th Brigade (First World War), 71, 89, 100, 105, 106, 114, 116, 118, 125, 126, 128

First Canadian Army (Second World War), 168, 233, 239
I Canadian Corps (Second World War), 168, 195, 217, 226, 227, 232, 233
II Canadian Corps (Second World War), 112, 168
1st Canadian Infantry Division (Second World War), 10, 150, 152–53, 163, 166, 170, 176, 180, 182, 184, 186, 190, 195, 197, 198, 201, 208, 216, 217, 234
2nd Canadian Infantry Division (Second World War), 152–53, 166, 170
3rd Canadian Infantry Division (Second World War), 165, 167, 170, 234
1st Canadian Armoured Brigade (Second World War), 170, 216
1st Canadian Infantry Brigade (Second World War), 150, 185, 186, 190, 192, 199, 203, 208, 217, 230
2nd Canadian Infantry Brigade (Second World War), 10, 150, 160, 171, 176, 178, 190, 197, 199, 203, 209, 217–18, 227, 247

3rd Canadian Infantry Brigade (Second World War), 150, 213, 217–18, 223

1st Commonwealth Division (Korean War), 256, 265
25th Canadian Infantry Brigade (Korean War), 246, 256, 264
27th British Commonwealth Infantry Brigade (Korean War), 255, 257, 264
28th British Commonwealth Infantry Brigade (Korean War), 264

1st Battalion PPCLI (1 PPCLI), 14, 16, 249, 268–69, 271–72, 277–78, 285, 287, 301–2
2nd Battalion PPCLI (2 PPCLI), 8, 10–11, 249, 251–52, 255, 264, 268, 277, 289, 293, 296, 298
3rd Battalion PPCLI (3 PPCLI), 12, 268, 271, 277, 279, 284, 285, 289, 292–93
4th Battalion PPCLI (4 PPCLI), 285

British Expeditionary Force (BEF), 34, 40, 76, 109, 119, 121, 162–63
Canadian Active Service Force, 148, 149, 150
Canadian Guards, 284
Canadian Military Headquarters, London, 159, 163
Calgary Highlanders, 12
Canadian Horse Artillery, 284
Canadian Mounted Rifles, 20, 75, 78
Canadian Scottish Regiment, 246
Carleton and York Regiment, 214
Department of Militia and Defence, 24, 31, 126, 131, 144
Department of National Defence, 144, 148
Department of Overseas Military Forces of Canada, 126
1st Special Service Force, 215–16, 225
42nd Battalion CEF, 71, 120
48th Highlanders (Toronto), 208–9, 214
49th Battalion CEF, 71, 91–92, 93, 118. *See also* Loyal Edmonton Regiment
Fort Garry Horse, 284 Fusiliers Mont Royal, 249
Hastings and Prince Edward Regiment, 166, 203, 208–9
Lord Strathcona's Horse, 25
Loyal Edmonton Regiment, 150, 151, 160, 176, 187–89, 192, 209–10, 213, 223, 224, 227, 247, 285
Mobile Force, 147–48
Ontario Tank Regiment, 213, 218
Originals, 1–2, 5, 57, 112, 120, 125, 200, 224
Perth Regiment, 228
Queen's Own Rifles of Canada, 284–85
Royal Canadian Regiment, 9, 71, 75, 93, 94, 111, 118, 120, 132, 141, 150, 190, 192, 213, 240, 249
Royal Highland Regiment of Canada, 21, 33, 284
Royal 22e Régiment, 9, 132, 150, 213, 218, 230, 240, 249
Seaforth Highlanders of Canada, 125, 150–51, 176, 186, 187, 201, 208–9, 213, 217
South Alberta Regiment, 167
Three Rivers Regiment, 188
West Nova Scotia Regiment, 228

GENERAL INDEX

Active Force. *See* Permanent Force
Adamson, Agar, 25, 42, 56, 58, 59, 64–66, 86–87, 93–95, 99, 100, 103, 108–9, 112–13,124
Adamson, Mabel, 25, 87, 95, 108
aid to the civil power, 136
Alderson, Edwin A.H., 35, 71
Alexander, Sir Harold, 171, 195–96, 226
Allard, J.V., 269
Amiens, Battle of, 114, 116
Annan, Bobby, 72
Ardelian, Don, 279
Arras sector, 116–21
  Cambrai, 119
  Canal du Nord, 116–17
  Drocourt–Queant line, 116–17
  Mons, 120–21, 123–24, 126, 135
  Tilloy, 117–19, 125–26, 165
Arril, Ken, 144–45
awards and decorations, 9, 11, 108, 115–16, 121, 151, 165, 189, 247, 260, 264, 270, 296
Barclay, 69
barracks, life in, 124, 153
Barwise, Ken, 261, 263
Bateman, Don, 271
battle exhaustion, 59, 217
battle honours, regimental, 9, 11, 264, 285, 296
Berton, Pierre, 257
Bessborough, Earl of, 142, 283
Bieler, Andre, 33, 69, 99, 106, 108
Boer War. *See* South African War
Bogert, M.P., 269
Bonar, A.A., 98, 99
Bordon, Robert L., 102, 109, 132
Bosnia. *See* Yugoslavia, collapse of former
Boss, Bill, 260
Bourassa, Henri, 25
Bradford, R.C., 77
Brain, Donald, 176, 177, 189, 210
Brice, Joe, 58, 59
Brown, George, 282
Buller, Herbert C., 3, 24, 46, 49–51, 59, 71, 76, 79–80, 134

Buonaparte, Eugene P., 80
Burke, B.A., 255, 257–59
Burke, J.J., 53, 57
Burns, E.L.M., 217,
Byng, Sir Julian, 85, 89, 96, 101, 142, 283

Cadieux, Marcel, 284
Calgary, 120, 137, 151, 240, 248, 249, 282, 284. *See also* Camp Sarcee; Currie Barracks; Museum of the Regiments
Calvin, Jim, 11, 293–97
Cameron, D.C., 241
Cameron, J.R., 268
Camp Hughes, 138
Camp Petawawa, 248
Camp Sarcee, 136, 138, 146
Camp Shilo, 138, 146, 148
Camp Valcartier, 8, 31, 32, 34,
Camp Wainwright, 249
Campbell, A.M., 219, 221
Campbell, K.L., 271
Canadian Corps (First World War), 8, 9, 71, 74, 85, 89, 94, 96–97, 101–2, 103, 105, 111, 113, 116, 117, 119, 125, 134,
Candy, G.W., 35, 43, 65
Canfield, Mel, 249
Carey, Rex, 189
Carmichael, Stanley, 271
Carr, Maurice, 262
Carriere, Felix, 154, 158, 171, 174, 176, 177, 189
Cassels, A.J.H., 265
Cave, John, 140
ceremonies, regimental, 1, 13–14, 17, 32, 133–34, 139, 142, 282–83, 285
Chute, C.H., 270
Christie, Jim, 28, 45
Christie, John, 120
Chrysler, William J., 252
Churchill, Winston, 159, 214, 226
Clark, John A., 124, 125–26, 128–30
Clark, Mark W., 195, 198, 216
Clark, R.P. "Slug," 175, 179, 183, 230, 236
Claxton, Brooke, 246, 247, 276
Coade, Basil Aubrey, 255
Cochrane, Harry, 78–79
Cold War, 241, 274, 275, 303
Coleman, Rowan, 188, 219, 223
Collins, John, 69
Colonel-in-Chief, 283
Colonels of the Regiment, 281–82, 285–86,
Colquhoun, W.G., 47, 141, 148, 149, 151–52, 154, 163, 165–66
Colville, Jock, 29
Comfort, Charles, 197
Conley, F.E., 98
Connaught, Arthur the Duke of, 19, 32
Courcelette, battle of, 88–93
Cousins, S.J., 189
Crerar, Harry, 233
Croatia. *See* Yugoslavia, collapse of former
Crofton, P.D., 210, 230
Crossman, Geof, 297
Currie, Arthur, 85–86, 96, 101, 104, 105, 106, 109, 114, 116, 121, 125, 168
Currie Barracks, 240, 249
Cyprus, 287–91, 292
  conditions in, 288–89

Davies, Bill, 243
Davis, Elmer, 221
Davis, Stanley, 92
Dearing, Rob, 289
de Chastelain, John, 282, 286
demobilization, 126–31, 133–34, 239–40, 275
Dextraze, Jacques, 249
D'Havet, Achilles, 182
Dickin, Donald, 248, 258
Dieppe, 169–70
Donaldson, Andrew G., 189, 206
Draycott, Walter, 37
Duggan, J.E., 113–15, 118, 135

Dumas, Rick, 289–90
Dumbells, 123
Dunphy, Kerry, 257
Dyer, Hugh, 113, 124, 125

Eaton, K.E., 228–29
Eddy, Robert, 225, 229, 231
Edgar, J.N., 117, 153, 165–66, 167
Edmonton, 1, 11, 13, 14, 16, 301–2
Eisenhower, Dwight D., 171, 273
Elizabeth II, Queen of Canada, 285
equipment, 12, 17, 24, 140–41, 161, 172, 175, 181, 234–35, 241, 255, 279, 292. *See also* weapons
  quality of, 9–10, 31, 136–37, 144, 146, 151, 255, 272–73, 279
executions, purported, 183–84
Eyre, Wayne, 289

families, 15–16, 140, 237, 240
Farquhar, Francis, 9, 22–24, 27, 29, 30, 32, 34, 50–51, 67, 121, 124, 134, 156, 299
  as C.O. overseas, 42, 45, 46–47
  killed in trench raid, 48–50
Farquhar, Lady Evelyn, 49
Ferguson, Howard, 94
Flynn, Brian, 294
Fort Osborne Barracks, 135, 137, 144, 145, 149, 151, 153–55
Foulkes, Charles G., 233, 241, 246, 251
Fox, Beatrice, 26
Franklin, Barclay, 244
Frost, Robert, 273
Frost, Sydney, 138, 169, 181, 193–94, 231, 234, 236, 277

gas, chlorine, 53–55, 81,
Gault, Hamilton, 8, 19–21, 33, 34, 49, 67, 94, 121, 124–25, 156, 213, 236–37, 241, 274, 282, 299, 303
  death, 281
  and demobilization, 128, 130–35
  1957 visit to Germany, 280–81
  overseas in World War I, 3, 5, 47–48, 59–60, 62, 64, 70–71, 79–80, 86–87, 112–13
  raising of regiment, 21–24
  retires from active service, 141
Gault, Marguerite, 19
Gawthorne, Ken, 252
Gemmell, N.M., 241
Germany
  Canada's contribution to NATO standing forces in, 277–80, 283
  life for soldiers in, 278
  surrender of, 120–21, 236
Gibson, T.G., 223, 224
Glassco, G.B., 79
Godwin, F.E., 52
Goodman, Charles, 279
Gower, Donald A., 12, 222, 224–25
Graham, Stuart, 282
Grant, George, 153, 235
Gray, Donald, 79
Green, Tyrone, 295
Grieve, Pat, 280

Haig, Douglas, 84, 88, 104, 105, 109
Haley, Jack, 204, 212
Hancox, George, 99,
Harding, Sir John, 216
Hastings, D.H., 270
Hendricks, Chester, 176
Herbert, H.R., 54
Hewson, C.W., 12, 282, 286
Hibbs, Donald, 252, 261, 270–71
Hill 70 (Lens), 103–4
Hill 145. *See* Vimy Ridge
Hill 677. *See* Kap'yong, battle of
Hitler, Adolf, 143, 147, 236
Hobson, R.B., 219
Hodder-Williams, Ralph, 56
Hoffmeister, Bert, 187, 203, 209, 211, 217–18
Holland, 10, 12, 233–36, 237
  IJssel River crossing, 234–36
  PPCLI transferred to, 233–34
Holten, Lou, 157, 177

Hughes, Sam, 8, 21, 24, 31, 34, 67, 68, 70, 131
Hunt, J.B., 211
Hyde, Gilbert, 145, 146, 160, 225

illness, 114, 158, 180
Italian Campaign, 12, 195–233, 236, 239. *See also* Sicily Campaign
  Campobasso, 199
  Gothic Line, 10, 226–29
  Hitler Line, 10, 215, 218–25, 299
  Liri Valley, 10, 215–19, 226
  Ortona, Battle for, 10, 199, 201–15
  Po River Valley, 226, 232
  Rimini Line, 229–32
  Romagna Plains, 232–33
  terrain and conditions, 195–97, 217, 227–28, 230–31

Jefferson, J.C., 187–88
Jones, Chuck, 264
Jones, Louise, 73–74, 80
Jones, Stanley Livingston, 36–37, 72–74, 76, 77, 80
Jordan, William, 66

Kap'yong, battle of, 11, 257–64, 299
Keane, Robert A., 249
Keller, R.F.L., 167
Kendall, F.J., 90
Kesselring, Albert, 196, 215, 225–26
Keys, N.A., 77
King, William Lyon Mackenzie, 147, 150
King George V, 111
Knight, Eric, 128–31
Korean War, 10, 17, 244–74, 275–76, 303
  background to, 244–46, 250–51
  Canadian Army Special Force, creation and recruitment of, 246–49
  conditions and terrain, 253–54, 258–59, 268
  domestic attention to, 273
  Jamestown Line, 266–73
  Kap'yong, battle of, 11, 257–64, 299
  Operation "Piledriver," 264–65
  training for, 249–51, 254–55
  voyage to Korea, 252–53
Kosovo. *See under* Yugoslavia

Lacombe, Oscar, 12
Laurier, Sir Wilfrid, 25, 26
Leese, Sir Oliver, 216, 226–27
Leonard, Brenda, 15
Leslie, Andrew, 14
Levy, Mike, 262–63
Lilley, C.V., 260, 261
Lindsay, R.A., 152, 167, 178, 183–84, 188–92, 193–94
Lipsett, Louis, 89, 113
Little, G.W., 118
London Blitz, 164–65
Lucas, J.P., 216

MacDonald, Bruce, 262
Macedonia. *See* Yugoslavia, collapse of former
MacKenzie, Lewis, 285, 287
Mackie, Jock, 140, 155, 157, 175, 180, 190
Maclachlan, M.F., 268
MacLean, D., 103
Maddison, H.P., 29, 52
Malone, R.S., 182
Mann, C.C., 242
Marsden, W.S., 26–27, 30
Martin, A.G., 79
Martin, S.F., 90
McArthur, Douglas, 245, 251, 254, 264
McCarthy, Rev. T., 133
McDonald, George, 68
McDougall, Colin M., 174–75, 178, 183, 230
McGreer, A.H., 80–82
McGreer, Stanton, 80–82
McKay, Sydney, 140, 155, 172, 175, 183, 197, 224

McKenzie, Hugh, 108
McNaughton, A.G.L., 143, 152, 160, 163, 168
Mercer, Malcolm S., 71, 77
Merchant, Livingstone T., 285
Middleton, Rod, 248, 253
Miller, Bill, 98, 99
Mills, J.G.W., 262, 263
Milne, A.R., 90
Mitchell, W.R., 260
Mitchener, Roland, 285
Mobile Command, 284
Mobile Striking Force, 242
Molson, Percival, 68, 103
Montgomery, B.L., 166, 170, 184, 190, 195, 232, 233, 237
Mortimer, A.N.B., 133
Mullin, G.H., 108
Munro, Brian, 258, 259
Munro, Don, 12
Munro, Jack, 29
Museum of the Regiments, 13, 282

Netherlands. *See* Holland
Newman, Steve, 17
Newton, D.O., 25, 38
Nivelles, mutiny, 126, 128–30, 132, 133
Niven, Hugh, 43, 51, 59–60, 64, 66, 67, 76–79, 107, 141, 280
Nixon, H.C., 204
Nordick, Glenn W., 292–93
North Atlantic Treaty Organization (NATO), 14, 245, 275, 277–80, 284, 287, 298, 301–2
Norway, PPCLI and planned operation, 159–62

O'Connor, H.F., 281
Oliver, W.M., 91
Ottawa, 17, 23, 24, 34, 113, 120, 121, 132, 133–35, 275, 282
Otter, Sir William D., 131

Papineau, Talbot, 25–26, 48, 49, 67, 107, 112
Pariseau, Jean, 247
Parrot, Don, 145, 146, 149, 150, 156, 164
Parvillers, assault on, 115–16
Passchendaele, Battle of, 104–9, 113, 114, 152
Patricia, Princess (Duchess of Connaught), 6, 17, 23, 32, 94, 95, 111, 133, 134, 282–83, 299
Patricia Comedy Company, 94–95
Patricia Edwina Victoria Mountbatten, Lady (Countess Mountbatten of Burma), 12, 17, 283, 285
Patton, George S., 171, 172, 186
pay, 139–40, 153, 241
peacekeeping, 286–99. *See also* Cyprus; Yugoslavia, collapse of former
Peacock, Charlie, 57
Pearkes, George, 151, 156, 160
Pearson, A.G., 9, 119, 124, 130, 281
Pearson, Lester B., 276, 286
Pelly, Raymond, 25, 67, 71, 86–87, 89–90, 93
Permanent Active Militia. *See* Permanent Force (PF)
Permanent Force (PF), 9–10, 131–32, 135–36, 138, 141, 144, 148–52, 165, 240, 276. *See also* Regular Force
Pitts, Herbert, 282, 285
Popey, W.J., 28, 61, 64–65, 120
Potentier, A.L., 87, 91
Potts, Arthur E., 87, 138
Prentice, Rocky, 270
Pusch, David, 15

Quartly, George, 221

Ramsay, A., 134
Rawlinson, Sir Henry, 83
recruitment, 24, 27–31, 145, 149–53, 167, 246–49
Regimental Association, 241, 281

regimental colours, 5–6, 8, 23–24, 32, 66, 133, 142, 236–37, 282–83, 285–86. *See also* "Ric-a-Dam-Doo"
Regimental Headquarters (RHQ), 13, 135
regimental heritage and traditions, 133, 236–37, 241, 284, 303
regimental system, 6–8, 142–43, 284
Regular Force, 285
Reid, Jim, 220, 222
Reilly, W., 189
"Ric-a-Dam-Doo," 13, 17, 33, 131, 133, 174
Richards, Gerald, 198, 199, 207, 211–12
Richardson, John, 269, 270
Richardson, Tracy, 28–29, 62
Riddel, W., 206
Ridgway, Matthew, 256, 263, 265
Robertson, Ken, 272
Robertson, R.F.S., 202–6
Rockingham, John Meredith, 246–47, 249, 251, 253, 264, 269
Roffey, William, 36
Ross, H., 260
Rosser, D.H., 224, 226, 228, 230
Rowley, Roger, 271
Ruttan, Clarence, 260–61

St. Laurent, Louis, 246
Salmon, H.L.N., 170, 171
Sansom, E.W., 160
Saul, W.J., 243
Schaen, Andy, 173–74, 176, 182, 211, 222
Scot-Brown, Charles, 249
Scott, Lewis, 38, 48, 54, 63
Seggie, Jim, 296
"shell shock." *See* battle exhaustion
Sicily Campaign, 10, 12, 151, 167, 170–95, 236. *See also* Italian Campaign
  Agira, 10, 191
  Leonforte, 10, 186–90
  Modica, 181–84
  Mount Seggio, 192–94
  Nissoria, 190–91
  Pachino landings, 173–78
  preparation for, 171–2
  terrain and conditions, 178–81, 185
Simonds, G.G., 112, 170, 172, 182, 183, 186, 190, 192, 197, 198
Sladen, Arthur, 25
Smith, Wallace, 225, 229
Smith, "Snuffy," 236
snipers, 45–46, 47, 108, 205
Somme, Battle of, 83–85, 92–93, 114. *See also* Courcelette, battle of
songs, 2, 133, 174, 225, 253
South African War, 20, 21, 22, 25, 27, 32, 38
Southern, K.J., 188
Spall, Robert, 115–16
Spellum, Mike, 294
sports, 139
Stalin, Josef, 244–45, 273
Stevens, J.F., 180
Stewart, Charles, 90–92, 112–13, 117, 124, 125, 134
Stewart, J.H., 23–24, 282
Stone, Jim, 10, 247, 249, 253–55, 257–58, 261, 263, 264, 271
Strathcona, Lord, 21
Stuber, John, 248
Stursberg, Peter, 179, 182
Sung, Kim II, 244–45
Sutherland, J.R.G., 189
Sutherland, William, 282
"Sweetbriar" exercise, 243–44

tactical innovation, 85–86, 113
Tait, Mike, 16
Ten Broeke, M.R., 107, 141
Thompson, George, 28
training, 8, 10, 12, 68, 96–97, 113–14, 146, 153–44, 157–59, 168–69, 171–72, 249, 250–51, 269

airborne, 242–43, 277
of militia and Army Reserves by PPCLI, 10, 136–38, 241
NATO, 278–79
northern operations, 240–44
trench raids, 47–48, 50
trench warfare, conditions of, 4, 36–38, 42–45, 51, 56–57, 59–60, 72, 75
Trenholme, Greg, 295
Triquet, Paul, 213
Truman, Harry, 245, 264
Turner, Richard, 88

Umpherville, Ken, 248
unit citations. *See* battle honours, regimental
United Kingdom
PPCLI in, 34–35, 156–72
voyage to, 155–56
United Nations (UN), 286–88, 290–93, 295–98
University Companies, 67–70, 80, 86, 94, 103

Van Fleet, James A., 263–65
Vaughan, J.W., 52, 62, 63
veterans, 12–13,
Villiger, Ken, 278
Vimy Ridge, Battle of, 85, 93–94, 95–102, 109, 113
Vokes, Chris, 151, 166, 167, 172, 178, 179, 182–84, 187–88, 190–91, 193–94, 198, 203, 208, 211, 212, 223

Waldock, D.A.G., 272
Walker, Walton H., 254, 256
Walker, William, 27
Walls, G.E., 145
Waniandy, Jim, 261, 262
Ware, Cameron B., 10, 194, 201–8, 210–11, 213, 219, 222–24, 226, 240, 241, 282
Watson, "Bucko," 177, 179, 191, 202, 205, 206, 210, 219, 221
weapons, 10, 17, 47, 74, 241, 270–72
Bren gun, 151, 158, 176, 191, 261, 270
Browning .30 and .50 calibre machine guns, 258, 261
Lee-Enfield rifle, 31, 35, 146, 151, 158–59, 255, 270–72
Lewis gun, 84, 115, 131, 138, 139, 146, 151
Ross rifle, 31, 35
Sten gun, 255, 272
Tommy guns, 255, 271
Willets, C.R.E., 141
Wilson, R.W., 106
Wilson-Smith, Norman, 268
Winnipeg, 135, 145, 148, 151, 153–55, 283. *See also* Fort Osborne Barracks
Wood, H.F., 268
Work Point Barracks, Esquimalt, 135, 137, 145, 148, 151

Young, F.G., 27, 43
Ypres Salient (Belgium), 3–5, 34–38, 39–42, 50–51, 70–71, 72–74, 85, 152, 299
Bellewaerde Ridge, 1–2, 3, 8, 59–67, 135, 141, 281, 299
Passchendaele, Battle of, 104–9, 113, 114, 152
St. Eloi, 42–50, 72
Sanctuary Wood, 8, 75–82, 86–87, 111–13
Second battle of, 52–67
Yugoslavia, 14, 16, 291–303
collapse of former, 291–92
Kosovo, 14–17, 301–2
Medak Pocket, 8, 11, 294–98, 299
NATO's Kosovo Force (KFOR), 301–2
NATO's Stabilization Force (SFOR) in, 298
United Nations Protection Force (UNPROFOR) in, 292–98
war crimes investigations in, 297–98, 302